PRAISE FOR STUPIDITY AND PSYCHOANALYSIS

"Can stupidity be avoided? Should it be? Can and should psychoanalysis make the subject less stupid? In attempting to answer these questions the present volume is anything but *naïve* or indifferent. Rather contributors maintain that psychoanalysis renews stupidity within moral and political contemporary debates. Stupidity has a long record of being dismissed and overlooked especially since the function of western philosophy is born out of the desire to eradicate it. Here the mastery of the philosopher is to signify truth. However, this book very originally argues that stupidity is not mere intellectual disability.

Freud liked to praise his patients – especially his first female patients – for their intelligence. In many ways, Freudian psychoanalysis has relied on the analysand's ability to make sense of the seemingly insignificant, the uncanny of the dream, the ascription of meaning to the slip of the tongue or the symptom. And yet as one contributor justly points out, the analytic cure which was invented by Freud and based on the principle of free association, makes room for the experience of stupidity. Analysands find themselves confronted with the stupidity of their discourse as well as discover the stupidity of their relationship to language and their engagement with *jouissance*. Freud himself acknowledged the libidinal investment of a one very specific kind of *Witz*: stupid jokes – also explored in this collection. While Freud registered and analysed the psychic function of stupidity, he nevertheless struggled with it.

Unlike Freud, Lacan fully embraced stupidity – the springboard thinker for many contributions in this remarkable collection. For Lacan, stupidity has more than one name ranging from foolishness (*bêtise*) to nonsense (*hors-sens, pas-de-sens*). Lacanian psychoanalysis, as the collection brilliantly illustrates, conceives of stupidity as a crucial part of the analytic cure and as inseparable from the experience of the unconscious. Whether the big Other should be considered stupid, or whether the problem lies in the stupidity of the signifier, or rather, the dumbness of the Real, the subject of the unconscious is necessarily duped, turned stupid – if not stupefied.

Stupidity, as contributors all maintain, is not a mere failure but an experience that needs to be approached, if not accepted, in the analytic cure. To confront one's stupidity may be – as the collection strongly suggests – one of the quite unavowable but very serious aims (and means) of psychoanalysis.

In this collection internationally renowned psychoanalysts, philosophers, literary critics all put to work 'the importance of being stupid' as not in praise of a position that can turn out to be tragic but rather as an acknowledgement of an experience constitutive of our very being – our *être parlant* which requires to be critically addressed."

— Isabelle Alfandary, philosopher and psychoanalyst, Sorbonne Nouvelle University, Paris

"Lacan contends that the human animal as the 'animal that supposes to know' remains structurally if not biologically afflicted by stupidity. In this broad sense, we are all not *sapiens* but *folie*-sophers. Famously, he also claims that the alleged non-stupid err the most. Dumb *or* dumber, it would seem. Is psychoanalysis then a question of fatalistically accepting this false choice and opt for ready-at-hand dumbness, trying not to know too much? Or is it instead a renewed Socratic method that turns such generic dumbness into wise ignorance, as a pacifying sublation achieved by the few who, erring the most, still somehow manage to know best? Problematising such clichéd alternative, in *Psychoanalysis and Stupidity*,Cindy Zeiher sapiently brings together a wide-ranging and entertaining collection of pungent essays whose provisional endpoint might be: Dumb *and* dumber, dialectically, or both are worse!"

— Lorenzo Chiesa, Newcastle University and European Graduate School

"Cindy Zeiher has provided us here with an erudite collection of irreverent reflections on a topic of no small importance! In these pages, the reader will find Freud glowingly characterized as the world's first Professor of Stupidity, and psychoanalysis as at times a *fool*osophical enterprise that takes human stupidity as its main object of study. Thought by some to be excessively cerebral, Lacan nevertheless invites us – analysands and analysts alike – to dwell and even revel in stupidity. In this collection, the contributors evince studied stupidity by allowing themselves to remain dupes of the unconscious."

— Bruce Fink, Lacanian psychoanalyst, author of *A Clinical Introduction to Lacanian Psychoanalysis: Theory and Technique*

"A wonderful collection of essays that highlights the central role that stupidity has played in psychoanalytic theory and practice – from the nature and function of such psychoanalytic concepts as the signifier, the symptom, the death drive, and jouissance, to the psychoanalytic understanding of humor, knowledge, being, and sexuality. While reading the essays collected herein, one will marvel at just how stupid we have been not to have realized stupidity's significance for psychoanalysis sooner. A truly critical intervention."

— Russell Sbriglia, Seton Hall University

Stupidity and Psychoanalysis

Stupidity and Psychoanalysis

Lacanian Perspectives on New Subjectivities and Social Forms

Edited by Cindy Zeiher

ROWMAN & LITTLEFIELD
Lanham • Boulder • New York • London

Rowman & Littlefield
Bloomsbury Publishing Inc, 1385 Broadway, New York, NY 10018, USA
Bloomsbury Publishing Plc, 50 Bedford Square, London, WC1B 3DP, UK
Bloomsbury Publishing Ireland, 29 Earlsfort Terrace, Dublin 2, D02 AY28, Ireland
www.rowman.com

British Library Cataloguing in Publication Information Available

Library of Congress Cataloging-in-Publication Data

Names: Zeiher, Cindy, editor.
Title: Stupidity and psychoanalysis : Lacanian perspectives on new subjectivities and social forms / edited by Cindy Zeiher.
Description: Lanham : Rowman & Littlefield, [2024] | Includes bibliographical references and index.
Identifiers: LCCN 2024041782 (print) | LCCN 2024041783 (ebook) | ISBN 9781786616203 (cloth) | ISBN 9781786616210 (ebook)
Subjects: LCSH: Stupidity. | Psychoanalysis. | Lacan, Jacques, 1901-1981.
Classification: LCC BF431 .S872 2024 (print) | LCC BF431 (ebook) | DDC 153.9--dc23/eng/20241113
LC record available at https://lccn.loc.gov/2024041782
LC ebook record available at https://lccn.loc.gov/2024041783

For product safety related questions contact productsafety@bloomsbury.com.

♾™ The paper used in this publication meets the minimum requirements of American National Standard for Information Sciences—Permanence of Paper for Printed Library Materials, ANSI/NISO Z39.48-1992.

Contents

Acknowledgements

It is a tall order to ask respected colleagues to put something like stupidity to work for the world to pick up and read. I thank those who have been willing to take stupidity seriously by contributing to this collection. Gratitude is warmly extended to the community of Lacanians both international and in Aotearoa, especially the CLA (Aotearoa/New Zealand Centre for Lacanian Analysis), where stimulating debates and conversations are actively fostered. Thank you to my colleagues at Te Whare Wānanga o Waitaha/University of Canterbury and to my students from whom I learn so much.

Thank you to editors, Yu Ozaki and Natalie Mandziuk from Rowman and Littlefield, for their infinite patience and consistent support.

Heartfelt love and thanks are extended to my wonderful immediate family in Aotearoa – Reuben Derrick – and our daughters, Naima and Iris Derrick, as well as my parents (in-law), Judy and Nick Derrick, with whom I have great discussions and debates! And to my Yorkshire family, especially Frances Carr, who always looks after me when I am visiting.

Eternal gratitude to my dear friends inside, outside and on the periphery of academia. Special mention goes to Tamara Smith, Richard Boothby, Emma Agnew, Jan Völker, Ed Pluth, Todd McGowan and Jenny Woods.

Also to my musician, artist and poet friends: my deep respect for trying to keep the world a bit less stupid and for calling out stupidity for what it is. Ka pai!

Introduction

Why We Should Listen to Stupidity's Bad Reputation

Cindy Zeiher

In *Seminar IV* (1958),[1] Lacan depicts imaginary objectification in terms of the subject in pursuit of the image it seeks to subsume, rendered stupid in the mirror stage through being drawn and quartered over the four corners of the mirror. In this context it would indeed make sense to consider the big Other as necessarily stupid, firstly because it is forever beyond the subject's lucid possession and, secondly, the subject is anyway unable to either entertain the possibility of its complete nonexistence. It seems therefore that stupidity cannot be avoided, neither should it be.

There are two kinds of stupidity: lack of cleverness and naïvety posed by the innocent question. But for the Lacanian subject, there is simply stupidity because these two kinds are closely held together through the speech act being inescapably linked to what is attempting to be articulated. The subject is born to be stupid and thus bound to make wrestling with it their life's mission. It is tempting to argue that the enlightened Lacanian subject could learn not to be stupid. But no, this subject instead strives to handle their stupidity and that of others with a different knowledge. This is the kernel of stupidity, which is revealed in a mixture of the actuality and the ideal of life, in both what is or is not said and in what doesn't or cannot. Here, we need to submit to the inescapability of linguistic structure yet also be willing to break from it.

Certainly, stupidity harbours false, overdetermined problems or is even unable to comprehend them at all. It seems that stupidity, in being unable to demarcate mistake/error from lack, is simply misrecognizing its failure in dealing with structural inconsistency by insisting on its own unique inconsistency as the other side to something more coherent. Here, at least, stupidity, belonging to everyone, has the function of making life a bit more tolerable.

As an orientation of knowing, Hegel's expression 'shapes of consciousness' describes ways of life which challenge our struggle in thinking these because of discontinuities and errors. At the same time, such knowing is not always shaped solely by consciousness, which can be known because the ever-present unconscious can, when least expected, provoke of all sorts of (ill)intentioned and (mis)directions. Here, the unconscious makes us look rather stupid. One such shape of the (un)conscious is *jouissance*; we do and say all sorts of stupid things in the name of preserving the dignity of our unique *jouissance*. In this way, *jouissance* is stupid both in character and content, which can't be adequately explained or escaped from. It is tempting to excuse stupidity as merely some sort of deficit, notwithstanding its highly visible presentations as lack of will, insight, courage, thinking, action and so on. Yet, despite its lack being stunningly obvious, stupidity can prevail through self-perpetuating versions of itself such as 'common sense' or even 'fake news'.

One usually acts with the knowledge one supposes one possesses, without intending this to be stupid. But we are nevertheless stupid insofar as we spend a lot of time stalking the forbidden veiled *objet a*, which fascinates us, mustering up courage to one day pull the veil aside, only then to realize that the desired object was never there. We were all along being duped. There never was a sublime object for us to revel in, and we always were in the realm of the imaginary. The opaque veneer of the veil covering that which held our desire presented a surface past which it was difficult to see clearly. This well illustrates not only the function of the imaginary but also the manner and extent to which we are willing to be dupes in its name. The hoped-for great revelation turns out to be a hugely disappointing and sobering moment of realization that we have been duped by the precise functioning of a stupid big Other, by a stupid fantasmatic *objet a*, nothing like the sublime Kantian one we had hoped for.

In reflecting its own causality, the Freudian *id* exhibits an infantile feature, both existing and insisting that because we are speaking subjects caught within our own division, we are therefore bound to utter stupidities when trying to distinguish between knowledge and truth. Here, the *id* reminds us that our existence is necessarily bound to our not speaking the truth. In this way, the emergence of the *id* marks a break with the illusion that merely being able to think renders us subjects-supposed-to-know. The *id* provides a space for the unconscious to deceive the subject-supposed-to-know by reminding them that even in their quest for knowledge in the realm of truth, they will remain stupid. Furthermore, the *id* compels the subject towards a space of disobedience to the law, thereby guaranteeing that it is not the subject who mediates knowledge and truth but something else entirely, for example God or nature. The subject is too stupid to be a mediator of truth-knowledge because the irrational forces which characterize its division present a chaotic order inimical to the rationality of knowledge and truth. In the absence of a unique formulation to their division, subjects spit out one stupidity after another in order to express a discourse. Yet this is not altogether a bad thing insofar as when on the couch, it is precisely what the subject ought to be doing. Only when willing to be stupid and remain stupid can the subject be a psychoanalytic subject, that is one willing to take up a very different position vis-à-vis knowledge.

We know what stupidity does to us, for we have all been there and suffered its effects. The essays in this collection all make attempts at thinking about the function of stupidity and its psychic plumbing. It seems as if stupidity renders the gap between knowledge and truth more apparent. By imposing its psychic as well as objective reality, stupidity reveals that without unconscious knowledge, truth remains anonymous. In this way, through its reorientation of the subject's consciousness, stupidity reveals a powerful, unconscious force within the subject.

On the couch, however, stupidity is put to work and becomes something else. In capturing the desire not to be stupid, to literally get to the bottom of stupidity, the analysand is compelled to be stupid. The demand for psychoanalysis for the analysand is personal and direct: 'something is not working and there is the possibility that it could work better'. The analysand does not know exactly what is not working or why but is curious to find out without appearing too stupid. On the couch, the analysand puts their unique stupidity to work and in so doing makes stupidity better for them because here the question of lack remains open as an unconscious, *extimate* category of otherness. The essays in this collection offer how, in understanding how stupidity situates lack (and authority), stupidity inevitably tells us something about ourselves.

Insofar as our stupidity manifests as being duped by apparent (or the symbolic appearance of) truths proffered by big Others, we will always remain stupid. The shaman encourages the symptom of repression as truth; God encourages the symptom of negation as truth; modern science encourages the symptoms of foreclosure as truth. We will always be stupid via these big Others because that is precisely the function of stupidity, to keep the master discourse circulating around the chosen master (signifier). Under such conditions, stupidity can be thought of as the residue of an excess, a stupid leftover which nevertheless tells us much about what is being stifled.

Freud's *Totem and Taboo*[2] places the unconscious repression of imagination at the heart of the social bond. In *Civilisation and Its Discontents*, he situates the experience of pleasure and unpleasure, including what he calls 'cheap pleasures' such as stupid jokes, as central to the essence of civilization. He even suggests that we are stupid, libidinal jokes of our own making: 'Man has become, so to speak, a god with artificial limbs. He is quite impressive when he dons all his auxiliary organs, but they have not become part of him and still give him a good deal of trouble on occasion.'[3] In *The Future of an Illusion*, Freud argues that religion is a universal neurosis which gives rise to anxiety and aggression and argues that the way out of the problems of God or nature has always been culture, including hostility towards it. Culture is the neutralizing force for stupidity, practical in orientation and allowing immediate, collectivized, narcissistic satisfaction.[4] The contributors in this collection wrestle with the signifier of stupidity to ask: What does stupidity bestow on the individual psychoanalytic subject whose identifications with the social bond, beliefs, idealism and so on, fail? Perhaps far from asserting ignorance, stupidity has the important function – through keeping the subject fully present in speech – of igniting the subject's very curiosity.

NOTES

1. Jacques Lacan (1994 [2020]), *The Object Relation: The Seminar of Jacques Lacan, Book IV*, trans. Adrian Price, Cambridge, Polity.
2. Sigmund Freud (1913), *Totem and Taboo*, trans. James Strachey, Boston, Beacon Press.
3. Sigmund Freud (1929 [1930]), *Civilisation and Its Discontents*, trans. James Strachey, London,W. W. Norton and Co., p. 36.
4. Sigmund Freud (1927–1931), *Future of Illusion*, trans. James Strachey, London, W. W. Norton and Co., p. 13.

Chapter 1

Stupid Jokes

Jean-Michel Rabaté

IT'S THE (PSYCHIC) ECONOMY, STUPID!

I'll begin by stating my astonishment facing Freud's lack of astonishment about a joke on the issue of astonishment. This happens relatively early in the Jokes book, when Freud quotes a famous witticism by Lichtenberg: 'He wonders *that cats should have two holes cuts in their fur in the very place where they have eyes*.'[1] Freud introduces the sentence in those terms: 'A joke of Lichtenberg assumes a very special position among these stupidity jokes (*Dummheitswitzen)*.' His conclusion is similar: 'But to wonder at something self-evident, at something which is actually only the statement of an identity, is certainly foolish *(eine Dummheit)*.' However, Freud is not naïve enough to have taken the *Witz* at face value, for he contrasts it with a true expression of stupidity that he finds under the pen of the French historian Michelet. Freud believes that Michelet gushed in characteristically naïve terms: 'How beautifully Nature has arranged things, so that as soon as a child comes into the world it finds a mother ready to take it to her!' (JRU, p. 49). Happily for him, Michelet never wrote that silly remark, even if he often praises Nature in his impassioned and feminist-leaning prose-poem, claiming moreover that women are 'divine'.[2] By contrast, Freud adds that Lichtenberg only pretended to be stupid. Why? For what aim? Freud leaves the answer for later, writing rather mysteriously: 'Lichtenberg's is a joke which makes use of foolishness (*der Dummheit)* for some purpose, and which has something hidden behind it. But what? At this moment, it is true, that is something we cannot tell' (JRU, p. 49).

In fact, Freud never answers his own question directly; he never explicitly lets the cat out of the bag, which gives his book on jokes this well-known aspect of a maze full of circuitous detours, strange contradictions, moments of pure insight and passages of insipid dullness. Freud can indeed explain that there is a psychic economy at work; he compares the mechanism of jokes with that of the dream with its basic techniques of condensation, displacement and apparent absurdity, but he cannot say what was hidden behind the fur in the joke of the pierced cat fur.

A little later, Freud extols Lichtenberg's wit in his 'rich selection of shrewd and witty metaphors' (JRU, p. 69). Lichtenberg regularly takes a worn metaphor and then endows it with a new and literal meaning, which creates a funny clash, as when he exclaims that the 'torch of truth' cannot be carried in a crowd 'without singeing someone's beard' (JRU, p. 69). But the cat joke does not reveal any metaphor: we are just talking about real cats' furs and wondering how they have been made. Where is the unmasking announced? A later section is devoted to the unmasking of what has been hidden in a tendentious joke, as with those of Jewish marriage brokers blurting out the unsavory truth about the young women they are trying to pass off as beauties. They are just letting the truth slip through their lips; the joke has functioned as a revelation of what had been concealed. Freud praises the 'psychological insight of deep penetration' thus revealed: 'Without some assent of this kind, no one would allow themselves to be overcome by the automatism that brings the truth to light in these stories' (JRU, p. 101). In a note, he equates this mechanism with the slip of the tongue and self-betraying phenomena, an entire psychopathology of everyday life (JRU, p. 112).

What had been concealed, masked or unmasked in the joke about cats' furs? What is hilarious about the remark that pretends to be naïve in order to make us laugh is that we suddenly imagine a skinned cat trying to don a more or less fitting fur that, like a tailored suit, has to be cut to size. This sends us to visual jokes like those we find in early animated cartoons when, to express the force of a blast, animals would be pictured shivering, naked and without hair, feathers or even skin, or – why not? – to Derrida's impassioned meditation on what nakedness can mean for his cat in *The Animal That Therefore I Am.* Is the joke a covert meditation on the fact that erogenous zones have the structure of a hole, or rather of the rim circling a hole? Is he adding a chapter on scopophilia by recycling this old German joke about cats? Surely this same fur must have other holes – however, this is not Lichtenberg's point, this is not his preferred cut.

Derrida is helpful in his meditation on animals and the untranslatable French word *bêtise*, half-way between stupidity and bestiality, a bestiality that is only addressed to humans, of course. The first volume of his seminar on *The Beast and the Sovereign* examines at some length the semantics of stupidity. Derrida takes his cue from Avital Ronell's book on the topic, *Stupidity,* in which she claims that stupidity might be a 'quasi-concept'.[3] Ronell had posited an equation between Heidegger's recognition that his years of service as a Nazi chancellor had been a great *Dummheit*, the French bêtise, and the English stupidity. *Dummheit* shares an etymology with 'dumb' for both call up the sense of being mute, unable to speak, dumbstruck in stupefaction. I cannot repeat the way Derrida declines all the variations and nuances of the terms.[4] What interests me in this context is that Freud needs an animal, a cat, to give the best example of what he calls a *Dummheitswitz*. It is as if the dumbness had migrated from the eyes to the mouth, to refer to Freud's remark that in German *stumm* (mute) and *Stimme* (voice) would be linked as two antithetical meanings of a single primal radical.[5]

Why, then, would Freud want to classify this *Witz* among 'stupid jokes' if he really thinks that Lichtenberg is pretending to be stupid? One reason may be that it discloses the mechanism of automatism itself, which is why this joke offers a good example of a Bergsonian mechanism. The key is the subtle interaction between a passive verbal construction of 'cut' (*geschnitten)* and a plural noun in the dative, along with the active verb expressing the ability to see by 'having' eyes. Let us look at the original sentence: 'Er wundere sich, *daß den Katzen gerade an der Stelle zwei Löcher in den Pelz geschnitten wären, wo sie die Augen hatten.*'[6] Joyce Crick has perfectly rendered this passive with 'have two holes cut' but cannot render the dative (literally: '. . . **to** the cats/ **for** cats . . . two holes in the fur **were** cut, where they **had** eyes'). The cats 'have' their eyes, they own them in an active mode, while their fur remains in the passive. A precise technical requirement is contained in *gerade an der Stelle* – just at the spot where – which intervenes before the verb; a more correct word order would be '*daß den Katzen zwei Löcher in den Pelz, gerade an der Stelle wo sie die Augen hatten, geschnitten wären*'. Of course, this banal syntax would partly kill the joke.

This carefully crafted sentence evokes a fantasied image of a living organism appearing either as man-made or as machine-produced. Cats' furs would be seamless bags or continuous envelopes into which a violent gesture would have made cuts, creating holes that appear magically in front of the eyes. The effect of the *Witz* is to make us imagine a factory in which cats' furs would be 'cut' by machines or by the great couturier, Nature itself. The wonder is about the precision of these crucial cuts that appear precisely where the eyes will be. We see the production of an animal fur as a coat as if it had not been growing along with the eyes but brought in later. As Bergson's famous formula states, here we see the mechanical 'plated' (*plaqué*) on the living (*le vivant*), but what becomes ludicrous in the process is any type of teleology. Or rather, teleology is undermined by an unstoppable sense of wonder, which is, after all, the origin of all philosophy. There is no reason why the pseudo-naïve or childish series should stop: Why do cats have a third eyelid? What is the function of that 'haw' placed between their lower eyelid and their eyeball? Why can humans close their eyes but cannot close their ears or noses? Why do most cats have fur and many dogs don't? Do we 'have' a body the way cats 'have' eyes, or *are* we our sentient bodies?[7]

Has Freud failed to analyse the joke because he was not convinced by Bergson's logic? It looks as if Freud had caught up with Bergson rather late in the writing of his book and had not grappled with his formula so early in the writing. It is only in his last chapter that Freud quotes Bergson at some length. He first quotes Bergson quoting Pascal: the latter had noted that we laugh when we see two faces that are alike, but not when we see them in isolation (JRU, p. 201). Freud assumes that Bergson's 'persuasive argument' can fit easily under his main headings (JRU, pp. 201–2) but his efforts at harnessing Bergson's concept of 'rigidity' and making it serve for his economic theory of a saving in psychic energy, or of a comparative difference between two expenditures, are so much at odds with Bergson's logic that it does not sound convincing in the end.

A little later, Freud returns to Bergson and again quotes him in French. Bergson's main concepts, the 'mechanization of the living' and the 'substitution of the artificial for the natural' (JRU, p. 214), would move by way of a 'neighboring connection of thought from automaton to the automata', thus leading us to 'the faded memory of a childhood toy' (JRU, p. 215). As soon as Freud has stated Bergson's main principle, he shifts, forgets the binary natural/artificial and enthuses on the topic of childhood; he then develops the idea that a child's pleasure with playful activities shows that even if they are repetitive in themselves, they remain for all joyful, spontaneous and free of censorship.

However, when he pretends to agree with Bergson on the theme of childhood, Freud reveals that he has not accepted a logic predicated on the conflation of the living and the mechanical. He shows this when he uses the main example that had been taken as a starting point by Bergson: Why do we laugh when we see someone trip and fall? For Bergson, this shows that we suddenly see a reduction of the human to the machine; the pompous exhibition of social distinction is all of sudden reduced to a disarticulated puppet – hence a rather cruel laughter. For Freud, on the other hand, such a childish mirth can be justified because it derives from a sense of omnipotence:

> For instance, if someone slips and falls in the street, we laugh because this impression – why, we do not know – is comical. The child will laugh out of a feeling of superiority or *schadenfreude*: 'You've fallen down – I haven't'. We adults seem to have lost some of the motives for pleasure that the child has and, instead, under the same circumstances, we are aware of the 'comic' feeling as a substitute for what we have lost. (JRU, pp. 216–17)

It is curious to see Freud resorting to the superiority theory of laughter, which clashes with his general sense that laughter operates by some kind of psychic relief, and this almost nostalgic appeal to the lost paradise of childish enjoyment. The child's laughter is a laughter of 'pure pleasure' (*reiner Lust)* (JRU, p. 216), and adults replace this pleasure with a more sophisticated sense of the comic – a sense that is lacking in children.

Here, at the end of the book, the child's emphatic naïvety rephrases what had been called simple stupidity at the beginning, although many concepts have shifted in between. Hence, it will be important to get a better grasp of the complex genealogy of the Joke book. If Bergson appears only at the end, we need to remember that it is both in a chapter that Lacan felt was below the usual level of Freud's book. We may also remember that Lacan was severe when he discussed Bergson's theory of laughter in his seminar on the Formations of the Unconscious, a seminar beginning with an examination of Freud's analysis of jokes. When Lacan mentions Bergson's 'theory of the mechanical appearing in the midst of life', he waxes sarcastic:

> His work on laughter reapplies in a condensed and schematic way the myth of vital harmony, of *élan vital*, characterized by its supposedly endless novelty and permanent creation. You cannot fail to appreciate how outrageous this is when you read that one of the characteristics of the mechanical as opposed to the vital is said to be its repetitive character – as if we don't piss in the same way every day, or go to sleep in the same way, or as if one is reinventing love whenever one has a fuck.[8]

Lacan has a strong point here, for his Bergson is the classical philosopher tainted by idealism, not yet the thinker revamped by Deleuze to usher in desiring machines. What is more, Lacan notes that Bergson's very theory of laughter ends up generating systematic repetition: 'This explanation by means of the mechanical appears throughout the book like a mechanical explanation. What I mean is that it lapses into a lamentable stereotype that entirely leaves out what is essential in the phenomenon' (FU, p. 118).

Lacan opposes this Romantic view with the analysis of marionettes by Kleist, who understands how an ideal of pure grace can be achieved by mechanical contraptions. What Bergson has glimpsed but not well conceptualized is that laughter is indeed created by repetition:

> Laughter effectively touches everything that is an imitation, a doubling, a *Doppelgänger* or a mask, and if we look at it more closely it's not just a matter of masks, but of unmasking – and unmasking at moments that are worth thinking about. You go up to a child with your face covered by a mask, he laughs in a nervous or embarrassed way. You move a bit closer, a manifestation of anxiety starts to appear. You take off the mask, the child laughs. But if you are wearing another mask beneath this mask, he won't laugh one bit. (FU, p. 118)

Lacan hits the issue on the nail by focusing on the curious proximity between laughter and anxiety that one finds in the phenomenon of the uncanny. As Freud was aware, many examples of the uncanny could function as jokes – as what Jensen had analysed before him, the story of the explorer who is sitting on an old branch and suddenly discovers that it is a huge snake.[9] Lacan decides to follow Freud's insight, which is why he goes back to what is Freud's main example, the *Witz* provided by Heinrich Heine on the rich man who behaved so 'famillionairely' with him. I will have to make a detour via the intellectual genealogy of this analysis.

THOSE STUPEFYING MILLIONAIRES

We know how much Freud's book on jokes owes to the excellent book by Theodor Lipps, his *Comic and Humor* from 1898.[10] Freud had begun by gathering an anthology of Jewish jokes with the view of demonstrating the proximity between the mechanisms of dreams and wit. Lipps follows a more academic method, typical of the German mode of investigation at the time: he surveys the critical literature on the psychology of humor, and refutes all his predecessors one after the other, adding what he had put forward in his earlier *Grundtatsachen des Seelenlebens (Foundations of psychic life)*, published in 1883. Freud repeatedly praised Lipps in his letters to Fliess.[11] In fact, Freud was afraid of discovering that Lipps had anticipated all his own findings, the main principle being that most psychic processes are unconscious.[12] In September 1898, Freud explained that Lipps's vocabulary expressed exactly what he had understood about consciousness and the unconscious, quality and quantity. [13] Lipps is quoted three times in the first version of the *Interpretation of Dreams.* Freud quotes his best-known motto: the question of the unconscious is not a question of psychology; it is *the* question of psychology.[14]

In his book on humor and the comic, Lipps begins with Ewald Hecker, who thought that laughter was caused by a competition between two affects, pleasure and unpleasure. The resolution of this tension would be marked by laughter. Lipps has no difficulty criticizing the idea of pre-existing affects, for as he stressed it, laughter is instantaneous and creates affect, but does not reflect it. He then examines theories of Karl Groos, Johannes Ziegler, Emil Kräpelin, Hermann Lotze, Karl Herkenrath, Friedrich T. Vischer and finally Gerardus Heymans. Lipps retains from these diverging interpretations of the phenomenon of laughter a number of terms, like the idea of a 'contrast' between opposed affects, the concept of a reduction of the big to the small, the fact that laughter emerges when one catches consciousness coming to itself in *statu nascendi* and the idea of a momentary stupefaction (*Verblüffung)* caused by the *Witz*. However, because he has been unable to find a coherent affective theory of laughter, he decides to attack it from the angle of comedy.

Lipps begins by illustrating the comic via one example that is not politically correct, and that one could include in the category of stupid jokes or jokes about stupidity: a German peasant laughs wholeheartedly when he sees a black man for the first time. Why? He thinks that his face has been painted (KH, pp. 39–41, 51–52, 64). Incidentally, this naïve hilarity is also one of the most embarrassing examples analysed by Bergson in *Laughter*, in a passage in which he quotes Lipps.

> Why do we laugh when we see dark hair turned blonde? What causes the comic aspect of a purple nose? Why do we laugh at a negro? The question is embarrassing, it seems, for psychologists like Hecker, Kraepelin, and Lipps have posed it one after the other and answered differently. I wonder whether the answer was not given to me one day when I heard in the street a simple coachman insulting a black customer who was sitting in his coach of being 'unwashed' ('*mal lavé*'). Unwashed! A black face would thus be for us in our imagination a face daubed with ink or soot.[15]

This stupid laughter, which seems to be at the root of a certain knee-jerk racism, derives from the clash between the artificial (make-up, paint, soot) and the living: once more, the paint seems to have been directly 'plated' on a black man's face. Happily, Lipps moves on and examines more subtle jokes, mostly from Lichtenberg. In chapter VI, which he devoted to the 'subjective comic or witticism (*Witz*)', Lipps finally exposes his own concepts, and does this with the joke he finds in Heine: 'I was sitting next to Salomon Rotschild and he treated me like an equal, in quite a *famillionaire* manner.' He reconstructs the logical structure of this *Witz and* uses objections that had been presented by Heymans earlier.

Heymans had accused Lipps of not discussing one important feature of the Heine joke: he did not specify that the word *famillionaire* did not exist in the dictionary. For Heymans, the key to the specific effect achieved by Heine is strong surprise, amazement or stupefaction (*Verblüffung*). One first perceives that *famillionaire* is an obscure coining, a word that seems at first to be a mistake; then one will see meaning emerge: when light is made, there is a sudden 'enlightenment' *(Erleuchtung)* and it undoes the effect of the previous stupefaction. Laughter comes at this instant, crowning the intellectual discovery that this word had a meaning, or rather two meanings at once.[16] In short, Heymans reminded Lipps that he had forgotten to be astonished by the funny portmanteau word.

When he gathered his previous essays in his book, Lipps included this discussion in the chapter.[17] To respond to Heymans, Lipps divided his analysis of the *Witz* into three moments. The first stage is intellectual, in which one identifies the cognitive content of the joke. To understand the message, one must see who the butt of the joke is – clearly, in this case, it is the rich man of whom Heine makes fun, at least because he is usually so hard to reach. A second moment is when the 'stupefaction' caused by an invented word is assuaged by our mind, which is able to see the genesis of the portmanteau word. The effort of the mind is brought to nothing when we grasp the meaning in the apparent non-sense. Laughter frees an affect entailed by a useless effort. The comic comes from a meaning reduced to almost nothing, as Kant has defined it earlier. The real meaning consists in understanding how non-sense is not absurd. The third moment of the *Witz* appears when one understands that all this relies on an interaction between two persons. The *Witz* is then perceived as a gesture, a rapid performance, a single act. The meaning in that stage is given by the situation of enunciation. Here is where Lipps sees a movement from the 'quantitative' to the 'qualitative' in his analysis of unconscious psychic economy.

Freud quotes Lipps's main observation, which is couched in a concise and elegant sentence: 'The joke says what it says, not always in a few, but always in too few words, that is, in words that in strict logic or in the ordinary way of thinking and speaking are not sufficient to say it. It is ultimately able to say it outright, by not saying it at all' (JRU, p. 5).[18] Freud will likewise hesitate between 'few words', an expression in which one can see the first principle of saving in psychic expenditure, and a more complex, paradoxical and an economic 'too few', which introduces surreptitiously another kind of expenditure. Freud's psychic economy is a concept that had already been fully formulated by Lipps. What counts in fact is the excess pleasure gained in the process. There is a productivity of excess, whether it goes in the direction of 'more' or of 'less', as Bataille discovered a little later in London when he met Bergson in person but first had to read – to his intense disappointment – his short book *On Laughter*.

To illustrate this concept of the 'too few words', Lipps analyses another *Witz* by Heine that is not quoted by Freud. Heine was chatting with the same 'famillionaire' baron who wondered why the waters of the Seine are clean upstream above Paris but dirty and polluted downstream. Heine then replied: 'Oh, but your father too was a truly honorable man' (KH, p. 78). His ironical parallel implies that the son was 'dirty' because he was a true robber baron, whereas the father had made his fortune in a clean manner. Thus, a river can flow with transparent waters until it gets polluted. Freud does not quote this witticism, which is curious, since he quotes again all the other Heine quotes in Lipps. Did he find that Heine had really not said enough, and thus remained too obscure? The witticism sounds quite aggressive once deciphered and would not trigger even a faint smile today. In the failure of the joke, we find the Aristotelian mechanism of the enthymeme, the truncated syllogism that is so important when one analyses political rhetoric.

This is the logic that Freud calls a 'syllogistic façade' (JRU, p. 147), which forces the mind to work hard to fill in the gaps, as when one must guess the meaning of a riddle. It is clear that at this point in chapter V in which Freud analyses jokes as a social process, he abandons his earlier economic theory predicated upon a tendency to spare intellectual energy: 'The syllogistic façade splendidly fulfils the aim of capturing our attention by setting it a task. Even while we are beginning to consider what might be wrong with the reply, we are already laughing; our attention has been caught on the hop; the release of the liberated inhibitory charge is accomplished' (JRU, p. 147). This analysis combines an Aristotelian rhetoric and Lipps's main intuition about the third moment of the joke when it appears as a social and relational gesture. A joke requires an audience, hence leads to a rhetoric, which is often sexual or political, and not a poetics of short forms founded on an economic mechanism of sparing. The formulations of wit only work if they are corroborated or vetted by listeners. If then, as Lipps had argued, the deployment of wit presupposes the unconscious, it is indeed a social unconscious.

When he developed his dialectics of the quantitative and the qualitative, Lipps showed how the feeling of the great presupposes the feeling of the small. Comedy can always be generated by the reduction of the big to the small. Thus, a comic object will transform itself into psychic energy, which lets the subject engage in play and feel freer (KH, p. 120). A sense of the comic accompanies the perception of an excess of psychic force, and then this surplus, or more precisely 'surplus weight' (*Übergewicht*), generates a sense of psychological and ontological lightness. Curiously, it is an excess of weight that triggers lightness and cheerfulness. Comedy is predicated upon an unstable balance between the light and the heavy, between the fullness and the emptiness of meaning. A sudden resolution provokes relief when previous tension is let loose. In Lipps's striking formulation, the release (*das Losgelassene*) turns into an unbound or unknotted energy (*das Unbändige*) (KH, p. 128). Here is what triggers the affect of gaiety, which in the end generates laughter.

Lipps does not remain within the psychic parameter that he sketches in these precious pages, and then goes astray in the second part of his book when he attempts a sort of encyclopedia of all the forms of the comic. He examines the naïve, the comic of characters, situations, the burlesque, the grotesque and so on. Only in the last pages does he return to the unconscious when he tackles humor as a release from what he calls a 'psychic damming-up' (*psychische Stauung*) (KH, p. 198). The expression is taken up by Freud when he analyses the dialectical interaction between damming (or repression) and the sudden release of laughter freed from its social constraints:

> Anything baffling summons up in the listener that state of energy-distribution which Lipps called 'psychical damming-up', and no doubt he is also right to assume that the 'release' (*Entladung*) turns out to be all the more powerful, the greater the prior damming. It is true, Lipps's account is not concerned expressly with jokes, but with the comic in general; but it seems to us very likely that the discharge (*Abfuhr*) brought about in jokes, which released (*entladet*) an inhibitory charge of energy, is increased in the same way by the damming-up. (JRU, p. 148)

Clearly, Freud's Road had been mapped by Lipps. He would simply have to rethink the main examples of jokes, and Heine's coining offered a perfect verbal equivalent of the unconscious condensation evinced by dream images. Then he had to systematize the links between these verbal or oneiric manifestations and the agency of the unconscious. However, the first principle put forward by Freud was insufficient, as we have seen.[19] The first point I wanted to make here is to show how much Freud owed to the conversation between Lipps and Heymans when tackling his key example, Heine's quip of 'famillionaire', a new phrase that moreover seemed to condense the economic metaphor he was constantly resorting to. Lipps gave him the concept of relief (*Erleichterung*) that, as he concedes at the end of chapter V, should replace the principle of economy (JRU, p. 151). This is the relief that Lipps had posited as the consequence of the comic when it generates a sublime movement towards lightness of being in the lifting of all inhibition. And such a mechanism requires the intervention of a third person:

> The process in the joke's first person produces pleasure by lifting inhibition, reducing local expenditure; it does not seem to come to rest until, by the introduction of the mediating third person, it has obtained general relief by means of a discharge (of energy). (JRU, p. 151)

My second contention is that the choice of the coining had a more personal resonance for Freud. After the rather long technical analysis of the formation of the compound *famillionaire*, we have a second take in a later chapter, when Freud expatiates on the context of Heine's joke. This takes place in chapter V, when he addresses the social process behind jokes and gives more details about the biographical background. Heine had indeed a very rich uncle who was called Salomon, like the Rothschild in the joke. He was indeed a member of the family of millionaires, but the rub was that he wanted to marry his cousin. As Freud notes, Heine was treated *famillionairely*, which meant, in fact, that he was considered a poor and excluded family member. Freud then tells a family anecdote: 'I recall an old aunt of mine, who had married in the Heine family, telling of how, as a good-looking woman, she found herself one day sitting at the family table next to a fellow-guest who seemed to her rather unprepossessing and was treated with some disdain by the others' (JRU, p. 136). In fact, Freud has displaced the family relationship: it was his wife Martha who was related to the Heine family in Hamburg. This old aunt was Martha Bernays's aunt. Martha's grandfather was linked with the Heine family by marriage. Bernays was a famous rabbi whose renown had reached even Karl Marx. Actually, Marx's own mother, Henrietta Pressburg, shared a great-grandfather with Heine. When Marx had to go in exile to Paris, he found Heine, who had preceded him in 1831. When both lived in Paris, they would meet often; when Marx left for London, he wrote to Heine that he would be the person he would miss most. In Paris, Heine married a French woman, Augustine Mirat, whom he renamed Mathilde. Mathilde was from a low social background, much younger, very beautiful, but obviously not extremely intelligent. Until the last, she believed that her husband was non-Jewish and a practicing Protestant.

One can surmise that Heine's famous *Witz* hits at the core of the symptom: the link between incest and money, a knot that denounces his own stupidity. The rich uncle had been quite helpful for a while and wanted to help his nephew, but he was also defending his daughter against this quasi-incestuous attraction. Besides, Amalie Heine, the beautiful cousin, did not reciprocate Heine's feelings. Salomon Heine, who had first been quite generous with his nephew, decided to cut him off when he observed the failed love affair. Of course, this exclusion from the rich family had the desired effect: Heine was very sad and found his inspiration in this melancholia. What is the key to the link between money and incest? It has been well defined by James Joyce when he has Stephen Dedalus recycle Freud's reading about *Hamlet.* Launched in a peroration about Shakespeare's private life, he delivers a paradoxical proof that the bard must have been Jewish:

> Saint Thomas [. . .] writing of incest from a standpoint different from that of the new Viennese school Mr Magee spoke of, likens it in his wise and curious way to an avarice of the emotions. He means that the love so given to one near in blood is covetously withheld from some stranger who, it may be, hungers for it. Jews, whom Christians tax with avarice, are of all races most given to intermarriage.[20]

One need not allude to race and Jewishness to talk about endogamic desires. A rich, literary-minded and Protestant young man accomplished what had been forbidden to Heine and married his first cousin with terrible consequences. This is the well-known love story of André Gide that has been analysed at some length by Lacan. Gide was aware of his own male pedophilia and yet insisted on marrying his cousin. The outcome was dramatic, not only for the incident of the burnt correspondence so well discussed by Lacan, but also because their sexless union quickly ravaged Madeleine Rondeaux, who was always taken as the writer's mother.[21] Like Heine, Gide had made a joke about millionaires. Gide made Zeus, the main god of the classical pantheon, a modern capitalist, a banker in his very strange novel entitled *Prometheus Misbound.*

Lacan summarizes its convoluted plot in the second session of *Formations of the Unconscious* in the context of Freud's analysis of the *'famillionaire'* joke (FU, pp. 43–44). Gide's *Prometheus Misbound* develops an absurdist story that revolves around the meeting of Prometheus and Zeus. Zeus is presented in a modern version as a rich banker called 'the Miglionaire'.[22] Lacan gives the interesting precision that, according to him, this word should be pronounced as an Italian word (FU, 36), thus with a soft /gli/ sounded as /lii/. Gide, who had read Freud closely but critically, no doubt alludes to Heine's famous coining. In the play, Zeus experiments with the concept of 'gratuitous act' (*acte gratuit*, which means both 'unmotivated action' and 'free gesture'). Zeus the Miglionaire wants to prove that no action is 'free', which means 'free of debt'. Hence Prometheus will only be 'untied' when he ends up eating his own eagle, but his friend Coclès must die first.

CRIMINAL AND POLITICAL STUPIDITY

I wish to re-knot a few themes that have tended to go in different directions: the links between stupidity and stupefaction; the way a *Witz* can denounce the stupidity of the subject who thinks his or her intelligence has been revealed; the link between Freudian themes like incest, money and castration; the difference between stupidity and other forms of foolishness; and finally the role played by stupidity in politics.

In a book that Derrida commented on at some length in a seminar on the death penalty, Theodor Reik, a good disciple and younger friend of Freud, discusses the numerous occurrences of stupid behavior observed among criminals who had planned all the details of a murder. They leave compromising envelopes, their address is on a paper stuffed in the clothes of the victim, they go to an extreme of disguising themselves but leave behind their wallets and so on. The facts are so consistently surprising that such apparent negligence is often referred to as 'criminal stupidity.'[23] As Reik writes: 'Crimes carefully planned and calculated in advance are often betrayed by a "stupid" chance' (CC, p. 42).

Among the many examples Reik gives, one of the most amazing is that of the famous Colonel Redl, who had caught many spies as Chief of the Austrian Intelligence Department. But he was himself a spy for Russia, and in 1913, he received large sums of money in two envelopes, managed to escape but left the case of a penknife with his initials in the cab that had been traced to the letters. Reik concludes: 'Criminal psychology has summed this up in the doctrine of "the one stupid mistake" committed in almost every serious crime.' (CC, 47). It seems as if divine retribution was there to confuse the criminals, making them betray the deed by one singular blunder. Of course, all these signs of 'carelessness, negligence and improvidence' betray a general tendency that Reik identifies as the 'compulsion to confess', or an unconscious wish to expiate by provoking punishment for the deed. The tendency to self-punishment is a general feature of unconscious life; Reik's main theses were first disclosed in 1927 in a German book on *Geständniszwang und Strafbedürfnis* (*Compulsion to Confess and Need of Punishment*).

It is quite possible that Lacan had heard of it when he wrote his doctoral dissertation, even though he does not quote Reik but quotes Hesnard and Laforgue, who knew of Reik's work with criminals.[24] Here was the main motivation he saw underpinning the criminal action of the woman he called 'Aimée' (Marguerite Pantaine, born Jeanne Donnadieu). He heard in her first statements that Aimée had wanted to murder herself when stabbing the actress Duclos; she also displayed a huge sense of culpability.[25] The concluding chapter following the exposition of her case (she had tried to murder the actress because she was jealous) identifies a wish to obtain punishment – it is a 'paranoia of self-punishment'.[26] He even sees in her case a wish to punish the superego.[27] She wanted to destroy what she was hoping to become, this beautiful actress who had an affair with the Prince of Wales, of whom she was in love in an erotomaniac manner.

Whether Lacan knew Reik's thesis or not is not crucial – both follow a Freudian logic in which the subject acts like a Dostoevsky character whose crime is simply a search for punishment and redemption. His insights have powerful consequences: he militates against the death punishment, because he sees that on the contrary it is an incentive to crime: 'The prospect of punishment does not deter the criminal, but unconsciously drives him to the forbidden deed.' (CC, p. 295). But the deed has been accomplished because it provided an emotional relief for the sense of culpability: 'Crime is felt as an emotional relief because it can connect the unconscious feeling of guilt to something real, actual' (CC, p. 292). And then it has been 'confessed' by another act that functions like a parapraxis.

A short story by Edgar Poe condenses this mechanism. In the 'Imp of the Perverse', we discover a man who accomplishes a murder just because he thinks he has found a way that will never be detected. He leaves a poisoned candle next to his chosen victim's bed. No one suspects foul play, and for a while he is glad to have been undetected; for many years, given that he has 'left no shadow of a clue', he is unsuspected even though he inherited a lot of money. He basks in the assumption of an 'absolute security'.[28] He ruminates on this sense of 'being safe', he must repeat that sentence regularly. One day, walking in a street, he pursues the thought and brings it to its extreme conclusion: 'I arrested myself in the act of murmuring, half aloud, these customary syllables. In a fit of petulance, I remodelled them; thus, "I am safe – I am safe – yes – if I be not fool enough to make open confession!"' 'The very utterance of the idea that he could be stupid enough to denounce himself is sufficient to make him act upon it. He calls this moment a "fit of perversity"' but we know that it is his remorse that tries to find a way out. He even conflates his 'imp of the perverse' with the ghost of the dead man. From now on, he is lost – he starts running like a madman, then people pursue him, not knowing why. What follows produces the climax of this compulsion to denounce himself: 'The long-imprisoned secret burst forth from my soul. They say that I spoke with a distinct enunciation, but with marked emphasis and passionate hurry, as if in dread of interruption before concluding the brief, but pregnant sentences that consigned me to the hangman and to hell.'

What Poe has described so cogently under the term 'perversity' is a common enough phenomenon, often described as stupidity for want of another term. Its main feature is accomplishing a gesture that is both dreaded and desired. American culture is replete with stories of 'sick jokes', unfortunate 'jackass' stunts that end up maiming the protagonists, last selfies taken by a grinning person who then falls to his death from a cliff, a tower or a pole. I had started collecting them, but the abundance was such that I had to renounce cluttering my files. One that I find delightful is this one: 'Gun Enthusiasts Celebrate Man Who Shot Himself in the Balls as Their King.'[29] The victim was in San Diego and belonged to a group of gun enthusiasts who, to spurn the usual guidelines that insist on security, take selfies showing loaded weapons pointed at their genitals. He shot himself accidentally in the testicles, then was hailed as their hero. This happened in August 2020. The member of the group called 'Loaded Guns Pointed at Penis' posted a video of himself pointing a loaded .45 handgun at his crotch. There's a brief pause before the gun discharges. The video of the man shooting himself was subsequently deleted, but members of the group captured the video and then disseminated it widely.

It sounds too simple to read this as an unconscious desire for castration – but who could resist it? Even the inventor of literary criticism, Origen, castrated himself in a moment of enthusiasm he may have regretted later. T. S. Eliot captures well the endless ironies entailed by this action:

Polyphiloprogenitive
The sapient sutlers of the Lord
Drift across the window-panes.
In the beginning was the Word.

In the beginning was the Word.
Superfetation of τὸ ἕν,
And at the mensual turn of time
Produced enervate Origen.[30]

This anecdote directs us to the widespread function of stupidity in groups like the army, churches and more generally, political groups. Because stupidity always has something to do with stupefaction, it points to moments when we hesitate between blissful or ignorant peace and the fear of some punishment for our innate guilty feelings. This is evident in a famous passage of Machiavelli's *Prince* when he explains how his main political mentor, Cesare Borgia, managed to pacify the province of Romagna that he had just acquired. Chapter VII of The *Prince* describes how Borgia saw that the province was unruly, rife with fighting factions and endless vendettas that created a state of general anarchy. He dispatched a ruthless captain, Remirro de Orco, with the mission of re-establishing order by all means. 'A swift and cruel man' Remirro de Orco tortured, burnt, killed, plundered and reduced the rebellious families to abject submission. Borgia had noted that a certain resentment, even hatred towards his rule, had been created. Here was his elegant solution, much admired by Machiavelli:

> And because he knew that the past severity had caused some hatred against himself, so, to clear himself in the minds of the people, and gain them entirely to himself, he desired to show that, if any cruelty had been practiced, it had not originated with him, but in the natural sternness of the minister. Under this pretense he took Ramiro, and one morning caused him to be executed and left on the piazza at Cesena with the block and a bloody knife at his side. The ferocity of this spectacle caused the people to be at once satisfied and dismayed.

More literally, this action kept the people 'at once satisfied and stupid' (*La ferocità del quale spettacolo fece quelli popoli in un tempo rimanere soddisfatti e stupidi*). Can one be satisfied other than by being stupid? Were the people of Romagna terrorized, thus momentarily stupefied or were they more lastingly happy because of a peace they saw finally at hand, or else did they only pretend to be stupid? Nothing would be simpler than this: they just needed to be there and say nothing.

Time and space lack to develop this idea, so I'll just refer to the excellent book jointly written by Dany Nobus and Malcolm Quinn, *Knowing Nothing, Staying Stupid.*[31] They begin by distinguishing their point of view from that of Avital Ronell, who had stated at the outset in her *Stupidity* that, according to her, stupidity consisted in the absence of a relation to knowledge, whereas Nobus and Quinn rightly claim that stupidity defines a knowledge that is no longer relational, and that it even 'disrupts the relational quality of any discursive structure'.[32] While fully endorsing their astute remarks on what can be called the *docta ignorantia* of Lacanian psychoanalysis, I'll make two minor objections: first, transference has little chance of beginning if an analysand believes the analyst to be stupid and second, most of the time, especially in Seminar XX, when Lacan talks about the stupidity of the signifier, or the sublimity of stupidity, he is in fact analysing *bêtise*, the beastliness of the signifier, which as we have seen, is not exactly the same thing.[33]

I will end by mentioning the possibility of political resistance thanks to another type of strategy that resembles stupidity. In fact, this strategy has taken many names, as we know via Jaroslav Hašek's famous Soldier Švejk: as soon as the epic story begins, we are told that Švejk has been officially called an idiot, a certified imbecile, and that all the legal and medical authorities have demonstrated that he is totally stupid. Indeed, at first, he sounds moronic, as if his attitude was to mimic and echo the stupidity of institutions like the army, the police or medical knowledge.

I'll quote a passage in which Švejk fends off attempts by the policeman to lock him up in jail for some disturbance he is supposed to have caused; in fact, he was just being a patriot on the eve of the declaration of war: 'wasn't it stupidity, Mr Švejk [. . .] when, according to the deposition of the police officer [. . .] you caused a crowd of people to collect in front of the war proclamation which was posted up at the corner, and you incited people with shouts of "God Save Our Emperor Franz Joseph! The war is already won!"'[34] Here, Švejk is presented as 'honest' and a 'lamb' throughout this passage, whereas the official is a 'black and yellow wolf'. The official cannot believe that Švejk, who was escorted to jail by policemen, could have uttered those words seriously: 'After all you know very well that you were under police escort and that a patriotic pronouncement like that could and must have been regarded by the public as ironic rather than serious' (GSS, p. 45). But Švejk's response is disarming and leads to his being dismissed without further ado: 'When a chap is being led under police escort, answered Švejk, it is a very hard moment in his life. And if a man, even in such a difficult moment as that, doesn't forget what he ought to do when there's a war on, I think he's not so bad after all' (GSS, p. 45). Thus, to conclude, Švejk presents a better form of resistance than Bartleby, who remains too smart for his own good. Švejk keeps on spouting banalities like this, drawing on a wide knowledge that is often accurate, but presented with a tone of voice that sends it up. However, one never knows whether he is a total idiot who, because he goes to all the length of the silly ideologies he reflects, can undermine them, or a very smart anarchist like his creator, who just makes fun of the absurdity of all repressive systems. Stupidity is a powerful weapon in Hašek's satire. It is by considering such a double-edged castrating operation that we can have access to the deepest sources of humor.

NOTES

1. Sigmund Freud, *The Joke and Its Relation to the Unconscious,* trans. Joyce Crick, New York, Penguin, 2002, p. 49.

2. Roland Barthes analyses what he calls Michelet's lesbianism in the chapter entitled 'Her majesty the Woman' in his *Michelet*, trans. Richard Howard, Berkeley, University of California Press, 1987, pp. 147–57. See also Jules Michelet, *La Femme,* Paris, Hachette, 1860. The quoted sentence is not in the original. It may have been due to a mistranslation in the German version quoted by Freud. However, similarly ludicrous formulations often appear in books and essays on attachment theory.

3. Avital Ronell, *Stupidity,* Champaign, University of Illinois Press, 2002; Jacques Derrida, *The Beast and the Sovereign,* vol. 1, trans. by Geoffrey Bennington, Chicago, Chicago University Press, 2009, p. 173.

4. Derrida, *The Beast and the Sovereign,* vol. 1, pp. 136–86.

5. Sigmund Freud, "The Antithetical Meanings of Primal Words," in *Standard Edition*, vol. XI, ed. James Strachey, London, Hogarth Press, 1957, p. 159.

6. Sigmund Freud, "Der Witz und seine Beziehung zum Unbewußten," in *Psychologische Schriften,* Freud-Studien Ausgabe Bd. IV, ed. Ilse Grubrich-Simitis, Frankfurt, Fischer, 1970, p. 59.

7. This is the main question posed by Helmuth Plessner in his anthropology of human 'excentricity' predicated on a disjunction between 'being one's body' and 'having one's body'. For Plessner, this excentricity distinguishes humans from animals. See *Laughing and Crying, a Study of the Limits of Human Behavior,* trans. by James Spencer Churchill and Marjorie Grene, Evanston, Northwestern University Press, 2020, pp. 34–38.

8. Jacques Lacan, *Formations of the Unconscious, The Seminar Book V,* trans. Russell Grigg, Cambridge, Polity, 2017, pp. 117–18. Hereafter FU and page numbers.

9. 'One can read now and then in old accounts of journeys that someone sat down in an ancient forest on a tree trunk and that, to the horror of the traveller, this trunk suddenly began to move and showed itself to be a giant snake.' Ernst Jentsch, "On the Psychology of the Uncanny" (1906), p. 8, www.art3idea.psu.edu › locus › Jentsch_uncanny

10. Theodor Lipps, *Komik und Humor,* 1898, reprint 2006, The Echo Library. Hereafter KH and page numbers.

11. See Freud to Fliess, 26 August 1898, in *The Complete Letters of Sigmund Freud to Wilhelm Fliess, 1887–1004,* trans. Jeffrey M. Masson, Cambridge, Harvard University Press, 1985, p. 324.

12. Ibid., p. 325.

13. Ibid., p. 329.

14. Freud quotes a lecture given by Lipps in 1896 on "The Concept of the Unconscious in Psychology," *The Interpretation of Dreams*, 1st edition, trans. Joyce Crick, Oxford, Oxford University Press, 1999, p. 404.

15. Henri Bergson, "Le rire. Essai sur la signification du comique" (1900), p. 24, http: //www.exosens.fr/audio/text/Bergson/Le Rire. I translate.

16. Theodor Lipps had published a series of essays on the psychology of comedy, "Psychologie der Komik" in the *Philosophische Monatshefte,* XXIV (1888), pp. 385–422 and 513–29, XXV (1889), pp. 28–50, 129–60, 284–307, and 408–32. This was the basis for his Komik *und Humor* of 1898. The Dutch psychologist Geraldus Heymans examined Lipps's earlier analyses in a critical manner in "Aesthetische Untersuchungen im Anschluss an die Lippsche Theorie des Komischen," *Zeitschhrift für Psychologie und Physiologie der Sinnesorgane* II (1896), pp. 311–43 and 333–52.

17. Lipps analyses Heine's *Witz* first in KH, pp. 75–76 then expands the analysis on pp. 81–83 in a second passage in which he responds directly to Heymans's objection that he forgot to mention 'stupefaction'.

18. "Der Witz sagt, was er sagt, nicht immer in wenig, aber immer in zu wenig Worten, d.h. in Worten, die nach strenger Logik oder gemeiner denk- und redenweise dazu nicht genügen. Er kann es schliesslich geradezu sagen, indem er es verschweigt." KU, pp. 77–78.

19. I have tried to demonstrate this failure in "Can You Spare a Laugh? Lacan, Freud, and Marx on the Economy of Jokes," in *Lacan, Psychoanalysis and Comedy*, eds. Patricia Gherovici and Manya Steinkoler, Cambridge, Cambridge University Press, 2016, pp. 82–103.

20. James Joyce, *Ulysses,* ed. H. W. Gabler, New York, Random House, 1986, p. 169.

21. I have discussed this in Jean-Michel Rabaté, "The Youth of Gide, or the Letter and Desire," in *Reading Lacan's Ecrits: From "Signification of the Phallus" to "Metaphor of the Subject,"* New York, Routledge, 2019, pp. 92–199.

22. André Gide, "Le Prométhée mal enchainé," in *Romans et Récits*, vol. 1, ed. Pierre Masson, Paris, Gallimard, Pléiade, 2009, pp. 465–509.

23. Theodor Reik, *The Compulsion to Confess: On the Psychoanalysis of Crime and Punishment,* New York, Farrar, Strauss and Cudahy, 1959, p. 43. Hereafter CC and page numbers.

24. Angelo Hesnard and René Laforgue, *Les processus d'auto-punition* (1930), reprinted Paris, L'Harmattan, 2002.

25. Jacques Lacan, *De la psychose paranoïaque en rapport avec la personnalité* (1932), reprinted Paris, Seuil, 1980, p. 250.

26. Ibid., pp. 265–304.

27. Ibid., p. 302.

28. Online version at etc.usf.edu › pdf › passage › the-works-of-edgar-allan-poe/theimpofthe perverse.

29. Gun Enthusiast Points Pistol At His D*ck, Shoots Himself in the Balls, Lucy Connolly, 14 August 2020 14:08, https://www.unilad.co.uk/life/gun-enthusiast-points-pistol-at-his-dck-shoots-himself-in-the-balls/

30. T. S. Eliot, "Mr. Eliot's Sunday Morning Service," in *Collected ZPoems 1909–1962,* London, Faber and Faber, 1963, p. 57.

31. Dany Nobus and Malcolm Quinn, *Knowing Nothing, Staying Stupid: Elements for a Psychoanalytic Epistemology,* New York, Routledge, 2005.

32. Ibid., p. 5.

33. See Jacques Lacan, *Le Séminaire, Livre XX, Encore,* Paris, Seuil, 1975, pp. 18–19, and pp. 24–27.

34. Jaroslav Hašek, *The Good Soldier Švejk*, trans. Cecil Parrott, London, Penguin, 1973, pp. 44–45. Abbreviated as GSS and page numbers.

REFERENCES

Barthes, Roland, *Michelet,* trans. Richard Howard, Berkeley, University of California Press, 1987.

Bergson, Henri, "Le Rire: Essai sur la signification du comique" (1900), http://www.exosens.fr/audio/text/Bergson/Le Rire.

Connolly, Lucy, "Gun Enthusiast Points Pistol At His D*ck, Shoots Himself in the Balls," https://www.unilad.co.uk/life/gun-enthusiast-points-pistol-at-his-dck-shoots-himself-in-the-balls/.

Derrida, Jacques, *The Beast and the Sovereign,* vol. 1, trans. Geoffrey Bennington, Chicago, Chicago University Press, 2009.

Eliot, Thomas S. "Mr. Eliot's Sunday Morning Service," in *Collected Poems 1909–1962,* London, Faber and Faber, 1963.

Freud, Sigmund, *Standard Edition*, trans. James Strachey, vol. XI, London, Hogarth Press, 1957.

———, "Der Witz und seine Beziehung zum Unbewußten," in *Psychologische Schriften,* Freud-Studien Ausgabe Band IV, ed. Ilse Grubrich-Simitis, Frankfurt, Fischer, 1970, pp. 9–219.

———, *The Complete Letters of Sigmund Freud to Wilhelm Fliess, 1887–1004,* trans. Jeffrey M. Masson, Cambridge, Harvard University Press, 1985.

———, *The Interpretation of Dreams*, 1st edition, trans. Joyce Crick, Oxford, Oxford University Press, 1999.

———, The *Joke and Its Relation to the Unconscious,* trans. Joyce Crick, New York, Penguin, 2002.

Gide, André, *Romans et Récits*, vol. 1, ed. Pierre Masson, Paris, Gallimard, Pléiade, 2009.

Hašek, Jaroslav, *The Good Soldier Švejk*, trans. Cecil Parrott, London, Penguin, 1973.

Hesnard, Angelo, and Laforgue, René, *Les processus d'auto-punition* (1930), reprinted Paris, L'Harmattan, 2002.

Heymans, Geraldus, "Aesthetische Untersuchungen im Anschluss an die Lippsche Theorie des Komischen," *Zeitschhrift für Psychologie und Physiologie der Sinnesorgane* II (1896) pp. 311–43 and pp. 333–52.

Jentsch, Ernest, "On the Psychology of the Uncanny" (1906), www.art3idea.psu.edu › locus › Jentsch_uncanny

Joyce, James, *Ulysses,* ed. H. W. Gabler, New York, Random House, 1986.

Lacan, Jacques, *Le Séminaire, Livre XX, Encore,* Paris, Seuil, 1975.

———, *De la psychose paranoïaque en rapport avec la personnalité* (1932), reprinted Paris, Seuil, 1980.

———, *Formations of the Unconscious, The Seminar Book V,* trans. Russell Grigg, Cambridge, Polity, 2017.

Lipps, Theodor, *Komik und Humor* (1898), reprint 2006 by The Echo Library.

Michelet, Jules, *La Femme,* Paris, Hachette, 1860.

Nobus, Dany, and Quinn, Malcolm Quinn, *Knowing Nothing, Staying Stupid: Elements for a Psychoanalytic Epistemology,* New York, Routledge, 2005.

Plessner, Helmut, *Laughing and Crying, A Study of the Limits of Human Behavior,* trans. James Spencer Churchill and Marjorie Grene, Evanston, Northwestern University Press, 2020.

Poe, Edgar Allan, "The Imp of the Perverse," *etc.usf.edu* › pdf › passage › the-works-of-edgar-allan-poe/theimpofthe perverse.

Rabaté, Jean-Michel, "Can You Spare a Laugh? Lacan, Freud, and Marx on the Economy of Jokes," in *Lacan, Psychoanalysis and Comedy*, ed. Patricia Gherovici and Manya Steinkoler, Cambridge, Cambridge University Press, 2016, pp. 82–103.

———, "The Youth of Gide, or the Letter and Desire," in *Reading Lacan's Ecrits: From "Signification of the Phallus" to "Metaphor of the Subject,"* eds. Stijn Vanheule, Derek Hook and Calum Neill, New York, Routledge, 2019, pp. 92–199.

Reik, Theodor, *The Compulsion to Confess: On the Psychoanalysis of Crime and Punishment,* New York, Farrar, Strauss and Cudahy, 1959.

Ronell, Avital, *Stupidity,* Champaign, University of Illinois Press, 2002.

Chapter 2

Natural Born Dupes

A Lacanian Theory of Stupidity

Gioele P. Cima

BEYOND EXEGETICAL OBSCURITY: A BRIEF ANATOMY OF *SEMINAR XXI*

Seminar XXI, *Le non-dupes errent (1973–1974)*, is one of the most fascinating and at once most underrated moments in Jacques Lacan's teaching and one that over the years has unfairly received little attention among critics. For example, according to the French philosopher Jean-Claude Milner, after *Seminar XX* something in Lacan's teaching 'breaks'[1] and the splendor of the mathematical formalization and hyper-Bourbakism[2] of the very early 1970s gives way to the 'anti-mathematics' of the Borromean knot.[3] In this regard, it is highly symptomatic that in *L'Œuvre Claire* [The Clear Work] Milner, who is certainly not unfamiliar with the late and the very last Lacan,[4] denounces the breakup of the 'second Lacanian classicism' while omitting any reference to *Seminar XXI*, the obscure seminar in which knot and matheme coexist antinomically and form an almost monstrous hybrid. Restating this general exegetic penumbra, in his 'Dossier' Marcelle Marini only devotes a few lines to the presentation of the seminar, remarking that apart from its 'parodic or very abstract form', it has 'nothing really new'[5] to say. Hastly anticipating the introduction of the fourth Borromean ring at *Seminar XXI* (which was actually only to make its debut during *R.S.I. (1974–1975)*), Marini even goes as far as defining *Les non-dupes errent* as the seminar of the knot and of the 'fourth circle (the one that creates the knot)',[6] consequently neglecting most of its theoretical complexity. François Regnault also seems to make the same mistake when, deliberately skipping from *Seminar XX* to *Seminar XXII*, he states that 'the Name-of-the-Father is added to the knot as something more', as 'something added'[7] (a thesis that, as we shall see, entirely overlooks the main arguments of *Seminar XXI*). In contrast to Marini and Regnault,

Christiane Lacôte is one of the few commentators who does justice to the seminar, stressing the important mediating role it carries out between the seminars of the first and the second half of the 1970s: according to her, *Seminar XXI* equally offers both an extension of the previous and certainly better-known *Seminar XX* (of which it radicalizes certain crucial concepts, such as the role and function of writing, the ductility of the Borromean knot, the para-ontological formula 'there is no sexual relationship' and the modal logics) and an 'accelerated' rudimentary glimpse into the final period of Lacan's teaching (anticipating the irreverent tone and certain particular notions, such as the debilitating function of the Symbolic, the limits of science and the fragility of psychoanalytical practice).[8] However, my impression is that even Lacôte's meticulous reading fails to insist adequately on what makes this seminar an *unicum*: alongside its function as a filter, *Les non-dupes errent* contains intuitions that would never reappear in the later seminars, mainly because they are overshadowed by the hegemony of the Borromean knot or obscured by the notorious pervasive pessimism of Lacan's latest years. Schematically, we can summarize the main arguments treated in *Seminar XXI* by means of five essential hypotheses.

1. The three registers of the Real, the Imaginary and the Symbolic are immanent and 'strictly equivalent'. After introducing the Borromean knot in *Seminar XX*[9] and illustrating its fundamental property (the three rings are linked in such a way that if any one of them is severed, all three become separated[10]), Lacan adapts the mutual solidarity between the three rings to the Real-Imaginary-Symbolic triad.
2. The equivalence of the three registers allows us to reinstate the Real as a positive order, and no longer as what is excluded a priori and perpetually shut out: as we shall see, although he preserves the definition of the Real as the impossible and non-formalizable (the 'hole in knowledge', to use Luigi Francesco Clemente's effective phrase[11]), such a choice allows Lacan to exploit this tricky register as a benchmark on which to graft a psychoanalysis directed towards the Real and to define the ethical and political limits of an analytical practice that does not degenerate into fraud or imposture.
3. With the decay of hyper-Bourbakism, writing no longer simply consists of a pure literalization, of an infallible 'ground' for mathematical science, but coincides with a precarious flanking of the edge of the Real: as Lacan had already noticed in the previous year, the transmissibility of mathemes is no longer guaranteed because, even if their foundation claims to be literal and impersonal, 'nevertheless, they are not transmitted without the help of language, and that's what makes the whole thing shaky'.[12]

4. Language no longer carries out a humanizing function but, on the contrary, a profoundly *de-stabilizing* one. This change of direction turns the philosophical anthropology of the early Lacan into a negative, or even monstrous, anthropocentrism[13] in which the cut of the signifier no longer compensates for the impasse of the biological but produces an irreducible perpetual disorientation that the very last seminars would rename 'mental debility'.
5. Closely connected to the previous points, the unconscious is redefined as a knowledge [*savoir*] that has to be invented starting from the assumption of the hole of the Real: to invent this knowledge, and avoid becoming prey to the bottomless freedom of the psychotic, it becomes necessary to let oneself be 'duped' by the viscosity of structure, abiding by it as best as one can.

As we shall see, each of these points constitutes a fundamental premise to define the most important and seductive thesis of the entire seminar, a hapax in Lacan's teachings that I propose to call *The Lacanian Ethics of Stupidity*.

FROM *LES NOMS DU PÈRE* TO *LES NON-DUPES ERRENT*

As the title of the seminar emphatically indicates, there is a clear homophony between *Les non-dupes errent* (which for now we can translate as 'the non-dupes err') and *Les Noms du Père* (the Names-of-the-Father), a detail that links *Seminar XXI* to the so-called 'interrupted seminar' of 1963 on the Names-of-the-Father. During this tumultuous year, following the revocation of his role as a training analyst and his 'excommunication'[14] from the *Société Française de Psychanalyse*, Lacan is also asked to leave Sainte-Anne hospital, where he held the previous ten seminars. In the midst of this political and institutional commotion, he only manages to deliver a single cryptic lesson of the 1963 seminar, with the result that when in January 1964 the meetings resume in the premises of the *École Normale* with a different title (*The Four Fundamental Concepts of Psychoanalysis*) and program, the question of the Names-of-the Father falls silent (a silence that will last over six years).[15]

Though Lacan already began to rediscuss the concept in 1969, it is *Seminar XXI* that marks a crucial turn in the elaboration of the Names-of-the-Father and their hermetic plurality. It is a Seminar that marks an authentic watershed between the 'sacrilegious' lesson of 1963 (in which the function of nomination is first introduced) and the beginning of the final controversial period of the French analyst's teaching (ushered in by the reduction of these names, in *Seminar XXIII*, to mere symptoms or 'tools'[16]). In *Seminar XXI*, Lacan begins to direct psychoanalytic knowledge back to the Borromean knot; an operation that would be fulfilled – not without sudden reversals and remarkable contradictions – only the following year, in *R.S.I.* By staging the dizzying passage from the matheme (a key concept in the early 1970s) to the knot, *Seminar XXI* opens up an authentic grey area in which Lacan already has one foot out of the obsession for mathematical formalization, but hasn't yet plunged himself into what Roudinesco scornfully defines as the 'planet Borromeo'.[17] The importance of the seminar lies precisely in this ancipital form, in which the pluralization of the Names-of-the-Father and the postulate of the equivalence of the three registers produce an ephemeral but resounding overlapping that allows us to say that the Symbolic, the Imaginary and the Real really are the *true* Names-of-the-Father.[18]

With this thesis, Lacan is forced to make two further specific moves: on the one hand, to reappraise the Imaginary – the quirky register traditionally identified with misrecognition, alienation and delusion – and on the other, to put in check the (alleged) superiority of the Symbolic – doxastically the register of language and intersubjectivity. With regard to the latter, we can say that Lacan had *already* implicitly scaled down (if not even depreciated) the Symbolic in 1963 when he decided to state this pluralization: with this move, the Symbolic is not only divested of the transcendental principle of nomination but also dispossessed of its logical primacy, ending up relegated to the existential burden of the Word, which fatally upsets the condition of the human animal. It's precisely the semantics of *Seminar XXI* which, ten years later, exacerbates the consequences of this scaling down, transforming it into an authentic species-specific stigma: far from representing a pacifying harmonic instance, the Symbolic now exerts a debilitating function on man, one of mental exhaustion. This negative anthropocentrism, according to which the speaking animal is *de*-naturalized by language, represents an important change in direction from Lacan's philosophical anthropology theses of the early 1950s. Whereas in the first two seminars, Lacan's main argument was that the Symbolic and language come into play to *overcome* the condition of desperate biological helplessness of man (*Hilflosigkeit*) – the 'premature' mammal – for the late and very last Lacan, language and the Symbolic exert a *mutilating* action on the subject, consigning him to mental debility.[19] Whereas in *Seminar II* Lacan said that the animal is a 'jammed machine' because its parameters are frozen by the fixedness of its habitat, while man is a free animal because he is 'decomposed',[20] with this reversal of perspective, the decomposition the Symbolic turns the human animal into something *a*-typical, perennially maladjusted.

In the same way, during *Seminar XXI* both language and the unconscious are defined using almost Burroughsian[21] terms, as a 'canker' or a 'cloth', a parasitical organism that makes the speaking animal weak-minded.[22] The

Word does not simply limit itself to *de-naturalizing human beings*, separating them from all the other animals, but it transfigures them into something *un*-differentiated and scarcely recognizable, something monstrous:

> It is when the Word is incarnated that things really start going badly. [The speaking animal] is no longer at all happy, he no longer resembles at all a little dog who wags his tail or a nice monkey who masturbates. He no longer resembles anything. He is ravaged by the Word. [. . .] The speaking being is a sick animal. 'In the beginning was the Word' says the same thing.[23]

Instead of elevating the human animal above all the other simple animals, the establishment of language drains the subject of every distinctive feature, stigmatizing it as 'that bizarre speaking animal'.[24]

With regard to the Imaginary, Lacan is all the more explicit, if not even solemn:

> You have always comprehended – [. . .] but wrongly – that the progress, the forward step was to have marked the overwhelming importance of the Symbolic with respect to this misfortunate Imaginary.[25]

And again: 'people attribute it to me wanting the Imaginary to be excrement, muck [*caca, bobo*], a bad thing, and that what is supposed to be good is the Symbolic'.[26] Instead, the Imaginary is 'a *dit-mansion* [. . .] just as important as the others',[27] which should no longer be relegated to being a bone in the throat of the Symbolic, a white stain from which the subject has to be disalienated. Rather, if the Symbolic is codification, formalization, deciphering, the Imaginary is meaning [*sens*],[28] an essential component without which we couldn't live, appointed to carry out a double function. On the one hand, it 'stops the deciphering' of the Symbolic, thus moving from being its saboteur to its necessary suppressor, the 'froth' that seals the abyss of the Real. On the other, because 'there is always intuition in what the mathematician starts from', the Imaginary is also 'an intuition of what is to be symbolised',[29] what Daniel Dennett defines as *intuition pumps* and Henri Poincaré described as 'a small push at the right moment', which presents itself with 'brevity, suddenness and immediate certainty'.[30] In this new role, the Imaginary is at once the *halt* and the raw material of any possible symbolization, something that no longer needs to be cleaned up by the Symbolic, but that seems productively tied to it. It is precisely in this tension between the negative anthropocentrism of the Symbolic and the structurally indispensable nature of the Imaginary that the *Lacanian Ethics of Stupidity* takes shape.

WE ARE ALL DUPED: TOWARDS AN ETHICS OF STUPIDITY

As we shall see, not only are the two formulas *Les non-dupes errent* and *Les noms du père* are homophones but, as Lacan explains, they convey 'the same knowledge [*le meme savoir*]'.[31] To better grasp this suggestion, it is necessary to dwell on a further ambiguity of the seminar title: in fact, the syntagm *Les non-dupes errent* does not exhaust itself in the pantomimic reference to the Names-of-the-Father, but is also grafted onto the ambivalence of the verb 'err' (wander) and of the noun 'dupe' (fool). This is because, in French, 'err' can mean both the impetus [*lancée*], the inertial impulse of those who wander aimlessly, and the error, the *fiasco*, so that the title of the seminar can be read both as 'The non-dupes wander' and as 'The non-dupes are mistaken'. In a similar fashion, the 'dupe' (the 'stupid' that is easily fooled) is, etymologically, 'the bird one can trap, precisely because it is stupid'.[32] Prolonging this logic, then, non-dupes should be those who do not allow themselves to be fooled, who do not fall into the 'snare'. And yet, from the perspective of the unconscious, this naïve and linear distinction loses all its value, forcing us to rethink the relationship between dupes and non-dupes according to what Lacan, mocking his 'subject supposed to know', calls 'knowledge supposed subject [*savoir suppose sujet*]'[33]: a knowledge that ciphers and works unbeknownst to the subject.[34] This formula is not new to *Seminar XXI* and can already be found in the final stages of *Seminar XV*, where Lacan defines the unconscious as a 'knowledge without subject [*savoir sans sujet*]',[35] that is, a knowledge that is 'ciphered' without the supposition of an Other, that is, a decentralized and interrupted articulation.

It remains now to ask how Lacan manages to link this peculiar form of knowledge (one of the most extreme consequences of the inexistence of a metalanguage) with the 'wanderers' of *Les non-dupes errent*. What is it that a similar knowledge, desubjectivezed but at the same time unconscious, shares with the dupe, the fool who easily falls into a trap? On closer inspection, this relationship turns out to be much more crucial than it seems.

Indeed, on the one hand, Lacan specifies that the derivation of 'err' from 'to wander' (*itinerare*) is actually not correct, because it is the result of a linguistic contamination: rather, '*errer* comes from *iterare*, which has nothing to do with a journey, since it means "to repeat", from *iterum*'.[36] Therefore, the dupe that wanders must be understood first and foremost as someone who has remained stuck to a particular type of repetition. As Lacan demonstrates, using as an example the so-called 'errant knight', it is not the thirst for adventure that moves the subject, nor any hidden desire to know ('it is not desire that presides over knowledge, it is *horror*'[37]), but rather the thrust of the compulsion to repeat. Instead of a fervent, brave explorer, the latter is the hostage of a knowledge that, precisely because it can never be fully subjectivized, makes the subject run in circles.[38] Knowledge, like the object *a* and against the onto-theological imaginary readings inspired by the so-called *homo viator*, is not intentional (i.e. in front of the subject), but always behind his back, breathing down his neck:

> Life is that of the *viator*. Those who in this lower world – as they say – are in a foreign land. The only thing that they do not notice is that simply by bringing out this function of foreigner, they give rise at the same time to the third term, the third dimension, the one thanks to which they will never get out of the relationship of this life.[39]

On the other hand, although it undoubtedly constitutes the key term of *Seminar XXI*, it is not the first time that during such discussions Lacan uses the word 'dupe'. In particular, there are three significant recurrences of this term that we find in the Lacan of the late 1960s, all decidedly close to the notion of the 'knowledge supposed subject':

1. The first can be found, not surprisingly, precisely in the very last session of *Seminar XV*. Here, by describing the object *a* as an object that brings forth lack, distance (and not mediation or binding) between the subjects, Lacan emphasizes that it is this very mismatch that makes the relationship between the subject and the Other deeply 'asymmetric', out of focus. Because of this incommensurability between the subject and the other, even 'dialogue' (i.e. language as communication) turns out to be a 'duperie',[40] something that doesn't work or that does not produce the expected effects.
2. The following year, in *Seminar XVI*, the seminar on the Other's inconsistency and the automation of knowledge, the term returns with a decidedly more structured meaning. During the session of 5 March 1969, Lacan offers his audience a definition of knowledge that is surprisingly in line with that proposed in *Seminar XXI*: knowledge is 'a truth endowed with the property for which we cannot know anything about'.[41] In other words, knowledge is here elevated to a specific articulation that, while operating unbeknownst to the subject and outside of his awareness, nevertheless adheres to him with the same exclusive viscosity of a truth. Knowledge is a truth of which the subject knows nothing but by which at the same time he is continuously cheated. In the same session, in order to describe the way in which this unconscious knowledge works, Lacan speaks of '"duperie" of consciousness', of a scam that – he specifies – must in no way be confused with a *tromperie*, that is a deception.[42]

3. Finally, in *Seminar XVIII*, *duperie* is defined as the process through which the subject is 'captured' in the semblance of discourse. Even in this case, Lacan speaks of a 'fundamental scam',[43] that is, a complex mechanism whose unconscious dynamics unfolds throughout the subject's entire life. Afterwards, with an explicit reference to the theory of knowledge and alienation in Karl Marx, Lacan equates cognition tout court with a defective biological function, which would be used by the speaking animal as a precarious survival device (a point he will make even more emphatically in the last seminars). In a nutshell, we can summarize Lacan's position as follows: the *duperie* implemented by the semblance of discourse penetrates the most intimate folds of human biology, constituting both a defensive survival mechanism *and* a primitive scam, something that makes the human animal a fool for the entirety of his life.

Consequently, not only does the subject repeat something believing that he wanders (i.e. he mistakes the *iterative* logic of the signifier for an *itinerant* one), but it is precisely in this 'truth' articulated behind him that the deception (i.e. the fundamental duperie that precedes and conditions every possible form of wandering) lies.

However, the overlap between knowledge and repetition developed by Lacan between the late 1960s and early 1970s must not be confused neither with the repetition compulsion (*Wiederholungszwang*) described by mainstream psychoanalysis, nor with its francophone depleted variant, the repetition automatism (*automatisme de repetition*).[44]

Far from overlapping with some pre-established content, an ancestral meaning that should direct the vicissitudes of the subject in a sort of *destiny* (as in the case of Jungian analytical psychology), this relationship must be traced back to the pure differential logic of the signifier, that is, to a purely formal opposition without content: *duperie* is a cut, the fundamental break with which the saying [*dire*] is engraved on the subject.

This fundamental premise shows us that, unlike what some commentators believe, 'les non-dupes errent' does not simply indicate a desecration of the Names-of-the-Father, but designates the very formula of *structure*, namely the impossibility of separating man from the grip of language and the signifier. Lacan's hypothesis, in turn, implies two important corollaries, which are developed from the earliest sessions of *Seminar XXI*. First, the grip of language on the speaking animal, which in turn is inextricable from the establishment of the unconscious, 'never lets go':[45] since man is born already bathed in language, this structure must be grasped as coextensive with his own life, something that accompanies him from the very first cry to death. As already mentioned in *Seminar XVIII*, language is a scam with no exit. Second, since this mark is constitutively traumatic (amalgamating the words *trou* (hole) and *traumatisme* (trauma) Lacan says that language is a *troumatisme*, a corrosive and desperate replacement[46]), the speaking animal is unconsciously forced to resort to an 'invention' that can soothe his anxiety. The fact that there is a *saying*, that is, that the human animal is first and foremost a speaking animal, is there to cork the hole of the absence of the sexual relationship.

Further developing one of *Encore*'s central arguments, Lacan claims that in humankind, language is simultaneously both a cork and a barrier to the absence of a sexual relationship: not only is the fact that we speak an immediate consequence of our inability to write (logically) the sexual relationship, but it is precisely the presence of language that retroactively raises the question of the (im)possibility of this relationship.[47] It is language that produces and concomitantly obstructs the (possibility of the) sexual relationship as a *real* phenomenon. Consequently, this impasse opens a wound in the speaking animal that can be mitigated only with an injection of meaning [*sens*], and without which he would fall into total despair.

According to the Lacan of *Seminar XXI*, it is exactly this relationship between language (the Symbolic), the absence of the sexual relationship (the Real) and meaning (the Imaginary) that articulates the structure of the unconscious in the form of knowledge.[48] More precisely, structure is nothing but this specific 'relationship [of the subject] to a certain knowledge',[49] a sheer invention that screens the abyss of the Real.[50]

Returning to the formula of *Seminar XXI*, we can then see how, with the addition of the unconscious, the naïve distinction between dupes and non-dupes is completely subverted and, as a consequence of that, if escaping the 'snare' of the structure is an impossible task, then the speaking animal is always and necessarily also a fooled animal: a dupe. And yet, the fact that 'it is necessary to be a dupe, namely, to stick to structure' [51] drastically complicates the position of the non-dupes. Moreover, if the speaking animal is always already a dupe, what happens to non-dupes? At first, the necessity of the structure seems to unravel the one between dupes and non-dupes as a *false* dualism, that is, a fake binomial in which the position of the non-dupe becomes nothing but a mere 'hallucinosis' inscribed in the genetics of the dupe itself. For Lacan, non-dupes would be those who, convinced that they could escape the misunderstandings and the impasses of language, 'refuse to be captured by the space of the speaking being'.[52] To put it in the jargon of *Seminar XXI*: if the position of the dupe is the zero degree of subjectivity, of the one who errs (wanders/repeats) in the infinite *chicane* of language without ever being able to get out of it, then that of the non-dupe, who errs (is mistaken) precisely because he refuses to wander, seems to become an *impossible* position, namely a fraud. However, instead of locking itself into something unproductive and almost noumenal, the condition of the non-dupes is decidedly paradigmatic because it underlies – albeit negatively – the function of *choice* on which the relationship between subject and structure relies.

If, theoretically speaking, the position of the non-dupes is simply aporetic, from an ethical perspective the latter becomes that of those who choose *not* to choose; those who, under the illusion of being able to *reject* the knowledge of structure, think they are free and, for this reason, are in bad faith.

Deluding themselves that they can really escape from the grip of language and denying the existence of the unconscious, non-dupes do not realize how it is this very choice of not choosing that confirms their definitive capture in the snare of the structure.[53] This is why Lacan emphasizes that non-dupes are 'two times dupes':[54] once, as each speaking animal is constitutively a dupe, that is an animal 'deceived' by the 'parasite' of language; twice, because they delude themselves that they can remain indifferent to their inexorable condition.[55]

As opposed to sheer impostors, true non-dupes are always 'second-degree' non-dupes, namely non-dupes *among* the dupes: they are those who, coming to terms with the necessity of structure (and with the stupidity that this act entails), decide to err (wander) by getting themselves fooled by *a certain type* of knowledge. This further detail gives an unequivocal dialectical twist to *Seminar XXI*'s formula, which seems to be confirmed by Lacan himself when, stressing the double negation, he explicitly says that 'not to be a non-dupe [does not imply] coming back to be a dupe'.[56] But if the mark of duperie is something necessary, the same does not hold for the specific knowledge from which the subject (unconsciously) chooses to let himself be fooled.

It is at this point that the overlap between the Names-of-the-Father and the strict equivalence of the three registers comes into play: here, the Names-of-the-Father (the Symbolic, the Imaginary and the Real) act as the 'foundation of the saying [*du dire*]',[57] that is as the transcendental frame that contains and regulates the subject's discourse and his relationship with knowledge. The unconscious choice that every speaking animal is obliged to make upon entering language as a subject is (ethically) reversed in adhering to a *particular* type of knowledge, which is in turn embodied in one of the three registers of existence, namely in the Names-of-the-Father. It is this need to assume an (unconscious and contingent) Name-of-the-Father that turns the syntagm of *Seminar XXI* into 'an ethics [founded] on the refusal of being unduped',[58] that is, into an ethics of stupidity.

THE DIALECTIC SQUARE OF KNOWLEDGES, OR FOUR FORMS OF STUPIDITY

As well as introducing the re-conceptualization of the three registers and deepening the speculations on the Borromean knot, this seminar also dwells on an interesting review of the relationships between psychoanalysis, science and religion, which could be effectively integrated within Lacan's arguments on the constitutional stupidity of the human animal. As we will soon see, not only is this epistemic triad equivalent to three distinct ways of being 'fooled' by knowledge, but, in the light of the dupes/non-dupes dialectics, it reveals itself rather as a tetralogical set, that is a square, the fourth position of which is occupied by *cynical* knowledge, a form of non-knowledge based on the alleged *rejection* of stupidity.

During the second session of the seminar, Lacan states flat out that the limit of science is its not wanting to know anything about what 'does not belong [. . .] to its system'.[59] In the eyes of science, and of its ontological chauvinism, that which exists coincides entirely with the formalizable, while everything that lies outside this domain is not only devalued to a form of drab idealism but even denied the attribute of existence. Counting blindly only on the infallibility of its paradigms and the possibility to test and transmit every ounce of its *sapientia*, scientific knowledge repudiates the fact that its premises are based on an imaginary intuition.[60] As Lacan will state even more eloquently later, by disowning the irreducibility of meaning [*sens*], science pursues the illusion that it will achieve a *pure* formalization. But, given that writing the great book of Nature and its mathematical formulae is a purely mythical ambition, scientific knowledge is nothing more than a fooling [*edupation*] of the Symbolic, the knowledge of those who believe they can manipulate the Real so as to 'scratch away all the meaning'.[61] This is why the subject fooled by science is a *dupe* of *non-dupes*, someone who believes he can reduce the fundamental duplicity of language and the signifier to a corpus of all-explaining laws. With regard to religion, in *Seminar XXI* Lacan defines it as equivalent to metaphysics, as they both aim at producing an 'organizing thought', a totalitarian systematic knowledge centered around the existence of an alleged truth (God, Being) and the advent of its messianic fulfillment (the Apocalypse, Absolute Knowledge). Religion and metaphysics are 'on the same side'.[62] Both assume that 'there is a universe' and for this reason, those who unconsciously adhere to their knowledge are *dupes* of *dupes*, subjects who replace their constitutional stupidity with an overdose of meaning. According to Lacan, who in *Seminar V* already described idolatry as a form of symbolic imaginarization,[63] knowledges based on a semblance of the One (i.e. on the hypothesis of the Other as One) act by converting the differential laws of the Symbolic into an imaginary orgy fuelled by the punctual reflection between the subject and his truth (religion), or by the stainless correlation between thinking and the object being thought about (metaphysics). To paraphrase Marx, religion and metaphysics are the opium of *dupes*.

Though itself 'contingent' and the product of a necessary form of stupidity, psychoanalytic knowledge (as the knowledge of the unconscious) drastically differs from both scientific knowledge and religious/metaphysical knowledge. For Lacan, before anything else, psychoanalysis is a 'pratique'[64] that, instead of conforming to the rigid precepts of scientific knowledge or sealing its contradictions with the 'froth' of meaning, is oriented towards the Real. It 'give[s] rise to a type of meaning that illuminates the other meanings to the point of *putting them in question*',[65] a dramatic knowledge of the not-all, crossed by a perpetual disharmony. In parallel, the discourse of the analyst dominates other discourses even though it is logically subsequent to them;[66] so Lacan remarks that without the late emergence of psychoanalysis it would have been impossible to pose the question of knowledge and its unconscious work. In other words, it is only thanks to the *logical* and *chrono*-logical delay of psychoanalysis that a critique of knowledges could be posed, *après-coup*. Therefore, far from perfectly adhering to the domain of the other knowledges, psychoanalysis enters dialectics as a 'symptom', in the double acceptation of the word: first, in Marxian terms, as what denies and subverts the alleged universality of a given system; second, as something fragile and always on the brink of homologation, which constantly risks falling into line with other knowledges and being confused with them. It's because of this irreducible precariousness that the subject of psychoanalysis is a subject duped by the Real: a non-dupe between dupes erring between the perils of the impossible or, in Lacan's words, a 'good dupe'.[67]

The science-religion-psychoanalysis triad returns in an important press conference held a few months after the end of *Seminar XXI* and that Jacques-Alain Miller significantly entitled 'The Triumph of Religion'. This is a fundamental contribution that makes up for the limits of *Les non-dupes errent*: while impeccably describing the constitution of each of the three knowledges, the seminar doesn't go all the way and almost entirely neglects the way they interact and influence one another. Commendably filling this gap, 'The Triumph of Religion' sets forth a decisively subversive thesis: the common opinion that technical and scientific progress will extinguish the obscurantist knowledge of religion is false and has to be rediscussed from scratch. To make it even more interesting, there's the fact that Lacan's invective implicitly targets Freud too. Although monotheistic religions contributed to the development of civilization by suppressing aggressive instincts and supplying a shelter for humans against their impotence before nature, the father of psychoanalysis thought that religion is only a *delusion*. According to Freud, with the coming of the modern era, religion tout court revealed itself as a dangerous barrier against cultural progress, an obstacle to be torn down in order to favor the unbridled deployment of science.

Putting together the theses of *Seminar XXI* and those of 'The Triumph of Religion', we can isolate three important differences between Freud's vision and Lacan's: first, for Lacan, the relationship between science and religion is not an *aut-aut* (or a scientific demystification, or a religious obscurantism) but, as we shall see, a reciprocal complex articulation; second, where Freud thought that religion is reactionary and science progressive and emancipative, for Lacan (at least for the Lacan of *Seminar XXI*) the authentic delusion is scientific progress; third, whereas for Freud psychoanalysis is a science with a 'special status', for Lacan it represents a third pole, a bulwark between scientific and religious knowledge.

The first aspect to stress is that according to Lacan, religious knowledge doesn't consist in an easy mysticism coming from a distant past, but in a *threat* from the *future*. During the conference, he states that religion is incredibly 'powerful' and 'invincible',[68] and that this overwhelming power is by no means antithetical to scientific knowledge. On the contrary, the correlation between science and religion is not only positive, but also exponential, because as science 'will introduce all kinds of distressing things into each person's life'[69] little by little, religion will be called upon to supply a 'meaning' for each of these convulsions. The more science collides with the Real, revealing its most shocking aspects (from the atomic bomb to space travel), the more these discoveries will strengthen people's dependence on religious knowledge, which will have to 'give meaning to the oddest experiments'.[70] Paradoxical as it may sound, from the modern age onwards, it would have been science that produced the need for religion and fuelled its power. How to explain such a relationship? Put another way, how can it be that the clamor caused by a scientific discovery is overturned into a spasmodic need for meaning? To answer this, we need to stress a decisive turn which, although it represents a typical trait of the very last Lacan, is surreptitiously revealed in *Seminar XXI*. Since the late 1960s, two different conceptions of science seemed to coexist in Lacan: on the one hand, science as a practice of the Real, oriented towards a disillusion with religious obscurantism and the search for an effective praxis (physics, cybernetics and, to an extent, linguistics); on the other, science as the ideological and cultural paradigm in charge at a certain point in history, a set of beliefs, scientistic in nature and always 'twenty years late' compared to the first type, which aims at 'maintaining the functioning of such or such apparatus of the human organism'[71] (and in which we recognize naïve realism and the positivist and biogenetical sciences).[72] The principle of this division already appears in embryo in *Seminar XI*, where Lacan distinguishes between 'science', the science that's an 'object of the meditation of philosophers', for example, and 'Science *itself*', 'the science in which we are caught up, which forms the context of the action of all of us [. . .] and which the psycho-analyst himself cannot escape'.[73] If 'science' indicates the doctrinaire background noise of the concept of science (ideal science), which opposes progress and aims at preserving the status quo, 'Science *itself*' designates the unappeasable inclination of the human being towards a clarification of the Real and its laws (the ideal of science). In the very last Lacan, however, this distinction seems to gradually wear thin and disappear, with the result that sciences tout court becomes impotent, and the Real is consecrated as an inexorable and unreachable domain of which we can only seize a few 'pieces'. It's precisely the articulation of the seminars of the 1970s that stages this *Kehre*: on the one hand, as Milner states, 'second classicism' (of the matheme and the utmost trust in scientific formalization) withers away 'just when it seemed to come true'[74] in *Seminar XX*; on the other hand, from *R.S.I.* onwards, Lacan tries to find a remedy to the collapse of science with the Borromean knot – an attempt that finds its limits already in *Seminar XXIV*.[75]

In this succession, *Seminar XXI* is a critical juncture in which the difficulties in finding a referent to replace the matheme are evident, to the extent that for most of the seminar Lacan has to resort to improvisation. One could object that instead it's logic that holds the keys to the machinery of *Les non-dupes errent*, something that Lacan states explicitly himself ('logic is the science of the Real'[76]). But can we really be sure of that? Far from being the mainstay of the analytical practice, the notion of logic the seminar supplies is rather a pale ghost that can hardly stand on its own two feet. Not only does it come across as decisively muddled, insofar as it is still surreptitiously dependent on the matheme and on formalization, but its very definition seems to lack a core: Lacan seems to have an all but clear idea of what the fundamental principles of his supposed 'logic of the Real' should be. And though he boldly argues for the need to abandon the principle of contradiction and to rebuild a new logic capable of making the unconscious rational, he never actually tackles the issue thematically. The aphoristic and practically inconclusive declarations on the clapped-out logic of the Real suggest instead that logic serves as a *decoy*, a sort of theoretical veil covering Lacan's concomitant elucubrations on the knot – which actually become dominant the following year. Besides this function as an alibi, the image of science conveyed in *Seminar XXI* remains that of a machinery constantly jammed by the last irreducible specks of meaning intrinsic to any formalization. This block doesn't only reaffirm that there is an asymptotic unbridgeable distance between the human being and the Real but also reveals the fundamental 'futility'[77] of science. At this time, Lacan's disillusionment with the Real is such that, as he says himself a few months before *R.S.I.*, man wouldn't even be able to provide for his own extinction:

> I'm not a pessimist. Nothing will happen. For the simple fact that man is good for nothing; not even capable of destroying himself. Personally, I would find a total scourge promoted by man something wonderful. The proof that he has finally managed to get something done, with his own hands, his own head, with no divine intervention, or natural or of any of the kind. All that super-nourished

> bacteria roaming around the world like the locusts of the Bible would mean the triumph of man. But it will not happen. Science happily saunters through its crisis of responsibility. [. . .] And as I said, the real will win out, as always. And we'll be as fucked as we ever were.[78]

What's the place of psychoanalysis in this bleak scenario? For the Lacan of 'The Triumph of Religion', psychoanalytic knowledge is an 'impossible' one, drastically different from religious and scientific knowledge, because instead of trying to make something that will never work actually work (like science), or to sugarcoat this eternal malfunctioning with apotropaic narrations (like religion), it deals with 'what doesn't work'.[79] While science and religion agree that what 'goes round', 'what works is the world [*monde*]', psychoanalysis assumes as the object of its knowledge the 'revolting [*immonde*]'[80]: the absolute disharmony between the subject and the world, but also of the world with itself (a set of pieces that never becomes a whole[81]). But the ability of psychoanalysis to tolerate the inconsistency of the world is also the reason for its *immobility*,[82] its inability to prosper or perpetuate itself. If, as we said, psychoanalysis 'can only last as a symptom', that is as 'what isn't going well',[83] then religion is an *anti-symptom*, a knowledge made 'to cure men [. . .] so that they do not perceive what is not going well',[84] constantly fuelled by the impasse of science.

And what about philosophy? If in *Seminar XXI* religious knowledge is defined to be analogous to the metaphysical, should we then consider philosophy too as an anti-symptom? Based on Lacan's conference, we would have to say no. Whereas *Seminar XXI* equates philosophy and religion, attaching both to the same knowledge, 'The Triumph of Religion' shows how the management and distribution of these forms of knowledge are drastically different. While religion is 'invincible', a rising knowledge that, by parasitizing the achievements of science, will 'drown the symptom [of psychoanalysis] in meaning',[85] philosophical knowledge is diminished, incapable of achieving anything. For Lacan, not only does philosophy 'never say anything that interests everyone', but even when 'it does say something'[86] its work is at once swallowed up by the University, the ruthless market of knowledge.

Despite the disaccord between religion and philosophy, 'The Triumph of Religion' surreptitiously reaffirms the distribution of the *duperie* types of *Seminar XXI*, superimposing the *dupe/non-dupe* dialectics onto the Names-of-the-Father (the Symbolic, the Imaginary, the Real). To summarize, epistemologically, Lacan sets science and religion poles apart: where the dupe of non-dupes of science allows himself to be fooled by the Symbolic because he tries to make up for his structural stupidity by draining knowledge of any meaning and equivocation; the dupe of dupes of religion responds to the fraud of language by allowing himself to be fooled by the Imaginary and the opium of meaning. Psychoanalysis could replace these two positions as a knowledge of the non-dupes of dupes, a fooling of the Real that manages to sustain the ill-founded senselessness of the revolting [*immonde*]. However, if the relationship between dupes and non-dupes is a *dialectical* one, such a reading can only sound incomplete, because it neglects the fourth and last of the possible combinations, the non-dupes of non-dupes (an apparently impossible subjective position). Though Lacan doesn't deal with it explicitly, I think that, developing a sharp intuition by Alain Badiou, we could call this fourth pole *cynical* knowledge. As Badiou explains, the so-called 'non-dupes' are 'those who claim to know the negative heart of things and who cynically deny the possibility of emancipation'.[87] And yet Badiou's proposal seems to clash with the *dupe/non-dupe* dialectics at first: in proclaiming the impossibility of evading from the structure, from the inexorability of its hold, one would say that the cynic is absolutely right. Yet, if we further analyse the French philosopher's thesis, the two arguments don't seem too far apart. What 'possibility' of emancipation does Badiou allude to? Certainly not to emancipation in its most immediate, naïve, pseudo-subversive sense. Taking his position to the limits, we may notice how, from a dialectical point of view, this very idea of 'emancipation' is destined to assume an entirely different perspective: if the speaking animal is constitutionally duped and has no way of escaping from the structure, a non-banal emancipatory vision can only coincide with the very idea of 'wandering' as a form of programmatic participation. In other words, Badiou's cynic would be right in denying the possibility of a *direct* emancipation but would be wrong in denying the *absolute* possibility of emancipation, not realizing that the true emancipative practice is *ethical*, that is, intrinsically dependent on the *choice* the subject makes with regard to the structure. The only truly (and not utopianly) emancipative way must therefore go through the productivity of the structure's constraints, not through its instant negation (non-Badiousian cynic) or through the rejection of emancipation tout court (Badiousian cynic). This hypothesis finds support in Lacan's overall position with regard to cynical subjects.

Lacan never dwelt on cynicism, but it is interesting to note that his main references to the subject date back to before the 1970s: in *Seminar VII*, for example, he praised the 'heroism'[88] of such a position, while in the following seminar he associated it with the figure of Socrates, 'a tried and true cynic'.[89] Perhaps a little rashly, we could suggest that the disappearance of any further references to cynicism coincides with the apprehension that 'there is no metalanguage' ('There is no Other of the Other'), a conclusion Lacan came to during the 1960s. If the Other is inconsistent and one cannot come out of language, then even the cynical presumption to distance oneself from the structure and rise above it with a sort of ironic skeptical transcendence is a pure delusion: there is no 'outside', and the delusion of its hypothetical existence is an integral part of the deception of language. In other words, if from a logical perspective such a subject cannot exist because this assumption would necessarily reintroduce that of an Other of the Other, from an ethical one the subject of cynical knowledge would only *reaffirm* the viscosity of the structure and the inability to separate oneself from it.[90] Instead of incarnating a 'virgin' knowledge, prior to *duperie*, cynicism merely consists in a presumed and self-referential *rejection* of human stupidity – a form of non-knowledge that is contradictory, precisely because it believes it can touch the Real directly and with no mediation or, on the contrary, because it believes it cannot touch it at all. This is why Badiou deems the cynical position an 'imposture'.[91]

CODA: TOWARDS AN ABSOLUTE PSYCHOANALYSIS

The most stimulating aspect of Lacan's ethics of Stupidity is that the distinction between the different types of knowledge is not simply nominal but strictly practical: as Lacan explains during the intense session XII of *Seminar XXI*, just as science constantly risks degenerating into a religion (as in the case of Newton's law of gravity, which to justify the exact movement of the masses has to surreptitiously restore the 'God hypothesis'), so there are religions whose basic approach is decidedly scientific (as the Talmud, a book of formulas in which 'the saying [is emptied] of all its meaning', clearly demonstrates[92]). In other words, the distance between the three types of knowledge (i.e. psychoanalysis, science and religion) is never absolute because between them there is always a mutual encroachment, a continuous contamination that makes the modus operandi of the one slip under the 'label' of the other. The subject's choice to let himself be 'fooled' by a specific type of knowledge and not by another is never conscious, as evidenced by the fact that even the most strenuous of atheisms can prove to be supported by what Alenka Zupančič has appropriately defined as 'a God guaranteeing that there is no God'.[93] This persistent denaturalization of knowledge can be better understood if, pushing the speculations of *Seminar XXI* to the extreme, we apply the tetralogical set of Stupidity to psychoanalysis itself, that is, treating the latter as a real subject of *edupation*. In a certain sense, it is Lacan himself who, starting from *Seminar XXIV*, focuses thematically on the question of the legitimacy of the analytic discourse, engaging in what in his *Cours* on the very last Lacan Miller defined as an 'absolute psychanalysis'.[94] As is well known, Lacan has always insisted on the need to define the necessary limits and conditions so that psychoanalysis does not turn into an ideological hoax or a 'social drug'. However, in the last seminars, this critical stance is not limited to the usual invectives against post-Freudians but is extended even against Lacan's own psychoanalysis and against the Freudian one. The barbarization produced by the pseudo-liberal shift of Freud's heirs, as well as the adherence of the latter to the policies of conformism and social productivity, gradually took second place in Lacan's work, leaving more and more room for a surgical deconstruction of the analytic practice. Thus, the psychoanalysis described by *Seminar XXIV* is a precarious and easily alienating one, constantly on the brink of fraud [*escroquerie*] or delusion [*délire*]. With the decline of the matheme and the general decadence of the *EFP* (ever bigger and out of control), Lacan accuses psychoanalysis tout court of having transformed the unconscious into a hegemonic, imperialistic notion that is too often confused with a simple and inappropriate extension of consciousness:

> I only have an unconscious. That is even why I think about it all the time [. . .] I consist in an unconscious of which, of course, I think night and day, which means that the *une-bévue* becomes inexact.[95]

The result of this counterfeit is that, undergoing a sort of 'orthopedics' of his own unconscious, the very subject of psychoanalysis becomes 'always [a] rogue [*canaille*]'[96] (i.e. a weak-minded person who thinks he 'knows' something of his own and others' unconscious). It is on this scorching background that the clarification of knowledge in psychoanalysis takes on its full force. Firmly distinguishing an 'absolute' psychoanalysis oriented towards the Real (a psychoanalysis of the *non-dupes* of the *dupes*), that is, incessantly subjected to 'a recurrent see-sawing between institutional stabilization [. . .] and renewing dissolution[s]',[97] we could propose two further and crucial intersections between psychoanalytical knowledge and, respectively, science and religion/metaphysics: on the one hand, we would have a psychoanalysis completely absorbed by mathematical formalization, which forcloses the irreducibility of meaning and for this reason incurs the same deadlock of science (it is a psychoanalysis of the *dupes* of the *non-dupes*, in which the frantic search for mathematization 'at all costs' turns into its opposite, namely into a sensational form of idealization); on the other, we have a psychoanalysis based on meaning and Revelation, a sort of *Weltanschauung* or, as Lacan puts it more politically, a 'Church' (it is the psychoanalysis of the *dupes* of the *dupes*, of those who believe that the analytic treatment is equivalent to an enlightened path towards their own personal truth).

Finally, as Johnston suggested, we could also detect a cynical drift of psychoanalysis, whose identikit is given to us by Lacan himself in the earlier 'The Freudian Thing': that is the case of those psychoanalysts who, precisely because they combine a severe anti-intellectualism with the sloppiest pragmatism, are doomed to not err, namely 'never to move beyond the pre/non-analytic "reality" of quotidian common sense'[98] (it is a pre-Freudian 'psychoanalysis *without* psychoanalysis', a sheer paradox which treats every complexity – the death drive, or even the unconscious itself – like a useless cerebralism).

NOTES

1. J.-C. Milner, 1995, p. 164.
2. According to Milner's *L'Œuvre Claire*, Lacan's work can be divided into two large classicisms: the 'first classicism' is dominated by the structural laws of linguistics and the signifier; the 'second' relies on a mathematics devoid of deduction and of apagogic (i.e. purely literal). Since the second classicism radicalizes the major assumption of bourbakism (severing mathematics from any reference to quantity), Milner defines Lacan's bourbakism as a *hyper-bourbakism* (see *ivi*, pp. 132–40).
3. *Ivi*, p. 166.
4. One of Milner's main books focuses precisely on *Seminar XXII*: see J.-C. Milner, 2007. By 'the late Lacan' I mean the period that goes from the early 1970s – from *Seminar XVIII* (1971) onwards – to the end of *Seminar XXIII*, while by 'the last Lacan' I mean the so-called post-joycean Lacan, which goes from the end of *Seminar XXIII* (1975–1976) to *Seminar XXVII, Dissolution* (1980).
5. M. Marini, 1992, p. 237.
6. Ibid.
7. F. Regnault, 1995, p. 73.
8. See C. Lacôte, 2005, pp. 313–32.
9. Strictly speaking, the 'primal scene' of the Borromean knot – as Luke Thurston defines it – dates back to *Seminar XIX*, precisely to the session of 9 February 1972. Unlike *Encore*, however, here the knot plays a more parenthetical role: it takes part in the formalization of speech, embodying the inextricability of the verb from the phrase (see J. Lacan, 2018, pp. 75–77; L. Thurston, 2018, pp. 146–47).
10. See J. Lacan, 1999, p. 112.
11. See L.F. Clemente, 2018.
12. J. Lacan, 1999, pp. 128, 110.
13. On Lacan's monstrous humanism, see L. Chiesa, 2016a, pp. 100–114.
14. See J. Lacan, 2003, p. 3.
15. For a lucid analysis of these events and the link between the 1963 seminar and the seminars of the 1970s, see E. Porge, 2013, pp. 72–102. According to Jacques-Alain Miller, not only Lacan never wanted to take up the theme of the seminar thematically, limiting himself to making some indirect and fleeting references during the late seminars, but he will also oppose the publication of the text of this single session, which will come to light (by Miller's own decision) only several years after his death (see J.-A. Miller, 2006, pp. 3–4).
16. 'In the end, the Name-of-the-Father is something slight' that 'can just as well be bypassed' (J. Lacan, 2016, pp. 102, 116).
17. É. Roudinesco, 1999, p. 393.

18. That of the Names-of-the-Father is a particularly divided exegesis, which is split between those who attribute to this concept a sort of 'lost' and 'irrecoverable' knowledge, which will never re-emerge after the interruption of the 1963 seminar (as Miller would seem to think), and those who see in all this a simple transitional 'interpretive' silence, whose knowledge would have reappeared in an organic and exhaustive form in the early 1970s (as in the case of Porge). For my part, I think that both these hypotheses are partially true: it seems to me that the Names to which Lacan referred in 1963 were *not at all* the Symbolic, the Imaginary and the Real but, as Lacan himself cryptically anticipates during that session, the triad of enjoyment-desire-object: 'Can't we go beyond the name and the voice and take our bearings from what Freud's myth implies in the register that grows out of our progress, that of the three terms: jouissance, desire and object?' (see J. Lacan, 2013a, pp. 76, 77, 88). In this case, taking advantage of the interruption of the seminar, Lacan could have exploited the so-called *hype* effect, to then re-elaborate his theory almost from scratch in conjunction with the Borromean knot. That being the case, it is only starting from *Seminar XXI* that an effective equivalence between the three registers and the Names-of-the-Father would be fulfilled.

19. Lacan will definitely unfold this hypothesis in the infamous *Seminar XXVII*, with the notion of the unconscious as *malentendu* (literally, 'mis-understood'), a form of mental dumbness that is virulently transmitted from generation to generation. However, some important precursors of the malentendu can be isolated already from the years of *Seminar XXI*. For example, during a conference held on 30 November 1974, Lacan says: 'The unconscious is this: that already before there were two people marked by the *parletre*, marked by this *distorsion in thought* [. . .] which depends on the fact that there is something of the *parletre*.' And then: 'there is an unconscious because these beings of *parletre* are such that it will not be possible that their learning of *lalangue* [. . .] is not [. . .] polarized by what is already oriented by the *parletre* in their parents' (Lacan, 1998, my emphasis).

20. J. Lacan, 1991, p. 31.

21. 'The word is now a virus. The flu virus may once have been a healthy lung cell. It is now a parasitic organism that invades and damages the lungs. The word may once have been a healthy neural cell. It is now a parasitic organism that invades and damages the central nervous system' (W.S. Burroughs, 2010, p. 39). In *Seminar XXIII*, Lacan will put it even more explicitly: 'language eats into the real' (J. Lacan, 2016, p. 21).

22. See J. Lacan, 1973–1974, session XV.

23. J. Lacan, 2013a, pp. 74, 77.

24. In critical terms, the leap from the hyper-humanist and pro-Heideggerian Lacan of the 1950s (who tried to separate as much as possible the 'simple' and 'stupid' animal from the – presumably free and autonomous – speaking animal) to the so-called anti-humanist Lacan of the 1970s (in which the human being would differ *negatively* from other animals precisely because the former is 'stupefied' by language) demonstrates the overall precariousness of his philosophical anthropology: indeed, not only at the end of the day Lacan's presumed late inhumanism turns into an even more radical (negative) anthropocentrism, but it is precisely this radicalism

that precludes an effective problematization of the severing between man and animal. However, an important exception to these tendencies (that of the 1950s and that of the 1970s) can be found in *Seminar XIX*, in which Lacan seems to question the 'punctuality' of animal instincts and to suggest that, even in their case, there may not be a sexual relationship (see J. Lacan, 2018, pp. 96–98, 110; L. Chiesa, 2016b, pp. 24, 29, 60, 192).

25. J. Lacan, 1973–1974, session I.
26. *Ivi*, session X.
27. *Ivi*, session I.
28. The immediate equivalence between meaning and the Imaginary is only temporary: after *Seminar XXI*, Lacan will redefine meaning as the product of the overlap between the ring of the Symbolic and that of the Imaginary, that is, of what, according to the Borromean logic, is *excluded* from the Real.
29. Ibid.
30. Quoted in A. Pagnin, S. Vergine, 1974, pp. 121–22.
31. J. Lacan, 1973–1974, session I.
32. Ibid.
33. *Ivi*, session XI.
34. In the 'Introduction à l'édition allemande d'un premier volume des *Écrits*', appeared shortly before the beginning of *Seminar XXI*, Lacan writes that 'Freud's discovery [is that] the unconscious works without thinking, nor calculating, nor even judging' and that the 'upshot' of this work is 'a knowledge that is only to be deciphered because it consists of a ciphering' (J. Lacan, 2001a, p. 556).
35. J. Lacan, 2001b, p. 376.
36. J. Lacan, 1973–1974, session I.
37. *Ivi*, session XI, my emphasis.
38. According to Lacan, the figure of the 'errant knight' (as well as the knightly novel in general) should be subsumed in the broader tradition of the courtly love, that is, in that set of literary strategies that *repeat*, in the form of poetry, the impossibility of the sexual relationship. After all, isn't the errant knight really the one who errs around the lady without ever being able to lie with her?
39. *Ivi*, session I. The manifesto of this (imaginary, religious and phenomenological) reading of life as a journey is probably Gabriel Marcel's *Homo viator*.
40. J. Lacan, 1967–1968, session XVIII (Conference).
41. J. Lacan, 2006, p. 203.
42. Ivi, p. 208.
43. J. Lacan, 2007, p. 164.
44. On this point, see D. Evans, 1996, p. 164.
45. J. Lacan, 1973–1974, session I.
46. *Ivi*, session VIII.
47. See L. Chiesa, 2016b, pp. xi–xxiii.
48. 'We all know, because all of us invent something to fill up the hole in the Real. Where there's no sexual relationship this gives a *troumatisme*' (J. Lacan, 1973–1974, session VIII).
49. *Ivi*, session I.

50. 'If this knowledge must be invented in order for there to be knowledge, it is perhaps for that that analytic discourse may be of use' (*ivi*, session IX).

51. *Ivi*, session I.

52. Ibid.

53. Lacan addresses this topic already in *Seminar V*, where he discusses the relationship between the subject and the signifying chain:

> what is there at the tip of our fingers, is that in his relationship to signifier a subject may occasionally, insofar as he is asked to constitute himself in signifiers, choose not to do so. He can say, 'No, I will not be an element in the chain.' That really is what lies at the bottom of the matter. But the bottom, the back, is exactly the same thing as the front. What does the subject do, in effect, when he chooses, in some way, not to pay a debt that he has not contracted? He does nothing but perpetuate it. His successive refusals have the effect of making the chain rebound, and he always finds himself tied to this same chain even more. (J. Lacan, 2017, p. 229)

Once in language, that is, once duped, the subject can only utter his refusal from *within* the structure: the very fact of being able to *utter* this refusal presupposes that the subject has already had access to the circuit of choice.

54. J. Lacan, 1973–1974, session III.

55. In this regard, the real case that *exceeds* the dupes/non-dupes dialectic is that of the psychotic: because of the *forclusion* of the Name-of-the-Father, it is the very dimension of choice that would be missing in the psychotic. Consequently, rather than a non-dupe, the psychotic would be an *un*-duped, someone who is completely severed from the scam of language. Returning to the case of Hans, during session III, Lacan explains how it was only by being fooled by his phobia that the child succeeded (albeit in a precarious and problematic way) in accessing this dialectic, thus becoming neurotic sui generis.

56. *Ivi*, session XIII.

57. Ibid.

58. *Ivi*, session I.

59. *Ivi*, session II.

60. This thesis will be reaffirmed even a few months after *Seminar XXI*, during a conference held at the *Centre Universitaire Méditerranéen*. Here, Lacan denounces how the 'mathematical apparatus' has produced the illusion in scientists of being able to 'renounce the use of one's own intuitions', that is, of something 'emerged from the Imaginary'. Instead of contributing to the clarification of its principles, this extremization of mathematical formalization would only reiterate that science 'does not know which way to go' (J. Lacan, 1998).

61. J. Lacan, 1973–1974, session XII.

62. *Ivi*, session XIII.

63. See J. Lacan, 2013b, p. 62.

64. 'I define [psychoanalysis] as a symptom – something that reveals the malaise of the society in which we live. Of course, it is not a philosophy. [. . .] Nor is psychoanalysis a faith, and I am not keen on calling it a science. Let's say that it's a practice'

(J. Lacan, 2007, p. 13). See also https://www.versobooks.com/blogs/1668-there-can-be-no-crisis-of-psychoanalysis-jacques-lacan-interviewed-in-1974.

65. J. Lacan, 1973–1974, session XIII, my emphasis.

66. In the logical succession of the four discourses, the analyst discourse is the fourth and last, namely, the other side of the master discourse.

67. *Ivi*, session III.

68. J. Lacan, 2013b, p. 64.

69. Ibid.

70. *Ivi*, p. 65.

71. J. Lacan, 1967.

72. For a sharp critique of the animism of modern science, see “Biology Soul-loves” in L. Chiesa, 2016b, pp. 29–40. For instance: ‘Modern science nevertheless equally promotes *a new kind of animism*, that is, a form of naturalist reductionism for which the presumed totalizability of man’s body including his brain, could eventually be mathematized – e.g. by means of a synergy statistics, genetics, and cognitive sciences – as a numerical segment of the whole of nature. The alleged correspondence between thought and what is being thought is thus not eliminated, only displaced. Modern science tries to recompose, in a novel way, the cosmos as harmonic’ (*ivi*, p. 33, my emphasis).

73. J. Lacan, 2003, p. 231. This crucial distinction has also been analysed in J.S. Lee, 1991, p. 192.

74. J.-C. Milner, 1995, p. 167.

75. ‘Psychoanalysis is not a science. It has no scientific status – it merely waits and hope for it. Psychoanalysis is a delusion – a delusion which is expected to produce a science [. . .] it is a scientific delusion, but this doesn’t mean that analytic practice will ever produce a science’ (J. Lacan, 1976–1977, session I).

76. J. Lacan, 1973–1974, session VIII. After all, isn’t it precisely in *Seminar XXI* that Lacan introduces the modal category of the possible as what ‘ceases to be written [*cesse de s’écrire*]’ (*ivi*, session V)?

77. It is remarkable that the ‘futility’ of science mentioned by the very last Lacan is drastically close to the meaning of the term as we find it in cosmic pessimism, namely to the realization of how ‘behind the shroud of causality we drape over the world, there is only the *indifference* of what exists or doesn’t exist’. This ‘irrevocable chasm between thought and world’ (E. Thacker, 2015, p. 15) would be the reason why, in the end, ‘science turns in circles’ (J. Lacan, 1976–1977, session I): unable to face the pure indifference of the Real, science would limit itself to supplying us with gadgets, technological trinkets (from mass appliances to the latest hi-tech systems) so as to be able to suture our anxiety and powerlessness. Moreover, Thacker claims that futility is opposed to two other existential provisions of pessimism: *failure*, namely the infringement of a deterministic system due to ‘a fissure between cause and effect’, and *fatality*, which indicates on the contrary ‘the hermeticism of cause and effect’, the ultimate incapacity to avoid a predetermined and inevitable outcome (E. Thacker, 2015, p. 14). Similarly, for the very last Lacan this would be the definitive failure of science: since science repudiates its own failures and ruptures (inasmuch as it only authenticates what it is ‘sure of’, darkening everything else) and it is no longer able

to resort to the fable of fatalism (the teleological idea of an apocalyptic but unstoppable progress), science would have plunged into a nihilistic indifference, whose only spring of survival is represented by the secretion of futile technological devices, that is, of objects *a*.

78. J. Lacan, 2007, p. 19. See https://www.versobooks.com/blogs/1668-there-can-be-no-crisis-of-psychoanalysis-jacques-lacan-interviewed-in–1974

79. J. Lacan, 2013b, p. 61.

80. *Ivi*, p. 62.

81. For the late and the very last Lacan, what we call the 'world' is nothing but an arbitrary aggregation of 'pieces', to which our thought/cognition would only later give a semblance of unity.

82. *Ivi*, p. 67.

83. *Ivi*, p. 71.

84. *Ivi*, pp. 71–72.

85. *Ivi*, p. 67.

86. *Ivi*, p. 83.

87. See A. Badiou, É. Roudinesco, 2014, p. 27.

88. See J. Lacan, 1992, p. 183.

89. See J. Lacan, 2017b, p. 108.

90. A further evidence in favor of the logical impossibility of the cynical position is the non-existence of a *fourth* Name of the Father, that is of an additional register besides the Symbolic, the Imaginary and the Real.

91. A. Badiou, É. Roudinesco, 2014, p. 27.

92. 'How these masses could know the distance at which they were at from other masses so that they would be able to observe Newton's law? It is absolutely clear that God is required here'; 'It is quite clear that if the Talmud has a meaning it consists precisely in emptying this saying of its meaning, namely, of only studying the letter' (J. Lacan, 1973–1974, session XII).

93. A. Zupančič, 2014, p. 32. That's why according to Lacan the true formula of atheism is not 'God does not exist' but rather 'God is unconscious'.

94. See J.-A. Miller, 2006–2007.

95. J. Lacan, 1976–1977, session II. With the term 'une-bévue' Lacan indicates a purely phenomenal unconscious (i.e. an unconscious *without instance*), namely the unconscious *minus* its speculative lucubration [*élucubration*].

96. J. Lacan, 1976, p. 3.

97. A. Johnston, 2019a, p. 183.

98. J. Lacan, 2019b, pp. 13, 14.

REFERENCES

Badiou A., Roudinesco É., 2014, *Jacques Lacan, Past and Present: A Dialogue*, New York, NY, Columbia University Press.

Burroughs W.S., 2010, *The Ticket That Exploded*, London, Fourth Estate. Chiesa L.

2016a, *The Virtual Point of Freedom: Essays on Politics, Aesthetics, and Religion*, Evanston, IL, Northwestern University Press.

2016b, *The Not-two. Logic and God in Lacan*, Cambridge, MA, MIT Press.

Clemente L.F., 2018, *Jacques Lacan e il buco del sapere. Psicoanalisi, scienza, ermeneutica*, Napoli-Salerno, Orthotes.

Evans D., 1996, *An Introductory Dictionary of Lacanian Psychoanalysis*, New York, NY, Routledge.

Johnston A.

2019a, "Lacan's Endgame: Philosophy, Science, and Religion in the Final Seminars", *Crisis & Critique*, Vol. 6, no. 1, pp. 157–87.

2019b, "The Freudian Thing", in Hook D., Neill C., Vanheule S., eds., *Reading Lacan's Écrits: from "Freudian Thing" to "Remarks on Daniel Lagache"*, New York, NY, Routledge.

Lacan J.

1967, "La place de la psychanalyse dans la médicine", Lettres de l'Ecole freudienne de Paris, n. 1.

1967–1968, *Le Séminaire de Jacques Lacan, Livre XV: L'acte psychanalytique, 1967–1968*, unpublished typescript.

1973–1974, *Le Séminaire de Jacques Lacan, Livre XXI*: *Les non-dupes errent, 1973–1974*, unpublished typescript.

1974, *Freud per sempre*, English version in https://www.versobooks.com/blogs/1668-there-can-be-no-crisis-of-psychoanalysis-jacques-lacan-interviewed-in-1974.

1976, "Note liminaire", Supplèment à Ornicar? n. 7. La scission de 1953. La communauté psychanalytique en France I.

1976–1977, *Le Séminaire de Jacques Lacan, Livre XXIV: L'insu que sait de l'une-bévue, s'aile à mourre, 1976–1977*, unpublished typescript.

1991, *The Seminar of Jacques Lacan, Book II: The Ego in Freud's Theory and in the Techinque of Psychoanalysis, 1954–1955*, New York, NY, Norton.

1992, *The Seminar of Jacques Lacan, Book VII: The Ethics of Psychoanalysis, 1959–1960*, New York, NY, Norton.

1998, "Le phénomène Lacanien", *Les Cahiers Clinique de Nice*, Vol. 9, no. 1, pp. 9–25.

1999, *The Seminar of Jacques Lacan, Book XX: Encore, 1972–1973*, New York, NY, Norton.

2001a, "Introduction à l'édition allemande d'un premier volume des *Écrits*", in *Autres Écrits*, ed. Lacan, Paris, Seuil.

2001b, "L'acte psychanalitique", in *Autres Écrits*, ed. Lacan, Paris, Seuil.

2003, *The Seminar of Jacques Lacan, Book XI: The Four Fundamental Concepts of Psychoanalysis, 1964*, New York, NY, Norton.

2006, *Le Séminaire de Jacques Lacan, Livre XVI: D'un Autre à l'autre, 1968–1969*, Paris, Seuil.

2007, *Le Séminaire de Jacques Lacan, Livre XVIII: D'un discours qui ne serait pas du semblant 1970–1971*, Paris, Seuil.

2013a, *On the Names-of-the-Father*, Cambridge, Polity Press.

2013b, *The Triumph of Religion: precede by Discourse to Catholics*, Cambridge, Polity Press.

2016, *The Seminar of Jacques Lacan, Book XXIII: The Sinthome, 1975–1976*, Cambridge, Polity Press.

2017a, *The Seminar of Jacques Lacan, Book V: The Formations of the Unconscious, 1957–1958*, Cambridge, Polity Press.

2017b, *The Seminar of Jacques Lacan, Book VIII: The Transference, 1960–1961*, Cambridge, Polity Press.

2018, *The Seminar of Jacques Lacan, Book XIX: . . . or Worse, 1971–1972*, Cambridge, Polity Press.

Lacôte C., 2005, "Les non-dupes errent", in Safouan M., ed., *Lacaniana. Les séminaires de Jacques Lacan. 1964–1979*, Paris, Fayard.

Lee J.S., 1991, *Jacques Lacan*, Amherst, MA, University of Massachusetts Press.

Marini M., 1992, *Jacques Lacan. The French Context*, New Brunswick, Rutgers University Press.

Miller J.-A.

2006, "Nota", in Lacan J., ed., *Dei Nomi-del-Padre* seguito da *Il trionfo della Religione*, Torino, Einaudi.

2006–2007, *L'orientation lacanienne: Le tout dernier Lacan, 2006–2007*, unpublished typescript.

Milner J.-C.

1995, *L'Œuvre Claire. Lacan, la science, la philosophie*, Paris, Seuil.

2007, *Les noms indistincts*, Paris, Verdier.

Pagnin A., Vergine S., 1974, *Il pensiero creativo*, Firenze, La Nuova Italia.

Porge E., 1997, *Les noms du père chez Jacques Lacan*, Toulouse, Éres.

Regnault F., 1995, "The Name-of-the-Father", in Feldstein R., Fink B., Jaanus M., eds., *Lacan's Four Fundamental Concepts of Psychoanalysis*, Albany, NY, Suny Press.

Roudinesco É., 1999, *Jacques Lacan: Outline of a Life, History of a System of Thought*, New York, NY, Columbia University Press.

Thacker E., 2015, *Cosmic Pessimism*, Minneapolis, MN, Univocal.

Thurston L., 2017, "Ineluctable Nodalities: On the Borromean Knot", in Nobus D., ed., *Key Concepts of Lacanian Psychoanalysis*, New York, NY, Routledge.

Zupančič A., 2014, "Realism in Psychoanalysis", in Chiesa L., ed., *Lacan and Philosophy. The New Generation*, Melbourne, Re.press.

Chapter 3

'For to begin yet again'

Re-rising the Ground(s) of Stupidity in Deleuze-Schelling-Lacan

James Martell

THE GROUND RISES

As we know, the homophonous *jeu de mots* of the title of Beckett's late novel *Comment c'est*, translated literally as *How It Is*, but which also sounds like the infinitive French verb *commencer* (to begin) and its formal imperative *commencez* (begin!), exposes a crucial feature of his oeuvre: the inextricability and confusion of its ontological and genetic dimensions. In other words, Beckett's works present a constant confusion between the depiction of a world (or a subject) and that of a world (or subject) about to be created or born. This confusion is well exemplified by Beckett's obsession with a psychoanalytic case he heard about at a lecture of Jung he attended in London on 2 October 1935. At this lecture, Jung spoke of a young female patient whom he had seen, and who, according to the psychoanalyst, 'had never been born entirely'.[1] As is well known, this anecdote resurfaces in Beckett's work sometimes directly, like in the radio play *All That Fall*, and more often indirectly, like in *Footfalls* or in the unborn-like status of characters and voices in *The Unnamable*, *Texts for Nothing*, *Fizzles* and other short texts. Thus, one of the traits that makes Beckett's literature so puzzling and fascinating (in the original sense of being in front of a *fascinus*[2] with all that this connotes) is that, in the Beckettian corpus, as a locus of discourse, images and what happens in between them, the problem of the constitution and genesis of the world, a subject or individual, and what connects them to each other, is always at stake.

As the common initial response to Beckett's literature shows, the immediate reader's reaction to such an entanglement between ontology and genesis (or world and birth) is earnest confusion, followed sometimes by straightforward rejection and other times by fascination, if not obsession.[3] What is, however, not that commonly remarked is that such a reaction arises out of a reading or spectatorship experience where the subject feels not only confused but straightforwardly stupid. This experience of stupidity is not due to a lack of references or information (like it could happen when reading Joyce, T. S. Eliot, Pound or a neo-baroque author like Alejo Carpentier). This stupidity is rather born out of the precise nature of the Beckettian experiment, wherein both the world and its beginning, together with their pendants, the subject and its birth, are confused in a suspension – akin to a Husserlian epoché – where they cannot be properly *ex*-perienced since they have lost the limits between them, or between any inside and outside. In other words, in the Beckettian universe, the world and its beginning, as well as the subject and its birth, are no longer or not yet properly individualized. It is my contention that, because of this impossibility to distinguish and trace the proper limits of the world and/or the subject vis-à-vis their beginnings, the Beckettian experience of stupidity can be best understood through Deleuze's own explanation of stupidity in *Difference and Repetition*.

The problem of stupidity in this book is developed in chapter III, 'The Image of Thought'. From the very first lines of this chapter, it is clear that the problem of the dogmatic and traditional image of thought that Deleuze wants to criticize is a problem of beginnings: 'The problem of the beginning in philosophy has always – and rightly – been regarded as a very delicate problem, for beginning means eliminating all presuppositions.'[4] In a sense, the question of the beginning in philosophy – and its concomitant problems like elimination and forgetting – is a guiding problem in Deleuze's thought from as early as his 1956–1957 seminar 'What is grounding?' and up to his late book *What Is philosophy* (1991). In 'The Image of Thought', the question is how to open up a (new) beginning beyond the traditional image of thought that is based on recognition and identity instead of on difference and repetition. If stupidity is examined in this chapter, it is because, as a problem, it has an essential role in both moments, in the dismantling of the traditional image of thought and in the tracing of a new image of thought.

According to Deleuze, in the traditional image of thought, in which the cogito is both naturally good and thought is universal and guided by common sense, the negative always takes the shape of error. Even if this image of thought recognizes that madness, stupidity and evil are not exactly errors, by ascribing them to an exterior force it still believes that our falling for them is the consequence of an error. For Deleuze, it is rather the notion of error that, elicited always from artificial and puerile examples (7 + 5 = 13), is 'exterior' and projected onto the transcendental sphere of thought. Thus, the real transcendental structures of thought and the 'negative' that envelops them must be searched for elsewhere. If we want to properly approach them, we need to understand that '[c]owardice, cruelty, baseness and stupidity are not simply corporeal capacities or traits of characters or society; they are structures of thought as such'.[5] Embedded in the traditional image of thought, philosophy has always duped itself into not making of stupidity a transcendental problem. Consequently, it has been rather the best literature (Flaubert, Baudelaire, Bloy, says Deleuze) that has been haunted by stupidity and taken it to the doors of philosophy. From this threshold, it is now philosophy's turn to consider stupidity properly, not as the other's stupidity, but as a truly transcendental question.

At this point in the chapter, Deleuze explains the link between stupidity and beginning. How is stupidity and not error possible? 'It is possible by virtue of the link between thought and individuation'.[6] Yet, what makes more radically original (and originary) the transcendental character of stupidity here is that this notion of individuation (derived, as we will see, from Gilbert Simondon's work) describes something *previous* to any cogito or to any constituted 'I' or 'me'. For Deleuze, individuation is precisely what precedes and makes possible any ulterior human determination or specification into 'I' or 'Me'. In itself, individuation consists of 'fields of fluid intensive factors which no more take the form of an I than of a Self'.[7] In this way, its function is psychological, biological and ontological, and given that it comprehends the transcendent possibilities of stupidity, cruelty and madness, we can say social and political as well. But how does individuation function exactly? Here, Deleuze explains it in stratigraphic terms: individuation as such 'operates *beneath* all forms', yet it is not exactly at the bottom of this structure. It is 'inseparable from a pure ground that it brings to the surface and trails with it'.[8] As is well known, this ground is derived from Schelling's notion of the *Urgrund* (original ground), which is inseparable – and sometimes indistinguishable – from an *Ungrund* (un- or non-ground) and an *Abgrund* (abyss). Yet, in this stratigraphy, what is, or perhaps more importantly, where exactly lies stupidity?

Here is Deleuze's clearest definition of it:

> Stupidity is neither the ground nor the individual, but rather this relation [rapport] in which individuation brings the ground to the surface [*fait monter*] without being able to give it form (this ground rises *through the I*, penetrating deeply into the possibility of thought and constituting the unrecognized in every recognition). All determinations become bad and cruel when they are grasped only by a thought which invents and contemplates them, flayed and separated from their living form, adrift upon this barren ground. Everything becomes violence on this passive ground. Everything becomes attack on this digestive ground. There the Sabbath of stupidity and malevolence takes place.[9]

Stupidity is, thus, the relation [*rapport*] between individuation and the ground where the former fails to give form to the latter. Yet, in this description, this relation includes a third term, the I, *through which* the ground rises, and then possibly a fourth term, (the possibility of) thought, *where* it penetrates, constituting in this act the unrecognized of each recognition. In this way, while transcendent, stupidity cannot itself be completely originary. For the ground to rise and fail to receive a form by individuation, there needs to be an I through which it rises. This is why stupidity is connected to violence, attack and malevolence. Unformed and un-individualized, undistinguishable within the relation between individuation and ground, all determinations appear as invented by this narcissistic thinking-I that contemplates them.

But what exactly is this ground? And how does Deleuze configure it at the crossroads of Schelling's and Gilbert Simondon's work? The common trait of the 'ground' in these two thinkers is not only its genetic condition as ground*ing* but also its essential recurrence, the fact that it is a grounding as a beginning that never stops or achieves its inaugural action or event. In other words, it is an 'eternal beginning' constituted by its very repetition and failure as an ultimate, last and, consequently, real or true act of finished origination. For Simondon, this is the ground and grounding movement of individuation as the ontogenetic movement of *everything* that exists: non-organic and organic matter, plant, animal and human life, as well as intersubjective, cultural, and social configurations and structures. In other words, for him ontogenesis does not describe the genesis of only the individual but rather of every becoming of Being itself or of Being as pure becoming. In this way, if there is a ground from where and against which[10] individuals differentiate themselves, this ground as pre-individual reality is common to every being, including the beings of psychological life (subjects, but also structures, phantoms, fantasies, etc.). As a matter of fact, psychological life (as the life of human emotions and thought) is not so much, for Simondon, a higher degree of individuation, but rather 'a slowing down of the living being', a 'new *plunge* into pre-individual reality followed by a more primitive individuation'.[11] This is why Simondon sees in the passage from living to psychological life a 'neotenic amplification'[12] of the living being's genesis, or, in other words, a conservation of and resurgence of premature, fetal or prenatal potential. Consequently, psychological thought and emotions have as a condition of possibility and existence a certain pre-individualized reality or a kind of always renewed and renewable fetal life. This constant renewal and submergence in the pre-individual make the Simondonian subject a split subject: 'the psyche exists when the living being does not completely become concretized and conserves an internal duality'.[13] However, this duality or split is not particular to the psychological individual. It is, rather, as an incompatibility of the system of Being-as-becoming with itself, an essential trait of reality. If individuation exists at all, it is precisely as a response to this incompatibility: '*Individuation is thus considered ontogenetic only insofar as it is an operation of the complete being*. Individuation must then be considered as a partial and relative resolution that manifests in a system which contains potentials and includes a certain incompatibility with respect to itself, an incompatibility that consists of forces of tension and the impossibility of an interaction between the extreme terms of the dimensions'.[14] Thus, because any problem between individuation and the ground would involve the whole system (incompatible in itself), stupidity and/or malevolence cannot be here only a phenomenon of the subject or I (even if such events need to go *through* it), but they must also affect the entire system of reality.

This interconnectedness or inextricability between the ground of a singular (psychological) individuation and the ground(ing) of all beings can be seen as well in the complex process of grounding in Schelling's philosophy. As we know, the complexity of this process of commencement appears not only thematically throughout Schelling's work, but his oeuvre itself *is* – and performs – said complexity as a constant recommencement of a failed beginning or aborted cosmogony. From his early commentary on Plato's *Timaeus* (1794), through the three drafts of the *Weltalter* project (1811, 1813, 1814/1815), up to his more reactionary late work as an attempt to ground a more positive philosophy,[15] Schelling's obsession and focus are the (pre-)conditions of the beginnings of the world, the subject, thought, freedom and God. In his universe: '"every single individual comes to being [*entsteht*] through the same scission [*Scheidung*] through which the world comes to being, and therefore does so right from the beginning with its own epicenter of time" (WA, 79). Individuals emerge from the monstrously generative disparity, the dis-equal cut or gap, *die Scheidung*, between the *Ungrund* of eternity and the being of becoming'.[16] This – always contemporaneous, in and as its beginning – disparity, cut or gap, is the above-mentioned 'eternal beginning' (*der ewige Anfang*) threatening any distinction, identity or individuation with a 'relapse' or 'new plunge' into the *Urgrund* or *Ungrund*, the original ground or ungrounding prior to any constitution or individuation, what in Simondon is the prenatal or pre-individualized reality. Put differently, the threat of the ungrounding is the constant repetition of the original grounding, the coming back to the pre-individual in order to begin (yet) again. As a repetition or resurging of the ground that suspends distinctions and individuations, this is the threat of stupidity and malevolence described by Deleuze as the rising of the ground where individuation or forming is hindered, yet where such a (failed) relation is reflected in the I.

DUPES OF THE PLACE

I begin again! I am beginning again since I believed I could finish.

I am even beginning again, because I had believed I could finish.[17]

– J. Lacan. *Seminar XXI. Les non-dupes errent*

If, as Adrian Johnston[18] and others have well shown, Lacanian psychoanalysis (especially after Žižek and the Ljubljana school) resonates well with Schelling's philosophy, it is precisely because of this indistinction – at the beginning – of and among the beginnings of the subject, the world, thought, freedom and (at least the Judeo-Christian) God. This is an indistinction that we see performatively exemplified in the lines above from Lacan's *Seminar XXI*, 'Les non-dupes errent', where belief and the repetition of the beginning are knotted as essentially linked. But if we consider this indistinction, especially in its radical confusion of the ontological and the ontogenetic (and even the cosmogonic) dimensions, together with Deleuze's rising ground of stupidity and malevolence thesis, how would a Lacanian reading of this ground and grounding appear? To put it differently, can we compare Deleuze's reflection on transcendental stupidity (developed through Schelling and Simondon) with Lacan's own version of what could be an original and originary transcendent stupidity or stupidity as a transcendental question? The different elements of the essential confusion or indistinction in both thinkers already point to the difficulty of the task. If, with the rising of this original ground, the onto-logical and the onto-genetic get confused, it is because the distinctions between reason and words (Logos) and its preconditions of existence (genesis) or their own birth have also disappeared, or are, at least, suspended. In other words, on this rising ground, reason and language (the Symbolic) exist only in, as, and through their own act of a-rising. Here, reason and words exist in and as the threshold of their own beginning(s). Using a Beckettian image, we could say that they speak only in and through the suspension or epoché of their own birth. Now, what complicates even more the consideration of these beginnings and thresholds in the translation between Deleuze's and Lacan's terminology is that they also use different terms for 'stupidity'. Deleuze speaks in *Difference and Repetition* of '*bêtise*', and Lacan – in the seminar on which we will focus,[19] where he engages directly with the question of a necessary kind of stupidity, *Seminar XXI Les non-dupes errent* – of '*duperie*'.

If Deleuze's term, *bêtise*, seems more directly relatable to a reflection on animality or what is animal (*la bête*) in the human, Lacan's term *dupe*, affected by the significant homophony that exposes the relation of dupery to what he terms the names-of-the-father (that is to say, by the resonance of *les-non-dupes-errent* with *les-noms-du-père*), includes an etymological reference as well to an animal, *la huppe* (the hoopoe bird in English), which, supposedly, is easy to capture by luring it. This etymological-animal reference allows him to underline two aspects of dupery or stupidity as he exposes its structure: (1) the necessary inextricability of the Imaginary within language or the Symbolic, and (2) sexual difference as an essential factor in the conception of the dupery, since the dupe, in French, is always *la dupe*.

As is well known, Deleuze specifically declares animals potentially protected against this transcendent stupidity since, in a sense, they are 'forewarned against this ground, protected by their specific forms'.[20,21] This is because, through the Simondonian traits of this ground, animals are safer from this rising ground (although not completely safe, as shown when Deleuze considers in *L'Abécédaire* that certain animals do stupid things like barking, 'the most stupid cry in nature')[22] since they are not so much 'undermined by the fields of individuation which work beneath them'.[23,24] 'Not so much' means that they are still undermined by such fields, but less so since in them the psychological (*psychisme*) is less preponderant than the vital. At this point, Deleuze introduces the imaginary dimension of the capture of stupidity. If, in comparison to the animal, 'the I and the Self' are 'defenseless' against this pre-individuation, it is because the rising ground appears with or as a 'distorted or distorting *mirror* in which all presently thought forms dissolve'.[25] In this way, we have in both notions of stupidity, Lacan's and Deleuze's, an imaginary capture, which, non-unrelated to animality, yet distinguishes stupidity as a (mostly) human phenomenon.[26]

However, the nature of this imaginary capture is different in these two notions. While Deleuze's rising ground and failure of individuation or to give form still need an imaginary reflection performed by an I or self, the rising ground itself does not seem to be an independent agent. Here, stupidity is an *accidental* consequence of the subject's turning over [*remuer*] of the ground due to the attraction and/or terror it provokes. It is through this temptation to touch and alter the ground – to turn it over, shake it, investigate it and so on – that the ground rises *with* the subject, and even though it does stare at him, it does so without its own eyes, making its gaze just a distorted and distorting mirror. On the other hand, in the case of Lacan's (non)dupes of *Seminar XXI*, the agent of the dupery is clearly not accidental. All the opposite, it is the *necessary* structure of the Unconscious, the structure of the names-of-the-father (*les-noms-du-père*) that – duping us into believing in such a name or no (nom/non) as master signifier – allows for 'signification to proceed normally'.[27] This is why stupidity or dupery here is not necessarily the danger (the Sabbath) or the analogue to error, but rather the desired condition, and the attempt at being non-duped at all is, instead, the error/erring itself: 'If the non-dupes are those [*ceux ou celles*] that refuse to be captured by the space of the speaking being, if they are those who keep their hands free of it, as I might say, there is something that we must know how to imagine, which is the absolute necessity that results from it, not of wandering but of error.'[28] This error, however, as Lacan explains it by underlining its connections with the French verb *errer* and the Latin *iterare*, is not the classic Cartesian external or projected example criticized by Deleuze (7 + 5 = 13), but rather the subjective error of those who, attempting not to be duped by the signifying structure, must necessarily conceive of life as nothing more meaningful than a journey in a foreign land.

Now, in this particular belief on a simple journey, born out of the attempt to not believe in the structure, the non-dupes miss the structure's and its lure's inescapability, since, Lacan says: 'simply by bringing out this function of the foreigner, they give rise at the same time to the third term, the third dimension, the one thanks to which they will never get out of the relationships of this life, unless it is to be then still more duped than the others, by this locus of the Other [*l'Autre*] that with their *imaginary* they nevertheless constitute as such'.[29] Thus, given this inescapability of the structure's dupery, we must ask: What exactly is the agent of the dupery in this seminar? If, in Deleuze, the agent was the subject itself (I or self) that, through the temptation to turn over or investigate [*remuer*] the ground of individuation, produced – or, at least, allowed the emergence of – stupidity as *bêtise*, here the agent is the locus or topological place [*lieu*] of the Other, even though it is still constituted by the subject's Imaginary. But what exactly is this locus that Lacan calls the structure or knowledge [*savoir*], and that he assimilates to the Unconscious? What is this place that could allow us to – Lacan says – forge a new ethics, one founded not on the refusal to be duped, but rather on an increment of the dupery by the Unconscious 'which, when all is said and done, is our only lot in terms of knowledge'?[30] If the agent of dupery is a locus, a place [*un lieu*], perhaps the right question is not *what* is it, but rather – as the first question of Beckett's *The Unnamable* remarks in its order[31] – *where* is it?[32] Consequently, the question changes too from by what or by whom one should be duped, to (by) *where* should one be duped? Here, Lacan chooses to use as a prime example Freud himself, who 'was dupe of the Real. // He was a dupe of the Real even if he did not believe in it. And this indeed is what is at stake. The good dupe [*la* bonne dupe], the one who does not err/wander, there must be somewhere a Real of which she is the dupe'.[33]

What does it mean to be duped of/by a place or position, and particularly by such a place or space as the Real can be, especially when we consider its figuration in the development of Lacan's own use of topology?[34] And how could this dupery forge a new ethics? At the end of the seminar, Lacan summarizes what he says he wanted to say all year long by stating what 'les non-dupes errent' [the non-duped err/wander] ultimately means: 'anyone who is not in love with his unconscious errs'.[35] In this way, he introduces a new dimension to the dupery of the Unconscious, and consequently, of the Real. As he says, 'there is no need to know [*savoir*] that one is in love with one's unconscious in order not to err. One only has to offer no resistance, to be its dupe'.[36] Thus, the error's meaning shifts from simply being a resistance to be duped or fooled by, to a resistance to be in love with the place as agent of the dupery, the Unconscious. Here, to end the seminar, he introduces a historical change. For him, what distinguishes the present time of his seminar is that, while past epochs were also in love with their Unconscious, they thought that it was knowledge as *connaissance* – instead of the *savoir* of the Unconscious. For us, or rather for you [*vous*], he says, for 'the first time in history, it is possible for you, to you, to err, that is to say, to refuse to love your unconscious, since in short you know what it is: a knowledge [*savoir*], a knowledge that pisses you off [*emmerdant*]'.[37] Nevertheless – he continues – maybe in this *erre* or impetus, maybe it is here [*là*], in this place where the ship lets itself be moved or dragged, 'that we can wager on rediscovering the *Real* a little more in what follows, to perceive that the unconscious is perhaps no doubt discordant, but that perhaps it leads us to a little more of this *Real* than this very little of reality which is ours – that of the phantasy – that it leads us beyond: to the *pure Real*'.[38] Thus, we must ask, on this ship letting itself be moved, approaching the real agent and place of the dupery (and potentially of the amorous attachment), the Real, is this movement not like the one of the *Stultifera Navis* or Ship of Fools? In other words, is this approach beyond the phantasy into the Real not a going beyond the dupery or *stolidus* (inert, stupid) of the *stultus* (idiot) into the madness of the moving ground? What is it that, beyond the apparent solidity of the fantasy's dupery, can still hold together the subject in front of the Real as rising ground?

In her 2008 article 'Moments d'une histoire d'amour', Marie-Hélène Brousse describes the change brought about by the *Seminar XXI* in terms of the psychoanalytic solution: 'instead of the love of meaning [*sens*], Lacan proposes love as the medium to give consistence to the Real'.[39] This changes love for Lacan. From now on, it does not consist in 'covering the object with a beautiful image, nor in annulling the difference between the signifier and the body'.[40] It is not a marriage between jouissance and meaning anymore. In what, then, consists this love as dupery by the Real? She mentions two possibilities, not mutually exclusive: (1) To realize that, that which keeps the speaking-beings [*parlêtres*] together is the 'senseless object that, in its stupid and ineffable existence, materializes the link between the three rings of string [*ronds de ficelle*] [of the Real, the Symbolic, and the Imaginary] and causes desire'[41] and/or (2) to choose in an act (e.g. the passage through analysis, through each session), the Real which will hold since 'in this business we pay with our hide'.[42] But if the Real is this senseless, moving ground, or it is embodied in a particular, yet also senseless, stupid object, how can it be loved? Or, in other words, as a new beginning (be it an object or a choice), how do we begin – again[43] – to love the Real?

In order to conceive the beginning of the love of the Real, let us go back to the utmost beginning of Schelling's *Urgrund*/original ground or *Ungrund*/ unground(ing). As we know, the main problem of Schelling's cosmogonic or ontogenetic system is how to account for the beginning of what is supposed to be the absolute; in other words, how to conceive of the separation implied in any beginning or birth of an absolute being that allows for no further or previous separation. This question is presented in his system both ontologically and genetically, alternatively or simultaneously depending on the text and sometimes within the same text. The inextricability of the knot between these two dimensions exposes the unbreakable link of both interrogations. That is to say, the separation or non-separation within Being (*onto*logy) is necessarily connected with the separation or non-separation at the beginning as birth (onto*genesis*). In moral terms, this means that explaining evil as an eternal and present being must explain (it) too (as) the beginning of evil. In the same way, explaining the origin of nature must be equivalent to explaining its eternal constitution and necessity in Being or the Spirit as a whole. Consequently, the infamous Schellingian indivisible remainder (or never-rising-remainder, *der nie aufgehende Rest*[44]) or excess is precisely this necessarily disappearing (but only from view, into the ground, Hades or 'unseen') gap between ontology and ontogenesis, between the essential-eternal world and its ungraspable yet always resurging beginning.

As Schelling explains in his *Philosophical Investigations into the Essence of Human Freedom*, this inextricability between what exists (*onto*) and its beginning (*genesis*) or ground necessarily brings a duality into it and as its beginning. This duality, the split of the original *Ur-* and *Un*grund into two equally eternal beginnings, can be explained as the effect of a future event: the emergence of life, love and personal existence.

> The being of the ground, as of that which exists, can only be that which comes before all ground, thus, the absolute considered merely in itself, the non-ground [*Ungrund*]. But, as proved, it cannot be this in any other way than in so far as it divides into two equally eternal beginnings, not that it can be both *at once*, but that it is in each *in the same way*, thus in each the whole, or its own being. But the non-ground [*Ungrund*] divides itself into the two exactly equal beginnings, only so that the two, which could not exist simultaneously or be one in it as the non-ground, become one through love, that is, it divides itself only so that there may be life and love and personal existence.[45]

Thus, herein lies the loving dupery: the cause comes after its effect. *First*, as *Happy Days*' Winnie repeats continuously in her beautiful future perfect, 'It will have been a happy day!' of love, life and personal existence, and *then*, in a return to and *at the beginning*, the ultimate cause, the indifference at the *Un/Urgrund*, will split itself into light and dark, good and evil, God and nature. This is the dupery of love as an effect creating its own cause, or the dupery of the structure of the Schellingian beginnings as *Ur/Ungrund*. But how is this a dupery of the Real?

To answer this question, we need to remember the complicated and evolving character of the Real in Lacan. As we know, the notion of the Real evolves at a somewhat fast pace through his writings and seminars, from its early opposition to 'the realm of the image',[46] up to its unknowable/rational character in later seminars like *Les non-dupes errent*. Now, if at this later point it has primarily a structural function and meaning (to be duped by the Real is to be duped by the structure), this function does not mean that the Real has lost its genetic signification or 'game'. As Lorenzo Chiesa explains, 'the Real with which the symbolic Other is now in direct contact is a leftover, a remainder of the primordial Real: Lacan defines it as an object *a*, the "*peu de reel*" which is left to us'.[47] This is why the Real can be equated with the rising *Ur/Ungrund* or ground, in the sense that, like the holes on a surface for a trypophobic, it is constantly threatening to erupt and consume it all, bringing us back to the original chaotic presupposed lost unity we – like the ground in Deleuze – fear and desire. In light of these genetic and threatening dimensions, we can ask: How is it then that, in the refusal to be a non-dupe, that is to say, to not believe or love the Real as the structure, we can forge 'for ourselves a quite different ethics',[48] an ethics that – we would hope – would take us beyond the current stupidity and malice?

To finally consider this possibility for us, let us go back to the Deleuzian notion of stupidity as the 'relation in which individuation brings the ground to the surface without being able to give it form'.[49] According to Deleuze, after the rising ground shows a mirror to the I or self, stupidity becomes indistinguishable from malice, but also from melancholy, and, ultimately, from madness [*folie*]. Here, the birth of madness coincides with the ultimate reflection of the individual on the (back)ground [*fond*]. This reflection makes both terms – individual and ground – stupid(ity) but also cruel(ty), the indistinction between their adjectival and noun forms arising from the impossibility of distinguishing an individual both from the affects or actions it suffers or performs and from the landscape or ground where these affects/events take place (the Sabbath). For Deleuze, this is the birth of madness but also of melancholy because, through this reflection, a 'pitiful faculty' develops in the individual spirit, the faculty to 'be able to see stupidity and *no longer tolerate it*'.[50] This rejection of the reflection makes this most pitiful faculty a royal one 'when it animates philosophy as a philosophy of the spirit – in other words, when it leads all the other faculties to the transcendent exercise which renders possible a violent reconciliation between the individual, the ground and thought'.[51] Now, this violent reconciliation does not mean a disappearance of the ground [*fond*] nor consequently of its reflection on the I or self. As a matter of fact, through this, first most pitiful, then royal faculty, the ground [*fond*] is carried in and through thought, 'still as the unthought and unthinking'.[52] Nevertheless, transcendent as this ground and the stupidity therewith are, this unthought/unthinking ground becomes here, for Deleuze, the empirical form necessary in order to think the *cogitandum*. In other words, it becomes the 'transcendent element' that cannot be but thought. In Lacanian terms, we could say that the ground and its concomitant transcendent stupidity become the element or structure, the Real, in which we must not be non-duped. This is what gives the Deleuzian rising-ground, the Schellingian *Ur/Ungrund*, and the Lacanian Real their ethical and genuinely political dimension. As Alenka Zupančič explains: 'The Real is not an Idea – it is the conceptual name for what must go wrong in reality for an idea to appear at all. And this is also what relates thought to the political dimension proper, instead of confining it to the act of "understanding", "reflecting", "analysing" reality. It is also a genuinely "political" point in Lacan'.[53]

Now, is it possible to understand the question of stupidity as a transcendent and perennial feature of thought without understanding our own Real's political, contemporary dimension? In other words, is it possible to understand stupidity and malevolence as transcendent features of thought (the unthought/unthinking ground of thought) threatening us continuously throughout history, without understanding what exactly is going wrong in our political reality today, and especially in our own perception of it? If, as we have seen through Lacan's, Deleuze's and Schelling's grounding, the problem of an absolute ontology is inextricably linked to its ontogenesis,[54] this entails that the beginning of the world (of any world) keeps repeating itself at every moment and, consequently, at every moment keeps changing *as* its – this world's – beginning. This is thus the inescapable dupery of the ontological and ontogenetic structure, translatable best perhaps in these terms: we get the beginning we deserve to create and keep creating (for) ourselves.

IN THE BEGINNING WAS THE . . .

Let us go back to our question about the locus of stupidity or dupery and, paraphrasing again *The Unnamable*, ask: *Where* is stupidity now? Here are three extremely contemporary examples:

1) In a recent interview, when Žižek described COVID-19 as stupid, there was an interesting moment in the reaction of the interviewer who did not understand at first what or whom was called 'stupid'. It took a second for the interviewer to see how such an apparently personal adjective could be addressed to a non-human subject. But perhaps – to Žižek's dismay – what the interviewer could not understand was how a virus that seems so successful – up to the point of putting the whole world on

its knees – could be described as 'stupid' instead of 'smart' or highly 'intelligent'.

2) The American poet Claudia Rankine begins a section of her recent book *Just Us* titled 'boys will be boys', focused on the Brett Kavanaugh confirmation hearings in the context of the #MeToo movement, with a personal anecdote gathered at a gate in an airport: 'The gate agent announces we are ready to board. A man looks around. A woman comes running. She gets in line behind the man who has been tracking her. He seems to see only her as he asks sharply, "Are you stupid?"'[55] As Rankine continues reflecting in this section on the events around the Kavanaugh hearings, and especially within the context of the Trump presidency in 2018, she goes back to the anecdote and the effect that the word 'stupid' had on her. At some point, she tries to understand this puzzling effect through an apparent synonym of 'stupid', the word 'idiot', which – through its etymology – would link stupidity to the sphere of the private, in opposition to the public or general.
3) The third example is not of a single utterance but rather of what we could describe as a stupid scene or a scene of original or originary stupidity. This scene is included in the *New Yorker* video recorded by Luke Mogelson of the insurgence at the US Capitol on 6 January 2021.[56] Among the other scenes of violence of the 'insurgents' penetrating into the building, this particular scene happens at the Senate chamber, when the insurgents are confronted with the empty, recently vacated space of power. If one suspends for a moment the tragic aspects of the events (the people who died, the undermining of the principles of democracy, the exposed reality of poverty and lack of education in the United States, as well as the effects of demagoguery and right-wing fascist propaganda, etc.), it can be seen as a rather funny scene. It starts with the motley insurgent group opening the upper doors of the chamber, phones in hand, recording and yelling: 'is this the Senate?!' Then it moves on to some of them on the ground of the chamber, disagreeing with each other about what to do now that they are there. Here we see them taking pictures of papers they find on the desks as possible 'evidence', while one of them, the self-baptized 'QAnon Shaman', is on the second floor emitting what is supposed to be a war chant while tapping the floor with an American flag as somebody is taking pictures or video of him. At some point, they find Ted Cruz's objection to keep counting the votes of Arizona, freak out and explode, saying that he was going to sell them out all along, just to realize their mistake a couple of seconds later, saying 'oh no, that's a good thing! He's with us'. Towards the end, they get on the rostrum and decide to say a prayer, where they thank God for, among other things, filling the chamber with patriots 'who love you

> and that love Christ' and finally express their revolutionary dream of renewal: 'Thank you for allowing the United States of America to be reborn'. While the word 'stupid' is not pronounced during the video, as we know, it was – and keeps being – repeated quite often when describing the events of 6 January and some of its consequences.

These three examples could be seen as instances of Lacan's three rings of string, with Rankine's anecdote representing an instance of stupidity in the Symbolic, Žižek's an instance in the Real and the Senate Chamber scene one in the Imaginary – although, as with Lacan's inextricable rings, there is plenty of mobility and transduction here. What all the examples show, however, is that, even as a transcendent problem (of thought), stupidity is always transitive. In other words, something/somebody is always stupid for/to somebody/something else. This means that even the relation between the ground rising and individuation in Deleuze, or the original ground of Nature/God/Being in Schelling, is also a dupery to and for somebody/something. In other words, as Lacan knew, stupidity is always a lure where somebody gets caught for/(in)to somebody/something else: usually a Master, the Symbolic or the Imaginary order. But what happens when, as he questions in *Seminar XXI*, the lurer or duper is the Real or the structure of the Real? And what is more, what happens when we realize this, and that, consequently, in order to not completely err believing ourselves non-duped in a free journey of life, we need to be duped by the structure? What is the danger/liberation of this realization today when – in the middle of a resurgence and emergence of new and old fascisms and kinds of stupidity – as Cindy Zeiher notes in a recent article: 'It is the willingness to be duped by the strange, albeit false freedom proffered via the *objet a*, that politics in general and Trump in particular, exploit'?[57]

As we know, this willingness to be duped has to do with the will to jouissance. This is what Deleuze describes as the temptation to turn over [*remuer*] the ground, and what the beautiful writing and thinking style of Schelling performs and that makes us go back to him more and more these days. My final hypothesis here is that what these three notions of stupidity (Schelling's, Lacan's and Deleuze's) have in common is that they show how this jouissance in stupidity is always connected with the ultimate repetition, that of the origin or beginning itself. This is why both Trump's and Joe Biden's campaign slogans (as well as many other political slogans throughout history) called for a kind of rebirth or return to an original soul or body of the nation ['Make America Great Again (Again)' and 'Battle for the Soul of the Nation'].[58] The ridiculous emptiness of the slogan (which, in the case of Trump in 2016, duped many into believing – stupidly – that it had no chance to succeed) is rather what makes it so successful. To the rational, non-duped puzzled questions: 'What do you mean "Make America Great Again"? When exactly was it great and what does this greatness consist of?' the implied – conscious of the need for the dupery – answer was 'whenever *you* think it was great: when your economic conditions were better, when you felt comfortable expressing racist, homophobic or xenophobic views, or even just when you were younger, had better financial and physical health, etc.' The point is not about reasonable and well-explained political agendas, it is rather about the (empty) return itself, when in stupidity and malice, we see the chance for the self or ego to make the world its own reflection (again). The trap here, and the reason why the raising of this ground is an opportunity for stupidity and malevolence to appear, is that, as James Williams explains, this repetition or return is just a repression or a disavowal of what is being repeated (from statements like 'there is no racism in America', 'the Civil War was not about slavery', 'all lives matter', up to the rejection of human dignity – and with it, of empathy – to particular groups: immigrants, transexuals, the poor, etc.). As the ground rises, like Cadmus, we repeat the foundation of Thebes in the murdering of the Serpent, without realizing or acknowledging that the repetition of this foundation (in the existence of the city itself) implies that we will also become the murdered Serpent ourselves.

> We must express and work with the repetitions that become concentrated in us and come to make us since to repress them or to treat them as something external is to redouble their force. [. . .] In the postulates that define the image, philosophy, common sense and good sense become allied to cruelty, stupidity and malevolence in the name of opposing them. [. . .] How do we give form to difference and repetition without reducing them according to the postulates of the image of thought? How do we give form to that ground, rather than allowing it to work violently within our very attempts to escape it?[59]

As we saw earlier, for Deleuze, the escape from this trap lies in a particular kind of ipseic recognition, stupidity recognized by stupidity. However, even within the possibility of a 'violent reconciliation' between 'the individual, the ground and thought'[60] in this reflection, for Deleuze, the ultimate result, the *cogitandum* as that which can only be thought, has not been thought *yet*. In fact, at the end of 'The Image of Thought', it is rather described by him as what has not yet happened: '"the fact that we do not yet think" or "What is stupidity?"'[61] Trying to finally think it, or even worse, to believe that it is something that can be finally thought, that is what Lacan called 'la connerie', of which the attempt itself to escape it is its essential lure and, at the same time, our essence.[62] As an attempt to understand everything anew, our stupid [*con*] essence is an attempt to begin yet again our (own) understanding. In this way, our essence can best be illustrated by Goethe's Faust's attempt to – in the quiet night of his study – translate anew the beginning of the Gospel of

John, or in other words, to translate the beginning of the beginning – before the barking (the most stupid animal sound, for Deleuze) of a Mephistophelian poodle interrupts us and our rebirth, yet again.

One yearns for life's torrents,
Alas – for life's sources.
Snarl not, poodle! [. . .]
'In the beginning was the Word' [. . .]
'In the beginning was the Sense.' [. . .]
'In the beginning was the Force!' [. . .]
The spirit helps me! At once I see counsel,
And write confidently: 'In the beginning was the Deed!'
If I should share the room with you,
Poodle, stop the howling, stop the barking!
Such a disturbing companion
I do not fancy suffering near me.[63]

NOTES

1. Davyd Melnyk, "Never Been Properly Jung," *Samuel Beckett Today / Aujourd'hui*. Historicising Beckett / Issues of Performance / Beckett dans l'histoire / En jouant Beckett. 15 (2005): 358.

2. As we can infer, this inextricability between the ontological and the genetic dimensions in Beckett's oeuvre can be linked to the Roman *fascinus* as it is described, for example, by Pascal Quignard in *Le sexe et l'effroi* (Gallimard, 1994), and to the phallus in Lacanian psychoanalysis. For a recent study on Beckett and sexuality, see Paul Stewart, *Sex and Aesthetics in Samuel Beckett's Work* (New York: Palgrave, 2011).

3. In a recent guest tele-lecture, my students in an undergraduate seminar asked my colleague Arka Chattopadhyay what made him become a Beckett scholar. He told them that he shared the same confusion and puzzled reaction they were having, except that, in his case, it quickly became a life obsession.

4. Gilles Deleuze, *Difference and Repetition*, trans. Paul Patton (New York: Columbia UP, 1984), 129. G. Deleuze, *Différence et répétition* (Paris: PUF, 1968), 169. From now on, I will include the original French version's page with FR.

5. Deleuze, *Difference and Repetition*, 151; FR 196.

6. Deleuze, *Difference and Repetition*, 151; FR 197.

7. Deleuze, *Difference and Repetition*, 152; FR 197.

8. Deleuze, *Difference and Repetition*, 152; FR 197. My italics.

9. Deleuze, *Difference and Repetition*, 152; FR 197–8. Translation slightly modified. My italics.

10. Here, the different meanings of the term 'fond' in French exemplify better than the English term 'ground' the different positionalities and loci of the ground as soil or earth, as an unfathomable, yet essential abyss, or as the background in a painting or cinematic image.

11. Gilbert Simondon, *Individuation in Light of Notions of Form and Information*, trans. Taylor Adkins (Minneapolis: University of Minnesota Press, 2020), 177; G. Simondon, *L'individuation à la lumière des notions de forme et d'information* (Grenoble: Million, 2017), 165. My italics.

12. Simondon, *Individuation*, 177; FR 165.

13. Simondon, *Individuation*, 177; FR 165.

14. Simondon, *Individuation*, 3–4; FR 25. My bolds, Simondon's italics.

15. For an examination of the later reactionary Schelling in relation to the influence that the earlier Schelling had on a notion of philosophy as construction relatable to Deleuze's and Guattari's, see Alberto Toscano, "Philosophy and the Experience of Construction," in *The New Schelling*, eds. Judith Norman and Alistair Welchman (New York: Continuum, 2004), 106–27.

16. Jason M. Wirth, *Schelling's Practice of the Wild* (Albany: SUNY Press, 2015), 87.

17. Jacques Lacan, *Seminar XXI, Les non-dupes errent*, trans. C. Gallagher. Unpublished Manuscript, Lesson 1. 1973–1974, 1; J. Lacan, *Séminaire XXI, Les non-dupes errent*. Unpublished Manuscript, Lesson 1. 1973–1974, 4, accessed, 3 March 2021, http://www.valas.fr/Jacques-Lacan-Les-non-dupes-errent-1973–1974,249 Translation modified.

18. See, for example, Johnston's "Repetition and Difference: Žižek, Deleuze and Lacanian Drives," in *Lacan and Deleuze*, eds. Bostjan Nedoh and Andreja Zevnik (Edinburgh: Edinburgh UP, 2016), 180–202, and especially his "Ghosts of Substance Past: Schelling, Lacan, the Denaturalization of Nature," in *Lacan. The Silent Partners*, ed. Slavoj Žižek (New York: Verso, 2006), 34–55, as well as chapter V "Against Embodiment: The Material Ground of the More-than-Material-Subject" of his *Žižek's Ontology: A Transcendent Materialist Theory of Subjectivity* (Evanston: Northwestern UP, 2008), 45–66. Needless to say, Žižek's own work is essential here, especially his most direct study on Schelling and psychoanalysis: *The Indivisible Remainder: An Essay on Schelling and Related Matters* (London: Verson, 1996).

19. While Lacan examines dupery in other seminars like *Seminar XI: The Four Concepts of Psychoanalysis*, we will focus on *Seminar XXI* because it is there where, engaging with the possibility of a dupery of the Real instead of the Symbolic, we find an analogous notion to Deleuze's idea of the problem (and opportunity) of stupidity for philosophical and ontological thought.

20. Deleuze, *Difference and Repetition*, 152; FR 197.

21. Ever since Derrida commented on this passage of *Difference and Repetition* in his seminar *La bête et le souverain* (2001–2002), the question of stupidity (as *bêtise*) in Deleuze as yet another essential distinction of the human in its hierarchical position in nature has been examined to see if Derrida's assessment of Deleuze's ultimate anthropologocentrism – at least on this particular issue – is right or wrong. Besides Derrida's own seminar, three articles that examine this question are: Bernard Stiegler, "Doing and Saying Stupid Things in the Twentieth Century: bêtise *and animality in Deleuze and Derrida*," *Angelaki* 18, no. 1 (2013), 159–74; Tano Posteraro "Transcendental Stupidity: The Ground Become Autonomous in Schelling and Deleuze,"

Symposium 20, no. 2 (Fall 2016), 1–21; and my own "The Animal Mirrors: The Human/Animal Divide in Derrida and Deleuze," *Mosaic* 48, no. 3 (September 2015), 175–89.

22. Gilles Deleuze and Claire Parnet, *L'Abécedaire*, directed by Pierre-André Boutang and Michel Pamart (1996, Paris: éditions Montparnasse/Absolut MEDIEN, 2015), DVD.

23. Deleuze, *Difference and Repetition*, 152; FR 197.

24. Like Deleuze, Simondon does not make an essentialist claim on stupidity or thinking for the human. In his own terms, the psychological (*psychisme*) is more preponderant in the human, just as the purely living is more preponderant in the animal, but ultimately, both share in both of these dimensions. See Simondon, *L'individuation*, footnote 7, 165.

25. Deleuze, *Difference and Repetition*, 152; FR 197. My italics.

26. Perhaps the most significant expression of the possibility of this stupidity as a rising of the ground that un-distinguishes both the animal and the human is the story of the evil Tereus in Ovid's *Metamorphoses*, where he begins by duping his wife, father and sister-in-law, and ends up not only being duped himself (into eating his own son) but also turned into the dupe bird itself, the hoopoe or epsos.

27. Dylan Evans, *Dictionary of Lacanian Psychoanalysis* (London: Routledge, 1996), 119.

28. Jacques Lacan, *Les non-dupes errent*, Lesson 1. 1973–1974, 13; FR 16. Translation modified.

29. Lacan, *Les non-dupes*, Lesson 1, 14; FR 17. Italics original French transcription.

30. Lacan, *Les non-dupes*, Lesson 1, 16; FR 19.

31. The first question 'Where now?' is the only one that keeps its place in the shift they suffer between the original French and the English version.

32. Here, perhaps, we can understand better Lacan's statement in *Les non-dupes errent*, according to which, ultimately, we lack depth, since we are beings 'you as well as me, of two dimensions, despite appearances'. Jacques Lacan, *Les non-dupes*, Lesson 3, 3; FR 48. What makes us two-dimensional is this inseparability of the question of the subject from its place within a surface (or ground), literally *da*-sein, being the *there*. This is also why the Real is better understood as knots within a topographic structure, namely, as the moment when the bidimensional surface implodes.

33. Lacan, *Les non-dupes*, Lesson 3, 19–20; FR 67. Translation modified.

34. As we know, the spatiality of the Real, as well as that of the Symbolic and the Imaginary, is linked to Lacan's insistence on the need to conceive them in topographic terms. As the three rings of string show, their topographic spatiality is essentially connected, which means that the dupery of the Real is always a dupery also by/through the Imaginary and the Symbolic.

35. Lacan, *Les non-dupes*, Lesson 15, 20; FR 282.

36. Lacan, *Les non-dupes*, Lesson 15, 20; FR 283.

37. Lacan, *Les non-dupes*, Lesson 15, 20; FR 283. Translation modified.

38. Lacan, *Les non-dupes*, Lesson 15, 20; FR 283.

39. Marie-Hélène Brousse, "Moments d'une histoire d'amour," *La cause freudienne* 1, no. 68 (2008): 16. All translations from this article are mine.

40. Marie-Hélène Brousse, "Moments d'une histoire d'amour," 17.

41. Marie-Hélène Brousse, "Moments d'une histoire d'amour," 17.

42. Lacan, *Les non-dupes*, Lesson 4, 8; FR 75.

43. 'Again', since, as we know, even if necessarily fictional, for the sake of Lacanian, psychoanalytic and perhaps any theory, there must have been, in the (or a) beginning, a blissful loving stage/place.

44. Friedrich Wilhelm Joseph Schelling, *Philosophische Untersuchungen über das Wesen der menschlichen Freiheit und die damit zusammenhängenden Gegenstände* (Berlin: Berliner, 2016), 26.

45. Friedrich Wilhelm Joseph Schelling, *Philosophical Investigations into the Essence of Human Freedom*, trans. Jeff Love and Johannes Schmidt (Albany: SUNY Press, 2006), 69–70; original German (quoted above) 66. Schelling's italics.

46. Dylan Evans, *Dictionary of Lacanian Psychoanalysis*, 159.

47. Lorenzo Chiesa, *Subjectivity and Otherness. A Philosophical Reading of Lacan* (Cambridge: MIT UP, 2007), 122.

48. Lacan, *Les non-dupes*, Lesson 1, 16; FR 19.

49. Deleuze, *Difference and Repetition*, 152; FR 197.

50. Gustave Flaubert, *Bouvard et Pécuchet*, quoted in *Difference and Repetition*, 152. My italics.

51. Deleuze, *Difference and Repetition*, 152; FR 198. Translation slightly modified.

52. Deleuze, *Difference and Repetition*, 153; FR 198.

53. Alenka Zupančič, "The Death Drive," in *Lacan and Deleuze*, ed. Boštjan Nedoh and Andreja Zevnik (Edinburgh: Edinburgh UP, 2016), 175.

54. As I have tried to show, this means not only that any world/subject description is threatened by the contemporaneity of its genesis, but also that any causality is undermined by the contemporaneity of its present description. In Lacanian terms: 'Although it may seem that the relationship between structural conditions of the symbolic order (within which the subject exists) is transcendental, in the sense that the condition pre-exists what steps into the place emptied by the primary repressed signifier, Lacan explicitly states that we should grasp this logic of causality not as one of genesis but as one of immanent synchrony.' Boštjan Nedoh and Andreja Zevnik, "Introduction: On a Disjunctive Synthesis between Lacan and Deleuze," in *Lacan and Deleuze*, ed. Boštjan Nedoh and Andreja Zevnik (Edinburgh: Edinburgh UP, 2016), 4.

55. Claudia Rankine, *Just Us* (Minneapolis: Graywolf Press, 2020), 257.

56. "A Reporter's Footage From Inside the Capitol's Siege," *The New Yorker*, 17 January 2021, accessed, 6 March 2021 https://www.newyorker.com/news/video-dept/a-reporters-footage-from-inside-the-capitol-siege

57. Cindy Zeiher, "Trump, Our Favourite *Jouissance*," *Continental Thought & Theory. A Journal of Intellectual Freedom* 3, 1: Special Issue: The Problem of Trump, (2020), 206.

58. Interestingly, the new Democratic candidate's campaign, Kamala Harris's, has begun using an almost counter-genetic or counter-originary slogan at the time I write

this (July 2024). Instead of making the country great *again* (or *again again*) or bringing back its original 'soul', her slogan is 'we are not going back!' Which is not exactly a promise of a better future, but an affirmation and movement against a recognized violent and chaotic past.

59. James Williams, *Gilles Deleuze's Difference and Repetition. A Critical Introduction and Guide* (Edinburgh: Edinburgh UP, 2013), 135.

60. Deleuze, *Difference and Repetition*, 152; FR 198.

61. Deleuze, *Difference and Repetition*, 153; FR 198.

62. Lacan, *Les non-dupes*, Lesson 3, 3–4; FR 49.

63. Johann Wolfgang von Goethe, *Faust*. My translation.

REFERENCES

Brousse, Marie-Hélène Brousse. "Moments d'une histoire d'amour." *La cause freudienne* 1, no. 68 (2008): 14–17.

Chiesa, Lorenzo. *Subjectivity and Otherness. A Philosophical Reading of Lacan*. Cambridge: MIT UP, 2007.

Deleuze, Gilles. *Difference and Repetition*. Translated by Paul Patton. New York: Columbia UP, 1984.

———. *Différence et répétition*. Paris: PUF, 1968.

Evans, Dylan. *Dictionary of Lacanian Psychoanalysis*. London: Routledge, 1996.

Goethe, Johann Wolfgang von Goethe. *Faust*. Munich: Wilhelm Goldmann, 1962.

Lacan, Jacques. *Seminar XXI, Les non-dupes errent*. Translated by C. Gallagher. Unpublished Manuscript, Lesson 1. 1973–1974.

———. *Séminaire XXI, Les non-dupes errent*. Unpublished Manuscript, Lesson 1. 1973–1974.

Melnyk, Davyd. "Never Been Properly Jung." *Samuel Beckett Today / Aujourd'hui*. Vol. 15, Historicising Beckett / Issues of Performance / Beckett dans l'histoire / En jouant Beckett (2005): 355–62.

Nedoh, Boštjan and Andreja Zevnik. "Introduction: On a Disjunctive Synthesis between Lacan and Deleuze." In *Lacan and Deleuze*, edited by Boštjan Nedoh and Andreja Zevnik, 1–12. Edinburgh: Edinburgh UP, 2016.

Rankine, Claudia. *Just Us*. Minneapolis: Graywolf Press, 2020.

Schelling, Friedrich Wilhelm Joseph. *Philosophical Investigations into the Essence of Human Freedom*. Translated by Jeff Love and Johannes Schmidt. Albany: SUNY Press, 2006.

———. *Philosophische Untersuchungen über das Wesen der menschlichen Freiheit und die damit zusammenhängenden Gegenstände*. Berlin: Berliner, 2016.

Simondon, Gilbert. *Individuation in Light of Notions of Form and Information*. Translated by Taylor Adkins. Minneapolis: University of Minnesota Press, 2020.

———. *L'individuation à la lumière des notions de forme et d'information*. Grenoble: Million, 2017.

Williams, James. *Gilles Deleuze's Difference and Repetition. A Critical Introduction and Guide*. Edinburgh: Edinburgh UP, 2013.

Wirth, Jason M. *Schelling's Practice of the Wild.* Albany: SUNY Press, 2015.
Zeiher, Cindy. "Trump, Our Favourite *Jouissance.*" *Continental Thought & Theory. A Journal of Intellectual Freedom* 3, no. 1: Special Issue: The Problem of Trump, (2020): 200–216.
Zupančič, Alenka. "The Death Drive." In *Lacan and Deleuze*, edited by Boštjan Nedoh and Andreja Zevnik, 163–179. Edinburgh: Edinburgh UP, 2016.

Visual Media

Deleuze, Gilles and Claire Parnet. *L'Abécedaire.* Directed by Pierre-André Boutang and Michel Pamart, 1996; Paris: éditions Montparnasse/Absolut MEDIEN, 2015. DVD.
"A Reporter's Footage From Inside the Capitol's Siege." *The New Yorker*, 17 January 2021. Accessed 6 March 2021. https://www.newyorker.com/news/video-dept/a-reporters-footage-from-inside-the-capitol-siege

Chapter 4

Stupidity of the Signifier

Samo Tomšič

PSYCHOANALYSIS: CRITIQUE OF PURE STUPIDITY

In the second lecture of *Seminar XX*,[1] Lacan brings up the rumour that the seminar's topic was nothing other than love. The rumour itself is not false, but on closer inspection, the problematic of stupidity (*bêtise*) seems to be far more central in this and the other lectures of the seminar. *Encore* is a rightly famous seminar that proposes a series of significant epistemological developments: the elaboration of a theory of knowledge; reflection on mathematical formalization; valorization of knot theory; account of the relation between truth, knowledge and enjoyment; the limits of structural linguistics and so on. Although the discussion of stupidity assumes a less prominent place among these grand topics , the very emergence of the term in carefully premeditated moments provides the epistemological developments a critical edge. It gives Lacan's presumed scientism – the accent on mathematical formalism, the engagement with the modern scientific revolution, the so-called Borromean turn and so on – a somewhat ironic tone, while also explaining his increasingly negative stance towards philosophy.[2] Already a superficial reading of this seminar may show that stupidity offers a particular entry point or segue into a knot consisting of ontology, epistemology and politics – whereby the main intersection of these regions remains language, and specifically the relation between the signifier (epistemology), being (ontology) and enjoyment (politics). It is this intersection, that is, the examination of this knot, that I wish to pursue in the following through a closer reading of Lacan's *Seminar XX*.

Stupidity stands at the foreground of both introductory lectures, where it is explicitly associated with the basic unit of language – 'The signifier is stupid' (20) – and implicitly with enjoyment, defined as 'what serves no purpose' (3).

The formulation *ce qui sert à rien*, 'what serves for nothing' or 'what is good for nothing', may offer a first characterization of stupidity: stupid is what serves no purpose. This purposelessness or uselessness is not characteristic of every mode of enjoyment. The formulation targets above all enjoyment understood as surplus, *plus-de-jouir*, surplus-enjoyment. Lacan famously argued that this surplus is homologous to another prominent surplus, *plus-value*, surplus-value.[3] This leads straight to the main feature of the capitalist mode of production. The latter revolves around a surplus, which lacks usefulness rather than purpose, for Marx explicitly states that the purpose of the capitalist organization of social production is the constant increase of value. This is only possible if production becomes its own purpose, 'production for the sake of production',[4] precisely useless production. The capitalist imperative of perpetual economic growth, its organization of social production around the imperative of the constant increase of value and the organization of libidinal economy around the endless demand of pleasure (for the sake of pleasure) – the *encore* in the title of Lacan's Seminar – share the same uselessness and, consequently, the same stupidity.[5]

Further developments in the seminar approach the uselessness of enjoyment from the viewpoint of solitude: *jouissance solitaire*, solitary enjoyment. This expression is no less carefully chosen since it connotes masturbation. Articulated around a surplus, enjoyment inherently tends not only towards uselessness but also towards solitude, which can be understood in two distinct manners. First, in the obvious and most superficial sense of the absence of partner: satisfaction without a libidinal bond to another body. This detachment is indicated in the German term for masturbation, *Selbstbefriedigung*, self-satisfaction, which alludes to the centrality of the 'self' in enjoyment, more precisely to Freud's *Lust-Ich* (pleasure ego). In other words, narcissism. The second aspect of this solitude concerns the destabilization and potential dissolution of social links through the pursuit of useless surplus. One could argue that, in this problematic tendency towards solitude and uselessness, enjoyment turns *asocial*.[6]

Due to the ambiguity between these two states of solitude, it would be too rash to conclude that every enjoyment is stupid. This is because stupidity is characteristic of phallic enjoyment, which remains enjoyment of the organ, and in which the other body, the partner in enjoyment, is reduced to object *a*, the embodiment of surplus-enjoyment.[7] The hypothesis of 'other enjoyment' that Lacan examines in relation to femininity in general and feminine mystics in particular may point out the limits of stupidity, insofar as this mode of enjoyment contains a shift in the relation between language, enjoyment and the body. In distinction to the phallic localization of enjoyment, which seems stuck in masturbatory self-satisfaction, the 'other enjoyment' would imply a different scenario. For lack of better formulation, Lacan somewhat enigmatically speaks of the 'other satisfaction'. Although it should immediately be added that this 'other satisfaction' and 'other enjoyment' are anything but immunized against backlashes into self-satisfaction and solitude. They can turn into the self-sufficient enjoyment of language, 'satisfaction through babbling' (56, transl. modified), which is no less stupid than the masturbatory phallic enjoyment.

In its double role as signifier of enjoyment and signifier of castration, the phallus organizes production of enjoyment around the vicious circle of lack and surplus. Indeed, *plus-de-jouir* can be translated both as 'more enjoyment' and 'no more enjoyment'. This organization necessarily pushes the subject into an endless, useless chase for 'more', giving rise to a dissatisfying self-satisfaction. In 'other enjoyment', the latter is dispersed throughout language, as Lacan's examples strive to demonstrate: mystical literature, Joyce's *Finnegan's Wake* and Lacan's own writings. As already indicated, this scenario equally comprises a masturbatory drift of enjoyment, only that what is masturbated here is language itself. Against Aristotle, language is an organ-tool (*organon*) of enjoyment, rather than an organ-tool of communication.

Lacan's examples nevertheless aim to make a more complicated critical point. Mystical literature is not just empty babbling but a testimony; Joyce's literature is not only absurd scribbling but an invention of a new literary form by means of linguistic equivocity; the proverbial baroque style of Lacan's *écrits* is not simple obscurantism but a demonstration of the psychoanalytic method in an exoteric context; and, last but not least, the direction of speech in a psychoanalytic setting aims at working through the intricacies of enjoyment. All these are attempts at breaking with the alienation that affects the subject caught up in an endless production of discursive enjoyment, in other words, attempts at working through stupidity.

If the topic of Lacan's *Seminar XX* is indeed love, which is a form of bond – 'love is always reciprocal' (4, transl. modified) – then this topic cannot be addressed without its inversion, stupidity, a form of un-bond, for which one could claim, 'stupidity is always solitary', a one-way street that does not prevent it from being shared.[8] Love and stupidity describe two different ways in which enjoyment is organized and economized in a social link. Here and again, in line with the Freudian Eros-Thanatos couple: love expresses the conversion of enjoyment into a bond, whereas stupidity signals the destabilization and potential dissolution of social links through the pursuit of enjoyment for the sake of enjoyment.

While love '*makes* a sign' (*fait signe*, ibid.) – in the double sense of producing a sign and being one – stupidity *is* a signifier – the 'dimension of signifier at work' (*dimension en exercice du signifiant*, 21). Love and stupidity thus seem to relate to each other in a homologous way, as a sign does to a signifier. From Saussure, we know that the signifier is a differential component of the sign, which is arbitrarily tied to the signified. This means that the construction of this bond is not grounded in the signifier itself – that, considered in itself, the signifier is non-relational, and this is ultimately its 'stupidity'. The term 'love' would then signify a specific struggle, an attempt at working through the signifier's stupidity. This is the task of transference love in the psychoanalytic setting, which is why Freud insisted that there is no qualitative difference between everyday love and 'artificially produced' transference love. If love indeed *makes* a sign, then this sign expresses that a specific conflict takes place in the subject, a struggle with and against a problematic and ultimately stupid mode of enjoyment. The sign of love carries stupidity in its core, striving to embed it in a link or relation and thus transform its affectivity.

Love, as what *makes* (more or less smart) signs (out of stupid signifiers), then has to economize the signifier's stupidity and the non-relation that goes along with this stupidity.[9] Love creates a link, bond or relation, something that ties the stupid signifier to a signified and one enjoying body to another, allowing enjoyment to be more than self-satisfactory. (Again, Freud already saw in Eros a force that binds, although this bonding does not always end up positive for the subject.) The signified of the love-sign would be nothing other than the link or relation itself, whether social or libidinal. As economization of non-relation, love inevitably implies work, the notorious 'work of love', which ultimately comes down to constructing a relation that does not pre-exist, and whose actuality entirely depends on this ongoing work. Indeed, relation is arguably always a work-in-progress, a process rather than a result.[10] In this respect, love is also an attempt at working through the deadlocks imposed by the situation in which the stupidity of the signifier and the solitude of enjoyment mirror the fact that no 'them' (amorous couple) and no 'we' (political collective) are guaranteed in advance.[11]

By associating stupidity with the signifier, Lacan signals that the problematic must be examined in a structural rather than psychological manner. Instead of characterizing individuals, stupidity concerns the very fundaments of language and the relation between language and the body, epitomized in the problematic of surplus-enjoyment. Stupidity comes over as a specific figure of negativity, which in its own manner contributes to the consistency of discourse. However, Lacan insists that the complicated link between discourse and stupidity becomes evident only in the case of analytical discourse, whereas other discourses are grounded on the avoidance of stupidity:

> And yet it's impossible, given our experience, not to question something regarding analytic discourse: doesn't this discourse hold together by basing itself on the dimension of stupidity? [. . .] It is nevertheless true that there is a status to be granted to this new discourse and to its approach to stupidity. Surely it comes

> closer, since in other discourses stupidity is what one flees. Discourses always aim at the least stupidity, at sublime stupidity, for 'sublime' means the highest point of what lies below. (12–13, transl. modified)

Why does the privilege in highlighting stupidity come exactly to psychoanalysis, rather than, say, philosophy? It all comes down to the way psychoanalysis relates to language in general and to the signifier in particular. This attitude is sufficiently indicated in the etymology of the word 'sublime'. The Latin *sublimis* means 'lifted' or 'elevated'; the prefix *sub-* connotes 'beneath' and *limen* 'threshold'. Hence sublime is the point of contact between the highest and the lowest. To talk about the stupidity of the signifier goes against an entire philosophical tradition that saw in *logos* (word, language, reason) the highest quality of human being. The thinking of thinking, an activity that philosophers always valued as the ultimate ideal, is examined from the viewpoint of the zero level of thinking that philosophers would consider to be the level of stupidity.

This point is indeed central for understanding the reasons for Lacan's turn against ontology in his final years. The science of being goes back to a gesture, which is closely entangled with the signifier's stupidity but nevertheless overlooks it completely, Parmenides' distinction of being and non-being: 'It is precisely because he was a poet that Parmenides says what he has to say to us in the least stupid of manners. Otherwise, the idea that being is and that nonbeing is not, I don't know what that means to you, but personally I find that stupid. And you mustn't believe that it amuses me to say so' (22). Parmenides remained blind to the excess that is inherent to the very act of separation between being and non-being and to the prohibition of the discourse of non-being: the leaning of ontology on the master's discourse (that Lacan in *Seminar XX* writes *m'être* in order to accentuate the kinship between 'master' and 'being'). Here, a more fundamental quarrel concerns the status of stupidity itself – rather than being avoided, the signifier's stupidity is the foundation of ontological discourse especially because the signifier demonstrates the *ontological in-difference of being and non-being*. For this reason, Lacan sides with Heraclitus against Parmenides (114), hence with the idea of ontological change and becoming in contrast to the 'conventional' ontologies of being and order.

In contrast to ontology, psychoanalysis confronts stupidity directly because it traces thinking and being back to their logical and material bedrock, the signifier: 'The subject is not the one who thinks. The subject is precisely the one we encourage, not to say it all, as we tell him in order to charm him – one cannot say it all – but rather to utter stupidities. That is the key' (22). Free association, the analytic imperative of avoiding censorship and reporting everything that comes to mind, is the main strategy to access the unconscious:

'for it is with those stupidities that we do analysis, and that we enter into the new subject – that of the unconscious' (ibid.). This time an inversion of Cartesianism is at stake: thinking does not require the subject's conscious attention, doubt or intentionality; it is enough to utter stupidities, to associate more or less freely, in short, to speak. In free association, intentionality without consciousness is manifested, the intentionality of language, which shows that free association was an illusion (albeit a necessary one) and impossibility (albeit a real one). In the end, free association – 'uttering stupidities' – turns out to be a compulsive process. Contrary to philosophical obsession with the 'thinking of thinking', psychoanalysis brings about its disenchantment by reducing thinking to speaking. Stupidity is not simple absence of thought but presumably uncensored uttering, where signifiers reveal their stupidity. Further, what is indeed most crucial in the analytic process is not so much to think oneself thinking, but rather to hear oneself talking. Therefore, the point of free association is not in the imperative of 'saying all' but in reducing thinking to speaking, which seems to unfold by itself.

At this point, it may be worth recalling Lacan's introductory lines from his *Letter of Dissolution:* 'I speak without the slightest hope – specifically of making myself understood. I know that I do so – by adding thereto whatever it entails of the unconscious. That is my advantage over the man who thinks and does not perceive that, to start with, he speaks. An advantage which I owe solely to my experience.'[12] The demarcation line between philosophy and psychoanalysis is again at the core: 'The man who thinks and does not perceive that, to start with, he speaks' would be a suitable definition of the philosopher. Consequently, the oblivion of speaking would be a more fundamental gesture, on which philosophy is grounded, certainly more fundamental than the 'oblivion of being' (Heidegger) or the oblivion of enjoyment. This is also where Lacan's so often repeated *ça parle* (it speaks) enters the picture. By descending to this zero level of thinking, where thinking is indistinct from speaking, psychoanalysis confronts stupidity directly in the guise of the master-signifier. To recall another crucial formula: 'The unconscious is the fact that being, by speaking, enjoys, and [. . .] does not want to know nothing more about it' (104–5). To rephrase, the speaking being resists knowledge, it actively rejects it and in doing so enacts one of the three fundamental passions (next to love and hate): ignorance, a passion characteristic of stupidity.

Just like the sublime, substance, too, stands for both the highest and the lowest, something that lies underneath, but also something most fundamental and essential. Pertaining to the basic unit of language, stupidity must therefore be substantiated: 'analytic discourse introduces an adjective made into a noun, "stupidity", insofar as it is a dimension of the signifier at work (*dimension en exercise du signifiant*)' (21). The activity of the signifier that is of relevance here is its causing of enjoyment in the living body, which is why

Lacan's next move introduces the 'enjoying substance'.[13] This third mode of substance aims to overcome the Cartesian dualism of thought and extension, whereby enjoyment pinpoints the *ontological in-difference of thinking and extension.*

Since stupidity is no longer understood in its subjective or psychological dimension but becomes substantiated as the defining feature of the signifier, this makes psychoanalysis more than simply a 'talking cure'.[14] Psychoanalysis is also a cure of talking, a therapy of language. Its clinical practice therefore intersects and competes with logic, which has perceived itself as a therapy of language ever since Aristotle, but also with linguistics, understood as *the* scientific treatment of language.

PARTING WAYS: PSYCHOANALYSIS AND LINGUISTICS

In his tribute to Roman Jakobson, which introduces the second lecture of *Seminar XX*, Lacan remarks 'that it is difficult not to speak stupidly about language. That is nevertheless what you, Jakobson, manage to do' (14). In which respect did Jakobson break with the philosophical and scientific tradition of 'speaking stupidly' about language? One part of the answer may be found in Jakobson's focus on poetic language, which remained in the background of Saussure's work. Saussure's fascination with anagrams became known in the 1950s and immediately revealed an unusual flipside to his semiological project. The publication of other manuscripts only confirmed that there was an inner tension in Saussure's work, tarrying between linguistic synchronicity and diachronicity. Under the structuralist label, it was Saussure's synchronic linguistics that triumphed over the diachronic: the actualization of the system in the present became more important than its metamorphosis through time and the stabilization of structure more central than its instability and becoming.

Jakobson's emphasis on poetic language drew attention to significantly more dynamic and unstable aspects of language. Furthermore, Jakobson introduced other phenomena in linguistic consideration, which may be considered the margins of language, such as child language and aphasia. Both phenomena allow linguistics to observe language in becoming and language in dissolution, and thereby challenge the predominant views on fully developed linguistic capacity.[15] For Jakobson, these vicissitudes of language should not be seen as simple pathologies, deviations from linguistic norms and disturbances of otherwise regular and stable linguistic structures. Rather, it is from the viewpoint of these linguistic margins that the so-called normal functioning of language must be highlighted. More precisely, from the perspective of poetic language, child language and linguistic disorders, the distinction between the normal and the pathological must be questioned in the field of language and rejected from the field of linguistics. It was the path opened up by Jakobson that inspired Lacan's link between language and the unconscious, another non-stupid attempt in talking about language – with the addition that Lacan introduced in his account of language an object that, strictly speaking, does not belong to the field of linguistics, or with which linguistics does not know what to begin with – precisely, enjoyment. Thus, it is no surprise that the closing session of *Seminar XX* proposes some wide-reaching critical comments regarding the scientific ambitions of linguistics.[16]

The normativist approach to language that guided grammatical, logical and philological tradition until structuralism and theories of performativity assumed that language *ideally* contains no surplus (non-sense, non-relation, enjoyment) and that the underlying function of language consists in communication and the representation of reality. By restricting the productive dimension of language, the philosophy of language and a majority of linguistic schools removed the stupidity of the signifier from the picture. Lacan addresses the issue in the following manner: 'language is merely what scientific discourse elaborates to account for what I call lalanguage [. . .] language [. . .] is the pondering of knowledge on lalanguage' (138–39, transl. modified). This scientific pondering tries to make of lalanguage (language as it *dis*functions in the living body) something 'more', an ordered system that can be used in a regular manner. In doing so, linguistics blends out the causal link between language and the unconscious, and more specifically between signifier and enjoyment, which would otherwise make language appear as a specific type of disequilibrium or disturbance in the living body. The pondering of scientific knowledge strives to separate language (*langue*) from the activity of speaking (*parole*) and thus from the body. In doing so, the science of language repeats the fundamental gesture of all those philosophies of language, which refuse to deal with the 'life of language' – lalanguage – and instead direct their attention to something like an ideal or model language – a language in which the signifier is presumably not stupid, because it sustains communication, adequate representation of reality and differentiation between truth and falsehood.

In contrast to this endeavour, which walks straight into the trap of stupidity while trying to escape it, departing from the signifier's stupidity indeed contains its restriction and lays ground for a materialist theory of language (Lacan names it *linguisterie* in order to mark its distinction, not simply from linguistics, but from the analytical and positivist tendencies in the science of language). Because of its systematic focus on the *dis*functioning of language in the living body, psychoanalysis cannot be satisfied with providing grammatical or logical analyses only. Nor can it embark on the hermeneutic quest for sense and meaning, the search for 'words beneath words', as Saussure did in his fascination with anagrams.[17] By inventing psychoanalysis, Freud indeed introduced his own take on language, as well as his own language. Against this background of singularity, Lacan eventually insisted that his formula 'the unconscious is structured like a language' does not belong to the field of linguistics. The question beckons, however: Does this mean that Lacan ended up rejecting or abandoning the structuralist research programme? Not necessarily. But he did reject linguistic normativism and its hypothesis of the central role of communication in language:

> It is generally said that language serves to communicate. [. . .] Communication implies reference. But one thing is clear – language is merely what scientific discourse elaborates to account for what I call lalanguage. Lalanguage serves purposes that are altogether different from that of communication. That is what the experience of the unconscious has shown us, insofar as it is made of lalanguage, which, as you know, I write with two la-s to designate what each of us deals with, our so-called mother tongue (*lalangue dite maternelle*), which isn't called that by accident. If communication approaches what is effectively at work in the enjoyment of lalanguage, it is because communication implies a reply, in other words, dialogue. But does lalanguage serve, first and foremost, to dialogue? As I have said before, nothing is less certain. (138, transl. modified)

If dialogue is the paradigm of communication and more fundamentally the ultimate figure of relation or link, in which no negativity is contained or economized, then linguistics constructs its object by rejecting the non-relationality *of* and *from* language. The linguistic object is an idealization, an epistemic fiction, which certainly exists in the register of knowledge, but for which linguistics claims a status that is homologous to the 'epistemic' object of ontology, being. It is for this reason that Lacan never got tired of repeating that the big Other (language) does not exist. This clearly does not mean that lalanguage does not exist. Lalanguage exists precisely as an ongoing symbolic activity in the speaking body. However, this activity never amounts to a fully constituted, ontologically complete result; differently put, speech never stands for the practical realization of the epistemic object that is fabricated by linguistics. The true opposite of the abstract *langue* is not just any form of living language, but the maternal *lalangue*, with all the weight and ambiguity that the reference to motherhood entails in the psychoanalytic framework – the first one being that the maternal *lalangue* is a *libidinal* bond, and therefore an unstable, internally broken and inevitably conflicted relation. In turn, the epistemic object of linguistics, *langue*, is a delibidinized link without any trace of negativity that accompanies the life and the enjoyment of language.[18] Furthermore, the opposite of communication is not a disordered and headless babbling. The narrative arguing that outside communication there is only linguistic nonsense or language in dissolution is the founding myth of normative philosophies of language. The false opposition between communication ('language of being') and non-sensical language ('language of enjoyment') traverses the history of philosophy ever since Aristotle.[19] And it reflects the ongoing desire of science and philosophy to establish mastery over language.

With his focus on the poetic function of language, Jakobson opened up a path that pertains neither to the communicative dialogue nor to a presumable language monologue. Poetics exemplifies something that psychoanalysis equally aims at: the discursive handling of enjoyment caused by the 'signifier at work'. Although Jakobson personally never thematized enjoyment of language, his take on exemplifications of linguistic disequilibrium (again child language, aphasia and poetry) paved the way for something like a *non-relational linguistics* – a linguistics that engages in a depsychologization of language and no longer departs from the communication model only in order to return to it. By putting linguistic phenomena that demonstrate the inherent instability of linguistic structures at the centre of attention, Jakobson indeed moved away from the assumption of an *ideal language* (language without negativity and without surplus) and thereby implicitly posited that linguistics must bring about a thorough decentralization of language. If there were such a thing as the 'Galilean science of language' (as Jean-Claude Milner would put it), then such a science would have to detach language from the conscious intentionality of its presumable users, but not from the living body, hence from the activity of speech. It would have to replace the pragmatic conception of language (language as *organon*) with a thorough materialist take on the link between signifier and enjoyment. Since this material activity challenges the linguistic assumption that language predominantly serves the purpose of communication, the task of *linguisterie* consists in pinpointing in the incompatibility between *langue* and *lalangue* a concrete limit of linguistics.

Saussure's detachment of *langue* (language) from *parole* (speech), which still guided the majority of structuralists, failed to accomplish the necessary decentralization in the field of language. Only when language has been thoroughly detached from the intentionality of its conscious users, structural instability, or rather, structure as organized disequilibrium, could become the central problem and the privileged entry point in the science of language. Lacan's structuralism embarked on this path twice, first by establishing the link between language and the unconscious and later by introducing the notion of *lalangue* for marking the exact opposite of Saussure's notion of *langue*, the fusion of the signifier and the body brought to the point in the production of enjoyment. Again, this is what underpins Lacan's compulsive repetition that the big Other does not exist. What does not exist is language as a stable epistemic object, fabricated by the science of language and presumably actualized in the activity of speaking. To put it in Aristotelian terms, language is not *ergon* but *energeia* – an activity that does not amount to a completed result. One could say that humans speak *because* language does not exist. But at the same time, they also speak in order to make this inexistent language exist. Speaking provides the inexistent language a minimum of consistency, reality and being. In short, it provides inexistent language with a body.[20] The activity of speaking stands for language in becoming, or in the process of emergence, rather than for a simple usage of a pregiven linguistic tool. Again, contrary to Saussure, there is no *langue* outside *parole*; there is only *lalangue*, on the level of which *langue* and *parole* are indistinct. The activity of speaking generates the 'language-effect', the fantom of a completely constituted language.

Pursuing his criticism of the Saussurean take, Lacan suggested defining the signifier in spatial terms, which again points out the cause of its stupidity: 'Indeed, the signifier is first of all that which has a signified effect (*effet de signifié*), and it is important not to elide the fact that between signifier and signified effect there is something barred that must be crossed over' (18, translation modified). What at first glance seems to merely repeat Saussure's decomposition of the linguistic sign in fact moves beyond the Saussurean framing. The first important difference consists in determining the signified as the effect of the signifier – and since the definition is supposed to be topological, the term 'effect' must be understood in correlation with the effect at stake in the curved or twisted surface such as the Möbius strip. The signified effect has the same status as the flipside effect of the Möbius strip. This places Saussure's comparison of the relation between the signifier and the signified with a sheet of paper in a different light. While in Saussure we have a two-sided surface, which is moreover static (there is no activity that would produce a signified effect), in Lacan we have a one-sided active surface, which indeed brings about a signified effect.[21]

Understood as a system of active differences, language creates an objective appearance of relationality, referentiality and parallelism between signifier and signified, which is nevertheless not there. What is there is the signifier's causality. Hence, Lacan's second emphasis that there is a barrier between the signifier and the signified that must be crossed over in order to move from one to the other, just as there is a margin on the Möbius strip that delays the passage to the flipside. But this transition is never accomplished, since the Möbius strip does not have a flipside; the latter is an effect of the torsion of its surface. Or, perhaps better, the Möbius strip is simply this torsion, which pinpoints the activity of this topological object. Similarly, in language, we never pass over to a signified, which would not be an effect of the signifier, and more importantly, which would not be inherently unstable and shifting. This, of course, does not mean that the signified is a simple illusion. The signified is a dynamic effect, sliding along the curvature that is the signifier. And the stupidity of the signifier comes down to this discrepancy, this limping or dysfunctional relation with the signified:

> Signified effects seem to bear no relation to what causes them. That means that the references or things the signifier serves to approach remain approximate – macroscopic, for example. What is important is not that it's imaginary – after all, if the signifier allowed us to point to the image we need to be happy, that would be fine and dandy, but it's not the case. At the level of the signifier/signified distinction, what characterizes the relationship between the signified and what serves as the indispensable third party, namely the referent, is precisely that the signified misses the referent. The collimator doesn't work. (20, transl. modified)

A collimator is a technical device which is used for narrowing down a beam of particles or waves. It allows directing the motion of these particles and causing alignments or changes in their movement. But the signifier is a malfunctioning collimator. Its curvature causes the 'signifying wave' to deflect from the targeted reference. Hence, it does not serve for determining directions and orientation but rather for deliberately causing breaks, deviations and disorientations. The signifier contains a fault and is made of unstable and flexible material. Structural linguistics encountered this 'stupidity' when it separated the signifier from its assumed function of meaning. But again, the notion of arbitrarity did not yet grasp the causality of the signifier. This is to say nothing of the double character of this causality: on the one hand, the causing of an incorporeal signified, and on the other, the causing of corporeal enjoyment.

It is at this juncture of the signified and enjoyment that the dimension of the body finally enters the picture – a body parcelled by the signifier, which marks various corporeal regions as privileged supports of enjoyment. Erogenous zones are the bodily parts where the signifier becomes most material and its function of signification indistinguishable from corporisation.[22] In *Seminar XX*, the ultimate exemplification of this signifying action is Bernini's sculpture of the ecstasy of St Theresa. Elsewhere in the seminar, the facial expression of the angel, whose arrow pierces the saint's chest, provides an image of the signifier's stupidity:

> 'The signifier is stupid. It seems to me that this could lead to a smile, a stupid smile, naturally. A stupid smile, as everyone knows – it suffices to visit cathedrals – is an angel's smile. [. . .] If an angel has such a stupid smile, that is because it is up to its ears in the supreme signifier. To find itself on dry land would do it some good – perhaps it wouldn't smile anymore. It's not that I believe in angels [. . .] it's just that I don't believe they bear the slightest message, and it is in that respect that they are truly signifying. (20–21)

The angel's face is the perfect counterpart to St Theresa's expression of ecstasy. Her face remains undecided between pleasure and pain, while her body is thrown into a state of cramp. In turn, the angelic smile is enigmatic because it creates the impression of a coded message that the angel's presence is supposed to reveal. The smile is indicated, suggested, discreet, a mere semblance of a smile, whose appearance coincides with its disappearance. This gap between emergence and disappearance, the discrepancy in which the emptiness of the angelic smile is settled, is also the 'place' of stupidity. The smile gives rise to speculations that try to fill it with meaning. In doing so, these speculations only intensify the smile's enigma, which strictly speaking hides nothing, no secret, cipher or divine detail. Moreover, the stupid smile illustrates the function of the master-signifier, signifier without signified but with a signified effect – a signifier which signifies the fact that it signifies. It gives an order, produces the signified effect and in the same gesture causes enjoyment. In linguistics, this redoubling of the signifier's causality, together with the dislocation of the speaking body brought about by linguistic disequilibrium, remains out of the picture. Whereas linguistics seems to be on the side of the angel, speculating on its enigmatic smile, psychoanalysis sides with the saint and draws its lessons from her testimony of the experience of ecstasy.

PARTING WAYS: PSYCHOANALYSIS AND PHILOSOPHY

In the church Santa Maria della Vittoria in Rome, where Bernini's sculpture is located, there is an interesting detail that Lacan failed to mention. Directly opposite of Bernini's Saint Theresa there is Domenico Guidi's 'Saint Joseph's dream'. In this less famous and less dramatic work, we see the saint sleeping in the presence of an angel, who visits him in his dream. The angel in Guidi's sculpture exemplifies another aspect of the stupidity of the signifier, for which Lacan uses the term feeble-mindedness (*débilité mentale*) and which radicalizes his critical stance towards philosophy in his final years.[23] Whereas Bernini's sculpture gives shape to the bifurcation that the 'stupid signifier' causes in the speaking body, Guidi's evokes the earliest Freudian reflections on the link between dreams, language and hallucinatory satisfaction of unconscious desire.

Again, if psychoanalysis sides with the mystic's testimony and her attempt at working through the experienced ecstasy in writing, philosophy appears to be on the side of dreamwork. In a quote much appreciated by Freud, Heinrich Heine mockingly describes philosophy as an intellectual activity, which consists of patching up the gaps in reality.[24] Looking again at the contrast

Figure 4.1 Bernini, Gian Lorenzo. *The Ecstasy of Saint Theresa* (1652), Church of Santa Maria della Vittoria (Rome, Italy). *Source*: Photo by Samo Tomšič.

between Guidi and Bernini's sculptures, one could add that philosophy presupposes, if not disembodiment, at least a body in the state of rest. In order to achieve this, philosophy, too, needs to fabricate an ideal language, in which the signifier will cause no turbulences or disequilibrium, in other words, a language which will be separated from the body. To bring about this separation is traditionally the task of logic, ever since its Aristotelian foundation.

According to Barbara Cassin, Aristotle's entire philosophy and the influence it exercises well into the present can be brought down to a fundamental 'decision of sense',[25] which determines the sense of speaking and the basic function of language in the background of the opposition between meaningful communication and nonsensical babbling. This decision takes place in *Metaphysics,* Book Gamma, where Aristotle delimits discourses that are similar in appearance but opposed in their content and method, philosophy and sophistry. The whole procedure consists of deciding the direction that philosophy

Figure 4.2 Guidi, Domenico. *The Dream of Saint Joseph* (c. 1694), Church of Santa Maria della Vittoria (Rome, Italy). *Source*: Photo by Samo Tomšič.

must take and determining the path of sense as the direction or orientation of philosophical thinking (the French *sens* means both sense and direction). This necessarily initiates the fabrication of an ideal language accompanied by an ideal speaker (presumably actualized in the figure of the philosopher).

The discourse of sophistry is rejected as an exemplification of confused speech, even a dissolution of language. This rejection makes sophistry interesting for psychoanalysis while also drawing attention to the procedures by means of which philosophical discourse constituted itself both historically and logically. It is not unusual that the refutation of sophistry stands at the very entry into ontology. The preontological condition of ontology is the decision on whether language is fundamentally relational or non-relational, apophantic or performative, in other words, whether language unveils true being or merely produces semblances and enjoyment in speaking. For philosophy, there is no such thing as 'enjoyment of being', and the fundamental task of ontology, this science of being qua being, consists in maintaining being and semblance, as well as language – the signifier – and enjoyment apart. The Aristotelian position is the perfect opposite of what Lacan argues in Seminar XX: *là où ça parle, ça jouit, et ça sait rien*, where there is speech, there is enjoyment and there is no knowledge. For logic, the contrary is the case: where there is speech, there is no enjoyment and there is only knowledge.[26] The condition of scientific knowledge (insofar as we understand ontology in its classical sense of the science of being) is a strict separation of language and enjoyment, prohibition of enjoyment in and of language.

In Aristotle, this separation obtains the familiar logical phrasing in the principle of non-contradiction: 'It is impossible for the same to belong and not belong to the same with respect to the same' (Met. 1005b 19–21).[27] For Aristotle, there is no split or difference on the level of sameness. Such difference is excluded, projected onto sophistry, a discourse that is in perpetual contradiction and therefore non-identity with itself. Aristotle argues that the sophists 'speak for the pleasure of speaking' (following Cassin's translation), or in English translation: 'For those who speak for the sake of words, the refutation is to heal their speech in the voices and what is said in the words' (Met. 1009a 21–22). The main scandal of sophistry consists in speaking for the sake of speaking. Its speech is empty since it does not enunciate anything, except that it enunciates. In this framing, empty speech would be something like the stupidity of the signifier articulated, stupidity that speaks.

The principle of non-contradiction thus associates linguistic inconsistencies with the enjoyment of speaking. Inconsistencies, paradoxes and contradictions are signs of the enjoyment of language. They signal that *logos* lost its apophantic function, the unveiling of being, that it ceased to be the language of being and became a factory of enjoyment. Aristotle insists that the refutation of those who speak for the sake of speaking has a therapeutic effect. It is the cure against the presumable closure of *logos* into babbling. The separation of sophistry from philosophy constructs an inconsistent and contradictory figure of speech:[28] on the one hand, the sophist personifies enjoyment in speaking and on the other, the same excess makes the sophist indistinguishable from a plant (Met. 1008b 7–12). The sophist is thus a paradoxical synthesis of contraries, a talking plant. It is indeed symptomatic that Aristotle makes this unusual shift from babbling, which displays anything but the speaker's numbness, even if that speaker does not enunciate anything, to the plant as the embodiment of silence. Yet this position is explained through the fact that for Aristotle speaking means as much as speaking about something in particular, and more specifically, about something that *is*. Those who speak must necessarily enunciate something; their speech must signify something true, otherwise 'there would be no language, neither in relation to themselves or in relation to others' (Met. 1006a). Language is either apophantic or it does not exist.

The true significance of sophistry is that its relation to language is marked by a certain irony. Contrary to the philosopher's struggle to fabricate a stable and univocal language of being, sophistical practice demonstrates that language does not exist.[29] The scandal of sophistry comes down to its choice of the performative function of *logos*, which blurs the border between being and non-being, reverts Parmenides' ontological decision and introduces movement into what *is*. Whereas speech acts actively produce the realities they speak about, for Aristotle, speaking must remain a *passive* activity. Talking about non-being inevitably makes us fall into the overlapping of being and enunciation. Further, in contrast to the ontological ideal of the language of being, sophistical irony shows that language is non-being, or more precisely, that the *signifier is non-being, which has the effect of being, but which nevertheless insists outside being*. It is this ambiguous placement that sustains both the relationality and non-relationality of the signifier. And further, rather than striving for language without negativity and productivity, one of the main efforts of psychoanalysis consists in inventing an intelligent use of the stupid signifier.

Of course, Aristotle's philosophy is not immunized against the excessive dimension of language that it strives to prohibit. The distinction between *to ti esti* (what is) and *to ti en einai* (what must be) clearly valorizes the latter over the former. What does this distinction say about the language of being? If ontology never merely speaks but commands how reality must be, then the imperative signifier returns at the core of the science of being. There is no 'being *qua* being', only commanded being, being as a specific kind of surplus product of linguistic activity.[30] This imperative signifier undermines the very idea of ontological stability, epitomized by the link between duration and being. In the same line as the remark on the university discourse's 'eternal dream', Lacan's neologism *êtrernel* mocks the metaphysical category of 'being that is eternal and is in itself'. The true opposition to *êtrernel* is not 'being that is not eternal and is not in itself' but 'being that is not eternal and *is* in itself'. For classical ontology, such modality of being is complete nonsense. But it is precisely this 'nonsense' that is actualized by the signifier:

> [N]o signifier is produced as eternal. That is no doubt what, rather than qualifying it as arbitrary, Saussure could have formulated – it would have been better to qualify the signifier with the category of contingency. The signifier repudiates the category of the eternal and, nevertheless, oddly enough, it is intrinsically. Isn't it clear to you that it participates, to employ a Platonic approach, in that nothing on the basis of which something entirely original was made *ex nihilo*, as the creationist idea tells us? (40, transl. modified)

The onto-theological framing is right about one thing: there is no being that is not eternal and is in itself. It is exactly the excluded 'isn't' from Parmenides' axiom. And so, we are back at the signifier as being-producing non-being (difference).

Aristotle's metaphysics defined the presumable eternity of being as the immovability of the divine sphere. It is this ordering of the real into a closed, spherical world that Lacan eventually called 'Aristotle's dream': 'Aristotle thinks [. . .], he thinks the world, and this he dreams like what we call the whole world, people. He dreams the world that he thinks, like everyone who speaks. The result is that it is the world that thinks. The first sphere is what he calls *nous*.'[31] Consequently, the psychoanalytic clinic deals with the maladies of Aristotelianism:

> The psychoanalysand sometimes syllogizes, that is, aristotelizes. Thus Aristotle maintains his domination. Which is not to say that he lives – he survives in his dreams. In every psychoanalysand there is a disciple of Aristotle. But it must be said that the universal is sometimes realized in babbling. Insofar as the psychoanalysand dreams, the psychoanalyst must intervene. Is it in order to wake up the psychoanalysand? But he does not want it in any case – the psychoanalysand dreams, that is, he sticks to the particularity of his symptom.[32]

Once again, the oppositional couple of logic and babbling enters the picture. In contrast to this false opposition, the psychoanalytic technique of interpretation implies another decision, which thoroughly rejects the Aristotelian 'decision of sense' and its underlying opposition between normal and pathological language. Against the Aristotelian choice of sense against nonsense, psychoanalysis chooses equivocity, the overlapping of sound and sense, as well as the overlapping of sense and enjoyment (epitomized in Lacan's neologism *joui-sens*, enjoyed-sense). But psychoanalysis has not always been consistent in this choice. In Freud, interpretation is still supposed to reveal a hidden sense of the analysand's symptoms. Freud consistently brought in archaeological metaphors in order to illustrate his technique of listening and interpreting the analysand's speech: excavation and reconstruction of forgotten elements of the subject's history. One could say that for Freud the analyst's function remains tied to *Aufklärung*; the analytical intervention must reveal sense where the analysand sees nothing but nonsense. This move already entails an inversion of Aristotelianism, but when, for instance, Freud in his analysis of jokes emphasizes their technique of drawing sense out of nonsense, he in some way outlines his understanding of the analytical situation as well.

Lacan followed this path only in order to bring about an inversion in priorities, the fusion of sense and enjoyment, indicated in the already mentioned neologism *joui-sens*. Consequently, the focus on equivocity changed the aim of the analyst's intervention: 'Analytical interpretation is not made to be understood; it is made to cause waves (*vagues*).'[33] One meaning of *vagues* is troubles and confusions. Analytical interpretation thus aims at producing difficulties in understanding, subjecting thinking to forcing and thus making the analysand work through the symptom's nonsensical perseverance, rather than simply understanding its signification. The ambiguity that accompanies the analyst's intervention due to the use of equivocity introduces a minimum of disturbance, which challenges both the ongoing syllogizing and babbling in the activity of speaking and thinking.

The analysand suffers, but this suffering nevertheless comprises a certain satisfaction. Freud was clear enough in this regard: there is organized resistance against psychoanalysis, whose ultimate expression is flight into illness and pursuit of *Lustgewinn* (pleasurable profit, surplus-enjoyment) from the illness itself. Lacan translated this paradox with the comment that the subject of the unconscious is defined by happiness. In order for analysis to remain effective, it must produce the obstacles that the analysand's thinking keeps running into. In the analysand's speech, it must detect pieces of a problematic stupidity, which are returned to the analysand through equivocity. Here it becomes clear in which respect Freud did not accomplish the break with Aristotelianism he initiated by recognizing the link between language (equivocity) and the unconscious.

In order for psychoanalysis to part ways with at least a certain problematic form of philosophy, another effort was needed. Lacan's teaching strived to accomplish this step. But this does not mean in any way that this 'divorce' of psychoanalysis from philosophy failed to create the conditions for a wide-reaching metamorphosis of philosophy, on the contrary.

NOTES

1. Jacques Lacan, *Seminar, Book XX, Encore*, trans. Bruce Fink, New York: Norton, 1999. All references to this edition are included in the text (page numbers in brackets).

2. In 1974, the term 'antiphilosophy' eventually appears in a context where Lacan describes the university discourse as a 'persistent collection of imbecilities' (Jacques Lacan, 'Peut-être à Vincennes . . .', in: *Autres écrits*, ed. Jacques-Alain Miller, Paris: Seuil, 2001, p. 315). Whatever it may be in substance, antiphilosophy certainly engages in a thorough critique of stupidity that presumably characterizes the knowledge promoted by the modern university (the 'market of knowledge', as Lacan occasionally called it).

3. *Plus-value* was the old translation of *Mehrwert* into French. Nowadays, the term *survalue* is more common.

4. See, for instance, Karl Marx, *Capital,* Vol. 1, London: Penguin Books, 1990, p. 735.

5. Perhaps as a brief reminder: the homology between surplus-enjoyment and surplus-value does not imply that enjoyment must be 'accumulated' somewhere in the mental apparatus. What they have in common, logically and structurally, is the mutual conditioning of lack and surplus that pushes the subject into the vicious circle of *dissatisfaction* (which is ultimately a form of satisfaction, one that cannot come to an end and becomes its own purpose). Marx and Freud both associated this mode of endless satisfaction – satisfaction qua dissatisfaction – with a force they named *Trieb*, drive.

6. Freud associated this tendency with the death drive, the destructive libidinal force, whose ultimate horizon is the dissolution of libidinal and social bonds, whereas Eros is said to sustain their reproduction. Freud's schema nevertheless contains an interesting twist, according to which the death drive strives for renewing or re-establishing an ideal state of equilibrium (absence of excitation, ultimately death), whereas Eros preserves the organized disequilibrium that is the state of life.

7. See the lower level of the masculine formulas of sexuation (78). The implicit suggestion would then be that masculine sexuality, with its proverbial phallocentrism, is overtly marked by stupidity. This, of course, does not imply that women and other subjective positions in the field of sexuality are immunized against stupidity. A closer look at the formulas shows that, while the 'masculine' position is onanistic, the 'feminine' position is antagonistic (this is indicated by the split of the 'feminine' subject between the phallic function and the signifier that marks the Other's inconsistency and incompleteness). I am putting the terms 'masculine' and 'feminine' in quotation marks because they ultimately do not designate bodily phenomenology ('sex').

8. Example: populism, where stupidity is shared through aggressivity and resentment directed against the sexual, racialized or economic other. Another example: economic liberalism, where competitiveness is equally accompanied by aggressivity and resentment. One could argue that capitalism grounds its social bond – which is more like a social un-bond – on the coupling of stupidity and resentment. The consequence of this combination can only be the proliferation of structural and physical violence.

9. It is no coincidence that the axiom 'there is no sexual relation' plays a prominent role in *Seminar XX*. We could put this axiom right next to 'the signifier is stupid'.

10. With the centrality of surplus-value in the economic sphere, capitalism logically strives for social non-relation and environmental disorder. Climate breakdown may just be the ultimate surplus-product of capitalism, a striking demonstration of its fundamental uselessness, systemic stupidity and antisociality.

11. To put it in Lacan's technical terms, the stupid signifier (S_1, the master-signifier) guarantees only one 'signified', and that is surplus-enjoyment (*a*). As sign and bond, love is always-already a discourse of love, in which an overcoming of narcissism takes place. A striking difference between Freud and Lacan is at stake here. According to Freud, the ultimate horizon of love is always narcissism; Lacan inverts the perspective by arguing that love is always reciprocal, and in this reciprocity, it can stand for a form of work, which counteracts the resistance of narcissism and destabilizes its libidinal fixation on self-satisfactory enjoyment. Psychoanalysis as a form of amorous labour – transference – is a possible cure against the stupidity of enjoyment.

12. Jacques Lacan, *Television*, ed. Joan Copjec, New York: Norton, 1990, p. 129.

13. For a well-pointed account of the term, see Joan Copjec, "The Sexual Compact", *Angelaki: Journal of the Theoretical Humanities*, 17:2, 2012, pp. 41–44.

14. As described by Josef Breuer's patient Bertha Pappenheim [Anna O.], whose 'case history' is discussed in Freud and Breuer's *Studies on Hysteria.*

15. See Roman Jakobson, *Langage enfantin et aphasie*, Paris: Minuit, 1969. The longest essay in this collection – originally written in German, *Kindersprache, Aphasie und allgemeine Lautgesätze* – was published in Uppsala in 1939.

16. Comments, for which one can add that they in many ways resonate with or even anticipate Deleuze and Guattari's critique of linguistics in *Mille plateaux* (1980). See Gilles Deleuze and Félix Guattari, "November 20, 1923: Postulates of Linguistics", in: *A Thousand Plateaus,* trans. and foreword by Brian Massumi, Minneapolis: University of Minnesota Press, 1987, pp. 75–110.

17. 'Words beneath words' was the title of Starobinski's essay on Saussure's anagrams. See Jean Starobinski, *Les mots sous les mots*, Paris: Gallimard, 1971.

18. It is not surprising that analytic philosophers of language and linguists like Noam Chomsky show such a strong aversion to so-called continental philosophy, and particularly to French structuralism and post-structuralism. The continental philosophy of language overtly stresses the aspect of language – the enjoyment of maternal *lalangue* – that resists integration into the normalizing tendencies of linguistic positivism.

19. The critique of this opposition lies at the core of Barbara Cassin's work. See, for instance, Barbara Cassin, "Parle, si tu es un homme", in: *La décision du sens*, eds. Barbara Cassin and Michel Narcy, Paris: Vrin, 1989, pp. 9–60.

20. "What has a body and does not exist? Answer – the big Other." Jacques Lacan, *Seminar, Book XVII, The Other Side of Psychoanalysis*, trans. Russell Grigg, New York: Norton, 2007, p. 66.

21. One familiar way of illustrating this activity would be the performative function of language, the capacity of language to actively produce reality rather than simply representing it, as is still the case in Saussure's arbitrary yet perfectly stable and motionless relation between the signifier and the signified.

22. Here, another feature of the signifier that must be thought together with its stupidity enters the picture, its imperative nature: 'Every dimension of being is produced in the wake of the master's discourse – the discourse of he who, proffering the signifier, expects therefrom one of its link effects that must not be neglected, which is related to the fact that the signifier commands. The signifier is, first and foremost, imperative' (32). Twentieth-century linguistics pinpointed this imperative nature of the signifier under the name of performativity. Only that Austin's theory of speech acts did not move beyond the conscious intentionality of the speaker, even if the very notion of performativity challenged the predominance of the communicative function of language.

23. Feeble-mindedness is a most problematic notion, used in psychiatry and eugenics throughout the late nineteenth and well into the twentieth century for labelling social and learning deficiencies in individuals. For a recent critical and historical account, see Gerald V. O'Brien, *Framing the moron. The Social Construction of*

Feeble-Mindedness in the American Eugenic Era, Manchester: Manchester University Press, 2013. The role feeble-mindedness played in the hereditarian theory of IQ is discussed in Steven Jay Gould, *The Mismeasure of Man*, New York: Norton, 1996, pp. 188–204.

24. See Sigmund Freud, *New Introductory Lessons on Psychoanalysis*, in: *The Standard Edition of the Complete Psychological Works of Sigmund Freud*, Vol. 22, London: Vintage, 2001, p. 161. The connection between thinking and dreaming leads back to the very foundations of psychoanalysis in Freud's *Interpretation of Dreams*. There, Freud famously outlines his understanding of dreams as substitute satisfactions of repressed unconscious desire and as products of an ongoing work of the mental apparatus. Freud's thesis is that dreams and waking are marked by the same intellectual activity. If this is the case, awakening is, strictly speaking, impossible and thinking as such comes down to resistance against awakening. Lacan ("Peut-etre à Vincennes. . .", op. cit., p. 315) picks up on this thread, when he speaks of 'antiphilosophy', an effort of exposing the 'indestructible root [of the university discourse], its eternal dream'. Whatever antiphilosophy may be, it most certainly strives to force a 'particular awakening' of thinking from the 'persistent collection of imbecilities' that characterize the university discourse, including a certain form of philosophy.

25. See again, Barbara Cassin and Michel Narcy, *La décision du sens, op. cit.*

26. Aristotle in fact commits a betrayal of Socrates here. Looking at Plato's dialogues we can hardly overlook that Socrates' main lesson seems to be that speech does not lead to anything other than the recognition and acceptance of one's own non-knowledge. Plato also leaves no doubt that Socrates enjoys talking. His aporetic method comprises a comic economization of enjoyment. Moreover, this is the function of *philia* in philosophy, love for knowledge, which is supposed to establish a link between the epistemic and the libidinal (of course, Freud and Lacan renamed this link transference). This is where Socrates indeed deviates from the figure of the sophist, without therefore automatically becoming an Aristotelian type of philosopher.

27. All references are from the following edition: *The Complete Works of Aristotle*, Vol. 2, ed. Jonathan Barnes, Princeton, NJ: Princeton University Press, 1995.

28. Cassin recalls that sophistry is both a historical fact and a structural effect produced through the solidification of philosophical discourse. And there is discrepancy between the two images of sophistry. See Barbara Cassin, "Who's Afraid of the Sophists?: Against Ethical Correctness", in *Sophistical Practice. Toward a Consistent Relativism,* New York: Fordham University Press, 2014, pp. 25–43. Plato is not yet part of this tradition, since his dialogue on the *Sophist* demonstrates the impossibility of differentiating or separating sophistry from philosophy. To some extent, sophistry remains a dialectical inner other of philosophy, and the ultimate exemplification of this immanent split of philosophical thought is none other than Socrates, the thinker, who had trouble sleeping (which, from the Lacanian perspective, is a significant detail).

29. More generally, what the discourse of irony repeatedly demonstrates is the inexistence of the Other. See Jacques-Alain Miller, "Clinique ironique", in: *La cause freudienne*, no. 23, Paris: Navarin, 1993, pp. 7–13. It should nevertheless be recalled that the position of psychoanalysis is not irony, since its entire clinical practice deals with the fact that the Other's inexistence nevertheless causes material, corporeal consequences.

30. Looking back at the debates that have surrounded the short-lived fashion of speculative realism, one can say: yes, there is an absolute correlation between language and being; it cannot be otherwise. But this does not imply that this correlation covers *all* reality. Lacan's concept of the real stands precisely for the aspect of reality that cannot be mapped onto the correlation of language and being.

31. Jacques Lacan, "Le rêve d'Aristote", in: *Colloque pour le 23e centenaire d'Aristote*, ed. M. A. Sinaceur, Paris: Unesco Sycomore, 1978, p. 23.

32. Ibid.

33. Jacques Lacan, "Conferences et entretiens dans des universités nord-americaines", in: *Scilicet*, Vol. 6–7, Paris: Seuil, 1976, p. 35.

Chapter 5

Lacan, Pigeons and Hedgehogs in Barbery and Achache's *The (Elegance of the) Hedgehog*

Antonio Viselli

For Claudio

Pigeons and hedgehogs are more commonly found overlooking, or even squashed on, French streets rather than in the pages of psychoanalytic literature. Nonetheless, these two less-than-brilliant animals do hold a certain gravitas in notorious passages in Freud and Lacan's writings, particularly with regard to Freud and Schopenhauer's 'hedgehog dilemma', as well as Lacan's analysis of the mirror stage. Furthermore, they are front and centre in a French novel and film which also explicitly reference psychoanalytic thought. This chapter will explore the convergence of these animal signs, the pigeon and the hedgehog, and the role they play in relation to the topic of stupidity in the following literary and filmic corpus: Muriel Barbery's breakthrough novel, *The Elegance of the Hedgehog* (2008) and its cinematic adaptation by Mona Achache, *The Hedgehog* (2009).

Psychoanalysis is cloaked in caricature in both of these works, with an explicit critique of Lacan in Barbery's novel. Nonetheless, Lacanian thought more specifically, and psychoanalysis more broadly, offers an intriguing pathway into the exploration of stupidity in these works. Therefore, in keeping with a specular dynamism, through close readings of the various manifestations of stupidity in these works, I will offer both a moderate Lacanian reading of Barbery and Achache's creations, balanced with the latters' representations of psychoanalysis in their works, in an attempt to demonstrate the harmony between apparently diverse conceptual views. Through this structure, psychoanalysis is offered the opportunity to speak back on the topic of stupidity, as it becomes the lens through which to examine examples of being *bête*,[1] the *lalangue* of stupidity and what we could conceive of as becoming *linguistruck*.

This chapter contributes primarily to the realm of literary studies, with attention to close readings of key passages in which stupidity is conceptualized first and foremost through its semantic relevance, before any discussions of its metalinguistic and psychoanalytic resonances transpire. Therefore, I will focus on the genres present in this corpus and how they relate to the psychoanalytic process; how intertextuality functions as a way to enmesh various discourses, including references to Lacan and Freud, among a library of other authors, as well as intermedial narratives relevant to Lacanian thought. This chapter reflects as much on notions of stupidity as on its antonym: the complex definitions and examples of intelligence.

Stupidity is often interpreted as a lack. Whether it be of sense or judgement, of smarts or intelligence, it is defined negatively, and in true structuralist form, as a binary. Theorists such as Avital Ronell and Jacques Derrida have examined stupidity as a concept that exceeds thought and knowledge, one that subverts spatial and contextual boundaries and measures; one that is unrelated to knowledge.[2] Malcolm Quinn positions Lacan's conception of stupidity as 'anything at all' in, on and through language: 'Lacan's comments on Bentham locate stupidity as a specialised position *of* language, and not as a concept that is defined by adopting a specialised position *on* language, of the kind that we take up when we say "I have just said something stupid".'[3] He adds: 'Linguistics inside language gives us *linguisterie* and *lalangue*, in which a metalanguage commentary is renamed as a product of language that refers to the unconscious, and not to a non-scientific, cultural or "ordinary" language object. As Lacan nearly said, the unconscious is structured like linguistricks.'[4] In both the novel and film, the limitations of language are evident, as Renée and Paloma reflect on meaning in language with reference to medieval texts through to foreign-language acquisition. Furthermore, the eponymous hedgehog in Barbery and Achache performs and embodies a linguistrick, as back bent, it stoops face down and retreats to safety, following the instinctive impulses of the id: it is quite simply stoop-id. Stupidity, in this corpus, is also manifest through its etymological signification: that which produces awe, amazement and that which stuns. As a result, stupidity at its very core is sublime, as it constantly negotiates a threshold, straddling a fine line between subject and object or between the subject and itself.

STUPIDITY IN *THE (ELEGANCE OF THE) HEDGEHOG*: A SUMMARY

Stupidity and intelligence are a recurring duality that rhythms the narratives in Barbery and Achache's respective novel and film. In both instances, novelist and director juxtapose the voice of the young Paloma Josse, whose existential crisis culminates in the choice to commit suicide on the day of her thirteenth birthday,[5] and the mundane quotidian of a highly cultivated caretaker, Renée Michel, who must play dumb in order to maintain the perfect image of the anonymous subaltern.

Paloma and her family live on the fifth floor of an apartment complex managed by Renée, a building that resembles a bourgeois panopticon. The Josse family nucleus is made up of the youngest member, Paloma; her older sister, Colombe, a university student researching medieval literary history; an anxious and depression-prone mother, Solange, who has been in analysis for ten years; a 'very serious Minister of the Republic' father, Paul; and two cats, Constitution and Parliament.[6] Paloma paints a syllogistic sketch of her family's social standing, while also accentuating the difference between intelligence ('genius') and education:

> I am twelve years old, I live [. . .] in an apartment for rich people. My parents are rich, my family is rich and my sister and I are, therefore, as good as rich. My father is a parliamentarian and before that he was a minister: no doubt he'll end up in the top spot, emptying out the wine cellar of the residence at the Hôtel de Lassay. As for my mother . . . Well, my mother isn't exactly a genius but she is educated. She has a PhD in literature. She writes her dinner invitations without mistakes and spends her time bombarding us with literary references ('Colombe, stop trying to act like Madame Guermantes', or 'Pumpkin, you are a regular Sanseverina').
>
> Despite all that, despite all this good fortune and all this wealth, I have known for a very long time that the final destination is the goldfish bowl.[7]

Education and intelligence are incompatible for Paloma, who interprets the causal effect of her mother's PhD as serving a socially performative end – with the quintessential French novelists Proust and Stendhal synecdochically referenced via their aristocratic characters: Madame Guermantes and the Duchess Sanseverina, a fictional world detached from reality in which the bourgeois stupidity of her mother radiates in Paloma's eyes. She further expands on these characteristics in later chapters:

> My mother, who has read all of Balzac and quotes Flaubert at every dinner, is living proof every day of how education is a raving fraud. All you need to do is watch her with the cats. She's vaguely aware of their decorative potential, and yet she insists on talking to them as if they were people, which she would never do with a lamp or an Etruscan statue. (112)

Disillusioned by education, politics and the Parisian bourgeoisie that her family metonymically represents, Paloma resigns herself to suicide as the sole method to escape the goldfish bowl and the laws of society – or Name-of-the-Father – that it represents. Paloma better fits the paronomastic play present in Lacan's '*non-dupes errent*', which *Žižek* describes as 'those who do not let themselves be caught in the symbolic deception/fiction and continue to believe their eyes are the ones who err most'.[8]

The metaphor of the goldfish bowl is significant in both the novel and film, as it epitomizes entrapment, in which the subject becomes an object under surveillance, participating in life as an imprisoned bystander. Aspirations and growth, in this context, only become synonymous with restriction in space and liberties, in which one quickly becomes subjected to the gaze through a distorted, convex glass. In the following passage, the adolescent's frame of mind blurs together the spherical planet on which she lives, the stars and the goldfish bowl:

> All our family acquaintances have followed the same path: their youth spent trying to make the most of their intelligence, squeezing their studies like a lemon to make sure they'd secure a spot among the elite, then the rest of their lives wondering with a flabbergasted look on their faces why all that hopefulness has led to such a vain existence. People aim for the stars, and they end up like goldfish in a bowl. I wonder if it wouldn't be simpler just to teach children right from the start that life is absurd.[9]

According to Paloma, wasting one's best years away studying is to become a simple bourgeois stereotype, and as stupid as a goldfish. Furthermore, the common definition of stupidity and its etymon overlap with the 'flabbergasted' and overly educated elite who are reduced to shocking stupidity. Determined to live her last days to the fullest and to guide the narrative that she leaves behind, she decides to make a film of her surroundings, from incognito recordings of family members and passers-by to individual interviews with her building dwellers. In so doing, Paloma ensures the gaze is not primarily turned towards her, and the fishbowl, in a sense, becomes an extension of the camera through which she controls the narrative, all the while recognizing or distancing herself through others. As Lacan explains, 'Sure, the picture is in my eye, but me, I am also in the picture' and it is 'this necessary redoubling of myself as standing outside and inside my picture, that bears witness to my "material existence"'.[10] In a striking scene, the susurration of Paloma's description of the goldfish bowl complements her actions: filming her sister in the kitchen, she places a glass of water in front of her at a distance, and the parallax view allows the spectator to witness Colombe as though she were trapped in the goldfish bowl, underwater. The camera and the fishbowl become two sides of the same lens of intersubjectivity, where transparency and reflection meet the death drive, as we will shortly demonstrate.

Two pivotal encounters eventually thwart Paloma's suicidal plans: these include bourgeoning friendships with both Renée Michel and the new neighbour, Kakuro Ozu, the latter becoming a catalyst for change in both Renée and Paloma's characters. Mr Ozu is a foreign element that interrupts Paloma and Renée's quotidian life alike, embodying at once the cultural other who also becomes the Other. He disrupts the storyline by moving into one of the apartments Renée manages, since the previous tenant recently passed away. The Japanese widower remodels the typically Parisian apartment in Japanese style, and despite bringing with him an air of positive transformation in the building, he is nonetheless metonymically shrouded in mortality. Similar to the Lacanian triad of the Real, Symbolic and Imaginary, each of these three characters allegorizes elements of the unconscious through their struggle with language, their drives and the complexities of their (inter)subjective transformations. Let us begin by unravelling a portion of this interweaving triplicity.

Although Mr Ozu is a common element in both Paloma[11] and Renée's lives, *The (Elegance of the) Hedgehog* is structured on the parallel narratives of Paloma and Renée. Renée is a book-devouring concierge who, according to Philippe Lançon, 'is a concierge pretending to be a concierge so that the rich folk in the building, all equally malicious, stupid and neurotic, don't realize that she speaks better and is worth so much more than them'.[12] Nowhere is this statement more evident than in the very incipit of the novel, which describes Renée's interaction with one of the youths in her building:

> 'Marx has completely changed the way I view the world', declared the Pallières boy this morning, although ordinarily he says nary a word to me.
>
> Antoine Pallières, prosperous heir to an old industrial dynasty, is the son of one of my eight employers. There he stood, the most recent eructation of the ruling corporate elite – a class that reproduces itself solely by means of virtuous and proper hiccups – beaming at his discovery, sharing it with me without thinking or ever dreaming for a moment that I might actually understand what he was referring to. How could the laboring classes understand Marx?
>
> [. . .]
>
> 'Whosoever sows desire harvests oppression', I nearly murmured, as if only my cat were listening to me.
>
> But Antoine Pallières, whose repulsive and embryonic whiskers have nothing the least bit feline about them, is staring at me, uncertain of my strange words. As always, I am saved by the inability of living creatures to believe anything that might cause the walls of their little mental assumptions to crumble.[13]

In a building that embodies social structure, Renée chooses to perform her class, and when it comes to playing dumb, she undertakes her role with aplomb in her 'semi-retarded concierge uniform'.[14] Renée performs stupidity so as not to disrupt the social order. The reader, nonetheless, receives a glimpse into her frame of mind through her intellectual, stream-of-consciousness musings and her sociopolitical critiques – the excerpt's ensuing paragraphs are a veritable critique of Marx – and yet these comments above also offer a window into her personal realm, for example, through the feline references. As her cats are the only ones to listen to her cogitations, she tends to perceive others according to a 'cat-lady' paradigm, comparing the pubescent boy to her companions, albeit degrading and dehumanizing him even more. This is one of Barbery's strategies of reversal in the complex anthropomorphizing and dehumanizing of subjects and objects.

Renée is unmasked, however, by Paloma and Kakuro, who see through her dupery. Paloma, who has discovered the secret of the hedgehog who curls inwardly to remain safe from danger, tells Renée: 'You have found a good hiding place.'[15] Renée's refuge is in her armchair, in a secret room surrounded by books. Nonetheless, Kakuro unarms Renée in a deliciously intertextual and metalinguistic first meeting. Jacinthe Rosen introduces Kakuro, the new tenant, to Renée, and the following scene, which merits a lengthy quotation, takes place on the threshold of Renée's door:

> 'Bonjour Madame', were his first and only words, in unaccented French.
>
> I am wearing my semi-retarded concierge uniform. We are dealing with a new resident here, and force of habit has not yet compelled him to assume that I am inept, so I must make a special pedagogical effort. I limit myself therefore to a refrain of asthenic yeses in response to Jacinthe Rosen's hysterical salvoes.

They had nearly surpassed the deluge of information Jacinthe spat at them, when Jacinthe adds:

> 'The doormat that was outside the Arthens's door hasn't been cleaned. Can you bring it to the cleaner's?' asks the hen.
>
> Why must the comedy always turn to tragedy? To be sure, I also misuse language on occasion, although I tend to use such abuses as weapons.
>
> [. . .]
>
> And yet, there is an element of tragedy: I flinched when she said *bring* and at that very moment Monsieur Something also flinched, and our eyes met. And since that infinitesimal nanosecond when – of this I am sure – we were joined in linguistic solidarity by the shared pain that made our bodies shudder, Monsieur Something has been observing me with a very different gaze.
>
> A watchful gaze.
>
> And now he is speaking to me.

> 'Were you acquainted with the Arthens? I have heard they were quite an extraordinary family', he says.
>
> 'No', I reply, on my guard, 'I didn't really know them, they were just another family, here'.
>
> 'Yes, a happy family', says Madame Rosen, who, visibly, is getting impatient.
>
> 'You know, all happy families are alike', I mutter, to have done with this business, 'there's nothing more to it'.
>
> 'Every unhappy family is unhappy in its own way', he says, giving me an odd look and all of a sudden, even if it's not for the first time, I shudder.
>
> Yes, I assure you. I shudder – but quite involuntarily. It just happened, there was nothing I could do, I was overwhelmed.
>
> As misfortunes never travel alone, Leo decides it is time to slip between our legs, rubbing against Monsieur Something on his way.
>
> 'I have two cats', he says. 'May I ask your cat's name?'
>
> 'Leo', replies Jacinthe Rosen in my stead.[16]

The first 'shudder' in this passage is originally from the verb 'sursauter' in French, which implies a leap or jump.[17] Renée and Mr Ozu literally both leap at a grammatical error, arguably the first leap of faith that will unite them in these stories. The second and third examples of 'shudder' are originally 'tressaille' in French, which means to quiver, twitch or vibrate.[18] Furthermore, the combinatory acoustic images of the two syllables, 'tresse' (which signifies tress or knot) and the sound 'aïe' (the French cry for pain), coupled with the locus of the conversation in the doorway, and therefore at the threshold (*sublimis*) of the concierge's chambers, create the sense of a sublime re-evaluation of self and other, of class structure, and the tress reinforces the knotted structure that binds Renée, Kakuro and Paloma.

From a shared grammar-flinching experience, the unexpected complicity between the concierge and the new guest intertextually breaks into the literary realm. The reference in this passage to 'unhappy families' is a direct quotation from *Anna Karenina*, whose author is also present here in feline form: Leo (Tolstoy). Such an allusion further underlines the fact that a looming deathly aura accompanies Kakuro, as the protagonist in Tolstoy's novel commits the act that Paloma is incapable of doing. Anna Karenina throws herself in front of a train, an act that intertextually foreshadows Renée's demise.

This meeting between Renée and Kakuro marks the beginning of a platonic friendship, but it also foreshadows Renée's untimely death, as she is struck by a cleaner's van in her attempt to save her homeless drunkard friend from being hit. Before this tragic ending, Mr Ozu courted Renée, inviting her out and over for dinner, thus disturbing the quiet and concealed lifestyle she had come to embrace. He had noticed her lack of stupidity, and Renée's hiding place was therefore burnt. As a result, Kakuro genuinely *saw* her, unlike the inhabitants of her building, who do not recognize her one evening as she exits the building arm-in-arm with Kakuro, dressed and coiffed for a night out: 'They didn't recognize me', she states, 'flabbergasted', to which Kakuro responds, 'It is because they have never seen you [. . .] I would recognize you anywhere'.[19] Renée had accepted Manuela, the Portuguese maid's assistance as she prepared for her night out, going to a hair salon for the first time in her life and borrowing a dress from the dry-cleaners which hadn't been retrieved because the previous owner had died.

The bourgeoning love between Renée and Kakuro would not last, and, despite her name – Renée means 'reborn' in French – neither would Renée's transformation. In one of the final scenes of the movie, Renée is struck dead by the 'Malavoin Cleaners' van, a 'punishment', as she describes it, for having borrowed and stained the dress.[20] This real stain can also stand in place of Lacan's stain, *la tâche*, which is the gaze qua object that resists any reductive interpretation. The stain is on the dress, which itself embodies transgression and death; as such, the stain becomes the dress. Renée's transformation enacts the expression of *faire tâche*, which means to stand out and be seen. Kakuro and Paloma are the only characters who truly see Renée's elegance prior to her makeover. Therefore, the split gaze of the *tâche*, in which the object's gaze is imprinted in the object, has a profound impact on Paloma, who, upon hearing the news of Renée's death, stares her own impending fatality in the face and recognizes her will to live.

Although Renée's death serves a narrative purpose in the film and novel – it functions in the Imaginary order, in specular relation to Paloma's fear of sociability, as she would much rather finish flattened like a hedgehog than in the goldfish bowl – it also serves as a socio-political critique. As soon as she dares to transcend the socially acceptable, stupid space of a concierge cliché, she is punished through a *Deus-ex*-cleaner-*machina*. Some things are simply forbidden, *interdit*, and this is precisely the adjective used in Lançon's critique of the film *Le Hérisson* when describing Renée.

> When 'old ma Michel'[21] enters Mr. Ozu's apartment, she is dumbfounded [*interdite*]. It is perhaps the best scene in the book. It reminds one of an old haiku by Ryôta: 'From them, no words come: the guest, the host, the white chrysanthemum.' But this delicacy does not last, and the heavy discourse begins once again: finesse and recognition come from the other, the stranger, that is the nice and perpetual message.[22]

This beautiful passage unites a Derridean notion of hospitality – in which the ambiguity of the French *hôte* (host) can denote at once the guest and host, thus confusing subjectivities – with the charged polysemy of '*interdite*' (dumbfounded). Whereas in English, dumbfounded combines 'confounded' and 'dumb', the inability to speak – and therefore the struggle with language in its most elementary form of utterance – in French, *interdite* can signify both a sense of shock and interdiction. Renée's stupidity is forbidden, and yet, once she transcends its boundaries, she ceases to exist. Her becoming – and being reborn (Renée) – is paradoxically redacted as it occurs, and her meaning, whether narratological, linguistic or otherwise, is fleeting. This is in part due to the very genres Barbery and Achache develop.

INTERSUBJECTIVE META-NARRATIVES

Psychoanalysis is not only relevant thematically as a topic of discussion and critique in Achache and Barbery's works; the genres and meta-narratives in both the film and novel also reflect a psychoanalytic process and engage in the intertwining of literary and psychoanalytic concepts.

The Elegance of the Hedgehog alternates first-person accounts of Renée and Paloma, beginning with the concierge, whereas *The Hedgehog* begins with Paloma, sequencing scenes in a mostly alternating fashion. In both instances, the audience is doubled: we, the readers and viewers, are the first, silent audience in whom Paloma and Renée confide. In written form, this passes primarily through a double diary which Paloma keeps, and in the film, we are on the receiving end of an intimate docu-diary. These narratives represent the monological talk therapy through which we can glean symptoms of the characters' struggles, thought processes and even their unconscious. Oftentimes, conversations between characters occur in dialogic – even interview – format. When it comes to Paloma, however, the monological narrative forces the reader to take on the role of the analyst, in a work that nonetheless heavily critiques the psychoanalytic process.

From a literary perspective, the dual protagonists and the introduction of the diary form within the novel create an intermedial effect, through which the genre of the novel reinvents itself. By suggesting another art form distinct from the one at hand, a hybridized aesthetics manifests itself, and this intermedial dynamism echoes the intersubjective ambiguities in the stories as well. *The Elegance of the Hedgehog* exceeds itself as a novel by pointing to its very inception and to the metalinguistic tools employed to create it – language – all the while destroying the traditional understanding of the genre. From the perspective of a mise-en-abîme, we are dealing with a text – or multiple texts – within a text; and in the film, a movie or documentary – and interviews – within a movie. The narrative frames are blurred and exceed themselves, and as such, so too is the discursiveness of the subject. I will argue that an invisible frame beyond the narrative and cinematographic frames, similar to Slavoj Žižek's bluff,[23] is an intermedial fugal framework which interweaves characters and their representations all the while maintaining the gap between them.

Mr Ozu is the crucial third element that links Paloma and Renée's narratives. The triangle, knot or chain that connects these three characters merits further exploration from both an intermedial and psychoanalytic perspective. The three interweaving voices, I will argue, recall the musical style of fugue, defined by Nadya Zimmerman as follows:

> Like the canon, fugue incorporates the method of imitation. In a fugue, the first voice enters playing the main theme, which [. . .] is called the subject. The second voice enters, perhaps a few measures afterwards, and takes that same subject, but modifies it by starting on a different note. The modification in the second voice [. . .] is called the answer. [. . .] the answer retains the same intervallic shape and melodic structure as the subject, yet it is said to be in a different key. When the second voice enters with the answer, the notes occurring simultaneously in the first voice are no longer considered part of the subject: they are referred to as the countersubject.[24]

This musical style is dialogic in nature, dependent upon the subject-answer dichotomy, which is a form of polyphony defined as counterpoint. A fugal meta-narrative highlights this very process, all the while blurring the boundaries of the diverse, contrapuntal subjectivities at play. Not only is fugue dialogic, but it is a form of imitation, which is relevant to both storylines in our corpus: Paloma avoids the theatricalities of everyday life, vowing to die before becoming a bourgeois cliché; Renée knows how a stereotypical concierge should act, and she does so until her ruse is revealed. As we will discuss, Renée and Paloma can both take on the eponymous metaphor of the hedgehog for different reasons and in different contexts. In addition to this statement, the fact that both characters share the role of alternating protagonist implies the terminology employed in fugal form is of further importance. Who is the subject and who is the countersubject? Which voice answers? The answer to these questions depends on the point of view, as a fugal poetics allows for a performance of distorted and muddled intersubjectivities, which oscillate between Renée, Paloma, Sakuro and even the reader.

In *An Introduction to the Structural Analysis of Narrative*, Roland Barthes describes an element that he deems quintessential to the novel, which enmeshes the linearity of narrative and a verticality of hidden temporality able to suggest simultaneity:

> *Le lecteur, lui, perçoit une suite linéaire de termes. Mais ce qu'il faut noter, c'est que les termes de plusieurs séquences peuvent très bien s'imbriquer les*

> *uns dans les autres: une séquence n'est pas finie, que, déjà, s'intercalant, le terme initial d'une nouvelle séquence peut surgir: les séquences se déplacent en contrepoint; fonctionnellement, la structure du récit est fuguée: c'est ainsi que le récit, fois, 'tient' et '"aspire'.*[25]
>
> [The reader, by contrast, perceives a linear succession of terms. But what calls for special attention is that some terms belonging to several sequences can easily dovetail into each other. Before a sequence is completed, the initial term of a fresh sequence can be introduced: sequences proceed according to a contrapuntal pattern. Functionally the structure of narrative is that of the fugue: narrative 'pulls in' new material even as it 'holds on' to previous material.][26]

The terms in the original French and the English translation to explain the structure and dynamism of the contrapuntal narrative are significant: '*s'imbriquer*' is translated as 'dovetail'. In the original French, the image Barthes offers of narrative fluidity and overlap is through bricks. In a novel and film in which the majority of the story takes place in a building – and which is about a bourgeois building and its hierarchies – such a motif is useful. In the English translation, the reference to dovetailing is also apropos, given Paloma's name signifies 'pigeon' in Spanish, and her sister's name, Colombe, is French for 'dove'. Although it is doubtful that Barbery paid such close attention to Barthes's conception of a fugal novelistic narrative, the fugacious element inherent to language – where signification in language is fleeting and unstable – is particularly attractive for this study. However, one can imagine an intertextual nod to Barthes and his death in our corpus: the philosopher and author of *The Death of the Author*, in a similar way to Renée, was killed by a cleaner van as he was walking home. Could Barbery be attempting to reclaim the legitimacy and authority of the author by grounding signification in the text through the subversion and critique of psychoanalytic principles? Although impossible to answer, if Barbery's voice were in harmony with Paloma's, such a claim would resonate true. Regardless of Barbery's stance, an oedipal attempt to (re-)kill the killer of authors allows signification to spiral into endless signification. As such, a writerly text and a fugal poetics have much in common, and we as readers could apply Barthes's literary criticism on fugue to interpret this corpus. This nonetheless falls beyond the scope of this chapter.

The three voices that thread together in fugal form, however, do suggest the overlapping nature of the elements that make up one's subjectivity. I will argue that the three characters, Paloma, Renée and Kakuro, on top of their fugal echoes, stand in as metaphorical placeholders for Lacan's Real, Symbolic and Imaginary. I have argued elsewhere that it would be fruitful to consider fugal form alongside Lacan's Borromean knot.[27] *The Hedgehog* and *The Elegance of the Hedgehog* offer a particularly propitious backdrop to consider such a parallel. In the following section on animals, it will become evident that Renée and Paloma alternatingly represent aspects of the Imaginary and the Symbolic in relation to images and language, whereas I will explore Sakuro's relation to the Real in the final section of this chapter. It is now necessary to return to the main topic of this chapter – stupidity – and to uncover the animalistic characteristics that relate to each character and the relevance of being *bête*.

BECOMING *BÊTE*

Animals are pervasive in Barbery and Achache's works, in which they occupy a discursive and metaphorical role. Primarily domestic animals, these include cats, dogs, hedgehogs, goldfish and pigeons. Even from a promotional and marketing perspective, these animals often grace the covers of various editions and translations of the novel as well as the film posters. For example, the Folio edition of *Le Hérisson* displays a cat – performing their quintessential nature according to Renée, who describes them as 'mobile decorative objects'[28] – seated on top of a stack of books; on the German advert for the film, the title of which is translated as *Die Eleganz der Madame Michel* – thus removing any reference to the hedgehog in privileging of the more concrete naming of Renée – appear several goldfish in the background as though the poster were within the fishbowl. Here, there is evidently a frame-beyond-the frame or better yet, a parallax view in which the spectator visualizes a shift occurring from the epistemological to the ontological: Paloma and Renée are seated on a couch, as the young girl films her adoptive mother figure Renée while the latter holds a cat, and a fishbowl with a goldfish sits between them. In this section, we will analyse the signifying chain of animal examples, the roles they play in relation to the fugacious characters and the topic of stupidity.

Through and alongside these animals, the reader and viewer gain a perspective on characters and their cogitations, as well as how they engage with the world. The analogies and comments regarding animals combine anthropomorphic and dehumanizing narratives. Furthermore, from a linguistic and deconstructionist perspective, the animal is (a) *bête* and a source of *bêtise*. In this section, I will unite elements in Jacques Derrida's writings that critique Lacan in an attempt to demonstrate how this dialogue also plays out in various ways in *The (Elegance of the) Hedgehog*. Derrida, in 'The Transcendental "Stupidity" ("*Bêtise*") of Man and the Becoming Animal According to Deleuze', explains that these terms ('*bête*' and '*bêtise*') are untranslatable: 'no English words – especially not "stupid" or "stupidity" and not even "dumb" or "dumbness" – [. . .] adequately translate "bête" or "bêtise." Even within the borders of the French idiom, there is no stable semantic context that could univocally guarantee a safe translation from one pragmatic use of "*bête*" or "*bêtise*" in a given context into another one'.[29] Indeed, '*bête*' can echo stupidity, naïvety, dumbness, shame, idiocy, distraction, a scatterbrain and context-dependent, its linguistic register can pertain to a range of meanings from the childishly playful to the condescending. French idiomatic expressions with dehumanizing characteristics abound in which animal parts take over the human body in metonymic fashion: telling someone to 'shut up' translates to shutting one's '*gueule*', which is the mouth of a carnivorous animal. The etymology of 'bête' links to the English 'beast' (via the Latin *bestia*), which does not have an evident connotation to stupidity other than their inability to use language in a similar way to humans. Beasts do, however, imply danger. Through the (mostly) domestic examples of animals, I will explore the intertwining signification of stupidity and danger in our corpus, especially when the metaphorical animal is considered individually as opposed to in a gregarious context. Lacan and Derrida would most likely agree on one thing: '*bête*' does not equal 'animal'. In the examples below, I wish to highlight the intersubjective elements at play in our corpus and the discursive, intertextual and psychoanalytic roles they represent.

Two critiques that Derrida makes of Lacan and animals are noteworthy here before we delve into the textual examples. The first is in fact an echo of Gilles Deleuze's rethinking of the Jung vs. Freud hierarchy in French thought. Deleuze writes of a categorization of animals:

> We must distinguish three kinds of animals. First, individuated animals, family pets, sentimental, Oedipal animals each with its own petty history, 'my' cat, 'my' dog. These animals invite us to regress, draw us into a narcissistic contemplation, and they are the only kind of animal psychoanalysis understands, the better to discover a daddy, a mommy, a little brother behind them (when psychoanalysis talks about animals, animals learn to laugh).[30]

He further explores the categories of 'animals with characteristics or attributes' such as State animals or those present in 'divine myths' from which we can extrapolate 'structures, archetypes or models'; and finally, the 'demonic animals, pack or affect animals' defined by their 'multiplicity'.[31] These categories are permeable, and the animals in question, although primarily domestic, do not all entertain Deleuze's critique of regression.

Second, in *The Animal That Therefore I Am*, Derrida explains:

> The animal will never be, as man is, 'prey to language'. Later, in 'The Direction of the Treatment', we read: 'It must be posited that, produced as it is by any animal at the mercy of language [*en proie au langage*], man's desire is

> the desire of the Other' (264). This figure of the prey symptomatically and recurrently characterizes the 'animal' obsession in Lacan at the very moment when he insists on dissociating the anthropological from the zoological: man is an animal but a speaking one, (120) and he is less a beast of prey than a beast that is prey to language. There is no desire, and thus no unconscious, except for the human; it in no way exists for the animal, unless that be as an effect of the human unconscious, as if the domestic or tamed animal translated within itself the unconscious of man by some contagious transference or mute interiorization.[32]

This example is important for our discussion of the mirror stage below. Humans may be prey to language; however, that does not discount the attempt to interrogate the very structure of language and semiosis – and therefore of the unconscious as well – and the parallels drawn in our corpus between characters and animals, domesticated as they may be. These are less examples of transference than they are of the gaze, of subject-object relations and of an aesthetic portrayal of intersubjectivity. For example, Paloma, whose name signifies 'pigeon', learns via her sister about the reproductive characteristics of the beehive. We are left with a perfect and quite literal example of the birds and the bees. Whereas her sister is infatuated with the idea of several bees copulating with the queen and dying – enmeshing copulation and castration; eros and thanatos – Paloma is struck not by the sex or death drives at stake, but rather by the notion of intelligence and its relation to language as structure: 'the fact that these insects have a coded language: all the claims that verbal intelligence is specifically human begin to seem rather relative'.[33] Here, a pseudo-mirror stage combines Paloma's coming of age with a reflection on subjectivity and codified language. Such an observation is not incompatible with Derrida's concept of 'animot', which blends animal and 'mot' ('word' in French) to create the acoustic image of animal in the plural ('animaux').[34] This parallel would merit further exploration than the scope of this study permits.

To continue with one final Derridean example, which is applicable to our corpus, the philosopher explores a coupling – an ontological, 'onto-zoo-anthropo-theologico-political copulation' between the two eponymous figures in his *The Beast and the Sovereign*.[35] With reference to the archetype of the wolf-tyrant, he claims 'la bête e(s)t le souverain' [the beast is/and the sovereign].[36] As Daniel P. Daly explains, '[b]y bringing the two figures of the beast and the sovereign into dialogue, it threatens to eradicate their hierarchical distance or to reverse it, to oppose them antagonistically with one another or to equate them. It is a typical aspect of Derrida's deconstructive logic to unleash all of these possibilities, to allow them to affiliate, in a troubling uncertainty, an undeniable familiarity within a landscape of difference, to revel in the interstitial space of the Freudian *unheimlich*'.[37] What I propose is to apply a similar blurring in the following statement: *La bête e(s)t Renée.* The polysemic resonances in this French phrase are numerous: (1) 'The beast [in the story] is Renée.' This is fitting for a character who describes herself in grotesque terms, such as a 'mammoth' (30). (2) 'The beast and Renée.' Such a statement blurs the boundaries of subjects: either Paloma or Kakuro could be the beasts who disrupt Renée's sovereignty, her hiding place. (3) 'The beast is reborn.' The name Renée is also the feminine past participle of the verb 'to be born'. In this statement, we can examine the relationship between cyclicality and specularity. Let us now explore these facets in context through references to poodles, cats, hedgehogs, goldfish and pigeons.

Cats and Dogs

Cats and dogs are on the opposite spectrum of human-animal interaction, with one representing fidelity and friendship, the other fickleness and independence. These seemingly incompatible traits both qualify Renée, who discusses intelligence and stupidity vis-à-vis both animals, but during two distinct periods in her life, two pillars or 'totems', as she names them. When describing her life when her husband was still alive and the concierge-duo dynamic, she portrays what the public expects as a stereotype for the concierge:

> In the collective imagination, the couple formed by married concierges – a close-knit pair consisting of two entities so insignificant that only their union can make them apparent – will in all likelihood be the owners of a poodle. As we all know, poodles are a type of curly-haired dog preferred by petit bourgeois retirees, ladies very much on their own who transfer their affection upon their pet, or residential concierges ensconced in their gloomy loges. Poodles come in black or apricot. The apricot ones tend to be crabbier than the black ones, who on the other hand do not smell as nice. Though all poodles bark snappily at the slightest provocation, they are particularly inclined to do so when nothing at all is happening. [. . .] Poodles are ugly and stupid, submissive and boastful. They are poodles, after all.
>
> Thus the concierge couple, as served by the metaphor of their totemic poodle, seems to be utterly devoid of such passions as love and desire and, like their totem, destined to remain ugly, stupid, submissive and boastful.[38]

The totemic poodle is shrouded in sarcastic cliché. To push the tone further, as one might imagine with a passage beginning with 'In the collective imagination', there is nothing real about the description above: Renée and her late husband never had a dog, but it goes without saying that they should blend into the monochromatic background of the collective imagination. However, although they do not own poodles, they *are* the poodles who feign stupidity and who remain faithful to the building dwellers.[39]

In truth, Renée is certainly more of a cat lady, and judging by the 184 results for the word 'cat' alone in the novel, Barbery seems to have a preference for felines as well. Renée is, according to the beggar, the archetypal 'Ma Michel' who lost her cat. The cat, as Barbery writes, is also a modern totem. Contrary to the stupid dog, however, members of the feline family are intelligent, yet also potentially decorative, as Paloma recounts:

> If you want to understand my family, all you have to do is look at the cats. Our two cats are fat windbags who eat designer kibble and have no interesting interaction with human beings. They drag themselves from one sofa to the next and leave their fur everywhere, and no one seems to have grasped that they have no affection for any of us. The only purpose of cats is that they constitute mobile decorative objects, a concept which I find intellectually interesting, but unfortunately our cats have such drooping bellies that this does not apply to them.[40]

These cats are totemic and, as such, represent a family dynamic and bloodline from a Freudian perspective. These praised and objectivized animals, whose wealth and pleasure are sublimated into immobility, transform them into a combination of literal and figurative meaning: they are quintessentially fat cats in a house of fat cats. Their emblematic totemism is what Paloma rejects, as she compares herself to her mother's interactions with their cats. To reiterate the previous quotation on Solange's interaction with the cat – and her firm belief in the cat's consciousness and soul as opposed to that of an Etruscan statue or a lamp – Paloma inverts the natural familial dynamic, in which she views her mother as the child: 'It would seem that children believe for a fairly long time that anything that moves has a soul and is endowed with intention. My mother is no longer a child, but she apparently has not managed to conceive that Constitution and Parliament possess no more understanding than the vacuum cleaner.'[41] Paloma witnesses an inverted image: she views the (m)other in lieu of herself and critiques Solange's actions and language all the while employing the same literary register she criticizes in her mother. The cat's supposed intelligence juxtaposed with Solange's education-as-stupid further enhances a blurred intersubjectivity. Paloma, due to her blind spot, is struggling with her own gaze and the redoubling inscription of herself within her mother, the cat as totem, as well as the goldfish stuck in the bowl.

From the example of Paloma's rich family, we move contrapuntally to Kakuro's household and his cats. As he too 'really is very rich (so they say)', the parallel between Paloma's personal world and Mr Ozu's is harmonious, as in the overlapping voices of the fugue.[42] The distinction between the two – and here, literary counterpoint underlines a point of difference as opposed to musical harmony – is that Kakuro's cats *are* decorative, which sparks a conversation on intelligence. In the example of Paloma's household, a conversation on intelligence and instruction (as a 'fraud') was juxtaposed with the treatment of the domestic feline pet. Paloma recounts her experience in Kakuro's flat as follows:

> I went to have tea at his place and meet his cats. On that point I'm really not any more convinced by his cats than by mine but at least Kakuro's cats are truly decorative. I explained my point of view on the matter, and he replied that he believed in the radiance and sensitivity of an oak tree, and all the more so where cats are concerned. We went on to discuss the definition of intelligence and he asked me if he could write down my formula in his moleskine notebook: 'It is not a sacred gift, it is a primate's only weapon.'[43]

Paloma views the world scientifically, primarily through an evolutionary lens, whereas Kakuro's comments leave room for the spiritual as well. From decorative cats to intelligent primates, Paloma is on the attack with her definition of intelligence as a 'weapon'. The term 'primate' suggests a primitive – and therefore preliterate – subject, a word that does not occur often in the novel. However, in the original French, the term 'monkey' is present, in a passage where Paloma distances herself from her mother and her peers:

> Where I'm concerned, just seeing my mother shooting up with her anti-depressants and sleeping tablets has been enough to inoculate me for life against that sort of substance abuse. Lastly, teenagers think they're adults when in fact they're imitating adults who never really made it into adulthood and who are running away from life. It's pathetic.[44]

What is lost in translation in this excerpt is the verb 'imitating', which in the original French is '*singeant*' (from the verb *singer*: to ape/act like a monkey). This passage further underlines the role reversal with the (m)other, and Paloma's sense of superiority among her pack: a performative oscillation between the Symbolic and the Imaginary.

Finally, cats have an intertextual role to play in *The (Elegance of the) Hedgehog*. As mentioned before, the catalyst to Mr Ozu and Renée's relationship is the recognition of a literary reference by Leo Tolstoy. The totemic feline sets off an unspoken complicity between these two characters, and the totem allows for a transcendence of any taboo: in this case, not an incestuous one, but the transgression of societal rules that Renée follows and which forbid a budding relationship between a concierge and a wealthy dweller in the building she manages. The cat, in these examples, therefore allows for a reflection on the gaze, on the (m)other-daughter dynamic, as well as the limits of language and the ways to supplement or bifurcate its (lack of) signification.

The Hedgehog

The eponymous animal is front and centre in the novel and film; however, the term 'hedgehog' appears only twice in the novel and in the same passage, with the exception of the title. In this passage, Paloma describes Renée as follows:

> She radiates intelligence. And yet she really makes an effort, like, you can tell she is doing everything she possibly can to act like a concierge and come across as stupid. But I've been watching her, when she would talk with Jean Arthens or when she talks to Neptune when Diane has her back turned, or when she looks at the ladies in the building who walk right by her without saying hello. Madame Michel has the elegance of the hedgehog: on the outside, she's covered in quills, a real fortress, but my gut feeling is that on the inside, she has the same simple refinement as the hedgehog: a deceptively indolent little creature, fiercely solitary – and terribly elegant.[45]

This passage attempts to reconcile an oxymoron: the combination of intelligence and stupidity or of fierceness and elegance. Renée's mask gives her the strength to perform her duties with diligence, and yet, she has her secret hiding place: her literary and imaginary universe of philosophy, literary theory and film.

A hiding place is paramount for the hedgehog's safety, but what of its sociability? Arthur Schopenhauer in *Parerga and Paralipomena* is the first to establish the hedgehog or porcupine's dilemma[46] which Barbery must have used as the foundation for her novel:

> One cold winter's day, a number of porcupines huddled together quite closely in order through their mutual warmth to prevent themselves from being frozen. But they soon felt the effect of their quills on one another, which made them again move apart. Now when the need for warmth once more brought them together, the drawback of the quills was repeated so that they were tossed between two evils, until they had discovered the proper distance from which they could best tolerate one another. Thus the need for society which springs from the emptiness and monotony of men's lives, drives them together; but their many unpleasant and repulsive qualities and insufferable drawbacks once more drive them apart.[47]

The question of how much intimacy is too much certainly corresponds to Renée's preoccupations, as she would rather recoil in the safety of her books than seek the intimacy of another person.

Sigmund Freud famously quipped that he was off to America 'to catch sight of a wild porcupine and to give some lectures'.[48] That he did, albeit a corpse, and returned to Vienna with a bronze statue of a porcupine. 'The expression "to find one's porcupine" became a recognized saying in our circle', explains Jones, thus becoming a shibboleth, according to Allouch, a recognition of the happy few in Freud's inner circle.[49] Lacan famously called his students and followers 'hedgehogs', as Jean Allouch explores in *Trans-maître; Jacques Lacan et son élève hérisson*.[50] Despite their acerbic critiques – which I will explore in the following section – could Barbery and Achache be considered hedgehogs, followers in a Lacanian lineage, or do they rather pledge allegiance to Jean Giraudoux's hedgehog,[51] an author Lacan also references in his discussion on hedgehogs? Giraudoux's play, *Electra*, certainly has the most resounding intertextual connection with Barbery and Achache, as a mendicant interrupts a serious discussion regarding the gods' intervention in our mundane lives, by tangentially derailing the narrative. After discussing the many reasons hedgehogs cross the road – from sustenance to reproduction – he pauses on the anomaly:

> Then suddenly you see one, a young little one, who isn't stretched out quite like the others, a lot less dirty, its little foot extended, its chops firmly closed, much more dignified, and in seeing that one there, we have the impression he didn't die like a hedgehog, but rather he was hit in the place of another, in your place.[52]

The mendicant has set up the ending in *The (Elegance of the) Hedgehog*, where Renée saves the beggar from being killed by the van and takes his place. This allusion draws a nearly perfect parallel between the two stories, while further emphasizing the Electra complex and tension between Paloma and her mother in our corpus. From Schopenhauer and Freud to Lacan and Giraudoux, 'the prick of intellectual influence' for Barbery and Achache could certainly have come from many a hedgehog.[53]

The Goldfish and the Pigeon

From being prey to language, we now shift to the cat's prey: the (gold)fish. I have already explained the metaphor of the goldfish bowl, which is central to Paloma's struggle. It crystallizes her desire to fully break from her mother (mirror stage) and the laws of the father (bourgeoisie). This pet also plays an important narrative and symbolic role in our corpus, as Paloma sedates her sister's goldfish using her mother's medication which she has been stockpiling in hope of overdosing on it. Once the fish floats lifelessly to the surface, Paloma flushes it down the toilet, only for it to appear later in Renée's bathroom. It is difficult not to smirk at the connection between Renée's name and the supposed death/rebirth of the fish, which, in Christian iconography, represents Christ through the enigmatic acronym of *ichthys*, which in Ancient Greek signifies 'fish'. Each letter stands for 'Jesus Christ, Son of God,

Saviour',[54] therefore acting as a symbol of recognition and belonging among a community, an iconic shibboleth per se, especially during times of persecution. In the following section, I cite Paloma's critique of psychoanalysis, which she compares to Christianity, stating: 'only psychoanalysis can compete with Christians in their love of drawn-out suffering'.[55] For Paloma, who wishes to avoid all suffering by ending her life, neither Christianity – and its discourse on abnegation – nor psychoanalysis – and its attempt to heal the self – are attractive solutions for the adolescent who does not cease to point the camera at others. She naïvely believes that she alone controls her narrative and the gaze, to return to Žižek's explanation of the *non dupes errent*.

The person Paloma most films without her knowing is her sister, Colombe. As explained earlier, the sisters' two animal alter egos are the dove and pigeon, which, when combined with Paloma's obsessive filming-gaze and the mirror stage, recall an interesting parallel in Lacan's seminars. Citing the examples from 'Harrisson' (the English translation writes L. Harrison Matthews), Lacan explains that previous

> experiments demonstrated that ovulation is triggered by a female pigeon's sight of the specific form of a member of its own species, to the exclusion of any other sensory form of perception, and without that member having to be male.
>
> Placed in the same room with individuals of both sexes, but in cages that are fabricated in such a way that the pigeons cannot see each other, although they can easily perceive each other's calls and smells, the females do not ovulate. Conversely, if we allow two pigeons to view each other – even if it is through a glass barrier that suffices to thwart the onset of the mating game, and even when both pigeons are female – ovulation is triggered within a period of time that varies from twelve days (when the separated pigeons include a male and a female) to two months (when the separated pigeons are both female). But what is more remarkable still is that the mere sight by the animal of its own image in a mirror suffices to trigger ovulation within two and a half months.[56]

With this passage in mind, the excerpt regarding the copulation of bees becomes even more glaring. Paloma is an adolescent, and her perception of herself – and the need for a doubling Colombe/Paloma – is incongruous with her belief system. Nevertheless, her obsessive filming of her sister is fundamental to Paloma's coming of age.

The truly transformative moment for the young protagonist occurs only in the final scenes of the story: Paloma may not yet be the ovulating pigeon in Lacan and Harrison's examples, but she has certainly displaced her mother figure (Electra complex), a surrogate for whom she finds in Renée Michel. Renée's passing therefore becomes a specular moment for Paloma, who experiences death first-hand for the very first time. She sees herself in the substitute (m)other who has now been taken from her, and this sparks a renewed interest in living life to the fullest. The pigeon and hedgehog may not be likely friends in the real world; however, in Barbery and Achache's creations, in which the semiotic, intertextual and psychoanalytic value of these animals is extremely rich, these connections are possible.

To conclude this section in Lacanian fashion, perhaps the hedgehog and the pigeon were already intertwined even in Lacan's thoughts. I mentioned above that in *Écrits*, in the original French, the pigeon theorist is referred to as 'Harrisson', whereas in the English translation, 'Matthews' is added to the patronymic. With a proper French accent, 'Harrisson' is not far at all from the French for hedgehog: *hérisson*.

Becoming Linguistruck and *Lalangue*

Paula Murphy describes the division of the Lacanian subject as constituting two halves: 'the subject of the signifier and the subject of *jouissance* or enjoyment. It is language that binds these two halves together in the form of linguistricks'.[57] Two examples of explicit Lacanian psychoanalysis in Barbery's novel demonstrate the struggle between these halves in Paloma, and more specifically her confrontation with the mother (tongue) and *lalangue*. Although Paloma distances herself from her mother, remnants of the mirror stage still infiltrate her commentary, seemingly unbeknownst to her, as we have already seen. In this section, I will scrutinize these two examples before expanding on the importance of *lalangue* and the linguistrick through the figure of Kakuro Ozu.

The first reference is to Solange's analysis from Paloma's critical perspective, and the second is an excerpt from a session between an analyst and Paloma at her mother's request. The following selection is particularly rich in references to Lacan:

> Maman announced at the dinner table last night, as if it were a pretext to let the champagne flow freely, that it was exactly ten years ago that she started her 'anaaalysis'. Everyone will agree that this is absolutely maaarvelous. As far as I can see, only psychoanalysis can compete with Christians in their love of drawn-out suffering. What my mother didn't say is that it's also been exactly ten years since she started taking anti-depressants. But apparently she doesn't see the connection. Personally I don't think she's taking the anti-depressants to ease her anxiety but rather to endure the analysis. When she describes her sessions, it's enough to make you want to bang your head against the wall. The guy says 'hmmm' at regular intervals, and repeats the end of her sentences ('And I went to Lenôtre's with my mother': 'Hmmm, your mother?' 'I do so

like chocolate.': 'Hmmm, chocolate?'). If this is how it is, I can set up shop as a psychoanalyst tomorrow. He gives her copies of lectures from the 'Freudian Cause' which, contrary to what you might think, aren't just some sort of rebus but are actually supposed to mean something. Fascination with intelligence is in itself fascinating, but I don't think it's a value in itself. There are tons of intelligent people out there and there are a lot of retards, too. I'm going to say something really banal, but intelligence, in itself, is neither valuable nor interesting. Very intelligent people have devoted their lives to the question of the sex of angels, for example. But many intelligent people have a sort of bug: they think intelligence is an end in itself. They have one idea in mind: to be intelligent, which is really stupid. And when intelligence takes itself for its own goal, it operates very strangely: the proof that it exists is not to be found in the ingenuity or simplicity of what it produces, but in how obscurely it is expressed. If you could see all the bum-fodder Maman brings home from her 'sessions' . . . Full of the Symbolic, and foreclusion, and subsuming the Real, with the help of a whole lot of mathematical formulae and dubious syntax. It's complete rubbish![58]

This lengthy excerpt is rich in its depiction of Paloma's perception of her mother, of language and especially of analysis. Through mimicry, Paloma performs a sort of inverted *lalangue*, in which the subject attempts to distance herself from the (m)other through language. If *lalangue* is the repetition and prolongation of sounds as meaningless lallation when the child's subjectivity is still enmeshed in the mother's, then Paloma's exaggerated impersonation of her mother – with the examples of 'anaaalysis' and 'maaarvelous' – is a mockery of the separation between subject and (m) other. This tension also arises with regard to the contradiction between content and syntax in this excerpt: whereas Paloma views analysis and life as cyclical, repetitive and absurd – such as taking antidepressants for ten years in order to endure analysis – the structure of her language is chiasmatic, thus further reinforcing the paradigm of the Imaginary via the mirror stage which she cannot completely surpass. The sentence '[f]ascination with intelligence is in itself fascinating' is a (distorted) syntactical mirror, with 'intelligence' mirroring 'itself', framed by 'fascination' and 'fascinating'. The binaries of self/other and stupid/intelligent collide in this linguistrick with a discourse on psychoanalysis as Paloma arguably looks at her mother while also seeing herself.

Following this excerpt, the specularity between Paloma and Solange becomes even more apparent:

That afternoon I was eating chocolate. I really like chocolate and it is probably the only thing I have in common with Maman and my sister. While I was biting into a bar with hazelnuts, I felt one of my teeth crack. I went to look at myself in the mirror and saw that I had indeed lost a little chip off my incisor.[59]

Paloma then recounts her mother's dream in which she loses her teeth, one by one. When Solange tells this story in analysis, her analyst, whose very Freudian name is Dr Theid, responds:

> 'Chère madame, a Freudian would tell you that it is a dream about death'. That's funny, no? It's not even the naiveté of his interpretation (falling teeth = death, umbrella = penis, etc.), as if culture did not have huge powers of suggestion that have nothing to do with reality. He thinks that in this way he will establish his intellectual superiority ('a Freudian would say') over mere erudition (he wants you to know he is distancing himself from Freud) – but you're left with the impression that it's a parrot who is speaking.[60]

The young protagonist is distancing herself once again from her mother and may therefore be more susceptible to the act of distancing which the other is also performing. What is most of interest in this passage, which prepares the battle for superiority between Paloma and her mother's analyst, is that the reference to the parrot echoes the semantic field of mimicry and language, further underlining Lacan's oft-quoted tenet of the unconscious being structured like a language as well as 'the discourse of the Other'. I shall return to this following the second explicit critique of Lacan in the novel.

Paloma finally agrees to sit down with Dr Theid, but she does not do so on the defensive. The exchange goes as follows:

> 'Your mother is very worried about you', he attacked, managing this time not to move even his lower lip. [. . .] So I decided to say something with a lot of gravitas: 'Do you think it has something to do with the foreclosure of the Name of the Father?' Do you think that made him move? Not a fraction. [. . .] 'Hmm?' he went, 'I don't think you understand what you are saying'. 'Oh yes, yes I do', I went, 'but there is one thing I don't understand in Lacan, it is the exact nature of his relation to structuralism'. He opened his mouth slightly to say something but I was quicker. 'Oh, yeah, and the mathemes, too. All those knots, it's a bit muddled. Do you understand any of it, this topology stuff? Everybody has known for quite a while that it's a scam, no?'[61]

This scene sets psychoanalysis up to fail, as the doctor leaves the room to confirm with Solange that her daughter is fine following Paloma's threats that she will smear the doctor's reputation among the elite that frequent her family, a comment she ends up deeply regretting.

As Eric Cabrot reminds us, a twelve-year-old girl would not likely have the capacity to process or conceptualize abstract thought.[62] Therefore, although it is difficult at times to consider Paloma a fictional character, this is precisely what she is. Whether her voice is that of Barbery's is arguable. There would certainly be room to have the critiques of psychoanalysis in her work outlined above juxtaposed with other literary and philosophical references, especially in a book written by a professor of Philosophy who seems to set psychoanalysis up to fail. To offset such a bias, one could posit that a Joycean logic is applicable here. For example, that of *A Portrait of the Artist as a Young Man*, in which the authorial and narrative voices, through examples of ironic distancing, clash with the young protagonist's, who already believes he is a writer. Who is to say that Paloma will not grow up to untangle the muddled knots she refers to, eventually making sense of Lacan and, why not, write her own *The Elegance of the Hedgehog*?

(FORE/CON)CLUSION

Until now, the focus has remained on the alternating protagonists of Renée and Paloma. Through the examples in this chapter, I have demonstrated that Paloma (mostly) represents the Imaginary through her struggle with the mirror stage, whereas Renée primarily represents the Symbolic through language/literature. It is now time to complete the Borromean knot with Kakuro Ozu. His foreignness puts him immediately in a position of other within these works. He becomes Other, however, when we consider his relation to the Real and to language. Kakuro, I have explained, is surrounded by death: from moving into the building following the death of a tenant, to being a widower, to engaging in a supposedly forbidden relationship with Renée, which leads not only to her transformation – and rebirth/Renée – but to her death as well, and finally, to the music that surrounds the spaces he inhabits. On this last note, a comedic scene takes place in which Renée uses Kakuro's high-tech bathroom in which Mozart's Requiem plays when one sits on the toilet. Such a musical genre is used during masses to lay souls to rest and therefore serves the narrative role of foreshadowing.

Mr Ozu is an element of disturbance for the subject and countersubject in our corpus. In the initial exchange between Renée and Kakuro, the reader/viewer witnesses Renée becoming *linguistruck*, if I may distort Lacan's term, by the Japanese man's 'unaccented French'. He speaks like a book, and the two grammar-purist bookworms bond intertextually. *Linguistruck* and charmed by Kakuro – as is Paloma, who has been learning Japanese for several years – Renée's transformation begins, and she slowly stops feigning stupidity and rather begins speaking eloquently. She can finally be herself. The relationship that arises is as much with Kakuro as it is with language. However, when we consider the film *The Hedgehog* alongside the novel, there is an irreconcilable distinction between Kakuro's role vis-à-vis language. Togo Igawa, who plays Mr Ozu in the film, is a Japanese actor who does not speak French. He learnt every line phonetically, and thus offers an excellent example of the split between the subject as signifier and the subject as jouissance. Furthermore, he is not much different than the parrot-like psychoanalyst, or the vessel-dummy of the true ventriloquist: the Real.

This example could be discussed through *lalangue* or through Lacan's 'subject *qua* S'. Quinn explains that,

> Lacan's wish was to 'put forward my stupidity (bêtise) in order to show that perhaps stupidity is not, as people think, a semantic category, but rather a way of collectivizing the signifier'. As Ed Pluth has put it, with reference to *lalangue*, '*Lalangue* shows us instead a kind of stupidity proper to language, something that concerns not the relation between thinking and language, and not the generation of unintended meanings, but rather a level of no meaning at all. A zombie-like level of language'.[63]

The deathly aura that surrounds Ozu and his embodiment of this 'zombie-like level of language' places him in the privileged position of 'subject *qua* S', that is, the subject that stands for nothing, or the subject that *is* absence. This final element is what allows for the signification of signifiers, and it ties the Borromean knot and fugacious narrative, which intertwines Paloma, Renée and Kakuro in a novel and film that seem to portray psychoanalysis as stupid when in reality, it offers it the chance to *poke* back.

NOTES

1. The term '*bête*' in French, as will be discussed, can translate as stupid, among several other terms. Its etymology recalls animalistic connotations – 'beast' – which allow us to scrutinize the important narrative, philosophical and psychoanalytic roles animals play in this corpus.
2. Ronell, Avital, *Stupidity*. Chicago: University of Illinois Press, 2002.
3. Malcolm Quinn, "Stupidity is Anything at All," *Parallax,* Vol. 19, No. 3 (2013), 70, DOI: 10.1080/13534645.2013.808016
4. Quinn, "Stupidity is Anything at All," 70.
5. In the film, Paloma is turning twelve.
6. Barbery, Muriel, *The Elegance of the Hedgehog*. Trans. Alison Anderson. New York: Europa Editions, 2008, 76.
7. Barbery, *The Elegance of the Hedgehog, 42*.
8. *Žižek*, Slavoj, "With or Without Passion: What's Wrong With Fundamentalism, Part 1," accessed 21 March 2021: https://www.lacan.com/zizpassion.htm
9. Barbery, *The Elegance of the Hedgehog*, 41.
10. Lacan, Jacques, *The Four Fundamental Concepts of Psycho-Analysis*. New York: Norton, 1979, 63.

11. Paloma is learning Japanese and has a keen interest in Japanese culture. She and Kakuro share similar scenes and dialogues that Paloma also has with Renée.

12. Lançon, Philippe, "Faut-il écraser le hérisson?" *Libération*, Last modified 5 July 2007: https://www.liberation.fr/livres/2007/07/05/faut-il-ecraser-le-herisson_97601/ My translation.

13. Barbery, *The Elegance of the Hedgehog*, 25–26.

14. Barbery, *The Elegance of the Hedgehog*, 328.

15. Barbery, *The Elegance of the Hedgehog*, 607.

16. Barbery, *The Elegance of the Hedgehog*, 329–33.

17. Barbery, Muriel, *L'Élégance du hérisson*. Paris: Gallimard, 2006, 196.

18. Barbery, *L'Élégance du hérisson*, 197.

19. Barbery, *The Elegance of the Hedgehog*, 756.

20. Barbery, *The Elegance of the Hedgehog*, 789.

21. Old ma Michel (la mère Michel) is a reference to a French children's song, wherein the old lady has lost her cat.

22. Lançon, 'Faut-il écraser le hérisson?'. My translation.

23. Žižek comments on a painting during an art roundtable and uses the concept of a 'frame beyond the frame'. He admits in *Fright of Real Tears* that this comment was a bluff; however, there might be an unintended desire to enmesh irony and stupidity in this concept, which he revisits in his later work. Slugan, Mario, "The Rhetorics of Interpretation and Žižek's Approach to Film," *Slavic Review*, Vol. 72, No. 4 (Winter 2013), 734.

24. Zimmerman, Nadya, "Musical Form as Narrator: The Fugue of the Sirens in James Joyce's *Ulysses," Journal of Modern Literature,* Vol. 26, No. 1 (2002), 110.

25. Barthes, Roland, *Introduction à l'analyse structurale des récits*. Paris: Seuil, 1981, 15.

26. Barthes, Roland and Lionel Duisit, "An Introduction to the Structural Analysis of Narrative," *New Literary History*, Vol. 6, No. 2, On Narrative and Narratives (Winter, 1975), 255.

27. See Viselli, Antonio, "This Novel Will Self-Destruct: (Un)Writing the Self in André Gide's *The Counterfeiters*," *Continental Thought & Theory: A Journal of Intellectual Freedom*, Vol. 2, No. 3 (2018), 224–239. https://ir.canterbury.ac.nz/bitstream/handle/10092/16380/CTT%20V2N3%2012%20Viselli%20.pdf?sequence=1&isAllowed=y

28. Barbery, *The Elegance of the Hedgehog*, 111.

29. Derrida, Jacques, *The Transcendental "Stupidity" ("Bêtise") of Man and the Becoming Animal According to Deleuze*, Vol. 2. Ed. Gabriele Schwab. New York: Columbia University Press, 2007, 35–36.

30. Derrida, "The Transcendental "Stupidity" ("Bêtise") of Man," 37; Deleuze, Gilles and Felix Guattari, *A Thousand Plateaus: Capitalism and Schizophrenia*. Minnesota: University of Minnesota Press, 2nd ed., 1987, 239.

31. Deleuze, *Plateaus*, 240.

32. Derrida, *The Animal that Therefore I am*. Ed. Marie-Louise Mallet. Trans. David Wills. Fordham University Press, 2008, 121.

33. Barbery, *The Elegance of the Hedgehog*, 502.

34. Derrida, *The Animal that Therefore I am*, 119.

35. Derrida, Jacques, *The Beast and the Sovereign, Volume 1 (The Seminars of Jacques Derrida)*. Trans. Geoffrey Bennington. Chicago: University of Chicago Press, 18.

36. Derrida, *The Beast and the Sovereign*, 39.

37. Daly, P. Daniel, "'La Bête e(s)t le souverain': Discuss with reference to the First Session of Jacques Derrida's *La Bête et le souverain*." *French Studies Bulletin*, Vol. 37, No. 140 (Autumn 2016), 63, https://doi.org/10.1093/frebul/ktw015

38. Barbery, *The Elegance of the Hedgehog*, 87–88.

39. Another point to explore would be Renée's discussion about distinct forms of intelligence, including manual vs. cerebral intelligence when she discusses the differences between herself and her husband: 56.

40. Barbery, *The Elegance of the Hedgehog*, 98.

41. Barbery, *The Elegance of the Hedgehog*, 99.

42. Barbery, *The Elegance of the Hedgehog*, 353.

43. Barbery, *The Elegance of the Hedgehog*, 353.

44. Barbery, *The Elegance of the Hedgehog*, 407.

45. Barbery, *The Elegance of the Hedgehog*, 302.

46. Although these are two distinct animals, their physical similarities allow Schopenhauer and Freud to draw similar conclusions.

47. Schopenhauer, Arthur, *Parerga and Paralipomena: Short Philosophical Essays*, Vol. 2. Oxford: Oxford University Press, 2000, 651–652.

48. Prochnik, George, "The Porcupine Illusion: Freud's Prickly Secret," *Cabinet Magazine* (Summer 2007): https://www.cabinetmagazine.org/issues/26/prochnik.php

49. Allouch, Jean. "Jacques Lacan et son élève hérisson," presented at a seminar in Cordoba (18–19 July 2020). Last accessed 21 March 2021: http://www.jeanallouch.com/pdf/361#:~:text=En%20psychanalyse%2C%20Lacan%20c'est%20de%20l'or.&text=Au%20moment%20d'apporter%20sa,munies%20de%20piquants%20(porcupine

50. Allouch, Jean. *Transmaître; Jacques Lacan et son élève hérisson*. Epel, 2020. Last accessed 20 March 2021: http://www.jeanallouch.com/pdf/354

51. For Lacan's mention of Giraudoux, see Allouch, Jean. "Fable de l'élève hérisson," *AG Elp* (June 2019). http://www.jeanallouch.com/pdf/354)

52. Giraudoux, Jean. *Électre*. Grasset, Paris, 1937, 47–48. My translation.

53. Prochnik, "The Porcupine Illusion."

54. Temperman, Jeroe, *The Lautsi Papers: Multidisciplinary Reflections on Religious Symbols in the Public School Classroom*. Martinus Nijhoff Publishers, Leiden, 2012, 43.

55. Barbery, *The Elegance of the Hedgehog*, 349.

56. Lacan, Jacques. *Écrits*. Trans. Bruce Fink, New York: W. W. Norton & Co., 2002, 154.

57. Murphy, Paula, "Linguistricks: Reading Lacan to the Letter," *International Journal of Baudrillard Studies,* Vol. 2, No. 2 (July 2005). Last accessed 21 March 2021: https://baudrillardstudies.ubishops.ca/linguistricks-reading-lacan-to-the-letter/#back5

58. Barbery, *The Elegance of the Hedgehog,* 349–51.
59. Barbery, *The Elegance of the Hedgehog,* 351.
60. Barbery, *The Elegance of the Hedgehog,* 352.
61. Barbery, *The Elegance of the Hedgehog,* 441.
62. Cabrot, Eric. "L'éloge de la concierge?" *Les fiches de lecture sur L'Élégance du hérisson.* Last modified 26 April 2007: https://www.lexpress.fr/culture/livre/les-fiches-de-lecture-sur-italique-l-elegance-du-herisson-italique_822119.html
63. Quinn, "Stupidity is Anything at All," 73.

Chapter 6

Errare Humanum Est

On Psychoanalysis as Morosophy

Dany Nobus

What does it mean for something or someone to be (called) stupid? Were this to be a stupid question, the answer would probably be glaringly self-evident, yet since the answer is everything but straightforward, the question may easily result in the designated replier feeling stupefied, dumbfounded and thus rather stupid, so that the very lack or deferral of a clear answer effectively provides the answer one was looking for all along. Since time out of mind, stupidity has been employed with reference to an existence *in defectu* – as the absence, loss or omission of a certain cognitive, affective and/or conative quality; a level of functioning below a certain average; or a state of being that is inferior to an agreed standard of normality, in short, a failure to be in possession of a capability that is considered to be ubiquitously present. Stupidity is what falls outside, and generally below the boundaries of common sense and what quite literally stands out as such because it cannot be recuperated within them. What was once accepted as wise may subsequently become stupid when the paradigms of wisdom shift towards new empirical or discursive truths, and what was once regarded as stupid may turn out to be wise when epistemic conditions, intellectual matrices, belief systems and power balances shift. Even though it was universally accepted for centuries as an undisputed fact, and continued to be enforced in the face of scientific evidence appearing to prove the contrary, the Ptolemaic geocentric perspective on the heavenly spheres has now been relegated to the dustbin of human stupidities.[1] Whereas persistent, seemingly excessive hand-washing was once perceived as distinctly stupid and possibly symptomatic of an underlying mental health condition, in times of a global, devastating pandemic, it might turn out to be one of the wisest things human beings can do in order to protect themselves and others against sickness and disease.

Maybe in order to avoid coming across as totally stupid, many clever people have of course examined this peculiar 'defective existence' more closely, generating more detailed descriptions and more careful distinctions, which has often resulted in fairly sophisticated theories of stupidity. When I was an undergraduate student during the mid-1980s, an eminent professor of psychiatry explained to us that, when it occurs in human beings, stupidity is not a uniform, monolithic condition, but a multifaceted state, with a rich, complex and diversified phenomenology. In sum, he posited that there is a well-established hierarchy of human stupidity – also known as 'mental retardation' – and that scientists had identified no less than four different types of stupidity, which are qualitatively similar yet quantitatively different in terms of their positioning on the intelligence scale. At the very bottom of the hierarchy, then, there is a state called 'idiocy', which is synonymous with profound mental retardation. All idiots allegedly have an intelligence quotient (IQ) below twenty. On the next level of the hierarchy, we find those who are slightly less stupid than the idiots and who generally have an IQ between twenty and fifty. These types of stupid people still suffer from severe mental retardation and are classified as imbeciles. The next bracket, which includes those human beings with a moderate mental retardation, represents IQ scores between fifty-one and seventy, and is commonly referred to as the category of the morons. Finally, the least stupid of all the stupid people are those with an IQ between seventy and (the normal, average score of) one hundred. In their case, there is only evidence of a mild mental retardation, which is also designated as debility. I do not recall any one of us questioning, let alone protesting against this classification and nomenclature, perhaps because we were only university students and therefore undoubtedly intelligent yet also still deeply ignorant, but more importantly because the professor's distinctions and the associated terminology had effectively been adapted from the ninth edition of the *International Classification of Diseases* (*ICD-9*), which had been published by the World Health Organisation in 1979.[2] It struck me, and maybe it struck other students too, that one should not argue with the scientific results of years of research conducted under the aegis of the world's most authoritative governing body on health and disease, at the risk of being perceived as being utterly stupid.

Many years later, I discovered to my surprise that the 'scientific' names given to the four different categories of human stupidity actually have a very long history and were, with one exception, originally not in common usage at all as descriptors of 'mental retardation', but rather as more generic terms for a condition or occurrence of frailty, defect or impairment. For example, in his moral essay *De Constantia Sapientis*, the first-century Roman Stoic philosopher Lucius Annaeus Seneca asserted that the wise man may occasionally be burdened by 'bodily pain and infirmity [*dolor corporis et debilitas*]', but that he is never overthrown by these events (*si non pervertunt*).[3] When, in one of his *Epistulae Morales ad Lucilium*, Seneca addressed the nature and source of human courage, he described the virtue as 'the impregnable fortification for human weakness [*Munimentum humanae imbecillitas inexpugnabile*]'.[4] Both in ancient and in modern Greek, the word ιδιώτης primarily refers to an individual with no official title, someone who is not involved in public affairs or merely acts in a personal capacity. In a similar vein, ιδιωτικός connotes privacy and could be used for someone who mainly keeps to himself. Only in a secondary sense was the meaning of ιδιώτης and ιδιωτικός extrapolated to include people whose profound lack of social engagement must indicate a certain degree of foolishness and stupidity. It is in this auxiliary sense that the word appears, *bis repetita placent*, in the first epistle of Paul to the Corinthians, where it is generally translated into English as 'unlearned'. For instance, in 1 Corinthians 14.16, Paul proclaims: 'ἐπεὶ ἐὰν εὐλογῇς πνεύματι, ὁ ἀναπληρῶν τὸν τόπον τοῦ ἰδιώτου πῶς ἐρεῖ τὸ Ἀμήν ἐπὶ τῇ σῇ εὐχαριστίᾳ; ἐπειδὴ τί λέγεις οὐκ οἶδεν'. In the King James version of the Bible, the phrase is translated as: 'Else when thou shalt bless with the spirit, how shall he that occupieth the room of the unlearned [τόπον τοῦ ἰδιώτου] say Amen at thy giving of thanks, seeing he understandeth not what thou sayest?'[5] The only word in the twentieth-century taxonomy of human stupidity that was originally reserved for foolishness, stupidity, sluggishness and placidity is μωρός, which also resonates with the Sanskrit मूर (muura), indicating the (human) characteristic of being dull, slow and dumb. This word appears in Paul's first letter to the Corinthians as well, in one of the most influential and controversial Christian axioms of all time. In 1 Corinthians 4.10, Paul describes himself and his fellow workers as μωροὶ διὰ Χριστόν, which the King James Bible renders as 'fools for Christ's sake', but which could perhaps be translated more accurately as 'fools through Christ', 'fools by means of Christ' or even 'fools via Christ's example'.[6] Paul's point is not that true Christians should be self-deprecating in honour of Christ's sanctity, but that Christ's earthly existence of persistent marginalization and humiliation accords spiritual value to foolishness and that the only true Christians are those who follow Christ's example.[7]

The specific, variegated terminology associated with (human) stupidity is thus of a relatively recent coinage and the same holds for the terms' connotations as diagnoses of (human) reason and intelligence. However, it goes without saying that these classifications are purely descriptive and do not provide any indication as to how some members of the human species may have ended up being as stupid as they are, and even less whether stupid people could be treated and cured. Yet here too, some of the world's cleverest individuals have sometimes tried to come to the rescue. In 2003, the American molecular biologist James D. Watson, then president of the world-renowned

Cold Spring Harbor Laboratory and co-discoverer, with Francis Crick, of the double helix structure of DNA, argued that stupidity is really a genetic (and therefore inherited) disease, for which bespoke screening programmes should be developed and rolled out, and which may eventually be cured with biotechnological tools.[8] For all I know, nobody went so far as to suggest that an incontestable genius is clearly also capable of committing stupidities, but Watson's statements on the matter elicited a violent backlash and eventually led to Cold Spring Harbor severing all ties with him in January 2019.[9] Although Watson's proposition of a possible genetic basis for stupidity in a sense only extended materialistic hypotheses that have become a staple of contemporary (biological) psychiatry, the mere suggestion that stupidity might run in families and that people might one day be cured of it through gene therapy was evidently a hypothesis too far.

Perhaps the key issue is not that we should avoid trying to identify the cause(s) of (human) stupidity, but that stupidity, as a measure of intelligence, is an extremely unstable category, so much so that a demonstrably stupid creature may very well be capable of the highest achievements and that the paragon of genius is by no means immune to intermittent bouts of stupidity. The first paradox was an important feature of Renaissance thought, in which it was most often epitomized by the trope of the donkey, as the quintessentially stubborn, stupid, servile and lowly animal. In this respect, the German Renaissance polymath Cornelius Agrippa declared, in the final chapter of his 1526 treatise *De incertitudine et vanitate scientiarum*, that 'there is no other animal than the ass which is so capable of divinity [*nullum animal tam esse divinitatis capax, quam asinum*]' and that 'nobody who has not first looked into an ass can ever be a philosopher [*ni primus è philosopho versus fuisset in asinum*]'.[10] The extraordinary value of asininity, as the unique vehicle of divine revelation, was extolled along similar lines, yet even more strongly by Giordano Bruno, in his 1585 dialogues *The Cabala of Pegasus*, in which it is argued that 'the ass or asininity is the symbol of wisdom', so that the best human beings can hope for is that God proves willing to grant them this amazing privilege: 'Pray, pray to God, O dear friends, if you are not yet asses that he make you become asses.'[11] Drawing on the elucubrations of another important Renaissance figure, the superbly christened Philippus Aureolus Theophrastus Bombastus von Hohenheim, who was more commonly known as Paracelsus, Carl Gustav Jung subsequently averred: 'Stupidity is the mother of the wise, but cleverness never.'[12] The latter point amplifies the second paradox mentioned above: being knowledgeable does not preclude profound stupidity, and self-identified or assigned genius may very well be directly proportional to relentless (accidental, unintended) flashes of it. The Austrian writer Robert Musil termed this condition 'intelligent stupidity' and James Watson's aforementioned views on the biological basis of stupidity would constitute an excellent instance of its occurrence.[13] Although it must have been known for centuries, Musil also offers the best description of it, in two lectures delivered before the 'Austrian Werkbund' in March 1937: '[I]ntelligent stupidity is what participates in the agitation of intellectual life, especially in its inconstancy and lack of results. . . . The stupidity this addresses is no mental illness, yet it is most lethal; a dangerous disease of the mind that endangers life itself.'[14]

At the beginning of his lecture, Musil very wisely conceded that he did not know what stupidity is, but he also admitted that he could not think of an 'investigation that has taken stupidity as its subject'.[15] Given his immersion in Viennese culture and his scholarly interests, it is a strange observation because Musil would have been perfectly placed to appreciate the significance of the first, and in many ways the only, discipline that had taken (intelligent) stupidity seriously until then – so seriously that it had advanced a revolutionary explanation for its multifarious occurrences and even articulated the foundational principles for its treatment. Maybe Musil's own ambivalence vis-à-vis some of the central tenets of this discipline prevented him from properly acknowledging its contributions.[16] In any case, he failed to ascertain what another Viennese citizen had so carefully laid out in his innovative account of the seemingly limitless scope of human (intelligent) stupidity. The man was called Sigmund Freud and he had endowed his theory and treatment of stupidity with the name psychoanalysis. Indeed, I wish to argue here that psychoanalysis was born through and developed alongside consecutive encounters with human stupidity and that, whatever else he may have been, Sigmund Freud was also the world's first professor of stupidity. I would even go so far as to say that psychoanalysis constitutes a genuine 'morosophy', that is, a wisdom of stupidity, which is not only represented at the level of its theoretical understanding of the human mind, but more dramatically in its clinical modus operandi, where it features on two distinct levels: the analytic act and the direction of the analytic treatment.[17]

At the risk of invalidating an argument before it has even been properly formulated, I should immediately concede that psychoanalysts have contributed relatively little to our understanding of stupidity if the latter term is confined to what would currently be designated as 'learning difficulties'. In 1909, the German psychiatrist and neuropathologist Leopold Löwenfeld published the only psychoanalytically informed monograph on the issue, which hardly received any attention from Freud and his circle of followers.[18] During the mid-1890s, Freud and Löwenfeld had clashed over the nosology of anxiety neurosis, which had resulted in the two men becoming friends, Freud writing a précis of *The Interpretation of Dreams* for a book series edited by Löwenfeld, and also contributing two papers at Löwenfeld's request to a comprehensive volume on obsessional neurosis and a collection on the influence of sexuality on nervous disorders.[19] Apparently, Löwenfeld did not think that Freud would have anything valuable to say on stupidity, or Freud himself declined the offer. During the 1920s and 1930s, the only psychoanalytic studies of what was also referred to as 'mental deficiency' and 'feeble-mindedness' were by the American psychiatrist L. Pierce Clark and the German physician Karl Landauer.[20] I think it is fair to say that none of these papers stand out for their originality or the brilliance of the ideas that are exposed therein. Perhaps the only contribution of note to the study of stupidity qua 'learning difficulty' that psychoanalysts made during those years concerns the identification and explanation of what was alternatively termed 'pseudo-debility' and the 'flight into stupidity'.[21] This peculiar condition was included by Otto Fenichel in his seminal 1945 treatise *The Psychoanalytic Theory of Neurosis*, as 'people [who] become stupid *ad hoc*, that is, when they do not want to understand, where understanding would cause anxiety or guilt feeling, or would endanger an existing neurotic equilibrium'.[22] Elsewhere in his book, Fenichel may have also captured the main reason as to why psychoanalysts were never particularly forthcoming in their approach to stupidity: 'Since analysis consists of making the ego face its conflicts, cases in which the capacity to do so is lacking cannot be analyzed. Feeble-mindedness is a contraindication [to analysis].'[23]

However, if stupidity is not reduced to the clinical spectrum of 'learning difficulties' and extended to encompass the intentional or inadvertent enactment of an uncommon thought process, the unexpected occurrence of a bodily or psychic event that defies epistemic conventions or the seemingly inexplicable eruption of a matter that challenges common sense, the theory and practice of psychoanalysis would not exist without it. More concretely, psychoanalysis would not have come into being had it not been for someone called Sigmund Freud refusing to dismiss these stupidities as meaningless imperfections of the human mind or insignificant corollaries of the human mind playing tricks on itself. As I shall show, Freud also came to realize that relieving the human condition of the most disruptive and painful of these stupidities required something other than the profession of knowledge. Utterly stupid as it may have seemed, including to himself, Freud was gradually forced to admit that ignorance is a better treatment for stupidity than any kind of expert reliance on established wisdom. Finally, with a little help from Jacques Lacan, it can even be argued that the overall purpose of treating stupidities psychoanalytically with ignorance is not to replace them with better, more rational or more realistic knowledge but to render the epistemic background against which they appear stupid too. In other words, the very acknowledgement of knowledge as intrinsically littered with stupidities is deemed more analytically productive than any attempt at exorcising stupidity by expanding the realm of conscious cognition.

Trained in neurology, Freud witnessed stupidity first-hand when he started attending the lectures and demonstrations of Jean-Martin Charcot in Paris during the Autumn of 1885, where he saw to his astonishment how hysterical men and women displayed symptoms that could not possibly be accounted for with the physiological and neuropathological theories of his day.[24] As he wrote in his obituary of the great French clinician, Freud learnt there the importance of carefully scrutinizing those clinical phenomena that do not fit into the established conceptual paradigms and steering away from uncritically reinforcing existing models of medical knowledge.[25] Confronted with the baffling clinical picture of one of Charcot's patients, Freud objected by saying: 'But that can't be true . . . it contradicts the Young-Helmholtz theory.'[26] It would have been an entirely reasonable comment to make, if only because what Freud observed was probably indeed incompatible with the theory in question, yet Charcot allegedly responded with a sentence that stayed with Freud for the rest of his life: '*La théorie, c'est bon, mais ça n'empêche pas d'exister*' (Theory is fine, but it doesn't preclude certain things from existing).[27] Stupidity already manifested itself at two different levels here. First, there was a whole range of bodily and psychic symptoms that simply did not make sense in terms of what was known about the operational mechanisms of the human body. And to add insult to injury, these nonsensical ailments were sufficiently debilitating for patients to be admitted to hospitals, where their clinical nonsensicality had been substantiated and existing therapeutic methods had been stretched to the breaking point. One could certainly have been forgiven for thinking that the patients presenting with these symptoms were ingenious malingerers who had somehow succeeded in persuading the medical establishment that there was something seriously wrong with them, merely in order to escape the drudgery of everyday life. However, Charcot taught Freud that these bizarre conditions deserved to be taken seriously and that their scrupulous examination might generate new explanatory hypotheses on their source and origin.[28] Second, there was the ever-present temptation to hold on to what was already known, to reaffirm the validity of epistemic frameworks, taxonomies, diagnostic systems and causal connections, even though the clinical observations seemed to point in a different direction. There was always the inclination to ignore the exceptions in favour of the preservation of the rule, or to reduce the exceptionality of the clinical picture in such a way that the rule could still apply. In this respect, Charcot suggested that consolidating a body of knowledge in the face of empirical contradictions was as nonsensical as the appearance of the contradictions themselves.

More importantly, though, hysteria was not just a stupidity because it undermined the very foundations of human physiology. Hysterical patients also purported to demonstrate that the human mind can be responsible for precipitating and perpetuating all kinds of (sometimes literally) crippling physical symptoms. We all know that the human body seems to have a mind of its own and that it can 'malfunction' to the point where its inhabitant is afflicted with a multitude of life-limiting and life-threatening diseases whose precise cause remains completely unknown. But why would anyone who is right in their mind make themselves ill? How can we explain that there is no objectifiable reason for some disorders at all, the only remaining option being that the ailment and the associated suffering must be psychological or psychosomatic?[29] How can a distinctly healthy body become dysfunctional for no other reason than the person's own state of mind? How stupid must one be to allow this to happen?

Within the space of this chapter, I cannot reconstruct in full how, during the 1890s, Freud crucially relied on his experiences in Paris for developing the theory and practice of psychoanalysis, which was as much an innovative clinical approach to the neurotic stupidities of the human mind as it was an account of the limitless expressions of human self-deceit. But before long, various other stupidities became the focus of Freud's attention – dreams, slips of the tongue, bungled actions and (stupid) jokes.[30] To many a contemporary scientist, these formations of the human mind are still as nonsensical and meaningless as they were to most of Freud's colleagues, yet Freud himself believed otherwise. Much like he had done with the puzzling symptoms of hysteria, he took them seriously, granted them meaning, attempted to explain them as manifestations of the unconscious and endeavoured to treat their disruptive occurrence with the technical tools of psychoanalysis. With the birth of psychoanalysis, these strange phenomena gradually became less stupid, more acceptable, less illogical, more common, less irrational, more normal. Freud never went so far as to claim that he had invented a technique to relieve the human mind of these stupidities for once and for all – as if anyone would even want to stop dreaming altogether – but that he had at least come up with a solid explanation for their emergence and an effective treatment for their most troubling varieties.[31]

At this point, the reader may accuse me of colonizing the Freudian text with my own lexicon, injecting stupidity into the psychoanalytic vocabulary in those places where what is at stake is effectively something else – repressed knowledge, unconscious representations or the return of the repressed – with a view to substantiating a thesis (psychoanalysis as morosophy) that is highly questionable at best and arguably stupid at worst. And indeed, I would have to admit that, for all their ostensible nonsensicality, Freud himself never explicitly referred to the formations of the unconscious that constitute the subject matter of his early psychoanalytic works as stupidities. But look, in January 1908, there came a five-year-old boy called Herbert Graf, whose father Max was a loyal participant in Freud's Wednesday seminars and whose mother Olga Hönig had been in analysis with Freud in 1897.[32] Freud had known 'this delightful little boy', whom he dubbed Little Hans, for quite some time and he had already mentioned his sexual developments in two previous papers.[33] Now he was consulted by the boy's father because the child had recently developed a phobia of horses, more specifically a fear that he would be bitten by a horse in the street.[34] For a period of five months, Freud conducted his analysis of the boy's phobia almost exclusively by proxy, the boy's father acting as his clinical intermediary. Over the years, much has been written about this case study, but there is one aspect of Freud's interventions that has been almost completely overlooked and which is both relevant to my argument and instructive regarding the direction of the psychoanalytic treatment.[35] Relatively early on in the father's vicarious analysis of his son, Freud intervened in a way that would prove highly momentous: 'I arranged with Hans's father that he should tell the boy that all this business about horses was a piece of nonsense and nothing more [*das mit den Pferden sei eine Dummheit, weiter nichts*].'[36] Freud did not provide a rationale for his intervention, which comes across as rather trivial, yet after Hans's father dutifully executed Freud's orders, the young boy readily adopted '*die Dummheit*' (the stupidity) as a name for his fear.[37] When Max Graf suggested to his son that they consult with Freud in person, the eminent clinician was even presented as the professor who can take the *Dummheit* away, and the entire subsequent analytic process could be seen as a treatment of Hans's stupidity.

I would venture the hypothesis here that Freud knew very well that, in rebranding Little Hans's phobia as a stupidity, the name would strike a chord in the young boy's mind. Realistically speaking, Hans's phobia was of course a stupidity because he would not have had any good 'objective' reason to be afraid of horses (biting him). As an irrational fear, the phobia was not conditioned by any known organic, anatomical lesion or physiological imbalance, and so from a strictly medical perspective too it could only be interpreted as a developmental anomaly. Furthermore, the young boy was sufficiently clever to realize that his phobia was senseless and illogical. In other words, he would have had the 'presence of mind' to acknowledge that his fear of (being bitten by) horses was totally absurd, much like most patients presenting with 'hysterical' or obsessional symptoms are quite willing to accept that their pathology really does not make sense.[38] Hence, in calling the phobia a stupidity, Freud merely rendered explicit what would have been already obvious to everyone, including to Little Hans himself. However, in designating the boy's fear as stupid and hoping that he would embrace the word as a new name for his problem, he also endowed it with a new meaning and indirectly appealed to Little Hans's own knowledge and self-image. It is as if Freud whispered into his ears that clever young boys may have phobias, but that they should not allow themselves to perform stupidities, let alone be stupid. In translating the phobia into a stupidity, it would not only have been easier for Little Hans to acknowledge, position and relate to his fear, but also to start investigating why and how a clever boy like him could have contracted this stupidity in the first place, and how he could possibly get rid of it.[39] Maybe it sounds a bit stupid to call a phobia a stupidity, but I think the effect was much more beneficial than anything that could have been achieved by calling it an *equinophobia* or a *hippodaknophobia*.

In 1908, when he was called upon as the eminent professor of stupidity, Freud very much adopted the position of a wise (old) man and did not hesitate to verbalize his precious wisdom to his young patient, much as he had done in the case of the Rat Man, whose obsessional neurosis he was trying to alleviate during the same period.[40] Nevertheless, it slowly dawned upon him that explaining to patients the repressed unconscious motives behind their stupidities, professing (psychoanalytic) knowledge, sharing expertise, offering 'intellectualist' interpretations and rendering representations conscious by articulating them for the patient rarely generate (immediate) effects. In some cases, patients' symptoms even exacerbate as a result. For example, during his analysis of the 'Wolf Man', Freud noticed that 'he [the "Wolf Man"] showed a habit of producing transitory "negative reactions"; every time something had been conclusively cleared up, he attempted to contradict the effect for a short while by an aggravation of the symptom which had been cleared up'.[41] At the end of his technical paper 'Remembering, Repeating and Working-Through', which was written during the time of the Wolf Man's analysis, Freud argued that 'giving the [patient's] resistance a name could not result in its immediate cessation'.[42] For the resistance to dissolve, he continued, the patient needs to engage in a process of 'working-through' (*durcharbeiten*), which requires time and which may test the analyst's patience. The problem was that Freud could not really explain what exactly this 'working-through' entails and whether it could have been facilitated or even expedited without the analyst's active intervention of naming the resistance. The patients' adverse reactions to the analyst's knowledge continued to bother Freud, even after he had revised his general outlook on the structure of the human mind with the introduction of the second topography (the distinction between the Ego, the Id and the Superego) in 1923. In the very same essay in which he first presented this distinction, he wrote: 'There are certain people who behave in a quite peculiar fashion during the work of analysis. When one speaks hopefully to them or expresses satisfaction with the progress of the treatment, they show signs of discontent and their condition invariably becomes worse.'[43] In a subsequent paper, he ascribed these paradoxical effects to the patients' unconscious sense of guilt and designated them as 'negative therapeutic reactions', yet the unconscious motive would not disappear as a result of the analyst's explanations of it: 'Patients do not easily believe us when we tell them about the unconscious sense of guilt.'[44]

More annoyingly, over and above some patients' unconscious sense of guilt there was also a more generic 'refusal to know' at work, which not only extends the duration of the analytic treatment, but curbs the overall clinical impact of the analyst's knowledge. Towards the end of a long psychoanalytic career, Freud stated in 'Analysis Terminable and Interminable':

> We tell the patient about possibilities of other instinctual conflicts, and we arouse his expectation that such conflicts may occur in him. What we hope is that this information and this warning will have the effect of activating in him one of the conflicts we have indicated, in a modest degree and yet sufficient for treatment. But this time experience speaks with no uncertain voice. The expected result does not come about. The patient hears our message, but there is no response. He may think to himself: 'This is very interesting, but I feel no trace of it.' We have increased his knowledge but altered nothing else in him.[45]

Apart from the fact that the analyst's professed knowledge of the patient's condition is not nearly as therapeutically effective as might be expected, and could even elicit an exacerbation of stupidity, there is at least one other reason as to why analysts must guard themselves against relying on their knowledge as a clinical tool. The principle follows directly from Charcot's bon mot that even the finest of theories never prevents certain things from existing and that it would therefore be foolish to hold on to a theoretical proposition if a clinical reality seems to prove the contrary. Knowledge should not make one blind to divergent empirical observations and alternative perspectives. Indeed, there is no reason why the patient's 'refusal to know' or 'not wanting to know' would not obtain equally for the clinician, even if the latter is not struggling to overcome disturbing unconscious conflicts. Despite his admiration for Charcot, Freud himself sometimes displayed symptoms of this type of stupidity, especially when it came to defending the universality of conceptual cornerstones such as the Oedipus complex, yet sometimes also with regard to postulates and ideas of which he knew very well that they were entirely speculative.[46]

Clinically, however, Freud insisted that psychoanalytic technique should never become entrenched in a rigid set of rules, that patients should never be reduced to clinical instances of an established type of condition and that each and every psychoanalytic treatment process should also present the clinician with an opportunity to acquire new knowledge. The first of these guidelines was formulated in the 1913 technical paper 'On Beginning the Treatment,' in which Freud suggested that the 'extraordinary diversity of the [patients'] psychical constellations . . ., the plasticity of all mental processes and the wealth of determining factors oppose any mechanization of the [psychoanalytic] technique'.[47] A psychoanalytic treatment, he maintained, is like playing chess: the opening moves and the endgame may be exhaustively described in clear, concrete strategies, but the 'infinite variety of moves' during the central part of the game far exceeds the boundaries of a generic rulebook.[48] The second guideline is implied in another technical paper from the same period, in which Freud divulged that the 'most successful cases are those in which one proceeds, as it were, without any purpose in view, allows oneself to be taken by surprise by a new turn in them, and always meets them with an open mind, free from any presuppositions'.[49] '[W]e ought not to cut ourselves from the possibility of testing what we have already learnt', Freud continued, 'and of extending our knowledge further'.[50] The third guideline is an extension of the previous one and appeared most poignantly in Freud's 1927 postscript to 'The Question of Lay Analysis'. After having proclaimed, rather duplicitously, that psychoanalytic knowledge had invariably resulted in therapeutic success, Freud went on to say: 'It was impossible to treat a patient without learning something new; it was impossible to gain fresh insight without perceiving its beneficent results. Our analytic procedure is the only one in which this precious conjunction [between cure and research] is assured.'[51] In sum, however knowledgeable psychoanalysts may have become on account of their theoretical instruction and clinical experience, when treating patients they should continuously guard themselves against becoming teachers and instead see themselves as lifelong learners. Taken together, patients' negative therapeutic reactions to the analyst's knowledge, their obstinate refusal to know and the analysts' own duty and responsibility to suspend their acquired knowledge so that they can be surprised by the provocations and challenges of a new clinical encounter can only lead to one conclusion. Rather than supplanting the patients' stupidities with their own wisdom, it is considerably better for psychoanalysts to play dumb or, better still, to accept their own dumbness. The professor of stupidity must also allow himself to be a stupid professor.

From the early 1950s, Lacan formalized the analyst's 'dumb' position in the treatment under the aegis of what he termed – with a little nod to the Indian Buddhist tradition of the *Dharmadhātustava* – 'the passion of ignorance'.[52] Contrary to what this notion may invoke, it should not be interpreted as an injunction for psychoanalysts to actively steer away from all sources of knowledge and to regard all theoretical schooling as superfluous, but rather as a professional commitment to acknowledging the intrinsic fractures of knowledge, the inherent stupidity of all forms of (doctrinal) knowing and a concurrent appreciation for the (clinical) value of not-knowing. Even though Lacan's outlook on the conceptualization of the analytic position changed dramatically over the years, he never compromised on the axiom of the psychoanalyst as one of the most advanced figurations of nonknowledge. At the very end of his first public seminar, he described the analyst's position in this respect as an *ignorantia docta*, a wise or learnt ignorance, a conscious knowledge of the partiality of all knowledge, an acknowledgement that some things exist – despite, Charcot would have said, all the fine theories we have at our disposal – without these things being already known and perhaps also without them ever being fully knowable.[53] The analyst's knowledge, Lacan asserted elsewhere, is but 'the symptom of his own ignorance' and this pathological manifestation of 'intelligent stupidity' – my term rather than Lacan's, here – can only be transformed into something valuable if the analyst is prepared to embrace the passion of ignorance, which 'must give meaning to all of analytic training'.[54] Lacan therefore also emphasized that it befalls those responsible for the transmission of psychoanalytic knowledge in vocational training programmes to ensure that analytic trainees are taught accordingly: 'The positive fruit of the revelation of ignorance is nonknowledge [*non-savoir*], which is not a negation of knowledge but rather its most elaborate form. The candidate's training cannot be completed without some action on the part of the master or masters who train him in this nonknowledge – failing which he will never be more than a robotic [read: an "intelligently stupid"] analyst.'[55] When, during the 1969–1970 academic year, Lacan introduced the discourse of the analyst as a unique social bond that is based on a distinct interconnection between four places and four functions – as opposed to the customary understanding of the 'analytic situation' as a dual relation between two people (the clinician and the patient) – he characterized the function of the analyst's knowledge (represented as S_2) as operating in the place of truth.[56] This is the only location from which it can be heard and employed as stupid, because the truth can only ever be approximated, never fully relayed in words without something of its truthfulness getting lost. For Lacan, it was another way of saying that, in order to preserve their position as psychoanalysts, clinicians must not think that their knowledge will ever be complete and act as if it is. Instead, they must approach their knowledge qua truth, accept that it will never be more than a fundamentally fractured body of ideas – in short, render it stupid.

So far, I have outlined two reasons as to why the theory and practice of psychoanalysis encapsulate a morosophy: psychoanalysis takes human stupidity as its main object of study (research and treatment) – all the more so as it attributes the stupid expressions of the human mind to repressed, unconscious motives – and in presenting a suitable treatment option for these stupidities, it effectively requires clinicians to keep their knowledge in a perennial state of failure.[57] To some, these two reasons may already suffice, yet I believe that, in psychoanalysis, there is a third pillar of stupidity at work, which clearly sets it apart from other (psycho)therapeutic modalities and which should seal the fate of Freud's brainchild as a morosophic creature for once and for all. Indeed, one might argue that psychoanalysis may very well have been (one of) the first discipline(s) to take human stupidity seriously, but that, in the endlessly proliferating therapy industry, it is by no means the only discourse in which stupidities have been recognized and given pride of place, and that a decent number of therapists out there may occasionally also enjoy playing dumb, irrespective of their professional denominations.[58] If we accept that these arguments are not totally stupid, then the two aforementioned reasons will probably be necessary, but evidently insufficient. The third reason, however, should take away any lingering doubt that psychoanalysis constitutes the one and only, genuine morosophy. Because unlike any other treatment paradigm, it does not only aim *at* stupidity but also *for* stupidity. Whereas the mainstream cognitive-behavioural therapist would try hard to exchange the client's cognitive distortions for better (more rational, more realistic, more acceptable and more 'intelligent') patterns of thought, the psychoanalyst would endeavour to accomplish exactly the opposite: turn the patient's epistemic narratives, against which the formations of the unconscious emerge as (painful, disruptive or even debilitating) stupidities, into a more stupid symbolic network of thoughts and representations.

I do not expect every reader (or indeed every psychoanalyst) to agree with me, yet the rationale for the psychoanalytic focus on stupidity as a clinical aim is exceedingly simple. Knowledge does not preclude the eruption of stupidities and even the knowledge of stupidity cannot protect anyone against committing stupidities.[59] To be clear: the knowledge that generates stupidity is not inherently flawed, illogical or inadequate. If anything, it might be ubiquitously acknowledged as a staple of robust, solid knowledge. After all, it is precisely because knowledgeable people continue to commit lots of stupidities that Musil invented the category of 'intelligent stupidity'. But if knowledge does not protect against stupidity, and excellent knowledge might even be directly proportional to excessive stupidity, how could anyone conclude that the latter could be reduced if the power of the former is progressively increased?

This is the question Lacan asked, albeit implicitly, in his 1972–1973 seminar *Encore*. Introducing François Recanati, a young French philosophy student, as the guest speaker on 12 December 1972, Lacan rekindled his formula of the analyst's discourse to wonder aloud what this discourse might produce on the side of the subject, that is, for the patient who enters the social bond as an analysand.[60] '[T]here is a status to be granted', he posited, 'to this new discourse [the analyst's discourse] and to its approach to stupidity [*la bêtise*]. Surely it comes closer, since in other discourses stupidity is what one flees . . . Where, in analytic discourse, is the sublimity of stupidity?'[61] As so often, Lacan did not provide an answer to his own question, yet the formula of the analyst's discourse he had constructed three years earlier indicates unambiguously what Lacan was alluding to: the fact that in the analyst's discourse the place of the (discursive) product is occupied by a master signifier (S_1).[62] What does it mean, then, for the discourse of the analyst to result in the product of a master signifier? How are we to understand the function of a master signifier in the place of the discursive product? Counter-intuitively, Lacan was not suggesting here that the prolonged process of a psychoanalytic treatment crystallizes, on the side of the analysand, into the conscious appearance of the ultimate thought, the cardinal word-representation, or the central sound image (signifier) that may be held responsible for all the stupidities that led the patient to start the process in the first place, even less that this 'entering into consciousness' of the master key would unlock the mystery of all the patient's trials and tribulations. If anything, he was insinuating that it was exactly the opposite. Like all human stupidities, the patient's symptoms are conditioned by an intricate symbolic network of representations (signifiers), a firmly established body of (repressed, unconscious) knowledge (S_2), which is controlled by a master signifier (S_1). The place of the product in the discourse of the analyst is simultaneously an instance of gains and a locus of loss; what patients stand to gain from the process is tantamount to what the process allows them to lose. Insofar as the master signifier occupies the place of product/gain qua loss in the analyst's discourse, patients are thus not being given the key to unlock their secrets and the key to their destiny, but relieved (delivered) from the injunction that has been keeping their secret under lock and key. Put differently, by situating the master signifier in the place of the product in the analyst's discourse, Lacan intimated that whatever power and meaning would have been accorded to a core representation in the patient's mind, the analytic process results in a gradual evaporation of the representation's authoritative, controlling force. Accordingly, the master signifier does not become more meaningful, but the overpowering meaning that had been attached to it becomes more and more nonsensical.[63] This is why Lacan could say that the analyst's discourse hangs together 'by basing itself on the dimension of stupidity'.[64] And when the master signifier is rendered stupid, the body of knowledge it has been ruling, organizing and structuring also becomes newly stupid, in the sense that its semantic spectrum becomes more creatively elastic, less disturbingly constrained, more inherently open-ended and less ponderously formulaic.

So, what does it mean for something or someone to be (called) stupid? For all that psychoanalysis has contributed, as morosophy, to our understanding of stupidity, the question remains as astute as it has ever been. But one additional, multilayered answer has imposed itself since the day Freud questioned Charcot about the nonsensicality of the hysterical symptoms the French master was demonstrating in his patients at the Salpêtrière. Stupidity is what drives people to consult psychoanalysts, especially after they have heard that the medical discourse cannot clarify the nature and identify the cause of their ailments; 'symptom-googling' has made them more addled and upset; and they themselves and/or their loved ones have reached the end of their tether. Stupidity is what psychoanalysts take seriously, even if they are not explicitly addressed as, or presenting themselves as, professors of stupidity who are capable of taking the stupidities away with a quick, ingenious sleight of hand. Stupidity is what psychoanalysts themselves epitomize and are expected to maintain, all the more so as most of their patients employ their own stupidities, and their ostensible lack of knowledge about what could have possibly triggered them, as a pretext for seeing their psychoanalysts as very knowledgeable people, expert clinicians, highly qualified practitioners or (as Lacan would have called them) subjects supposed to know.[65] Stupidity is another name for the position the psychoanalyst occupies in the treatment. Stupidity is what analysts in training should be taught by the hoary eminences in psychoanalytic training institutions. Most importantly, though, when they decide to initiate a clinical process, stupidity is what analysts aim for in the final instance. Stupidity is the best a patient may expect from a psychoanalytic treatment, at its end.

NOTES

1. On Galileo's famous recantation of heliocentrism before the Roman Inquisition, which refused to compromise on the absolute truth of the Holy Scriptures, see, for example, Thomas F. Mayer, *The Trial of Galileo, 1612–1633* (Toronto, Buffalo and London: The University of Toronto Press, 2012); Maurice A. Finocchiaro, *On Trial For Reason: Science, Religion, and Culture in the Galileo Affair* (Oxford and New York, NY: Oxford University Press, 2019).

2. World Health Organisation (Ed.), *International Classification of Diseases*, Vols 1 & 2 (Geneva: World Health Organisation, 1979). Following the initial release of these volumes, various revised editions of the general classification were issued under the heading 'Clinical Modification' (CM), and in quite a few cases, the volumes were also reissued with 'amendments and extensions' for specific countries. However, for all I have been able to establish, no substantive changes were made to the 'mental retardation' category in any of these revisions. The label was also retained in the tenth revision of the *ICD*, which was first released in 1994, as well as in the simultaneously published fourth edition of the *Diagnostic and Statistical Manual of Mental Disorders* (*DSM-IV*) and in the *DSM-IV Text Revision* of 2000, both courtesy of the American Psychiatric Association. However, two years after the publication of the *ICD-10*, the World Health Organisation published a separate *ICD-10 Guide for Mental Retardation* [*sic*], in which it was stated at the bottom of each of the document's eighty-two pages that the terms 'retardation' and 'retarded' were 'under consideration for a change in *ICD-11*'. When the *ICD-11* was published in 2019, mental retardation was indeed replaced with 'disorders of intellectual development', yet the debate continues whether these particular disorders should

be classified as a health condition, which is what is being implied by their inclusion in the *ICD*, or as a disability. The latter term is employed in the fifth edition of the *DSM*, originally published in 2013, alongside 'Intellectual Developmental Disorder'. For 'mental retardation' in the *ICD-10*, see https://www.who.int/classifications/ icd/icdonlineversions/en/. For the 'disorders of intellectual development' in the *ICD-11*, see https://icd.who.int/browse11/l-m/en#/http://id.who.int/icd/entity/605267007. See also World Health Organisation (Ed.), *ICD-10 Guide for Mental Retardation* (Geneva: World Health Organisation, 1996); American Psychiatric Association (Ed.), *Diagnostic and Statistical Manual of Mental Disorders*, 4th Edition (*DSM-IV*) (Washington, DC: American Psychiatric Association, 1994), 39–46; American Psychiatric Association (Ed.), *Diagnostic and Statistical Manual of Mental Disorders*, 4th Edition Text Revision (*DSM-IV TR*) (Washington, DC: American Psychiatric Association, 2000), 41–49; American Psychiatric Association (Ed.), *Diagnostic and Statistical Manual of Mental Disorders*, 5th Edition (*DSM-V*) (Washington, DC: American Psychiatric Association, 2013), 33–41. For background information on the replacement of 'mental retardation' in the *ICD-11* and the ongoing debate as to the precise status of 'disorders of intellectual development', see Luis Salvador-Carulla and Marco Bertelli, "'Mental Retardation' or 'Intellectual Disability': Time for a Conceptual Change," *Psychopathology* 41, no. 1 (2008): 10–16; Marco O. Bertelli, Kerim Munir, James Harris and Luis Salvador-Carulla, "'Intellectual Developmental Disorders': Reflections on the International Consensus Document for Redefining 'Mental Retardation-Intellectual Disability' in *ICD–11*," *Advances in Mental Health and Intellectual Disabilities* 10, no. 1 (2016): 36–58; Luis Salvador-Carulla, Marco Bertelli and Rafael Martínez-Leal, "The Road to 11th Edition of the *International Classification of Diseases*: Trajectories of Scientific Consensus and Contested Science in the Classification of Intellectual Disability/Intellectual Developmental Disorders," *Current Opinion in Psychiatry* 31, no. 2 (2018): 79–87.

3. Lucius Annaeus Seneca, "To Serenus on the Firmness of the Wise Man," in *Moral Essays*, Vol. 1. Trans. John W. Basore (Cambridge, MA and London: Harvard University Press, 1928), 80–81.

4. Lucius Annaeus Seneca, *Letters on Ethics*. Trans. Margaret Graver and A. A. Long (Chicago, IL and London: The University of Chicago Press, 2015), 449.

5. "The First Epistle of Paul the Apostle to the Corinthians," in *The Bible, Authorized King James Version with Apocrypha* (Oxford and New York, NY: Oxford University Press, 1997), 218. Without entering into a debate on Christian stupidity and the kingdom of heaven, Paul's statement appears to contradict Jesus's maxim in Matthew 5.3, where it is stated: 'Μακάριοι οι πτωχοί τω πνεύματι, ότι αυτών εστί η βασιλεία των ουρανών' (Blessed *are* the poor in spirit [πτωχοί τω πνεύματι]: for theirs is the kingdom of heaven). See "The Gospel According to St. Matthew," in *The Bible, Authorized King James Version with Apocrypha* (Oxford and New York, NY: Oxford University Press, 1997), 6. My thanks to Nektaria Pouli for alerting me to the passage from Matthew and for discussing the resonances of the πτωχοί τω πνεύματι with me.

6. "The First Epistle of Paul the Apostle to the Corinthians", 209.

7. The scholarly literature on Paul's paradigm of the 'holy fool' and the spiritual value of 'foolishness for Christ', which constituted the foundation for various religious orders and impacted upon the teachings of Francis of Assisi, Erasmus and Ignatius of Loyola, among others, is so vast that no selection could ever do justice to the embarrassment of riches. However, readers interested in pursuing the principle's ramifications will definitely benefit from John Saward, *Perfect Fools: Folly for Christ's Sake in Catholic and Orthodox Spirituality* (Oxford and New York, NY: Oxford University Press, 1980) and Sergey A. Ivanov, *Holy Fools in Byzantium and Beyond.* Trans. Simon Franklin (Oxford and New York, NY: Oxford University Press, 2006).

8. Shaoni Bhattacharya, "Stupidity Should Be Cured, Says DNA Discoverer," *New Scientist,* 28 February 2003, available at https://www.newscientist.com/article/dn3451-stupidity-should-be-cured-says-dna-discoverer/, accessed on 14 September 2020. Shocking as Watson's claims may have been, especially since they came from the mouth of an alleged genius, his hereditarian view on stupidity and intelligence was everything but new, because it simply rekindled perspectives first advocated by the American psychologist Henry Herbert Goddard during the early twentieth century. Apart from being credited with the rather dubious honour of having introduced the term 'moron' in the scientific vocabulary of intelligence testing, Goddard popularized the Binet IQ scale in the United States and championed large-scale eugenics programmes for removing morons from the gene pool, which subsequently informed American restrictions upon immigration and compulsory sterilization of the mentally unfit. See Stephen Jay Gould, *The Mismeasure of Man* (New York, NY and London: W. W. Norton & Company, 1981), 146–233; Stephen Jay Gould, "Carrie Buck's Daughter," in *The Flamingo's Smile: Reflections in Natural History* (Harmondsworth: Penguin, 1991), 306–318; Paul Lombardo, *Three Generations, No Imbeciles: Eugenics, the Supreme Court, and Buck v. Bell* (Baltimore, MD and London: The Johns Hopkins University Press, 2008).

9. Marilyn Simmons and Bruce Stillman, "Statement by Cold Spring Harbor Laboratory addressing Remarks by Dr James D. Watson in 'American Masters: Decoding Watson'," available at https://www.cshl.edu/statement-by-cold-spring-harbor-laboratory-addressing-remarks-by-dr-james-d-watson-in-american-masters-decoding-watson/, accessed on 9 September 2020.

10. Heinrich Cornelius Agrippa von Nettesheim, "Ad encomium asini digressio, in *De incertitudine et vanitate scientiarum declamatio invectiva* (The Hague: Adriaen Vlacq, 1662), cc4 – my translation. For more detailed readings of Agrippa's encomium of the ass, see, for example, Barbara C. Bowen, "Cornelius Agrippa's *De Vanitate*: Polemic or Paradox?", *Bibliothèque d'Humanisme et Renaissance* 23, no. 2 (1972): 249–56; Frances A. Yates, "The Occult Philosophy and Magic: Henry Cornelius Agrippa," in *Selected Works, Vol. VII: The Occult Philosophy in the Elizabethan Age* (London and New York, NY: Routledge, 1979), 37–47; Marc van der Poel, *Cornelius Agrippa: The Humanist Theologian and his Declamations* (Leiden: Brill, 1997), 99–102.

11. Giordano Bruno, *The Cabala of Pegasus*, Trans. Sidney L. Sondergard and Madison U. Sowell (New Haven, CT and London: Yale University Press, 2002),

39 and 26. For excellent disquisitions on Bruno's theory of asininity, see Vincenzo Spampanato, *Giordano Bruno e la letteratura dell'asino* (Portici: Premiato Stab. Tip. Vesuvio di E. della Torre, 1904); Frances A. Yates, *Giordano Bruno and the Hermetic Tradition* (London: Routledge and Kegan Paul, 1964), 285–326; Nuccio Ordine, *Giordano Bruno and the Philosophy of the Ass*, Trans. Henryk Baranski and Arielle Saiber (New Haven, CT and London: Yale University Press, 1996). In 1584, Bruno had already composed a *Sonnet in Praise of the Ass*, whose first lines ran as follows: "Blest asininity, blest ignorance,/o blest stupidity, pious devotion,/Able alone to set good souls in motion/That human wit and study can't advance", cited in Ingrid D. Rowland, *Giordano Bruno: Philosopher/Heretic* (Chicago, IL and London: The University of Chicago Press, 2008), 81. As Rowland points out, asininity in Bruno's works did not have the same resonances as *asinità*, which 'incorporated both the stubborn stupidity of pure ego and the divine simplicity of pure ignorance' and which was generally employed in a derogatory sense as the standard epithet of incorrigible pedantic figures occupying positions of power. See Rowland, *Giordano Bruno*, 79–80.

12. Carl Gustav Jung, "Paracelsus as a Spiritual Phenomenon," in *The Collected Works of C. G. Jung, Vol. 13: Alchemical Studies*. Ed. William McGuire. Trans. R. F. C. Hull (London: Routledge and Kegan Paul, 1967), 180. For an excellent, recent study of the life and works of Paracelsus, see Bruce T. Moran, *Paracelsus: An Alchemical Life* (London: Reaktion Books, 2019).

13. Robert Musil, "On Stupidity," in *Precision and Soul: Essays and Addresses*. Trans. Burton Pike and David S. Luft (Chicago, IL and London: The University of Chicago Press, 1990), 268–86.

14. Musil, *On Stupidity*, 284. Musil's 'intelligent stupidity' comes very close to Bruno's *asinità*, although it simultaneously reflects the gradual restriction of stupidity to measures of intelligence during the nineteenth century. Five years before Musil's lecture, in what is widely considered to be the first serious study of human stupidity in English, the American psychologist Walter B. Pitkin also stated that 'high abilities are often linked with serious stupidity' and this paradoxical confluence of genius and stupidity has now become a commonplace. See Walter B. Pitkin, *A Short Introduction to the History of Human Stupidity* (New York, NY: Simon & Schuster, 1932), 8; Robert J. Sternberg (Ed.), *Why Smart People Can Be So Stupid* (New Haven, CT and London: Yale University Press, 2002); Mario Livio, *Brilliant Blunders: From Darwin to Einstein—Colossal Mistakes by Great Scientists that Changed our Understanding of Life and the Universe* (New York, NY and London: Simon & Schuster, 2013); Theodore Dalrymple, *In Praise of Folly: The Blind-Spots of Our Mind* (London: Gibson Square Books, 2019). The title of Pitkin's book is sublimely ironic because it comes in at six hundred, densely printed pages. If I also wanted to draw the reader's attention to the volume by the arch-conservative psychiatrist cum critic Dalrymple here, it is mainly because its cover is adorned with the image of a sweet donkey, which demonstrates that the trope of the ass as an emblem of (wise) stupidity remains prevalent to this day. Other than that, his book focuses almost exclusively on the bizarre ideas of rather obscure authors of volumes Dalrymple himself picked up in some second-hand bookstores while on a trip to South-West Wales. In fact, without

acknowledging that he 'borrowed' his title from Erasmus and without elaborating on the donkey, the book is primarily about and in praise of himself, although his own blind spots clearly prevented him from recognizing the autobiographical nature of his work. See Desiderius Erasmus, *The Praise of Folly*. 2nd Edition. Trans. Clarence H. Miller (New Haven, CT and London, Yale University Press, 2003). For a fascinating historical exploration of changing conceptions of stupidity in the Western world, from the early eighteenth century until the present time, see Simon Jarrett, *Those They Called Idiots: The Idea of the Disabled Mind from 1700 to the Present Day* (London: Reaktion Books, 2020).

15. Musil, *On Stupidity*, 270.

16. See, for example, Eithne Wilkins and Ernst Kaiser, "A Conversation with Robert Musil", *The Transatlantic Review* no. 8 (1961): 9–24. Wilkins and Kaiser clarify in their preface to the transcript that theirs is an imaginary conversation, but that all the words spoken by Musil were taken from his published writings and manuscripts.

17. I am borrowing the term 'morosophy' from Erasmus, whose Folly at some point declaimed: 'Ingratum me Hercle et hoc hominum genus, qui cum maxime sint nostrae factionis, tamen apud vulgum cognominis nostri sic pudet, ut id passim aliis magni probri vice obiiciant. Proinde istos, cum sint *μωρότατοι* re, caeterum sophi ac Thaletes videri velint, nonne iure optimo *μωροσόφους* illos appellabimus?' In Clarence H. Miller's translation: 'An ingrateful crew if there ever was one: they are among my most loyal followers but are so ashamed of my name in public that they are always hurling it at the heads of others as a mark of the greatest opprobrium. Now I ask you, since these wretches are *most foolish* in fact but try to pass themselves off as wisemen and deep philosophers, what more fitting title could we find for them than "*foolosophers*"?' See Desiderii Erasmi Roterodami, "Moriae Encomium," in *Opera Omnia—Ordinis Quarti, Tomus Tertius* (Amsterdam and Oxford: North-Holland Publishing Company, 1974), ed. Clarence H., 74; Desiderius Erasmus, *The Praise of Folly*, 13. In all likelihood, Erasmus himself had taken the word from Lucian's *Ἀλέξανδρος ἢ Ψευδόμαντις* (*Alexander the False Prophet*), in which it appears as *τῶν μωροσόφων* (learned idiots), and which Erasmus had translated into Latin in 1505. See Lucian, "Alexander the False Prophet," in *The Works of Lucian*, Vol. IV, trans. A. M. Harmon (Cambridge, MA: Harvard University Press, 1961), 226–27; C. R. Thompson, "Some Greek and Grecized Words in Renaissance Latin", *The American Journal of Philology*, 64, no. 3 (1943): 333–35. Forty-two years after the first publication of Erasmus' *Praise of Folly*, the word morosophy was used as the title of an emblem book by Guillaume de la Perrière. In 2001, it was employed again by Matthijs van Boxsel – the world's leading expert on all things stupid – although van Boxsel never uses it with reference to psychoanalysis. The word also appears in a recent book by Steven Connor, yet Connor glosses it as 'the logos of the illogical, . . . a wise foolishness and a foolish or duncical philosophy', in an attempt to make sense of the μωροὶ διὰ Χριστόν. See Guillaume de la Perrière, *La morosophie* (Lyons: Macé Bonhomme, 1553); Matthijs van Boxsel, *Morosofie. Dwaze wijzen en wijze dwazen in Nederland en Vlaanderen* (Amsterdam: Querido, 2001); Matthijs van Boxsel, *The Encyclopaedia of Stupidity*. Trans. Arnold and Erica Pomerans (London: Reaktion

Books, 2003); Steven Connor, *The Madness of Knowledge: On Wisdom, Ignorance and Fantasies of Knowing* (London: Reaktion Books, 2019), 261.

18. Leopold Loewenfeld, *Über die Dummheit. Eine Umschau im Gebiete menschlicher Unzulänglichkeit* (Wiesbaden: Verlag von J. F. Bergmann, 1909).

19. In 1895, Freud published 'On the Grounds for Detaching a Particular Syndrome from Neurasthenia under the Description "Anxiety Neurosis"' in the *Neurologisches Centralblatt*. Shortly afterwards, Löwenfeld criticized Freud's views in a paper for the *Münchener Medicinische Wochenschrift*, to which Freud in turn replied in an article in the *Wiener klinische Rundschau* titled 'A Reply to Criticisms of my Paper on Anxiety Neurosis'. The synopsis of *The Interpretation of Dreams* entitled 'On Dreams' was originally written for *Grenzfragen des Nerven- und Seelenlebens*, a book series edited by Löwenfeld and Hans Kurella. In 1904, Freud contributed 'Freud's Psycho-Analytic Procedure' to Löwenfeld's *Die psychischen Zwangserscheinungen*, a volume which Freud later described as an 'exhaustive study' and 'the standard work' on obsessional neurosis, in a footnote to his case study of the Rat Man. One year later, Freud wrote 'My Views on the Part Played by Sexuality in the Aetiology of the Neuroses' for the fourth edition of Löwenfeld's *Sexualleben und Nervenleiden*. See Sigmund Freud, "On the Grounds for Detaching a Particular Syndrome from Neurasthenia under the Description 'Anxiety Neurosis'," in *The Standard Edition of the Complete Psychological Works of Sigmund Freud*, Vol. 3. Ed. and Trans. James Strachey (London: The Hogarth Press and the Institute of Psycho-Analysis, 1962), 85–115; Leopold Löwenfeld, "Ueber die Verknüpfung neurasthenischer und hysterischer Symptome in Anfallsform nebst Bemerkungen über die Freud'sche 'Angstneurose'," *Münchener Medicinische Wochenschrift* 42, no. 13 (1895): 282–85; Sigmund Freud, "A Reply to Criticisms of My Paper on Anxiety Neurosis," in *The Standard Edition of the Complete Psychological Works of Sigmund Freud*, Vol. 3. Ed. and Trans. James Strachey (London: The Hogarth Press and the Institute of Psycho-Analysis, 1962), 121–39; Sigmund Freud, "On Dreams," in *The Standard Edition of the Complete Psychological Works of Sigmund Freud*, Vol. 5. Ed. and Trans. James Strachey (London: The Hogarth Press and the Institute of Psycho-Analysis, 1958), 629–86; Sigmund Freud, "Freud's Psycho-Analytic Procedure," in *The Standard Edition of the Complete Psychological Works of Sigmund Freud*, Vol. 7. Ed. and Trans. James Strachey (London: The Hogarth Press and the Institute of Psycho-Analysis, 1953), 247–54; Sigmund Freud, "My Views on the Part Played by Sexuality in the Aetiology of the Neuroses," in *The Standard Edition of the Complete Psychological Works of Sigmund Freud*, Vol. 7. Ed. and Trans. James Strachey (London: The Hogarth Press and the Institute of Psycho-Analysis, 1953), 269–79; Sigmund Freud, "Notes Upon a Case of Obsessional Neurosis," in *The Standard Edition of the Complete Psychological Works of Sigmund Freud*, Vol. 10. Ed. and Trans. James Strachey (London: The Hogarth Press and the Institute of Psycho-Analysis, 1955), 221 – footnote 2. For Freud's own recollection of his public dispute with Löwenfeld, see Sigmund Freud, "Introductory Lectures on Psycho-Analysis. Lecture XVI: Psychoanalysis and Psychiatry," in *The Standard Edition of the Complete Psychological Works of Sigmund Freud*, Vol. 16. Ed. and Trans. James Strachey (London: The Hogarth Press and the Institute of Psycho-Analysis, 1963), 245. For an

obituary of Löwenfeld and his significance within the psychoanalytic community, see R., "Hofrat Leopold Löwenfeld," *Internationale Zeitschrift für Psychoanalyse* 10, no. 1 (1924): 103.

20. See L. Pierce Clark and T. E. Uniker, "A Psychological Study of the Nature of the Idiot," *Archives of Psychoanalysis* 1 (1926): 93–137; L. Pierce Clark, "The Psychology of Idiocy," *The Psychoanalytic Review* 19, no. 3 (1932): 257–69; L. Pierce Clark, "Psychoanalysis and Mental Arrest," *Proceedings and Addresses of the American Association for the Study of the Feeble-Minded* 37 (1932): 316–25; Karl Landauer, "Zur psychosexuellen Genese der Dummheit," *Zeitschrift für Sexualwissenschaft und Sexualpolitik* 16 (1929): 12–22 and 87–96; Karl Landauer, "Intelligenz und Dummheit," in *Das psychoanalytische Volksbuch*, Eds. Paul Federn and Heinrich Meng (Bern: Huber, 1939), 160–74.

21. See Berta Bornstein, "Zur Psychogenese der Pseudodebilität," *Internationale Zeitschrift für Psychoanalyse* 16, nos. 3–4 (1930): 378–99; Edmund Bergler, "Zur Problematik der Pseudodebilität," *Internationale Zeitschrift für Psychoanalyse* 18, no. 4 (1932): 528–38; Sandor S. Feldman, "Flucht in die Dummheit. Eine psychoanalytische Studie," *Psychoanalytische Praxis: Vierteljahrsschrift für die aktive Methode der Psychoanalyse* 2 (1932): 186–95. In *The Natural History of Stupidity*, Paul Tabori credited Alexander Feldmann [*sic*] as the only psychoanalyst who 'looked fearlessly upon stupidity'. Be that is it may, Feldman is now mainly remembered for his rather dubious, and demonstrably dumb views on the aetiology and psychoanalytic treatment of homosexuality. See Paul Tabori, *The Natural History of Stupidity* (New York, NY: Barnes & Noble Books, 1993): 2; Sandor S. Feldman, "On Homosexuality," in *Perversions: Psychodynamics and Therapy*, Eds. Sandor Lorand and Michael Balint (New York, NY: Gramercy Books, 1956), 71–96; Jonathan Dollimore, *Sexual Dissidence: Augustine to Wilde, Freud to Foucault* (Oxford: Clarendon Press, 1991), 171–73.

22. Otto Fenichel, *The Psychoanalytic Theory of Neurosis*, 50th Anniversary Edition (New York, NY and London: W. W. Norton & Company, 1996), 181.

23. Fenichel, *The Psychoanalytic Theory of Neurosis*, 576.

24. The most detailed record of Freud's stay in Paris, from 13 October 1885 until 26 February 1886, is contained in his almost daily letters to his fiancée Martha Bernays, which are preserved in the Sigmund Freud Papers at the Library of Congress in Washington, DC. The letters covering the period of Freud's Parisian studies are forthcoming in German as the fifth and final volume in the complete edition of these '*Brautbriefe*'. For an excellent discussion of this episode in Freud's life, see Peter Gay, *Freud: A Life for Our Time* (New York NY and London: W. W. Norton & Company, 1988), 47–53. For a more wide-ranging study of the Parisian origins of Freud's outlook on hysteria and neurosis in general, see André Bolzinger, *Freud et les Parisiens* (Paris: Campagne Première, 2002).

25. Sigmund Freud, "Charcot," in *The Standard Edition of the Complete Psychological Works of Sigmund Freud*, Vol. 3. Ed. and Trans. James Strachey (London: The Hogarth Press and the Institute of Psycho-Analysis, 1962), 7–23.

26. Sigmund Freud, Charcot, 13. In his obituary, Freud attributed the remark to 'one of us [students]', yet in a footnote to his translation of Charcot's *Leçons*

du mardi, he seemed to take full responsibility for it. See Jean-Martin Charcot, *Poliklinische Vorträge. I. Band: Schuljahr 1887–1888*. Trans. with notes Sigmund Freud (Leipzig and Wien: Franz Deuticke, 1894), 210 footnote 1.

27. Sigmund Freud, Charcot, 13. The aphorism reappeared in Sigmund Freud, "Fragment of an Analysis of a Case of Hysteria," in *The Standard Edition of the Complete Psychological Works of Sigmund Freud*, Vol. 7. Ed. and Trans. James Strachey (London: The Hogarth Press and the Institute of Psycho-Analysis, 1953), 115; Sigmund Freud, "Introductory Lectures on Psycho-Analysis. Lecture IX: The Censorship of Dreams," in *The Standard Edition of the Complete Psychological Works of Sigmund Freud*, Vol. 15. Ed. and Trans. James Strachey (London: The Hogarth Press and the Institute of Psycho-Analysis, 1963), 145; Sigmund Freud, "An Autobiographical Study," in *The Standard Edition of the Complete Psychological Works of Sigmund Freud*, Vol. 20. Ed. and Trans. James Strachey (London: The Hogarth Press and the Institute of Psycho-Analysis, 1962), 13.

28. For Charcot's own changing conceptions of hysteria, see Marcel Gauchet and Gladys Swain, *Le vrai Charcot. Les chemins imprévus de l'inconscient* (Paris: Calmann-Lévy, 1997). For broader studies of Charcot's life and ideas, see Jacques Gasser, *Aux origines du cerveau moderne. Localisations, langage et mémoire dans l'œuvre de Charcot* (Paris: Fayard, 1999); Catherine Bouchara, *Charcot. Une vie avec l'image* (Paris: Philippe Rey, 2013).

29. Hysteria has long since been removed from the medical classifications. Patients presenting with medically inexplicable mental and bodily symptoms are now routinely diagnosed as suffering from a 'functional neurological disorder' and referred to a mental health care professional on that basis.

30. Speaking to the French journalist Raymond Recouly in 1923, Freud stated: 'The starting-point [for psychoanalysis] . . . is to be found in Charcot's lessons at the Salpêtrière.' See Raymond Recouly, "A Visit to Freud," in *Freud As We Knew Him*. Ed. Hendrik M. Ruitenbeek (Detroit, MI: Wayne State University Press, 1973), 58. For dreams, slips of the tongue, bungled actions and jokes, see Sigmund Freud, "The Interpretation of Dreams," in *The Standard Edition of the Complete Psychological Works of Sigmund Freud*, Vols. 4/5. Ed. and Trans. James Strachey (London: The Hogarth Press and the Institute of Psycho-Analysis, 1958); Sigmund Freud, "The Psychopathology of Everyday Life," in *The Standard Edition of the Complete Psychological Works of Sigmund Freud*, Vol. 6. Ed. and Trans. James Strachey (London: The Hogarth Press and the Institute of Psycho-Analysis, 1960); Sigmund Freud, "Jokes and Their Relation to the Unconscious," in *The Standard Edition of the Complete Psychological Works of Sigmund Freud*, Vol. 8. Ed. and Trans. James Strachey (London: The Hogarth Press and the Institute of Psycho-Analysis, 1960).

31. In the final paragraph of *Studies on Hysteria*, Freud already conceded that psychoanalysis can probably do no more than transform hysterical misery into the unhappiness of everyday life. Even though the technique of psychoanalysis was revised and fine-tuned over the years, he never compromised on this initial belief. If anything, as he gained more clinical experience and his theoretical views progressed, he became even more sceptical as to the overall effectiveness of the psychoanalytic treatment, culminating in the pervasive therapeutic pessimism of the 1937 essay 'Analysis

Terminable and Interminable'. See Josef Breuer and Sigmund Freud, "Studies on Hysteria," in *The Standard Edition of the Complete Psychological Works of Sigmund Freud*, Vol. 2. Ed. and Trans. James Strachey (London: The Hogarth Press and the Institute of Psycho-Analysis, 1955), 305; Sigmund Freud, "Analysis Terminable and Interminable," in *The Standard Edition of the Complete Psychological Works of Sigmund Freud*, Vol. 23. Ed. and Trans. James Strachey (London: The Hogarth Press and the Institute of Psycho-Analysis, 1964), 209–53.

32. On Olga Hönig, see Mikkel Borch-Jacobsen, *Les patients de Freud. Destins* (Auxerre: Sciences Humaines Éditions, 2011), 74–79.

33. See Sigmund Freud, "The Sexual Enlightenment of Children (An Open Letter to Dr. M. Fürst)," in *The Standard Edition of the Complete Psychological Works of Sigmund Freud*, Vol. 9. Ed. and Trans. James Strachey (London: The Hogarth Press and the Institute of Psycho-Analysis, 1959), 129–39 and 134–35 in particular; Sigmund Freud, "On the Sexual Theories of Children," in *The Standard Edition of the Complete Psychological Works of Sigmund Freud*, Vol. 9. Ed. and Trans. James Strachey (London: The Hogarth Press and the Institute of Psycho-Analysis, 1959), 205–26.

34. Sigmund Freud, "Analysis of a Phobia in a Five-Year-Old Boy," in *The Standard Edition of the Complete Psychological Works of Sigmund Freud*, Vol. 10. Ed. and Trans. James Strachey (London: The Hogarth Press and the Institute of Psycho-Analysis, 1955), 1–149.

35. For critical commentaries on Freud's case study, its impact on the development of child analysis and biographical information on Herbert Graf, who would go on to become a famous opera producer, see Joseph William Slap, "Little Hans's Tonsillectomy," *The Psychoanalytic Quarterly* 30, no. 2 (1961): 259–61; Martin A. Silverman, "A Fresh Look at the Case of Little Hans," in *Freud and His Patients,* Eds. Mark Kanzer and Jules Glenn (New York, NY: Jason Aronson Inc., 1980), 95–120; Jules Glenn, "Freud's Advice to Hans' Father: The First Supervisory Sessions," in *Freud and His Patients,* Eds. Mark Kanzer and Jules Glenn (New York, NY: Jason Aronson Inc., 1980), 121–34; Josiane Praz, "Le Petit Hans et sa famille. Données historiques et biographiques," in *La sexualité infantile et ses mythes,* Eds. Jean Bergeret and Marcel Houser (Paris: Dunod, 2001), 121–39; Jean-Michel Quinodoz, "Analysis of a Phobia in a Five-Year-Old Boy ('Little Hans')," in *Reading Freud: A Chronological Exploration of Freud's Writings*. Trans. David Alcorn (London and New York, NY: Routledge, 2005), 78–87; Harold P. Blum, "Little Hans: A Centennial Review and Reconsideration," *Journal of the American Psychoanalytic Association* 55, no. 3 (2007): 749–65; Jerome C. Wakefield, "Max Graf's 'Reminiscences of Professor Sigmund Freud' Revisited: New Evidence from the Freud Archives," *The Psychoanalytic Quarterly* 76, no. 1 (2007): 149–92; Jean-Michel Vives, "'Little Hans': From His Phobic Episode to Becoming an Opera Director," *The International Journal of Psychoanalysis* 93, no. 4 (2012): 863–78. By far the most detailed analysis of the case study is to be found in Lacan's 1956–1957 seminar on object-relations: Jacques Lacan, *Le Séminaire. Livre IV: La relation d'objet.* Ed. Jacques-Alain Miller (Paris: du Seuil, 1994): 197–435.

36. Sigmund Freud, *Analysis of a Phobia*, 28. Although the German word '*Dummheit*' means stupidity, Strachey has translated it as 'nonsense', which would

render the German word '*Unsinn*'. In the more recent English translation of Freud's case study by Louise Adey Huish, '*Dummheit*' is translated inconsistently as 'silly', 'silly nonsense' and 'silly business', a decision that is all the more puzzling since the translator herself writes in her introduction that 'Freud's terms are deceptively simple'. See Sigmund Freud, "Analysis of a Phobia in a Five-Year-Old Boy ['Little Hans']," in *The 'Wolfman' and Other Cases*. Trans. Louise Adey Huish (London: Penguin Books, 2002), xxix, 21 and 46.

37. Sigmund Freud, *Analysis of a Phobia*, 30.

38. This principle does not apply in cases of psychosis, where the problem is exactly the opposite, notably that everything makes (too much) sense. As Daniel Paul Schreber wrote on three occasions in his *Memoirs of My Nervous Illness*: 'All nonsense cancels itself out' (*Aller Unsinn hebt sich auf*). See Daniel Paul Schreber, *Memoirs of My Nervous Illness*. Trans. and Ed. Ida Macalpine and Richard A. Hunter (New York, NY: New York Review Books, 2000), 168, 273 and 286.

39. Without entering into the clinical details of the case, it is noteworthy how it is only after Hans has rebranded his fear as a stupidity that he becomes interested in discovering how he 'got it' (*gekriegt hat*), in the sense of receiving or contracting it. At that point, Freud also becomes the professor who can take it away (*der dir die Dummheit wegnehmen kann*), as if the stupidity became an object in itself that could be part of an exchange and delivery process. In his *Seminar IV*, Lacan did not pay much attention to the term *Dummheit* as such, but noted how, at least in the French translation of Freud's case study, 'getting the stupidity' is rendered as '*attraper la bêtise*', whereby the verb '*attraper*' also invokes 'getting pregnant' (*attraper un enfant*), and thus at some stage of 'delivering' it. See Sigmund Freud, *Analysis of a Phobia*, 59 and 33; Jacques Lacan, *Le Séminaire. Livre IV*, 316–20 and 380.

40. The only time Freud saw Little Hans in person, during the afternoon of Monday, 30 March 1908, he effectively gave him a short lecture on the Oedipus complex, which ended with the words: 'Long before he was in the world . . . I [Professor Sigmund Freud] had known that a Little Hans would come who would be so fond of his mother that he would be bound to feel afraid of his father because of it.' Returning from Berggasse 19, Little Hans asked his father: 'Does the Professor talk to God . . . as he can tell all that beforehand?' See Sigmund Freud, "Analysis of a Phobia", 42–43. In the case of the Rat Man, Freud lectured his patient on the psychoanalytic theory of the displacement of affect as early as the fourth session. See Sigmund Freud, "Notes Upon a Case of Obsessional Neurosis," in *The Standard Edition of the Complete Psychological Works of Sigmund Freud*, Vol. 10. Ed. and Trans. James Strachey (London: The Hogarth Press and the Institute of Psycho-Analysis, 1955), 151–249.

41. Sigmund Freud, "From the History of an Infantile Neurosis," in *The Standard Edition of the Complete Psychological Works of Sigmund Freud*, Vol. 10. Ed. and Trans. James Strachey (London: The Hogarth Press and the Institute of Psycho-Analysis, 1955), 69.

42. Sigmund Freud, "Remembering, Repeating and Working-Through (Further Recommendations on the Technique of Psycho-Analysis II)," in *The Standard Edition of the Complete Psychological Works of Sigmund Freud*, Vol. 12. Ed. and Trans.

James Strachey (London: The Hogarth Press and the Institute of Psycho-Analysis, 1958), 155.

43. Sigmund Freud, "The Ego and the Id," in *The Standard Edition of the Complete Psychological Works of Sigmund Freud*, Vol. 19. Ed. and Trans. James Strachey (London: The Hogarth Press and the Institute of Psycho-Analysis, 1961), 49.

44. Sigmund Freud, "The Economic Problem of Masochism," in *The Standard Edition of the Complete Psychological Works of Sigmund Freud*, Vol. 19. Ed. and Trans. James Strachey (London: The Hogarth Press and the Institute of Psycho-Analysis, 1961), 166. A similar point appears in Lecture 32 of Freud's *New Introductory Lectures*: 'People in whom this unconscious sense of guilt is excessively strong betray themselves in analytic treatment by the negative therapeutic reaction which is so disagreeable from the prognostic point of view. When one has *given them* the solution of a symptom, which should normally be followed by at least its temporary disappearance, what they produce instead is a momentary exacerbation of the symptom and of the illness.' Sigmund Freud, "New Introductory Lectures on Psycho-Analysis. Lecture XXXII: Anxiety and Instinctual Life," in *The Standard Edition of the Complete Psychological Works of Sigmund Freud*, Vol. 22. Ed. and Trans. James Strachey (London: The Hogarth Press and the Institute of Psycho-Analysis, 1960), 109–10.

45. Sigmund Freud, "Analysis Terminable and Interminable," 233. The sentence in quotation marks alludes to a line from Goethe's *Faust*, in which the protagonist responds to the angels' chorus with the words '*Die Botschaft hör ich wohl, allein mir fehlt der Glaube*'. Stuart Atkins has translated it as 'Although I hear your gospel, I lack your faith'. See Johann Wolfgang von Goethe, *Faust I & II*. Ed. and Trans. Stuart Atkins (Princeton, NJ and London: Princeton University Press, 1994), 22.

46. On Freud's unshakeable belief in the universality of the Oedipus complex, in spite of Malinowski's evidence to the contrary, see, for example, Patrick S. Rivera, "'Freud's Speculations in Ethnology': A Reflection on Anthropology's Encounter with Psychoanalysis," *The International Journal of Psychoanalysis* 98, no. 3 (2017): 755–78. Given the topic of my essay, it might also be useful to mention that, on the occasion of a conference at New York University in March 1958, the American pragmatist philosopher Sidney Hook told the audience that he had once asked psychoanalysts what kind of evidence they would be 'prepared to accept which would lead them to declare in any specific case that a child did not have an Oedipus complex', and that the esteemed psychoanalyst Ernst Kris had responded to the question by saying that such a child 'would be one who acted like an idiot'. See Sidney Hook (Ed.), *Psychoanalysis, Scientific Method, and Philosophy* (New York, NY: New York University Press, 1959), 214; Murray L. Wax, "Oedipus as Normative? Freud's Complex, Hook's Query, Malinowski's Trobrianders, Stoller's Anomalies," *Journal of the American Academy of Psychoanalysis* 28, no. 1 (2000): 117–32. One of Freud's most bizarre justifications for refusing to abandon an idea, in this case his entirely speculative proposal of the death drive, occurs at the end of 'Beyond the Pleasure Principle', where he unapologetically declared:

> [P]eople are seldom impartial where ultimate things, the great problems of science and life, are concerned. Each of us is governed in such cases by deep-rooted internal prejudices,

into whose hands our speculation unwittingly plays. Since we have such good grounds for being distrustful, our attitude towards the results of our deliberations cannot well be other than one of cool benevolence [*ein kühles Wohlwollen*]. I hasten to add, however, that self-criticism such as this is far from binding one to any special tolerance towards dissentient opinions. It is perfectly legitimate to reject remorselessly [*unerbittlich*] theories which are contradicted by the very first steps in the analysis of observed facts, while yet being aware at the same time that the validity of one's own theory is only a provisional one.

See Sigmund Freud, "Beyond the Pleasure Principle," in *The Standard Edition of the Complete Psychological Works of Sigmund Freud*, Vol. 18. Ed. and Trans. James Strachey (London: The Hogarth Press and the Institute of Psycho-Analysis, 1955), 59–60.

47. Sigmund Freud, "On Beginning the Treatment (Further Recommendations on the Technique of Psychoanalysis I)," in *The Standard Edition of the Complete Psychological Works of Sigmund Freud*, Vol. 12. Ed. and Trans. James Strachey (London: The Hogarth Press and the Institute of Psycho-Analysis, 1958), 123.

48. Sigmund Freud, "On Beginning the Treatment," 123.

49. Sigmund Freud, "Recommendations to Physicians Practising Psycho-Analysis," in *The Standard Edition of the Complete Psychological Works of Sigmund Freud*, Vol. 12. Ed. and Trans. James Strachey (London: The Hogarth Press and the Institute of Psycho-Analysis, 1958), 114.

50. Sigmund Freud, "Recommendations to Physicians," 115. Freud made a similar point in Lecture 35 of the *New Introductory Lectures*, See Sigmund Freud, "New Introductory Lectures," 174.

51. Sigmund Freud, "Postscript to 'The Question of Lay Analysis'," in *The Standard Edition of the Complete Psychological Works of Sigmund Freud*, Vol. 20. Ed. and Trans. James Strachey (London: The Hogarth Press and the Institute of Psycho-Analysis, 1959), 256. For an in-depth discussion of Freud's 'conjunction' and its implications for psychoanalytic research, see Anna Ursula Dreher, *Foundations for Conceptual Research in Psychoanalysis*. Trans. Eva Ristl (London and New York, NY: Karnac Books, 2000), 37–64.

52. Jacques Lacan, *The Seminar. Book I: Freud's Papers on Technique (1953–'54)*. Ed. Jacques-Alain Miller. Trans. John Forrester (Cambridge: Cambridge University Press, 1988), 271 and 275. In his famous 'Rome discourse', Lacan indicated explicitly that he had adopted the passion of ignorance from the Buddhist tradition: Jacques Lacan, "The Function and Field of Speech and Language in Psychoanalysis," in *Écrits*. Trans. Bruce Fink (New York, NY: W. W. Norton & Company, 2006), 254. For a detailed consideration of ignorance in the *Dharmadhātustava* and other Indian spiritual treatises, see Donald S. Lopez, Jr., "Do Śrāvakas Understand Emptiness?" *Journal of Indian Philosophy* 16 (1988): 65–105. For discussions of the significance of the passion of ignorance in Lacan's work, see, for example, Alain Vanier, "Passion de l'ignorance," *Clinique Méditerranéennes* 70, no. 2 (2004): 59–66; Dany Nobus and Malcolm Quinn, *Knowing Nothing, Staying Stupid: Elements for a Psychoanalytic Epistemology* (London and New York, NY: Routledge, 2005), 20–35; Béatrice Gaillard, "Passion de l'ignorance. L'ignorance consentie ouvre les voies d'accès au (pas tout) savoir," *Essaim* 41, no. 2 (2018): 165–172.

53. Jacques Lacan, *The Seminar. Book I: Freud's Papers on Technique*, 278. As Lacan himself pointed out in a lecture at Sainte-Anne Hospital in Paris on 4 November 1971, he had borrowed the term *ignorantia docta* (or *docta ignorantia*) from the Renaissance theologian and philosopher Nicolaus Cusanus, who had introduced it in an eponymous 1440 book with reference to human beings' limited comprehension of the infinity of God and the determination of the universe. See Jacques Lacan, *Talking To Brick Walls*. Trans. Adrian R. Price (Medford, MA and Cambridge, 2017), 5; Nicolaus Cusanus, *On Learned Ignorance*. Trans. Jasper Hopkins (Minneapolis, MN: Arthur J. Banning Press, 1985). For a more detailed explanation of Cusanus' doctrine, including instructive comparisons with Buddhist thought, see Andrew Martin, *The Knowledge of Ignorance: From Genesis to Jules Verne* (Cambridge: Cambridge University Press, 1985), 29–42. Throughout his seminars and writings, Lacan continued to underscore the non-negotiable importance of learnt ignorance for the analyst's work. See, for example, Jacques Lacan, "Note italienne," in *Autres Écrits* (Paris: du Seuil, 2001), 309; Jacques Lacan, "De Rome 53 à Rome 67: La psychanalyse. Raison d'un échec," in *Autres Écrits* (Paris: du Seuil, 2001), 343; Jacques Lacan, "Introduction à l'édition allemande d'un premier volume des *Écrits*," in *Autres Écrits* (Paris: du Seuil, 2001), 558.

54. Jacques Lacan, "Variations on the Standard Treatment," in *Écrits*. Trans. Bruce Fink (New York, NY: W. W. Norton & Company, 2006), 297.

55. Jacques Lacan, "Variations on the Standard Treatment," 297. Much like the previous quotation, this passage appears in a section of the paper entitled 'What the Psychoanalyst Must Know: How to Ignore What He Knows'. As Lacan also disclosed in his 1971 lecture at Sainte-Anne, the idea of nonknowledge (*non-savoir*) had already benefited from the attention of Georges Bataille in quite a few of his writings. See Lacan, *Talking To Brick Walls*, 9; Georges Bataille, *The Unfinished System of Nonknowledge*. Ed. Stuart Kendall. Trans. Michelle Kendall and Stuart Kendall (Minneapolis, MN and London: University of Minnesota Press, 2001).

56. Jacques Lacan, *The Seminar. Book XVII: The Other Side of Psychoanalysis (1969–'70)*. Ed. Jacques-Alain Miller. Trans. Russell Grigg (New York, NY: W. W. Norton & Company, 2007), 35. Within the space of this essay, I cannot elaborate on Lacan's entire 'matheme' for the discourse of the analyst, let alone explain his theory of the four discourses. The secondary literature on Lacan's discourse theory, and the analyst's discourse in particular, is enormous, yet the uninitiated reader may start with Julien Quackelbeen, "The Psychoanalytic Discourse Theory of Jacques Lacan: Introduction and Application," *Studies in Psychoanalytic Theory* 3, no. 1 (1994): 21–43 and Paul Verhaeghe, "From Impossibility to Inability: Lacan's Theory of the Four Discourses," *The Letter: Lacanian Perspectives on Psychoanalysis* 4 (1995): 76–99. A general overview of Lacan's changing views on the analyst's position in the treatment and his formalization of the analyst's discourse in *Seminar XVII* can be found in Dany Nobus, *Jacques Lacan and the Freudian Practice of Psychoanalysis* (London and New York, NY: Brunner and Routledge, 2000), 56–105.

57. In the opening session of his 1976–1977 seminar, Lacan made a translinguistic pun by suggesting that the German term for the unconscious (*das Unbewußte*) could be rendered in French as '*l'une-bévue*', which may be retranslated into

English as 'the one-blunder'. In doing so, he condensed an argument he had already made in *Seminar XI*, when he changed the ancient medical maxim '*ablata causa tollitur effectus*' (the effects disappear when the cause is removed) into '*ablata cause tolluntur effectus*' (the absence of a cause enhances the effects). See Jacques Lacan, "L'insu que sait de l'une-bévue s'aile à mourre," *Ornicar?* 12/13 (1977): 4–16; Jacques Lacan, *The Seminar. Book XI: The Four Fundamental Concepts of Psychoanalysis*. Ed. Jacques-Alain Miller. Trans. Alan Sheridan (Harmondsworth: Penguin, 1994), 128. For a highly entertaining survey of the unconscious as a 'mental blunderbuss', see the posthumously published book by the Austrian-American psychoanalyst Edmund Bergler, *A Talent for Stupidity: The Psychology of the Bungler, the Incompetent and the Ineffectual* (New York, NY: International Universities Press, 1999). For the notion of 'knowledge in failure', see also Jacques Lacan, "Lituraterre," Trans. Dany Nobus, *Continental Philosophy Review* 46, no. 2 (2013), 329.

58. In the context of human stupidities being recognized, I cannot resist reminding the reader of the annual Darwin awards, even though they do not exactly count as 'therapeutic interventions'. Since roughly the mid-1980s, the American Darwin Awards Association has annually rewarded a small number of people around the world whose stupidity has been proven to be of an exceptionally high standard. In doing so, the organization intends to 'salute the improvement of the human genome by honouring those who accidentally remove themselves from it', whereby it is explicitly stated that all nominees should be 'free of mental defect'. One of the most notorious winners was the Brazilian priest Adelir Antõnio de Carli, aka Padre Baloeiro. Rather than describing his accomplishments here, I shall leave it to the reader to discover what earned him the coveted accolade. See https://darwinawards.com

59. Because the entire debacle is now in the public domain, I shall not be accused of entering into a polemic when I say that the most sublime example of how advanced knowledge of stupidity by no means erects a barrier against it has been offered by Avital Ronell, one of the leading academic experts on stupidity. After having written a seminal treatise on stupidity, Ronell was suspended from her professorship at New York University for the academic year 2018–2019, because she was found guilty of stalking and sexually harassing a male graduate student over a period of three years, during which time she had acted as his advisor. In her defence, many of her most illustrious academic friends then signed a letter in which it was stated that she should be exonerated owing to the significance of her academic contributions. In this particular case, one person's stupidity was tackled with repeated salvos of additional stupidity – one of her supporters, who shall remain nameless here, even went so far as to apologize for the utter stupidity of defending Ronell's stupidity on the grounds of her academic reputation – yet evidently not in a psychoanalytic sense. See Avital Ronell, *Stupidity* (Urbana and Chicago, IL: University of Illinois Press, 2002); Slavoj Žižek, "Is Avital Ronell Really Toxic?" in *A Left That Dares to Speak Its Name: Untimely Interventions* (Cambridge and Medford, MA: Polity, 2020), 265–70.

60. Recanati's intervention was not included when the text of Lacan's seminar was published in 1975, but was released as a stand-alone essay the same year: François Recanati, "Prédication et ordination," *Scilicet* 5 (1975): 61–87.

61. Jacques Lacan, *The Seminar. Book XX: On Feminine Sexuality, the Limits of Love and Knowledge*, 13.

62. In a footnote to this section of the seminar, Bruce Fink has helpfully included the full formula of the analyst's discourse, also providing the gloss that 'Lacan is suggesting here that the S_1 produced by analytic discourse is equivalent to stupidity or nonsense (*la bêtise*)'. See Lacan, *The Seminar. Book XX: On Feminine Sexuality, the Limits of Love and Knowledge*, 13 – footnote 47. Because the French word for stupidity (*bêtise*) also connotes animality, *bête* also meaning beast or animal, Jacques Derrida devoted a substantial portion of his 2001–2003 seminars on *The Beast and the Sovereign* to a deconstructive reading of it, also paying attention to Lacan's comments on *bêtise*. See Jacques Derrida, *The Beast and the Sovereign*, Vol. 1. Eds. Michel Lisse, Marie-Louise Mallet and Ginette Michaud, Trans. Geoffrey Bennington (Chicago, IL and London: The University of Chicago Press, 2009); Jacques Derrida, *The Beast and the Sovereign*, Vol. 2. Eds. Michel Lisse, Marie-Louise Mallet and Ginette Michaud, Trans. Geoffrey Bennington (Chicago, IL and London: The University of Chicago Press, 2011).

63. Lacan had made a similar remark in *Seminar XI*, yet the meaning of the sentence in which he did so is turned into its opposite in the English translation of it. In the original French text, Lacan comments: '*L'interprétation ne vise pas tellement le sens que de réduire les signifiants dans leur non-sens pour que nous puissions retrouver les déterminants de toute la conduite du sujet.*' Whereas Alan Sheridan has translated this phrase as 'Interpretation is directed not so much at the meaning as towards reducing the non-meaning of the signifiers, so that we may rediscover the determinants of the subject's entire behaviour', it should have been rendered as: 'Interpretation is not so much directed at meaning, but at reducing the signifiers into their nonsensicality, in order for us to rediscover the determinants of the subject's entire behaviour.' See Jacques Lacan, *Le Séminaire. Livre XI: Les quatre concepts fondamentaux de la psychanalyse (1964)*, Ed. Jacques-Alain Miller (Paris: du Seuil, 1973), 192; Lacan, *The Seminar. Book XI: The Four Fundamental Concepts of Psychoanalysis*, 212.

64. Lacan, *The Seminar. Book XX: On Feminine Sexuality, the Limits of Love and Knowledge*, 12.

65. 'Subject supposed to know' (*sujet supposé savoir*), which could also be rendered as 'supposed subject of knowing' is Lacan's formula for transference. See, for example, Jacques Lacan, "Proposition of 9 October 1967 on the Psychoanalyst of the School," Trans. Russell Grigg, a*nalysis* 6 (1995): 1–13. For 'supposed subject of knowing' as a translation of Lacan's concept, see Stuart Schneiderman, "Translator's Preface," in *Returning to Freud: Clinical Psychoanalysis in the School of Lacan*, Ed. and Trans. Stuart Schneiderman (New Haven, CT and London: Yale University Press, 1980), vii. At one point, Lacan referred to the attribution of the 'supposed subject of knowing' as a mishap or a bungled action in itself: Jacques Lacan, "La méprise du sujet supposé savoir," in *Autres Écrits* (Paris: du Seuil, 2001), 329–39.

Chapter 7

Responses to the Sexual Void

Capitalism, Paranoia and Disavowal

David Ferraro

THE PROBLEM OF STUPIDITY AND SYMPTOMS

Let us begin with an example. A middle-aged man has come to my clinic at the instigation of his girlfriend, who is reportedly dismayed with his drunken outbursts. He drinks too much every weekend, he says, and gambles more than he should, by way of his smartphone. It is because he is stupid, he says. Yet a little questioning reveals that he invests in large quantities of beer for his weekend binges and does not want to delete the app, which is the portal for his gambling. Whatever stupidity is present in his actions, at a certain level, he knows what he is doing and even plans to do it again. If 'stupidity' is the name for his symptom, then like other self-assessed names – 'laziness', 'selfishness' – it describes rather than explains a particular mode of self-destruction.

Consider another example. In the United States, Donald Trump won the 2016 election, in keeping with a raft of right-wing authoritarian governments from Russia, Brazil, the United Kingdom, Australia and Israel. Trump received the support of the wealthier Americans, particularly those who are white, whose class interests would be served by him. Yet Trump was also supported by a significant number of poorer voters, who will almost certainly be worse off – economically and environmentally – as a result of Trump's policies. One line of thought on this phenomenon of voters opting against their own apparent interests ascribes it to ignorance and stupidity. Trump, as one media outlet put it,[1] exploits his supporters through their lack of political education. In both of these examples, one clinical, the other political, a symptom supposedly arises from a lack of knowledge or a misuse of reason. 'Stupidity', then, lacks a positive content and marks the place of a lack.

A similar problem haunts the Marxist tradition. If the proletariat class consists of the majority of the population, how is it that this class has little or no representation in so many contemporary polities? Stupidity and ignorance are answers to this question and tend to take the problem back to the notion of 'false consciousness'. If one takes things at this level, the solution to self-destruction lies in education, or something like it, assuming that the lack in question is not structural. To take another example, cigarette packets in Australia are sold with grim warnings of the lethality of smoking, as well as graphic images of these ill effects on the bodies of smokers. There is evidence to suggest that these measures do, in fact, discourage smoking, but not entirely. What is happening for those smokers who persist in their habit despite warnings and education? Clearly, the problem can no longer be situated at the level of knowledge.

Psychoanalysis has something to contribute here, more so since consciousness, the 'self', and the ego are radically decentered, at least within the Lacanian psychoanalytic tradition. A symptom, at its simplest, is a mode of jouissance. 'Jouissance' is the name that Lacan gave to satisfaction, as distinct from pleasure. It refers to moments of intensity not bound by the homeostatic confines of the pleasure principle. Lacan produced multiple iterations of his teaching on jouissance (or multiple paradigms, as Jacques-Alain Miller[2] puts it). One such iteration can be found in Lacan's teaching of the late 1960s, in which Lacan, on the model of Marx's theory of surplus value, coined the term *plus-de-jouir*, or surplus jouissance.[3] Where previously, for Lacan, jouissance had been the outcome of a heroic transgression of the Law, as in *Seminar VII*,[4] it is now instead the result of a process of production. Just as Marx's surplus value denotes something largely invisible in contemporary economics and capitalism, not appearing on any balance sheet or forecast (as opposed to revenue or profit, for instance), so too does jouissance have no place within contemporary discourses on psychology or mental health. In the case of psychology in particular, conceptions of the mind are still oriented to pleasure and pain, punishment and reward, as if the nineteenth century, with its literary and philosophical depictions of pleasure in pain, and ennui in pleasure, never existed. Psychological scientism has not yet caught up with Romanticism. Surplus value and surplus jouissance only become audible when there is some failure to satisfy.

Lacan referred to the comparison between surplus value and surplus jouissance as a homology – 'the relation is not one of analogy'[5] – and it suggests further similarities between Marxism and psychoanalysis. Consider the base-superstructure distinction as it stands in the Marxist tradition, in which the base refers to the means and relations of production, and the superstructure to the institutional and ideological accompaniment to this production. By the same token, jouissance can be understood as the material 'base' for the subject of psychoanalysis, with fantasy and delusion constituting the superstructure. In the example of the clinic given above, the jouissance at stake was manifest in outbursts, and in excesses of drinking and gambling. 'Stupidity' in this vein is not the cause of this jouissance but part of the subject's fantasmatic infrastructure supporting the said jouissance. The jouissance at stake for Trump's supporters may be less identifiable, but one should consider the link that it may have to Trump's bullying mode of speech, and his references to the need to 'drain the swamp', 'build a wall', tackle 'Obamagate' and the like. There is an appeal here, through identification by Trump's followers with their leader, to a jouissance of revenge and *ressentiment*. Insofar as this is the case, Trump's followers support him not in spite of his viciousness but precisely because of it. The 'ignorance', prejudice and conspiracy theorizing of his supporters is in this manner the ideological support for a particular mode of satisfaction.

This approach to phenomena sometimes attributed to stupidity displaces the problem from that of knowledge and reason and instead makes it one of enjoyment and fantasy (or the psychotic equivalent to fantasy, delusion). As Camille Robcis put it:

> Attention to fantasy complicates a straightforward definition of experience as will or determination. With fantasy, identity is never unified or whole, but discontinuous and often contradictory. At the level of the group, fantasy is equally central but perhaps even more difficult to grasp. Historians of fascism, for instance, have tended to reduce it either to a 'failure of rationality' or to a political pathology if they are coming from a liberal perspective, or to a 'false consciousness', a displacement of a more accurate social reality, if they are informed by a Marxist viewpoint. In either case, what is missing from these accounts is an understanding of the actual desire expressed in these mass movements, the collective fantasy of a cleansing violence and a regenerated social body.[6]

In other words, the question of why somebody would choose to pursue a destructive jouissance or a nihilistic politics is a question of desire. As Deleuze and Guattari put it in relation to fascism, 'the masses were not innocent dupes; at a certain point, under a certain set of conditions, they wanted fascism, and it is this perversion of the desire of the masses that needs to be accounted for'.[7] Psychoanalysis is a procedure that can produce knowledge, but this knowledge is distinct from truth, and, increasingly over the course of his teaching, Lacan situated knowledge itself within an economy of jouissance. This may be why Lacan remarked that '*la psychanalyse est un remède contre l'ignorance; elle est sans effet sur la connerie*' ('psychoanalysis is a remedy against ignorance; it is without effect on bullshit').[8] In other words, without in any way promoting ignorance, it is clear that in psychoanalysis, knowledge is not a cure.

LACAN, STUPIDITY AND SEXUAL NON-RAPPORT

Lacan's remarks on the many varieties of human intellectual frailties are too numerous to be summarized here, but one particularly pertinent aspect of Lacan's teaching on stupidity and idiocy can be located in his *Encore* seminar. It is a seminar in which Lacan provides some of his most important positions as well as one in which he has quite a bit to say on stupidity. As ever, just as one must separate Freud from the Freudians, and Marx from Marxists, so it is necessary to encounter Lacan in his own words rather than through those who speak in his name.

'Stupidity', according to Lacan, 'is not, as people think, a semantic category, but rather a way of collectivising the signifier'.[9] Moreover, 'the signifier is stupid'.[10] This is particularly the case 'when we turn things into nouns', thereby presupposing a substance.[11] The term 'love' is instructive regarding this latter point. Most European languages distinguish between the verb 'love' and the noun 'love'. The former implies a relation to an Other, whereas love qua noun allows for the possibility of a love reducible to affect and narcissism. Free association in psychoanalysis is not the act of saying everything – which is impossible, in any case – but of speaking 'without worrying about saying something stupid'.[12] All the same, this stupidity stops short in common discourse, and 'to nourish oneself is part and parcel of stupidity', since this nourishment belongs to 'the imaginary dimension'.[13] The ontology of Parmenides, in which 'non-being is not', is said by Lacan to be stupid.[14] 'Parmenides was wrong and Heraclitus was right.'[15] The fundamental truth of the seminar – and Lacan calls this truth 'indisputable' – is that there is no such thing as a sexual relationship.[16] In the face of the absence of a sexual relationship – I will depart from Lacan's translator and instead use the term 'sexual rapport' – the discourse of the analyst may not necessarily be able to discern what is or isn't stupid, and may even itself 'hang together by basing itself on the dimension of stupidity'.

This sexual non-rapport and the discourses that arise in the face of it require some further elaboration. Lacan spent almost the entirety of his teaching criticizing psychoanalytic accounts of love that drew on a somewhat pious notion of 'oblativity', in which the loving subject, insofar as he or she relates to the Other via sexuality, would be engaged in a subject-to-subject relation rather than a subject-to-object, or a fetishistic subject-to-part-object relation. Lacan expresses this through Sade:

> As is emphasised admirably by the kind of Kantian that Sade was, one can only enjoy a part of the Other's body, for the simply reason that one has never seen a body completely wrap itself around the Other's body, to the point of

> surrounding and phagocytising it. That is why we must confine ourselves to simply giving it a little squeeze, like that, taking a forearm or anything else.[17]

This, in contrast to 'oblativity', means that the subject-other relation always reduces the other to the object *a* of fantasy (). Further, the lack of any sexual rapport between the sexes, particularly the heterosexual couple, is a repudiation of any notion that the sexes enjoy some 'natural' or complementary relation with each other. Masculinity and femininity, man and woman, are two different responses, two different organizational logics with respect to the sexual void. Lacan goes so far as to state that the analysand in the clinic speaking of his or her sexual object, 'about whom this gab about love is voiced', is, strictly speaking, giving voice not only to something about their partner but more precisely, about their relation to the real, to jouissance.[18] These two positions are depicted both in terms of their logical form and Lacan's mathemes in the graph of sexuation, also to be found in the *Encore* seminar:[19]

There is much to be said about this graph, but I would like to focus on the top lines featuring logical notation. The left and right sides of the table correspond to the masculine and feminine positions, respectively. The masculine portion of the table denotes a logic of the exception, whereas the feminine side articulates a logic of 'not-all'. On the masculine side, there are two apparently contradictory statements: namely, that all men are subject to x (i.e. castration), but that there is a man who is not subject to x and who is therefore a kind of founding exception. 'Castration' in this respect refers to subjection to the symbolic order, Law and language, and results in the kind of jouissance available to such subjects as being phallic in nature, in which the Other is enjoyed when inserted into the function of the object *a*. Structurally, this position has nothing to do with anatomy, and the sexual jouissance of the masculine subject will tend towards the fetishistic.[20] The feminine subject is in a different position since, according to the logic of the graph,

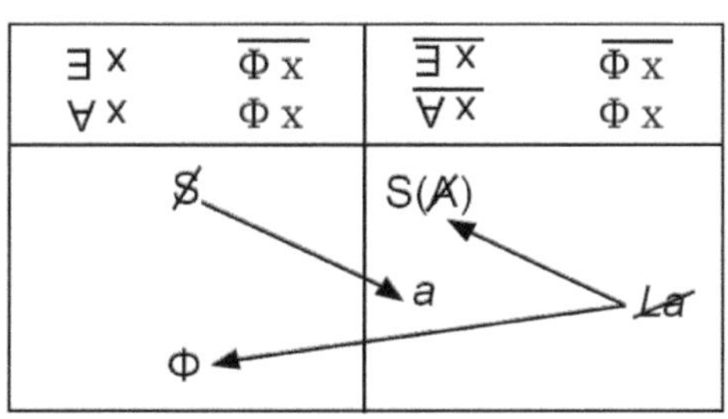

Figure 7.1 Graph of Sexuation. *Source*: Adapted from Jacques Lacan, *On Feminine Sexuality, the Limits of Love and Knowledge, 1973–1973. Encore. The Seminar of Jacques Lacan. Book XX*. Trans. B. Fink. (New York: Norton, 1998). 78.

her subjection to castration is 'not-all', which means that while she, too, can access phallic jouissance in accordance with the structure of her fundamental fantasy, she has the possibility of another jouissance. This other jouissance, outside of language, was linked by Lacan to mysticism.

To return to the masculine side of the graph, one can see that the universality of castration is haunted by the figure of the exception, raising the question of what or whom this exception is. It may appear logically as a sort of prime mover, but Lacan gave several ideas as to what is involved in the exception. The first can be found in *Seminar XVII*[21] in the figure of the father of the primal horde from Freud's *Totem and Taboo*.[22] The primal father is the one who supposedly has all the women to himself. Lacan regarded this as an impossibility, if not an obsessional neurotic fantasy, as it is difficult to hold onto even just one woman. There is a contrast with the figure of Don Juan who, rather than taking *all* the women – and the graph of sexuation clarifies that, when it comes to women, there is no 'all' to speak of – he approaches women one by one.[23] Precisely because there is no 'all' of the women, the figure of The Woman is another possible incarnation of the figure of the exception. In structural diagnostic terms, there are at least two broad responses to the exception to the Law. The first is the neurotic/perverse strategy of disavowal of castration, with the impossible fantasy that this is a method to obtain the place of exception. The other, psychotic strategy, is to incarnate this position of exception oneself, creating a subject who is not assimilated into the Law. These two respective approaches will be examined further below, and both can be considered as producing the destructive symptoms of the 'stupidity' mentioned previously.

THE IDIOT AND HIS ENJOYMENT

Just as there are the two places on the graph of sexuation, there are two modes of jouissance corresponding to them. As Lacan put it: 'There's no such thing as a sexual relationship because one's jouissance of the Other taken as a body is always inadequate – perverse, on the one hand, insofar as the Other is reduced to object *a*, and crazy and enigmatic, on the other, I would say.'[24] The latter refers to the speechless mysticism alluded to previously as the 'other' jouissance, available only to subjects on the feminine side of sexuation. The former, however, is designated as phallic jouissance by Lacan. It is, he says, 'the jouissance of the idiot'.[25]

What does Lacan mean by 'idiot' here? It is not a term that he used frequently. Put somewhat brutally, phallic jouissance, as applied to sexual enjoyment specifically, implies a fundamentally narcissistic relation to jouissance, in which the subject, strictly speaking, enjoys his or her own organ by way of the Other's body with the fantasy () as support. Sex is masturbation with an Other, in other words, an unsentimental outlook that can be contrasted with the supposed ecstasies of oblative sexuality. Notwithstanding the narcissistic implications of phallic jouissance, it is not entirely clear that Lacan intends the term 'idiot' as a pejorative. For instance, he alludes to the eponymous idiot of Dostoevsky's novel. Dostoevsky 'called on of his characters the Idiot, the one who conducted himself most marvellously, no matter what social field he was traversing and whatever embarrassing situation he found himself in'.[26] The idiot of Dostoevsky – 'идиот', in Russian – derives directly from Greek, and given Lacan's attention to Greek terminology elsewhere, there is good reason to suspect that Lacan has selected idiocy for its etymological associations. In the modern age, 'idiot' is one of several terms – 'cretin' and 'moron' are others – which were taken from classical languages and imported into psychiatry. In its origins, 'ἰδιότης' simply refers to a private citizen or peculiar quality and carries no particularly deprecatory ramifications.[27] In this vein, the jouissance of the idiot can be understood as the jouissance of the one body. This is the jouissance of the castrated speaking subject when there is no such thing as sexual rapport. Phallic jouissance means that, as far as sex is concerned, the two (or three, or four) never become one.

LACAN AND THE SOCIAL BOND

Is the speaking subject, then, merely speaking – and moreover, enjoying – into the void, as it were? While this is the conclusion that some Lacanian psychoanalysts have drawn, one should note that Lacan himself gave numerous indications that there are nevertheless relations between speaking beings, even if these relations cannot properly be called sexual. Love is one such relation, and Lacan's unsentimental view of sex can arguably be contrasted with his affirmative stance towards love. In addition, during the period between *Seminar XVII* and *Seminar XX*, Lacan described a number of discourses that can come to be in the place of sexual non-rapport. Lacan's definition of 'discourse' is simply that of a social bond or link (*lien social*) founded on language.[28]

Lacan introduced four such discourses in *Seminar XVII*.[29] These discourses are not an exhaustive list of the forms of social link, but rather, four specific social bonds:

Each term in the discourse represents, in overdetermined form, one of Lacan's algebraic terms, and when rotated, produces four different permutations, namely, that of the master, the university, the hysteric and the analyst, respectively. The discourse of the master is the elementary structure of discourse as such, in which the subject () is represented by a signifier () for

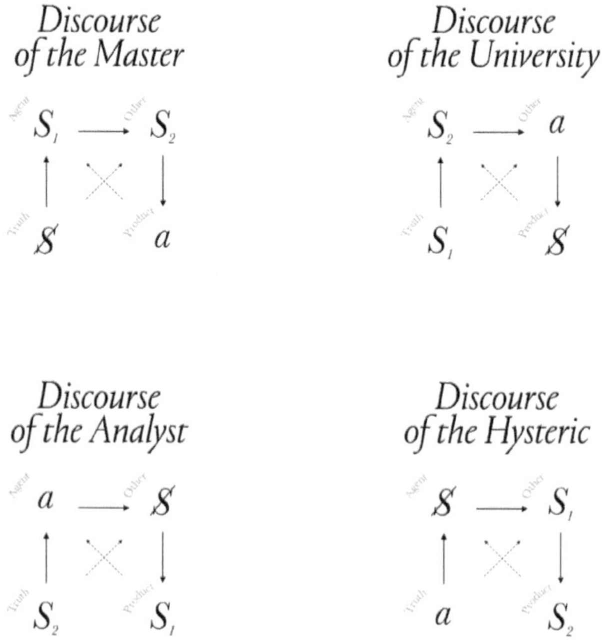

Figure 7.2 The Four Discourses. *Source*: Ross Sokolovski, Wikimedia Commons.

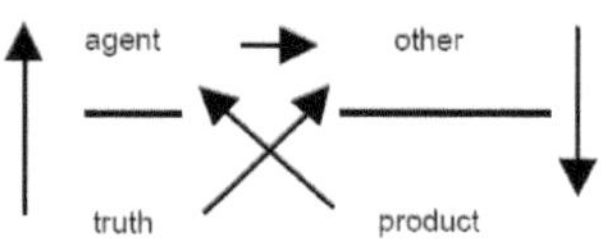

Figure 7.3 The Key to the Four Discourses. *Source*: Adapted from Jacques Lacan, *On Feminine Sexuality, the Limits of Love and Knowledge, 1973–1973. Encore. The Seminar of Jacques Lacan. Book XX*. Trans. B. Fink. (New York: Norton, 1998). 78.

another signifier (). Discourse as a material production generates an excess denoted by the *a*, which can be understood as the surplus jouissance discussed earlier as homologous to Marx's *Mehrwert*. The term in the upper left-hand corner indicates that in the name of which the discourse is animated:

There is a partnership formed by each of the discourses. The couples are, respectively, that of master and slave in the master discourse, teacher and student in the university discourse, hysteric and master in the hysteric discourse and analyst and analysand in the discourse of the analyst.[30]

Discourse does not eliminate the abyss of sexual non-rapport, but it can indicate a way of handling it. It may also be a way out of stupidity. Lacan's translator, Bruce Fink, tells us that Lacan's term for 'stupidity', '*la bêtise*', is the same as that which he used to translate the German word for 'stupidity' in the case of Little Hans.[31] This word is '*Dummheit*', and, as in English, the term for 'dumb' has the double meaning of both stupid and mute. Not every discourse consists of speech, of course, but the deployment of signifiers not only produces jouissance but can also – to an extent, at least – be a protection against its excesses.

Later, added another discourse, namely that of capitalism:

Here, the positions of and have been reversed, and what results might be more properly called a pseudo-discourse, in that the social bond that results – that of buyer and seller – is fleeting and unstable. What characterizes the discourse of capitalism is a radical rejection – a *Verwerfung* – of castration, in which the subject is 'burnt out'.[32] Lacan had read a good deal more of Marx than is sometimes appreciated, and in formulating the discourse of capitalism, he may have been suggesting that the subject qua workers enters it both as buyer and seller, a point that Marx makes repeatedly when discussing the fate of workers in the open market. The worker is at once a buyer (as consumer) and seller (of his or her labour power). The risk of burnout is on both sides here, in the form of hyperexploitation as worker or via excessive consumption. (Regarding the latter, consider the rise of addiction as a generalized mode of jouissance, with endlessly varying objects, whether in the form of literal substances, or gambling, or social media). Note here also the repudiation of castration. This replicates the position of the exception in the masculine side of the graph of sexuation, but it also has nihilistic consequences. An example could be found in the presumption of endless growth in economic models, which rejects the limitations inherent in deriving this growth, at least partly, from the bounties of the natural environment. Endless growth, limitless profit or jouissance without restriction

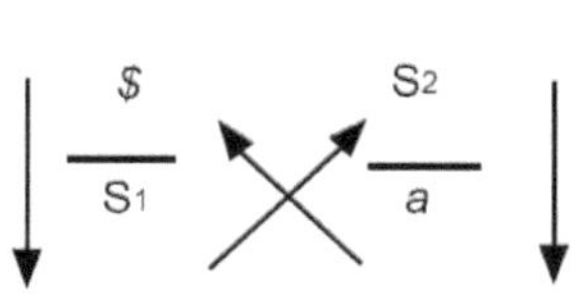

Figure 7.4 The Discourse of Capitalism. *Source*: Adapted from Lacan, J. (1972). 'Du discours psychanalytique,' in *Lacan in Italia 1953–1978*. En Italie Lacan, ed G. B. Contri (Milan: La Salamandra), 32–55.

all end up in the same place: 'It begins with a tickle and ends in a blaze of petrol.'[33]

MASTERY AND CAPITALIST RATIONALITY

The discourse of capitalism is a variant of the discourse of the master, and it is worth lingering on the question as to what Lacan refers to as a 'master'. The most obvious reference is to the dialectic of lordship and bondsman, otherwise known as the master-slave dialectic, in Hegel's *Phenomenology of Spirit*. This was transmitted to Lacan in the 1930s through the lectures of Kojève and unfolds in a dynamic interplay between the figures of master and slave, desire and recognition. As Hegelian scholars have noted, slavery became a potent metaphor for political oppression throughout modern Western political philosophy, though in the case of Hegel specifically, it was no mere metaphor. The trans-Atlantic slave trade was in swing, and some have argued that Hegel's dialectic was inspired, at least partly, by his readings of abolitionist authors as well as contemporary media accounts of the Haitian revolution.[34] As in Haiti, the master in Hegel's dialectic is trapped in an impasse, and the dialectic is resolved on the side of the slave.

In any event, the mark of Kojève and Hegel is discernible across much of Lacan's teaching, and not only in *Seminar I*, wherein Lacan produces a definition of desire that hinges on recognition,[35] which is to say, that it passes through the Other via the defiles of the signifier. In *Seminar X*, as Lacan is working out the relation of the object *a* to desire, Lacan revisits the master-slave dialectic, superimposing on it the dialectic of the barred subject and Other, and shifting the dialectic from a struggle between one consciousness and another to the unconscious,[36] and without any possibility of a synthesis.[37] Even as late as Seminar *XXIV*, Lacan dedicated a session of his teaching to a homage and critique of Hegel, rejecting the latter's 'absolute knowledge' but reaffirming the centrality of recognition to psychoanalysis, on this occasion, with reference to the Pass.[38]

There is at least one more philosophical reference to the master which Lacan makes use of, and that is the master of Aristotelian ethics. Aristotelian ethics, for Lacan, is aimed at the master. This master differs from the Hegelian master in that the latter already demonstrates signs of castration and already, according to Lacan, presages the disappearance of masters as such.[39] That Aristotle's ethical philosophy is addressed to masters can be taken in at least two senses. First, in a patriarchal society with a slave-based economy, the master was the head of the οἶκος or household, the other members of which had so little agency as to be, for Aristotle, sub-ethical. The second, more psychoanalytic sense in which Aristotle is writing for masters, is based on his ethics being founded upon the cultivation of virtues, which, in general, constitute a mean between two extremes. His ethics is oriented to the 'balance' or 'mean' of pleasure rather than the excess of jouissance, and this self-mastery is far removed from the divided, castrated subject of psychoanalysis. This bears a marked resemblance to Freud's pleasure principle, in which pleasure is both a resolution by homeostasis and the easing of a tension. The pleasure principle, however, only holds prior to the introduction of the death drive, and to what Lacan designated as jouissance. Aristotle assumes that, in principle, at least, a human subject can achieve this sort of virtue. When dealing with the subject of psychoanalysis, one who is radically and permanently divided and engaged in the production of surplus-jouissance, such mastery is mere fantasy. Thus, the figure of the master is impossible, but the fantasy of such a figure is nevertheless pervasive across all diagnostic structures. The fantasy may itself have something to do with Aristotelian logic, something which is also undermined by Lacan and by psychoanalysis more generally. As Barbara Cassin put it in her examination of Lacan's *L'etourdit*, 'your conscious mind is structured like a (generally) logical Aristotelian language. And your unconscious is structured like an ab-sent language, like a *lalangue*'.[40] The logic of sexuation in psychoanalysis is not a logic of non-contradiction.

The discourse of capitalism differs from that of the master of antiquity in several respects. As Lacan pointed out, the Aristotelian master was not a man of business, and the notion of virtue cultivated for base economic gain disgusted Aristotle.[41] The discourse should also be distinguished from capitalism itself, which dates back several hundred years in different parts of the world, depending on one's precise definition. The discourse of capitalism, in which the law of the market is positioned as the animating force of the discourse, has only really predominated since the 1970s and 1980s, if one is to identify it with the period that followed post-war Keynesianism and is now usually called 'neoliberalism'.[42] This era is characterized not by one but at least two dismal sciences: economics and psychology. Both coalesce to produce conceptions of the contemporary subject that are remarkably alike. From the economic perspective, the subject practices good, Aristotelian logic to rationally pursue his own self-interest. '*Homo oeconomicus* is an entrepreneur, and entrepreneur of himself.'[43] Suffering, in this paradigm, is a consequence of malinvestment, and to provide too much in the way of amelioration of suffering would, in effect, prolong this malinvestment. The role of politics is to provide an activist government that promotes competition, efficiency and the law of the market. This cannot be achieved by way of laissez-faire economic policies, since the latter tend towards centralization, monopolies and cartelization; hence this activism constitutes the 'neo' in neoliberalism.

The paradigm of *homo oeconomicus* under neoliberalism finds its counterpart in the discourses of psychology and 'mental health' that exist alongside it. The subject in these discourses shares with the Aristotelian subject the presumption of unified subjectivity that follows a logic of non-contradiction. Hence, conflicts and divisions are not structural in this model as they are in psychoanalysis; rather, they are examples of 'cognitive dissonance', essentially errors of thought. Suffering in this model derives from such logical errors, and its remedy is investment in work on the self, whether in the form of logical or empirical thinking exercises (to counter overgeneralization, or 'catastrophizing' and the like); distraction; relaxation exercises; a 'pleasant activity schedule' and so on. (Note, of course, that the accent is on the pleasant and pleasing, and not on anything like jouissance.) The cognitive subject presupposed by this discourse is modelled on the analogy of the computer. Language is reducible to mere data, and since computers are not embodied, there cannot be any space for something like *lalangue* within this paradigm. This tends towards radical individualism, a trait shared with the neoliberal economic paradigm, since language in this model is not particularly discursive in the Lacanian sense of constituting social links. The things of interest to psychoanalysts – dreams, fantasies, slips of the pen or tongue – are largely irrelevant in this paradigm. A conversation is a transmission of data rather than an exchange of speech, and still less is it a speech act in the 'performative' sense that this has for some linguists. Lacan agreed on this particular point with the linguists, saying: there is something distinct between speaking and saying. 'A word that founds a fact is a fact of saying, but speech functions even when it doesn't found any fact. When it gives a command, when it prays, when it insults, or when it voices a wish, it doesn't found any fact.'[44] Language from this perspective is discourse that touches the body and divides the subject, and not mere cognitive data. In contrast, in the cognitive model of modern mental health, the subject is not a born master but is someone who self-manages towards ideals of mastery, even if these ideals are, in the last resort, asymptotic.

What follows from this is that, if one is to take contemporary rationality as an antonym of stupidity, one is plunged into what Nietzsche once derided as 'that Socratic equation reason = virtue = happiness'.[45] The subject that works on itself via rationality is nonetheless driven by a fundamentally irrational moral directive and one which ignores the long tradition of linking truth (and the wisdom that acquires it) with suffering, rather than with happiness. Ancient examples include the *Oedipus* of Sophocles as well as *Ecclesiastes*. This latter tradition is more in keeping with psychoanalysis. As we saw earlier, 'in analytic discourse, what is involved is but that . . . not so much to say everything as to say anything, without worrying about saying something stupid'.[46] In following discourse wherever it leads, even if this entails 'stupidity', psychoanalysis is oriented to an ethics of truth, even if this truth is necessarily partial ('Saying it all is literally impossible'[47]), and necessarily situated at the same level as lies and fiction, which is to say, the symbolic order. Or, from another angle, self-destruction and the jouissance that opened this paper and which was attributed to stupidity, among other moral failings, is largely compatible with the rationality at play in the discourse of capitalism.

CAPITALIST BIOPOLITICS

The rationality at stake in the discourse of capitalism also determines the types of biopolitical interventions brought to bear on subjects. Technology in this discourse has extended the superego of the gaze to ever-increasing surveillance through the use of so-called 'smart' devices. These utilize the data of the psy-disciplines (except psychoanalysis, of course) to enact control in settings such as the school, the clinic and the workplace. One of the most striking features of this technology is the shift in accent from the qualitative to the quantitative, a point observed by William Gaddis back in 2002 when noting that 'digital machines' are used to make the primacy of quantity over quality 'the whole point' of aesthetic experience, for instance.[48] The speaking being is rendered dumb through psychometrics.

One way of reading these 'smart' devices is through Lacan's concept of the 'lathouse', introduced in Seminar XVII, of which he said: 'It is quite certain that everyone has to deal with two or three of this species. The lathouse has absolutely no reason to limit its multiplication. What is important is to know what happens when one really enters into relationship with the lathouse as such.'[49] The lathouse must be understood as a drive-object, and not an object of desire, which is to say that while it can and does produce jouissance, it can also cause anxiety. From a Lacanian perspective, all regression is structural, and not developmental or chronological. The omnipresence of the Other's gaze is one of several features of the neoliberal capitalist period that tends to cause a structural regression from the symbolic order to the imaginary (and simultaneously, producing real effects). Second, since the discourse of capitalism tends to devalue discourse itself in favour of numbers and to produce tenuous, fleeting social bonds, the biopolitical procedures undertaken in its name tend, above all, to individualize and privatize phenomenon. Massive rates of depression and anxiety, and increasing consumption of SSRI medications, can then be understood merely as growth in individual cases, rather than indicating a systemic problem, just as in Australia in early 2020 during catastrophic bushfires, the hyper-capitalist government and corporate media could depict the disaster as merely several instances within a long national history of bushfires, rather than as evidence of the effects of climate change. Third, the discourse of capitalism involves state activism to promote the primacy of the market, and while market exchange is symbolic, the reduction of human relations to market relations is premised on permanent competition and tends to reduce the Other to a paranoiac double. This is a point to which we shall return below. When considering this structural regression to the imaginary, it is worth recalling two points that Lacan made about it, one from early in his teaching and one late. The early point, from Lacan's paper on the mirror stage, is that the construction of a synthetic image of oneself grants the 'jubilant' illusion of mastery to the infant,[50] and from Lacan's later teaching, the imaginary order is what lends consistency to Borromean structure.[51] Imaginary devices allow for the illusion of totalization and the disavowal of castration.

Some examples of biopolitics under the discourse of capitalism may clarify what is at stake here. One could start with the Japanese manufacturer Hitachi, which claims that there is a positive correlation between happiness and physical activity, and which has therefore fitted its employees with an 'Employee Happiness Monitor', designed to gauge the workers' 'happiness quotient'.[52] On the one hand, this illustrates the extension of the quantitative gaze afforded by capitalist technology, but on the other, it showcases a number of dubious, if not outright stupid assumptions. These include the basis of the correlation itself, and the notion that 'happiness' is a measurable construct such that, within and between individuals, its proportions can be plotted across numerically homogenous units. Another example can be found in Britain's NHS, in which a 'digital future' is planned for the assessment and treatment of 'mental health' conditions. The proponents of this digital future envisage sweeping changes to service provision, including continual surveillance via smartphones, along with digital chatbots.[53] What is elided in these proposals is any consideration of the role of subjectivity or transference in mental health treatment. Note the contrast with psychoanalytic treatment. The latter is based on a long-term relationship, in which the patient can say anything, and which is – hopefully, at least – grounded in an ethics of care. The other is asocial, based on monitoring and suggesting, nudging a patient towards what the app designers believe is in his or her best interests. The social and structural dimensions of mental health care are reduced to pure technique and algorithm. There can also be paradoxical effects of the expansion of the gaze since this gaze has the potential to libidinize and make more symptomatic, as in the case, for instance, of the relation between binge eating and calorie counting. Even if the subject under such circumstances can successfully restrict his or her food intake, he or she is nevertheless upholding the centrality of oral jouissance by coupling it with this quantitative gaze.

While it is true that these technologies are becoming ever more totalizing and insidious, the very fact that they emerge from within the discourse of capitalism means they are structured by a foundational disavowal. This disavowal is multifaceted and denies lack, subjectivity, the unconscious, castration and the fundamentally relational structure of speaking beings' psychical life. The attempt at totalization therefore results, against the worst intentions of its progenitors, in a *pas-tout* phenomenon that always already creates the seeds of its own resistance within itself. A good literary example can be found in *Red Plenty* by novelist Francis Spufford.[54] The novel is set in the USSR of the 1950s and 1960s, in which the Soviet government is overseeing a period of economic growth. Administrators of the regime believe, with a touch of hubris, that the development of supercomputers will allow for the mathematical perfection of Soviet production and distribution. Naturally, the supercomputers fail to take into account the complexity of vast, interconnected economic systems and the tendency towards human error, and the project ultimately fails. Nonetheless, while the novel could be read as a critique of a kind of historical scientism, the context of its publication – the post-GFC world of 2010 – was one in which the world was reeling from a very similar conceit, this time on the part of bankers using computer technology to extract further profits from securities. This undertaking collapsed with the sub-prime housing crisis. This is another illustration that, despite disavowal, technology under capitalism produces its own impasses and resistances.

This reflects one of the overarching tendencies within the discourse of capitalism, namely, to construe the structural – whether in psychical or economic domains – as reducible to the technical. Bernard Stiegler, writing about Alan Greenspan, the former chair of the Federal Reserve in the United States who observed a 'period of euphoria' during the neoliberal period just prior to the GFC, noted that the reduction to pure technicity disavowed significant structural blind spots. As Stiegler put it:

> [T]he ideologues of this 'rational risk management' were undoubtedly not unaware of the limitations of their data sets. But they assumed that 'historic periods of stress' had occurred *only because these financial instruments did not exist during these periods*, or because competition was *not yet* 'perfect and undistorted'. Such was the concealed theory operating behind these robots, robots that supposedly 'objectify' reality and do so according to 'market rationality'.[55]

The stupidity and disavowal inherent in capitalist technology and biopolitical procedures is not merely an instance of imbecility, however, as it is harnessed to produce both surplus value and surplus jouissance, and is ultimately destructive. As Stiegler argued, algorithmic governmentality tends towards eugenics.[56] The deployment of biopolitical technology in this epoch seems to confirm a remark by Milan Kundera: 'Stupidity does not give way to science, technology, modernity, progress; on the contrary, it progresses right along with progress!'[57]

MANY STUPIDITIES, MANY RELATIONS TO THE OTHER

It is a matter of etymological curiosity and, moreover, a remarkable illustration of the dialectic between biopolitics and society that synonyms for 'stupidity' passed through antiquity into the discourse of medicine and psychiatry, before finally finding a place in colloquial vernacular as pejoratives and insults. As we have seen, the jouissance of the idiot could be an example of this and, given that it signifies a private, idiosyncratic jouissance, it would appear well adapted to the privatization and enclosure that accompanies the discourse of capital. Insofar as phallic jouissance operates on the one body, it is fundamentally narcissistic. A question arises then as to the significance of the relation to the Other in the context of a jouissance emerging from the one body.

To review Lacan's teaching for a moment, it is clear that desire cannot arise except via the Other. In Lacan's *Seminar I*, this operates in a Hegelian manner in which desire is desire for recognition by the Other. In *Seminar VII*, this is because desire and the Law are two sides of the same coin. Prohibition, up to and including that of repression, creates and is coextensive with the lack/desire that arises from the Law. There is therefore no way of reaching one's desire except via civilizational discontent, or what Kant described as 'the unsocial sociability of men'.[58] Jouissance might seem to escape this civilizational discontent, given its apparently solitary, masturbatory character, and this is indeed the argument put forth by Jacques-Alain Miller and his school. For Miller, jouissance is not merely idiotic but 'autistic', in the precise sense of being Otherless.[59] The late teaching of Lacan, according to Miller, involves a falling away of the Other, and the subject striving for sublimation undertaking a futile attempt at recognition from this Other, like a satellite orbiting a planet that no longer exists. What remains is the jouissance of the cynic, and Miller invokes Diogenes of Sinope, who famously masturbated in public in Athens, as the exemplar of this mode of jouissance.[60]

There are some difficulties here, however. It is true that the Other falls away for Lacan in his later work, but this Other is the Other qua guarantor of knowledge. (Without this guarantor, all knowledge and meaning-making takes on a broadly delusional character.) Lacan does several things to ensure that even if the Other is reduced to the level of semblant, or bare function, it is not dispensed with altogether. First, Lacan repeatedly insists on the function of discourse as both founding a social link *and* producing jouissance. Second, the structure of language itself is such that it is built upon the foundation of *lalangue*, a jouissance-laden babble that is at the heart of the symbolic register.[61] While this *lalangue* is particular to each subject, it is nevertheless described by Lacan as 'a common affair' in the first instance, and this is why psychoanalysis itself never merely descends into an *autism à deux*.[62] This is the case even if the communal nature of language produces singular, non-generalizable effects. The superego is an important reference point here, as Lacan never relinquished his use of the concept, and it clearly illustrates the extimacy at stake in *lalangue*. The superego is at once the voice of one's own drives and bears the irreducible mark of the Other. Finally, Diogenes of Sinope is a particularly curious example of autistic, solitary jouissance, since his masturbatory gestures are intended, like the rest of his philosophical activity, as a provocation to the Other. One might read this variously as perverse or hysteric, but in any case, an Other is already presupposed in the gesture. In other words, it is far from clear that the narcissism of jouissance allows it to escape the difficulties of civilizational discontent. Even for the autistic subject, jouissance in echolalia contains at least a minimal reference to the Other, and the radical insistence on a jouissance that is supposedly Otherless runs the risk of inadvertently recreating the pseudo-discursive logic of the capitalist discourse. The idiot may be narcissistic and a masturbator, but these alone do not render his enjoyments 'autistic', as idiocy by definition implies a relation to the Other.

What is often given in English as 'idiocy' or 'stupidity' often has a different etymological basis in Greek. Aristotle, for instance, in his *History of Animals*, spends a good portion of the text decrying animals – sheep, for example, and particularly swarm animals such as bees and wasps – with epithets given as 'slow', 'foolish', 'stupid', 'cowardly', but corresponding to the term μωρός, the basis of the English word 'moron'. When not abusing sheep, Aristotle, like Plato, discussed the human intellect with reference to 'nous', which becomes the cognate for a series of terms. 'Εὔνοια' becomes 'goodwill', and the lack of nous, ἄνοια, is associated with 'folly', 'want of understanding' or even something akin to dementia (which has a roughly similar etymological construction). More rarely, Aristotle invokes 'παράνοια', 'paranoia', translated as madness or insanity (in *The Athenian Consitution*, for instance).[63] Aristotle's use of the term is obviously broader than the psychoanalytic usage, and the latter – somewhat neglected in recent times – is crucial to grasping what is at stake in contemporary modes of auto-annihilation.

PARANOIA AND THE STATE OF EXCEPTION

Lacan commenced his psychoanalytic career with a study of paranoid psychosis, both in his doctoral dissertation and in the clinic with the case of Aimée. Paranoia, I will argue, is one possible response to the void of sexual non-rapport, and one of particular importance in contemporary times. Paranoia, in its classical expression, involves the subject incarnating the place of the exception as we saw in the graph of sexuation on the masculine side. What follows from this is that the subject in this position, and the Other which corresponds to this subject, is not fully barred. The Other is therefore able to enjoy the subject at the latter's expense, lawlessly, and without limit. From this starting point, an individual occupying the place of this lawless Other is liable to be construed as a persecutor. It is not, however, a matter of the paranoiac ever being able to do away with the Other qua persecutor, and rather like the Hegelian master-slave dialectic, any paranoiac who abolishes his or her persecutor will necessarily be on the precipice of abolishing themselves. The Other is necessary for the paranoiac's stability, which is founded on an imaginary consistency. The subject's own ego can maintain this consistency by way of projection into the Other, and the sort of relation that emerges is characterized by the competition and hostility of all imaginary relations. Both the absence of symbolic castration and this relentless imaginarization of the Other correspond very well to the pseudo-discourse of capitalism.

As Sylvia Plath wrote, 'It is the exception that interests the devil. / It is the exception that climbs the sorrowful hill.'[64] The paranoiac differs from the neurotic, particularly the obsessional, who merely fantasizes over the possibility of exceptionalism; the paranoiac embodies it. This exception varies according to time and place. Religious delusions in which the subject is not just *a* chosen one but *the* chosen one are common. In the USSR, according to Svetlana Alexievich, in 'the Kolyma prison camps, in the huts where they kept the madmen, people used to shout "I'm Stalin! I'm Stalin!"'.[65] In neurosis it is the object *a* which constitutes the exception, namely, that which resists assimilation into the symbolic order, but in paranoia, the object *a* is not clearly separated from the subject themselves, and is in the subject's pocket, so to speak. It cannot, therefore, function as an external source of fuel for desire and is instead a troubling internal element that psychotic subjects – paranoid, melancholic, schizophrenic or whatever – have to find a way to live with.

Incarnating the position of the exception, as we find it in Lacan, has some striking parallels with Giorgio Agamben's use of the term. The 'state of exception' is a suspension of the Law, or in psychoanalytic terms, of castration. In a modern context, it tends to be synonymous with fascism, or, at the very least, with an increasingly authoritarian bent on the part of states under the signifier of 'security'.[66] Republican Rome set limits on these exceptions, which is to say, self-imposed a symbolic castration, but contemporary exceptions tend towards excess rather than limit. The growing electability of aggressive fascist or proto-fascist leaders, who often campaign openly that their policies will come at the expense of their supporters, is the paranoiac response to impasses in the discourse of capitalism. Usually, these leaders either advocate conspiracy theories or at least foster them. The conspiracy theory is itself an exemplar of knowledge covering over a lack and is structurally indistinguishable from a delusion. Consequently, it is almost impossible to refute a conspiracy theory, since first, the interlocutor who attempts to do so will themselves be posited as part of the conspiracy; but second, the meaning-making underlying the theory is not the outcome of some dispassionate assessment of the facts, but rather, a metaphorical truth mistaken for a literal fact. Second, contradictory evidence is simply assimilated into the delusion, as in the case of GOP supporters in the United States who believe that COVID-19 death tolls are 'wildly exaggerated'.[67]

This in part accounts for the preconditions for authoritarian leaders to appeal to the paranoid subject. Note that Trump, Bolsonaro, Scott Morrison and others in this category never apologize or publicly admit to any failing. All criticism of them is derided as sheer malice on the part of the critic. This helps to maintain the image of pure consistency without lack, compatible with paranoid identification, while at the same time having the tendency of barring the Other. This barred Other is vilified as a persecutor who will be dealt with, even if, in the case of Trump at least, this is merely a rhetorical sideshow. The identification with the leader, for paranoiacs and non-paranoiacs alike, facilitates an aggressive jouissance by proxy, which is to say that arguments against these leaders appealing to reason or enlightened self-interest – they have been terrible for the economy, the environment, on COVID-19 – are beside the point.

The social links that can arise from this paranoiac structure and its identification with the aggressive leader are, however, limited and fleeting, and not such as to pose any challenge whatsoever to the machinations of capitalism either as discourse or mode of production. Compared to the mass uprisings in the face of police brutality in the United States, the paranoiac position tends to produce 'lone wolf' activism rather than parties. An alternative coupling of the void of sexual non-rapport and the discourse of capitalism is that of disavowal, which is often associated with fetishism or perversion but is, in this case, at least better identified with addiction under the catchcry of 'business as usual!'.[68] Instead of incarnating the exception, castration is not foreclosed but disavowed and transmuted into fantasies of one's own exceptionalism. When castration is disavowed rather than paranoiacally foreclosed, capitalist fantasies of exceptionalism abound. Consider, for instance, the tech industry entrepreneurs who imagine that they will escape environmental and civilizational collapse through the use of bunkers and security agents protecting them from the starving hordes,[69] as if a billionaire class can continue the status quo ante in the absence of a working class. This is the position of contemporary liberalism within the discourse of capitalism, which produces almost as much inequality and environmental destruction as the fascists but with the veneer of reasonableness. In this position, surplus value and surplus jouissance continue their accumulation, with the mounting destruction of this being a metaphorical can to be kicked down the road. In the absence of a third term, such are the meagre political positions linking jouissance and its idiocy with self-annihilation in our times.

NOTES

1. Ilya Somin, 'Trump Exploits Rational Political Ignorance', accessed 1 June 2020, https://www.usatoday.com/story/opinion/2015/10/04/trump-polls-immigration-taxes-column/72755896/
2. Jacques-Alain Miller, 'Six Paradigms of Jouissance' (trans. J. Haney), *Psychoanalytical Notebooks*, 34 (2020), 11–77.
3. Jacques Lacan, *The Other Side of Psychoanalysis. The Seminar of Jacques Lacan. Book XVII,* trans. R. Grigg (New York: Norton, 2007), 50.
4. Jacques Lacan, *The Ethics of Psychoanalysis. 1959–1960. The Seminar of Jacques Lacan. Book VII*, trans. D. Porter (New York: Norton, 1992).
5. Jacques Lacan, *Le Séminaire livre XVI. D'un Autre l'autre* (Paris: Seuil, 2006), 45.
6. Camille Robcis, 'What Is the Future of Psychoanalysis in the Academy?' *Psychoanalysis and History*, 20 (April 2018).
7. Gilles Deleuze and Felix Guattari, *Anti-Oedipus: Capitalism and schizophrenia*, trans. R. Hurley, M. Seem and H. Lane (London: Athlone, 1984), 29.
8. Jacques Lacan, 'Intervention aux conclusions des groupes de travail', *Les Lettres de l'École Freudienne,* 15 (1975), 235–244, 235.
9. Jacques Lacan, *On Feminine Sexuality, the Limits of Love and Knowledge, 1973–1973. Encore. The Seminar of Jacques Lacan. Book XX*, trans. B. Fink (New York: Norton, 1998), 20.
10. Lacan, *On Feminine Sexuality*, 20.
11. Lacan, *On Feminine Sexuality*, 21.
12. Lacan, *On Feminine Sexuality*, 27.
13. Lacan, *On Feminine Sexuality*, 14.
14. Lacan, *On Feminine Sexuality*, 22.
15. Lacan, *On Feminine Sexuality*, 114.
16. Lacan, *On Feminine Sexuality*, 12.
17. Lacan, *On Feminine Sexuality*, 23.
18. Jacques Lacan . . . . *or Worse. The Seminar of Jacques Lacan. Book XIX*, trans. A. Price (Cambridge: Polity, 2018), 134.
19. Lacan, *On Feminine Sexuality*, 78.
20. Jacques-Alain Miller, 'Of Distribution Between the Sexes' (trans. B. Wolf), *Psychoanalytical Notebooks*, 11 (2003), 9–27, 23.
21. Lacan, *The Other Side of Psychoanalysis*, 114.
22. Sigmund Freud, 'Totem and Taboo', in *The Standard Edition of the Complete Psychological Works of Sigmund Freud. Volume XIIIt,* rans. J. Strachey (London: Vintage, 2008), 1–162.

23. Lacan, *On Feminine Sexuality*, 10.
24. Lacan, *On Feminine Sexuality*, 144.
25. Lacan, *On Feminine Sexuality*, 81.
26. Lacan, *D'un Autre l'autre*, 175.
27. 'ἰδιότης', Logeion, accessed 24 June 2020, https://logeion.uchicago.edu/%E1%BC%B0%CE%B4%CE%B9%CF%8C%CF%84%CE%B7%CF%82
28. Lacan, *On Feminine Sexuality*, 17.
29. Lacan, *The Other Side of Psychoanalysis*, 29.
30. Colette Soler, *Lacanian Affects: The Function of Affect in Lacan's Work,* trans. B. Fink (London: Routledge, 2016), 39.
31. Lacan, *On Feminine Sexuality*, 11.
32. Stijn Vanheule, 'Capitalist Discourse, Subjectivity and Lacanian Psychoanalysis', *Frontiers in Psychology*, 7 (2016), https://www.frontiersin.org/articles/10.3389/fpsyg.2016.01948/full
33. Lacan, *The Other Side of Psychoanalysis*, 72.
34. Susan Buck-Morss, 'Hegel and Haiti', *Critical Inquiry*, 26 (2000), 821–65, 845.
35. Jacques Lacan, *The Seminar of Jacques Lacan. Book I. Freud's Papers on Technique. 1953–1954*, trans. J. Forrester (New York: Norton, 1988), 222–23.
36. Jacques Lacan, *Anxiety. The Seminar of Jacques Lacan. Book X*, trans. A. R. Price (Cambridge: Polity, 2014), 23–24.
37. Lacan, *Anxiety*, 270.
38. Jacques Lacan, *Séminaire XXIV (1976–1977): L'insu que sait de l'une-bévue s'aile à mourre*, trans. C. Gallagher, accessed 1 July 2020, http://www.lacaninireland.com/web/wp-content/uploads/2010/06/insu-Seminar-XXIV-Final-Sessions-1-12-1976-1977.pdf. 89.
39. Lacan, *Ethics*, 11–12.
40. Barbara Cassin, 'Ab-sense, or Lacan from A to D', in *There's no Such Thing as a Sexual Relationship. Two Lessons on Lacan*, eds. A. Badiou and B. Cassin and trans. S. Spitzer and K. Reinhard (New York: Columbia, 2017), 3–43, 25.
41. Lacan, *The Other Side of Psychoanalysis*, 82.
42. David Harvey, *A Brief History of Neoliberalism* (Oxford: Oxford, 2005), 13.
43. Michel Foucault, *The Birth of Biopolitics. Lectures at the Collège de France. 1978–1979,* trans. G. Burchell (New York: Picador, 2008), 226.
44. Lacan, . . . *Or worse*, 55.
45. Friedrich Nietzsche, *Twilight of the Idols*, trans. R. J. Hollingdale (London: Penguin, 1990). 42.
46. Lacan, *Encore*, 26.
47. Jacques Lacan, *Television. A Challenge to the Psychoanalytic Establishment*, trans. D. Hollier, R. Krauss and A. Michelson (New York: Norton, 1990), 3.
48. William Gaddis, *Agapē agape* (New York: Penguin, 2002), 4.
49. Lacan, *The Other Side of Psychoanalysis*, 162.
50. Jacques Lacan, 'The Mirror Stage as Formative of the *I* Function', in *Écrits*, trans. B. Fink, (New York: Norton, 2006), 75–81, 76.
51. Jacques Lacan, *The Sinthome. The Seminar of Jacques Lacan. Book XXIII*, trans. A. R. Price (Cambridge: Polity, 2016), 25.

52. Bea Kaye, 'Hitachi Introduces A Kafkaesque Workplace Happiness Monitor', accessed 7 June 2020, https://uproxx.com/technology/hitachi-introduces-a-workplace-happiness-monitor/

53. Tom Foley and James Woollard, 'The Ddigital Future of Mental Healthcare and It Workforce: A Report on a Mental Health Stakeholder Engagement to Inform the Topol Review', accessed 7 July 2020, https://topol.hee.nhs.uk/wp-content/uploads/HEE-Topol-Review-Mental-health-paper.pdf.

54. Francis Spufford, *Red Plenty: Inside the Fifties Soviet Union* (London: Bloomsbury, 2010).

55. Bernard Stiegler, *Automatic Society. Volume 1: The Future of Work*, trans. D. Ross (Cambridge: Polity, 2016), 2.

56. Stiegler, *Automatic Society*, 18.

57. Milan Kundera, *The Art of the Novel*, trans. L. Asher (London: Faber, 2006), 159.

58. Immanuel Kant, 'Idea for a Universal History with a Cosmopolitan Purpose', in *Kant: Political Writings. Second Edition,* trans. H. B. Nisbet (Cambridge: Cambridge, 2016), 41–53, 44.

59. Jacques-Alain Miller, 'Truth is Coupled with Meaning' (Trans. N. Boileau and R. Litten), *The Lacanian Review*, 2 (2016), 9–20, 19.

60. Jacques-Alain Miller, 'Psychoanalysis, the City, and Communities' (Trans. P. Dravers), *Psychoanalytical Notebooks,* 24 (2012), 9–27, 14.

61. Lacan, *Encore*, 138.

62. Lacan, *L'insu*, 112.

63. Aristotle, *The Athenian Consitution,* trans. P. J. Rhodes (London: Penguin, 2002), 102.

64. Sylvia Plath, 'Three Women', in *The Collected Poems* (New York: Harper, 1981), 176.

65. Svetlana Alexievich. *Boys in Zinc*, trans. A. Bromfield (London: Penguin, 2017), 143.

66. Giorgio Agamben. *State of Exception*, trans. K. Attell (Chicago: Chicago, 2005), 3.

67. Eliot Weinberger, 'The American Virus', *London Review of Books*, 42 (4 June 2020), 4–8.

68. David Ferraro, 'Burnt Out', *Lacanian Review Online* (15 January 2020), accessed 11 July 2020, http://www.thelacanianreviews.com/burnt-out/?fbclid=IwAR3vva8k-TQGW-QUBlLJna3CJMnnhkEQCGNJH91VCo66hBMNaUHBdMm1yz94

69. Douglas Rushkoff, 'How Tech's Richest Plan to Save Themselves after the Apocalypse', *The Guardian*, 24 July 2018, accessed 10 July 2020, https://www.theguardian.com/technology/2018/jul/23/tech-industry-wealth-futurism-transhumanism-singularity

REFERENCES

Agamben, G. *State of Exception*. Trans. K. Attell (Chicago: Chicago, 2005).

Alexievich, S. *Boys in Zinc*. Trans. A. Bromfield (London: Penguin, 2017).

Aristotle, *The Athenian Consitution.* Trans. P. J. Rhodes (London: Penguin, 2002).
Buck-Morss, S. 'Hegel and Haiti'. *Critical Inquiry*, 26 (2000), 821–65.
Cassin, B. 'Ab-sense, or Lacan from A to D'. In *There's no Such Thing as a Sexual Relationship. Two Lessons on Lacan.* Eds. A. Badiou and B. Cassin and Trans. S. Spitzer and K. Reinhard (New York: Columbia, 2017), 3–43, 25.
Deleuze, G., and Guattari, F. *Anti-Oedipus: Capitalism and schizophrenia.* Trans. R. Hurley, M. Seem and H. Lane (London: Athlone, 1984).
Ferraro, D. 'Burnt Out'. *Lacanian Review Online*, 15 January 15 2020. Accessed 11 July 2020. http://www.thelacanianreviews.com/burnt-out/?fbclid=IwAR3vva8k-TQGW-QUBlLJna3CJMnnhkEQCGNJH91VCo66hBMNaUHBdMm1yz94
Foley, T., and Woollard, J. 'The Digital Future of Mental Healthcare and Its Workforce: A Report on a Mental Health Stakeholder Engagement to Inform the Topol Review'. Accessed 7 July 2020. https://topol.hee.nhs.uk/wp-content/uploads/HEE-Topol-Review-Mental-health-paper.pdf.
Foucault, M. *The Birth of Biopolitics. Lectures at the Collège de France. 1978–1979.* Trans. G. Burchell (New York: Picador, 2008).
Freud, S. 'Totem and Taboo'. In *The Standard Edition of the Complete Psychological Works of Sigmund Freud. Volume XIII.* Trans. J. Strachey (London: Vintage, 2008), 1–162.
Gaddis, W. *Agapē agape* (New York: Penguin, 2002), 4.
Harvey, D. *A Brief History of Neoliberalism.* (Oxford: Oxford University Press, 2005).
Kant, I. 'Idea for a Universal History with a Cosmopolitan Purpose'. In *Kant: Political Writings. Second Edition.* Trans. H. B. Nisbet (Cambridge: Cambridge, 2016), 41–53.
Kaye, B. 'Hitachi Introduces A Kafkaesque Workplace Happiness Monitor'. Accessed 7 June 2020. https://uproxx.com/technology/hitachi-introduces-a-work-place-happiness-monitor/
Kundera, M. *The Art of the Novel,* Trans. L. Asher (London: Faber, 2006).
Lacan, J. *Television. A Challenge to the Psychoanalytic Establishment.* Trans. D. Hollier, R. Krauss and A. Michelson (New York: Norton, 1990).
Lacan, J. *Anxiety. The Seminar of Jacques Lacan. Book X.* Trans. A. R. Price (Cambridge: Polity, 2014).
Lacan, J. *The Ethics of Psychoanalysis. 1959–1960. The Seminar of Jacques Lacan. Book VII.* Trans. D. Porter (New York, Norton, 1992).
Lacan, J. *On Feminine Sexuality, the Limits of Love and Knowledge, 1973–1973. Encore. The Seminar of Jacques Lacan. Book XX.* Trans. B. Fink. (New York: Norton, 1998).
Lacan, J. 'Intervention aux conclusions des groupes de travail'. *Les Lettres de l'École Freudienne*, 15 (1975), 235–44.
Lacan, J. *Le Séminaire livre XVI. D'un Autre l'autre.* (Paris: Seuil, 2006).
Lacan, J. 'The Mirror Stage as Formative of the I Function'. In *Écrits.* Trans. B. Fink (New York: Norton, 2006), 75–81, 76.
Lacan, J. *The Other Side of Psychoanalysis. The Seminar of Jacques Lacan. Book XVII.* Trans. R. Grigg (New York: Norton, 2007).

Lacan, J. *Séminaire XXIV (1976–1977): L'insu que sait de l'une-bévue s'aile à mourre.* Trans. C. Gallagher. Accessed 1 July 2020. http://www.lacaninireland.com/web/wp-content/uploads/2010/06/insu-Seminar-XXIV-Final-Sessions-1-12-1976-1977.pdf.

Lacan, J. *The Seminar of Jacques Lacan. Book I. Freud's Papers on Technique. 1953–1954.* Trans. J. Forrester (New York: Norton, 1988).

Lacan, J. *The Sinthome. The Seminar of Jacques Lacan. Book XXIII.* Trans. A. R. Price (Cambridge: Polity, 2016).

Lacan, J. *. . . or Worse. The Seminar of Jacques Lacan. Book XIX.* Trans. A. Price (Cambridge: Polity, 2018).

Logeion, ἰδιότης'. accessed 24 June 2020. https://logeion.uchicago.edu/%E1%BC%B0%CE%B4%CE%B9%CF%8C%CF%84%CE%B7%CF%82

Miller, J-A. 'Of distribution between the Sexes'. Trans. B. Wolf. *Psychoanalytical Notebooks*, 11 (2003), 9–27.

Miller, J-A., 'Psychoanalysis, the City, and Communities'. Trans. P. Dravers. *Psychoanalytical Notebooks*, 24 (2012), 9–27.

Miller, J-A. 'Six Paradigms of Jouissance'. Trans. J. Haney. *Psychoanalytical Notebooks*, 34 (2020), 11–77.

Miller, J-A. 'Truth is Coupled with Meaning'. Trans. N. Boileau and R. Litten. *The Lacanian Review*, 2 (2016), 9–20.

Nietzsche, F. *Twilight of the Idols.* Trans. R. J. Hollingdale (London: Penguin, 1990).

Plath, Sylvia. 'Three Women'. In *The Collected Poems* (New York: Harper, 1981).

Robcis, C. 'What Is the Future of Psychoanalysis in the Academy?'. *Psychoanalysis and History*, 20 (April 2018).

Rushkoff, D. 'How Tech's Richest Plan to Save Themselves after the Apocalypse'. *The Guardian*, 24 July 2018. Accessed 10 July 2020. https://www.theguardian.com/technology/2018/jul/23/tech-industry-wealth-futurism-transhumanism-singularity

Soler, C. *Lacanian Affects: The Function of Affect in Lacan's Work.* Trans. B. Fink (London: Routledge, 2016).

Somin, I. 'Trump Exploits Rational Political Ignorance'. Accessed 1 June 2020. https://www.usatoday.com/story/opinion/2015/10/04/trump-polls-immigration-taxes-column/72755896/

Stiegler, B. *Automatic Society. Volume 1: The Future of Work.* Trans. D. Ross (Cambridge: Polity, 2016).

Vanheule, S. 'Capitalist Discourse, Subjectivity and Lacanian Psychoanalysis'. *Frontiers in Psychology*, 7 (2016). https://www.frontiersin.org/articles/10.3389/fpsyg.2016.01948/full

Weinberger, E. 'The American Virus'. *London Review of Books* 42 (4 June 2020), 4–8.

Chapter 8

A Mass of Fools and Knaves

Psychoanalysis and the World's Many Asininities

Adrian Johnston

LACAN'S RAZOR: TOO SMART FOR YOUR OWN GOOD

As regards all manners of theorizing, if the objects and others of theorizing are themselves stupid, then theorizing subjects' smart theories are at risk of being too smart for their objects/others (i.e. too smart for their own good qua truth). Excessive sophistication and subtlety can easily overshoot, and thereby foolishly miss their targets, when brought to bear on unsophisticated and unsubtle realities. This is especially important for psychoanalysis, given the centrality to it of recognizing a fundamental difference-in-kind between conscious and unconscious thinking (as per Sigmund Freud's core distinction between secondary and primary processes[1]). Insofar as the standards of smartness are set from the standpoint of the secondary processes of conscious thinking, the primary processes of unconscious thinking cannot but repeatedly seem to be stupid because of their disregard for and deviations from these standards.[2]

In 1967s '*Discours à l'École freudienne de Paris*', Jacques Lacan coins one of his many neologisms, a neologism highly relevant at this juncture: '*connerie-sens*', an invented word merging *connaissance* (knowledge qua acquaintance) with *connerie* (stupidity).[3] At this moment in 1967, he associates the conscious sense of knowing familiarity with the world with a state of deafness and dumbness, a complacent ignorance mistaking itself for real comprehension.[4] Both the theory and practice of Lacanian psychoanalysis aim at shaking this complacent *connerie-sens*.

Apropos this 1967 neologism, a distinction can and should be put forward between *connerie-sens* and *connerie* (and/or *bêtise*) as Lacan very precisely conceives the latter. Neither *connerie-sens* nor *connerie* straightforwardly equate to either stupidity or smartness. Instead, *connerie-sens* would be a stupid smartness. That is to say, it names cases of the proverbial 'being too smart for your own good'.

By contrast, *connerie à la* Lacan would amount to instances of smart stupidity. To be more exact, Lacanian theorists and clinicians (at least ought to) carefully calculate and calibrate their concepts and interpretations to be right at the level of the realities and Reals they seek to touch. For both Freud and Lacan, there is a fundamental *connerie/bêtise* of the unconscious: whether as Freud's primary process mentation, with its dreams, jokes, slips and so on, or Lacan's *jouis-sens* (enjoy-meant)[5] of the meaningless materiality of repressed, libidinally saturated signifiers. With this stupid unconscious as the central object of psychoanalytic theory and practice, analytically conceptualizing or interpreting this unconscious requires, among other things, not erecting metapsychological or clinical constructs whose complexity exceeds it or that see profound meaning where there is only superficial nonsense. The goal is not to outwit the unconscious, but to wit with and as it. Hence, for Lacan at least, *connerie* generally is preferable to *connerie-sens*.

At one point in *Seminar XVII* (*The Other Side of Psychoanalysis* (1969–1970)), Lacan implicitly distinguishes between bullshit (*déconnage*) and stupidity (*connerie*). More precisely, he declares:

> the discourse of the unconscious . . . imposes itself precisely by virtue of the fact that . . . it doesn't bullshit (*il ne déconne pas*). As stupid (*con*) as this discourse of the unconscious is, it is responding to something that stems from the institution of the discourse of the master himself. This is what is called the unconscious. It imposes itself upon science as a fact [*fait*].[6]

Given that this *connerie* of the discourse of the unconscious 'imposes itself upon science as a fact', as the brute facticity of the senseless, repetitive stupidity of the libidinal economy's primary processes, the only smart thing for the analyst (whether of libidinal and/or political economy) to do is to be equally stupid. That is to say, he/she must avoid projecting the standards and expectations of secondary-process-type cognition onto the unconscious, thereby seeing meaningful, intelligent rhyme and reason where there really is none. Such projected senses are tantamount to the bullshit of *connerie-sens* rather than true *connaissance* vis-à-vis the unconscious. Moreover, insofar as Lacan's theory of the four discourses derives those of the university, hysteric and analyst from that of the master (including the modern master as capitalist) as the *Ur*-discourse,[7] the discourse of the analyst must recognize its links with and parasitic dependence upon *la connerie du maître*, with the discourses of master and analyst paired as recto and verso[8] ('As stupid (*con*) as this discourse of the unconscious is, it is responding to something that stems from the institution of the discourse of the master himself').

Lacan could be said to wield a version of Occam's razor, one cutting short and cutting out all of the conscious mind's fascinations with intelligence, complexity, nuance and the like. These fascinations tend to interfere with registering an unconscious thinking utterly uninterested in such narcissistic obsessions. Indeed, Lacan's musings on the varieties of stupidity cut against an occupational hazard of virtually all academics and intellectuals: the anxious desire to be, or at least appear to be, the smartest person in any room. In order to be at the proper level to handle the foci of one's theories, one must traverse fantasies associated with this sort of desire. This desire and its fantasies all too often seduce the theorist into distorting these foci to fit his/her (self-)images of smartness. Under the shadow of Lacan's (rather than Occam's) razor, the truth usually is stupid, all other things being equal.

MADNESS, IMBECILITY, STUPIDITY: TAKE YOUR PICK

So, what about Lacan and stupidity? What exactly does he have to say regarding this topic? I ought to clarify a linguistic issue upfront. The passages in Lacan's *oeuvre* I will be mobilizing below generally involve him using two words in his native French tongue: *bêtise* and *connerie* (and these nouns' corresponding adjectival forms, *bête* and *con*/*conne*, respectively). Whereas *bêtise* straightforwardly translates into English as 'stupidity', *connerie* sometimes can and should be translated as, among other words, 'bullshit'. For an English speaker, bullshit is not necessarily equivalent to stupidity, particularly when someone is bullshitting in the service of crafty deception, artful manipulation and the like (indeed, as just seen, Lacan himself at one point distinguishes between bullshit [*déconnage*] and stupidity [*connerie*]). However, I would maintain, some instances of Lacan's use of *connerie* indeed ought to be rendered as 'stupidity' and taken as synonymous with his uses of *bêtise*. I believe myself to be justified in construing *connerie* as 'stupidity' in those passages featuring this word that I will be drawing on in what ensues.

Particularly in the later phases of *le Séminaire*, Lacan comes to associate closely psychoanalysis with stupidity. Already in *Seminar XIV* (*The Logic of Fantasy* (1966–1967)), he contends that both philosophy and psychoanalysis, when all is said and done, bottom out in stupidity (*bêtise*),[9] a contention he echoes thereafter.[10] As for philosophy, one need only call to mind such examples as Parmenides's foundational 'being is, nothing is not' (about which Lacan confesses 'personally I find that stupid (*bête*)'[11]), the tautological law of identity (A = A) and non-contradiction ($A \neq \sim A$) forming the basis of classical bivalent logic, G. E. Moore's 'here is one hand, and here is another' or even Alfred Tarski's '"snow is white" is true if and only if snow is white'.

Subsequent years of Lacan's seminar contain further observations about stupidity (as both *bêtise* and *connerie*) that begin to clarify what Lacan has in mind apropos the nature and status of the stupid in analysis. In *Seminar XVI* (*From an Other to the other* (1968–1969)), Lacan suggests, with a Heideggerian-style formulation, that 'the truth of stupidity is not without posing the question of the stupidity of truth' (*la vérité de la connerie n'est pas sans poser la question de la connerie de la vérité*).[12] This suggestion immediately raises the two-part question: What 'truth' (*vérité*) or sort of truth is at issue here and why might it be in some sense or other 'stupid' (*conne*)?

Seminar XX (*Encore* (1972–1973)) is particularly helpful in providing clues to answering this question. In the 12 December 1972 session of that seminar, Lacan speaks of the purportedly ultimate psychoanalytic truth according to which there is no sexual relationship (*il n'y a pas de rapport sexuel*).[13] He then promptly proceeds to remark, 'regarding analytic discourse: doesn't this discourse hang together (*se tient*) by basing itself on the dimension of stupidity (*bêtise*)?'[14]

The concluding paragraph of Freud's 1937 essay 'Analysis Terminable and Interminable' lurks implicitly in the background of Lacan's 1972 comments. Therein, Freud notoriously asserts that the castration complex, as organizing sexual difference, is the unmovable boulder against which any and every analysis pursued to its fullest conclusion runs aground – 'We often have the impression that with the wish for a penis and the masculine protest we have penetrated through all the psychological strata and have reached bedrock (*gewachsenes Fels*), and that thus our activities are at an end.'[15] The unsurpassable termination point of all analyses turns out to be, for the final Freud, a blunt given, a sheer factical matter as dumb as a rock.

Lacan clearly would not endorse Freud's characterization of this 'underlying bedrock' (*unterliegenden gewachsenen Felsens*) as 'a biological fact' (*eine biologische Tatsache*).[16] Yet, Lacan's idea of 'the dimension of stupidity' as the final truth grounding analysis tout court signals a strong endorsement of the assertion that contingent, senseless fact(s) (or, as Lacan phrases it in his *écrit* 'On a Question Prior to Any Possible Treatment of Psychosis', 'ineffable and stupid existence' [*ineffable et stupide existence*][17]) having to do with (more-than-biological) sexual difference enjoy some kind of finality for psychoanalysis. Statements in earlier years of *le Séminaire*, ones referring to foolishness and knavery, can be retroactively illuminated in light of the cross-resonance I am underscoring here between the Freud of 'Analysis Terminable and Interminable' and the Lacan of *Seminar XX*. These thus-illuminated statements in turn further buttress my interpretation of how and why Lacanian analysis grounds itself upon *bêtise/connerie*.

Throughout a number of the annual seminars preceding *Seminar XX*, Lacan, when discussing stupidity, invokes the category of '*canaillerie*'. This word usually is rendered by Lacan's translators into English as 'knavery'. However, as will prove important to note regarding Lacan's concept of the knave, it could also be translated as 'crookedness', 'coarseness' or 'vulgarity'.

In 1960, Lacan has recourse several times to the English word 'knave' (which he comes to translate into the French '*canaille*') as well as, and in relation to, the English word 'fool'. The fool, as Lacan points out in both *Seminar VII* (*The Ethics of Psychoanalysis* (1959–1960)) and the contemporaneous *écrit* 'Remarks on Daniel Lagache's Presentation: "Psychoanalysis and Personality Structure"', is he/she who tells the truth while playing the clown. Lacan appropriately appeals to the Shakespearean figure of the jester as uniquely enabled to speak truth to power (hence also Lacan's resort to the English language of the Bard in this context).[18] The Lacanian fool tells the truth in the guise of a lie (i.e. a mere joke, a jest not to be taken seriously, a harmless bit of irony or sarcasm safely encased in scare quotes and the like).

The Lacanian knave, by contrast, is the complementary inverse of the fool, namely, he/she who tells lies in the guise of truths. When introducing the opposed pair of the fool and the knave in the 20 March 1960 session of the seventh seminar, Lacan associates them with left-wingers and right-wingers, respectively.[19] On the one side, the left-wing fool presents truths critical of the established order. But, these critiques are doomed to inefficacy, since they are taken to be ridiculous flights of utopian fantasy or intellectualist nit-picking worth no more serious consideration than self-indulgent daydreams or armchair exercises. They pose no real threat to the status quo. If anything, such 'foolish' (center-)leftist criticisms usually even serve the powers-that-be in one or more of three ways: by providing a harmless release valve for discontent; by allowing this discontent to be complacently enjoyed as an end-in-itself rather than as a spur to acting (such as letting the jesters of late-night television shows, as Lacanian fools, lull one into remaining satisfied with the mere mockery, and nothing more, of those in power); and/or by providing a deceptive sheen of pseudo-democratic legitimacy to authorities apparently willing to tolerate such criticisms. As regards this last way, one need only remember former American president George W. Bush's co-opting of criticisms of his Iraq war as evidence of democracy's superiority – this alleged superiority purportedly justified the toppling of Saddam Hussein – since this democracy allows for such criticisms to be expressed without suppression.

On the other side opposite the fool, the right-wing knave poses as the sober, jaded realist, the thick-skinned enlightened pragmatist who simply says how things are in reality. Lacan elaborates:

> At a certain level of its usage, 'knave' may be translated into French as *valet*, but 'knave' goes further. He's not a cynic with the element of heroism implied by that attitude. He is, to be precise, what Stendhal called an 'unmitigated scoundrel' (le coquin fieffé). That is to say, no more than your Mr. Everyman (*Monsieur Tout-le-Monde*), but your Mr. Everyman with greater strength of character.[20]

He continues:

> Everyone knows that a certain way of presenting himself, which constitutes part of the ideology of the right-wing intellectual, is precisely to play the role of what he is in fact, namely, a 'knave'. In other words, he doesn't retreat from the consequences of what is called realism; that is, when required, he admits he's a crook (*une canaille*).[21]

Slavoj Žižek encapsulates Lacan's fool-knave couple as per *Seminar VII* thusly:

> the right-wing intellectual is a knave, a conformist who refers to the mere existence of the given order as an argument for it, and mocks the Left on account of its 'utopian' plans, which necessarily lead to catastrophe; while the left-wing intellectual is a fool, a court jester who publicly displays the lie of the existing order, but in a way which suspends the performative efficiency of his speech.[22]

Alain Badiou, in his short 2020 book *Trump*, depicts contemporary neoliberal capitalism in a fashion resonating with Lacan's and Žižek's just-quoted remarks. Without mentioning the Lacanian category of the knave, Badiou nonetheless highlights the knavery essential to today's apologists for capital. On Badiou's clear-eyed account, defenders of current capitalism behave like the Lacanian knave, openly acknowledging capitalism's various and sundry serious problems. However, as with all knavery, the capitalist variety seeks to sustain, in its confessions of capitalism's failures and vices, the background 'realist' assumption that, despite these flaws and shortcomings, 'there is no alternative' to capitalism (in Margaret Thatcher's words). Or, to paraphrase another former British prime minister, the neoliberal capitalist knave repeatedly proclaims: 'No one pretends that capitalism is perfect or all-wise. Indeed, it has been said that capitalism is the worst form of socio-economic system, except for all those other forms that have been tried from time to time.'[23]

Incidentally, the subject of Badiou's 2020 book, American president Donald J. Trump, definitely indulges in Lacanian knavery from time to time. As I noted above, the French word for knavery, *canaillerie*, also can be translated into English as 'crookedness', 'coarseness' or 'vulgarity'. Obviously, Trump is nothing if not a coarse, vulgar crook.

But, what is more, Trump periodically operates as a knave in the precise Lacanian sense. One example of this that comes to mind is Trump's now-infamous response to Bill O'Reilly during a 2017 Fox News interview when O'Reilly asks about Russian president Vladimir Putin. When pressed by O'Reilly about Putin's murderousness, Trump retorts, 'There are a lot of killers. You think our country's so innocent?'

Reacting to this particular 2017 instance as a simple, straightforward lie, of which Trump is known to utter many, is a major mistake (a reaction bound up with belief in the ideological myth of America as 'the shining city on a hill'). This is, rather, a case of knavery as lying in the guise of truth. The United States in fact has engaged in and continues to engage in plenty of violent skullduggery both at home and abroad. Trump is being factually correct about this. Yet, this is knavish insofar as Trump's admission of American murderousness is meant to mislead, to downplay and distract from his cosiness with Putin and the Russian mafia state apparatus. Moreover, Trump-the-knave, with his coarse, vulgar 'realism', wants everyone to abandon their (purportedly) idealist standards, to lower their expectations and resign themselves to the universal reign of thuggish authoritarian thieves as the permanent, unchangeable way of the world.

Overall, the essence of knavery (*canaillerie*) *à la* Lacan is the gesture of transforming a historically transient 'is' into an eternally natural 'ought'. The knave treats fleeting facts about currently dominant circumstances as always-already timelessly normative in their brute factuality. The inherently conservative *canaille* defends the status quo by removing the critical sting from inconvenient truths about it precisely through admitting them.

There is a resemblance here to the classical Freudian defensive manoeuvre of intellectually accepting the repressed specifically as a means of depriving the registration of the repressed of any power to induce change.[24] Indeed, the knave is troubled enough by inconvenient truths, often presented to him/her by those he/she takes to be fools, to be forced at least to defend against them. As Lacan remarks in *Seminar XXI* (*The Non-Dupes Err* (1973–1974)), 'The truth itches even those whom, without believing it too much, I call knaves' (*La vérité démage, même ceux que, sans trop y croire, j'appelle les canailles*).[25] With reference to the title of the twenty-first seminar, the knave certainly qualifies as erring, and as encouraging others to err, by playing the non-dupe, namely, the stoic representative of hard-nosed, unvarnished *Realpolitik* straightforwardly telling it how it is without any sugar-coating.

In *Seminar XVII*, Lacan returns to the topic of knavery in connection with that of stupidity (*bêtise*). He maintains that taking facts in their sheer factuality, as simply facts, is stupid.[26] However, in the manipulative hands of the knave, this is 'a prodigiously rich piece of stupidity' (*une bêtise prodigieusement féconde*).[27] Why? Lacan explains:

> There is no other metalanguage than all the forms of knavery (*la canaillerie*), if we thereby designate these curious operations derivable from the fact that man's desire is the Other's desire (*le désir de l'homme, c'est le désir de l'Autre*). All acts of bastardry (*Toute canaillerie*) are based on the fact of wishing to be someone's Other, I mean someone's big Other (*le grand Autre*), in which the figures by which his desire will be captivated are drawn.[28]

In this very same context, Lacan reminds the audience of his thesis according to which metalanguages are non-existent (*il n'y a pas de méta-langage*).[29] I will not delve into the topic of the Lacanian account of metalanguage here.[30] Suffice it for now to register that Lacan's conservative knave, in stating factual matters under the stupid (*bête*) assumption that description is immediately tantamount to prescription, pretends to be the established order incarnate. He/she feigns to occupy the meta-level position of directly embodying or giving voice to the status quo system itself (i.e. the big Other, the transindividual Third mediating all intersubjective relations). The knave is animated by 'wishing to be someone's Other', desiring to identify him/her-self with *le grand Autre*. Or, in the terms Lacan uses at one point in the seventh seminar, knaves try to pass themselves off as the anonymous, universal 'Mr. Everyman' (*Monsieur Tout-le-Monde*).[31]

Perhaps what makes knavery characterized thusly 'prodigiously rich' for Lacan is the similarity of its signature manoeuvre to one of the jokes recounted by Freud in his 1905 book on the topic. This now well-known bit of humor goes as follows:

> Two Jews met in a railway carriage at a station in Galicia. 'Where are you going?' asked one. 'To Cracow', was the answer. 'What a liar you are!' broke out the other. 'If you say you're going to Cracow, you want me to believe you're going to Lemberg. But I know that in fact you're going to Cracow. So why are you lying to me?'[32]

Of the second Jew, the one answering 'To Cracow', Freud promptly states, 'the second is lying when he tells the truth and is telling the truth by means of a lie'.[33] This joke about the two Jews in Galicia could be said to be celebrated by Freud as 'a prodigiously rich piece of stupidity', as something apparently 'stupid' (i.e. a joke) containing within itself intelligent insight. In *Jokes and Their Relation to the Unconscious*, he praises this joke's implicit theoretical sophistication:

> The joke . . . is pointing to a problem and is making use of the uncertainty of one of our commonest concepts. Is it the truth if we describe things as they are without troubling to consider how our hearer will understand what we say? Or is this only jesuitical truth, and does not genuine truth consist in taking the

> hearer into account and giving him a faithful picture of our own knowledge? I think that jokes of this kind are sufficiently different from the rest to be given a special position. What they are attacking is not a person or an institution but the certainty of our knowledge itself, one of our speculative possessions. The appropriate name for them would therefore be 'sceptical' jokes.[34]

Lacan not only credits *Jokes and Their Relation to the Unconscious*, along with *The Interpretation of Dreams* (1900) and *The Psychopathology of Everyday Life* (1901), as containing the breakthrough discoveries founding psychoanalysis proper – he heeds Freud's advice to accord the two-Jews-in-Galicia joke 'a special position'. In addition to the Lacanian version of the motif of 'lying in the guise of truth' (with knavery as a species of such dishonesty), one can see a cluster of Lacan's ideas as rooted in Freud's comments about this joke, including: the uniquely human double-feint (i.e. leaving true tracks to be taken as false tracks), the distinction between the subjects of utterance (the said [*dit*]) and enunciation (the saying [*dire*]), the stupidity of truth (*la connerie de la vérité*) and psychoanalysis as revolutionarily subverting 'the certainty of our knowledge itself' (as Freud puts it in the quotation above).

Like the second of the two Jews in Galicia, Lacan's right-wing knave, when engaging in knavery, is indeed 'lying when he tells the truth'. Recall that Lacan, in *Seminar VII*, notes of the knave (*la canaille*) that, 'when required, he admits he's a crook (*une canaille*)'. In short, the knave (as a crook, rogue, scoundrel, etc.) is knavish precisely in admitting that he/she is a knave. As with the Jew who answers 'To Cracow' in the Freudian joke, the knave confesses to being a knave so that his/her interlocutor will think him/her not a knave. Would a real knave, as dishonest, honestly own up to being a knave? As Lacan observes in the same context from the seventh seminar quoted above, 'Everyone knows that a certain way of presenting himself, which constitutes part of the ideology of the right-wing intellectual, is precisely to play the role of what he is in fact, namely, a "knave"'.

Thus, what the knave's interlocutor should do is respond as does the first Jew in the Freudian joke: 'If you say you're a knave, you want me to believe that you're not (so much of) a knave. But I know that in fact you really are a total knave. So why are you lying to me?' The same deserves to be thrown in the face of the knavish apologists for 'capitalo-parliamentarianism' (to borrow an appropriate term from Badiou for the neoliberal interface between capital and state). One ought to reply to them: 'If you say capitalo-parliamentarianism is bad, you want me to believe that it's not (so) bad given the admissibility of its faults. But I know that in fact capitalo-parliamentarianism really is bad. So why are you lying to me?'

In these instances, the smartness of the cunning knave, his/her clever anticipation of others' attitudes and hermeneutic dispositions towards his/her utterances, is the lure to be spurned by his/her addressees. The sophisticated reading of the knave's admission of being a knave is precisely what the knave counts on and, therefore, it is the trap to be avoided. Instead, the truth is to be found through refusing subtlety in favour of stupidity, specifically, the 'stupid' procedure of disregarding the 'prodigious richness' of the knave's feint and instead taking the knave literally at his/her superficial word. 'You say you're a knave. Well, yes, you really are a knave.' Or, Trump says he is a Putin-esque killer kleptocrat. Well, yes, he really is a bloodstained, wannabe-mafioso conman (in addition to being a pathetic garden-variety moron and compulsively lying malignant narcissist).

One even could come up with a knavish version of a clinical phenomenon highlighted by Freud. Certain analysands of Freud's and of his associates reported upsetting dreams depicting undesirable sets of circumstances. Freud then learnt that these analysands previously had become familiar with the ideas of *The Interpretation of Dreams*. Aware of Freud's thesis in that 1900 book, according to which all dreams express the fulfilment of wishes, these analysands expressed wishes that their analysts be mistaken through dreaming dreams appearing to contradict the central thesis of psychoanalysis's (early) theory of dreams. Freud labels these specific sorts of dreams 'counter-wish dreams' (*Gegenwunschträume*).[35]

Likewise, one readily could imagine an analysand already familiar with Freud's 1925 essay 'Negation' (*Die Verneinung*). On the basis of an awareness of the example therein of the unsolicited denial from the couch 'and the unidentified woman in the dream was not my mother',[36] this hypothetical analysand might preemptively declare in relation to similar dream content, 'and the unidentified woman in the dream must be my mother'. If this declaration is meant to prompt the listening analyst to conclude the opposite (i.e. 'and the unidentified woman in the dream was not the analysand's mother'), then the analysand in this case is behaving like a knave. This knave's analyst indeed should respond with a version of: 'If you say the unidentified woman in your dream must be your mother, you want me to believe that she is not your mother. But I know that in fact the unidentified woman in your dream is your mother. So why are you lying to me?'

On these sorts of knavish occasions, the application of interpretive cleverness to knaves' utterances would be too smart for its own good. Sometimes, the truth indeed is stupid. It can hide in plain sight. This makes the figure of the Minister in Edgar Allan Poe's 'The Purloined Letter', who conceals the letter purloined from the Queen out in the open, a variant of the Lacanian knave – and this before Lacan precisely conceptualizes knavery *comme canaillerie* starting in *Seminar VII* (i.e. several years after his mid-1950s analytic appropriation of Poe's story).

Lacan, at several points in his later work, characterizes knavery (*canaillerie*) as collapsing into foolishness (*sottise*)[37] and/or stupidity (*bêtise*).[38] This Lacan even insists that the discourse of the analyst, as per the theory of the four discourses introduced in *Seminar XVII* and the contemporaneous text '*Radiophonie*' (1970), is unique among the discourses in bringing about a reduction of knavery to stupidity (*bêtise*).[39] This insistence links back up with the somewhat cryptic statements I cited above about analysis and stupidity from the 12 December 1972 session of *Seminar XX*, statements that prompted my turn to the fool-knave pair in the first place. As seen, for Lacan, in both the nineteenth and twentieth seminars, as well as already in *Seminar XV* (*The Psychoanalytic Act* (1967–1968)),[40] the analyst's discourse 'culminates in' or 'bases itself on' *bêtise*.[41] Yet, how and why does analysis transform knavery into stupidity and/or foolishness? What does this amount to in more concrete terms?

Again in the 12 December 1972 session of *Seminar XX*, Lacan offers further specifications of what he has in mind apropos the stupidity at stake in psychoanalysis. He reminds his listeners, regarding 'analytic discourse' (i.e. the discourse of the analyst as per the four discourses), that 'I formulated' it 'to you as *a* with S_2 below it'.[42] He is invoking the matheme of the analytic discourse. Lacan then asks of this discourse 'what that questions on the side of the subject – in order to produce what, if not stupidity (*la bêtise*)?'[43] He immediately adds:

> It is nevertheless true that there is a status to be granted to this new discourse and to its approach to stupidity. Surely it comes closer, since in other discourses stupidity is what one flees. Discourses always aim at the least stupidity, at sublime stupidity (*la bêtise sublime*), for 'sublime' means the highest point of what lies below (*le point le plus élevé de ce qui est en bas*).[44]

In Lacan's theory of the four discourses, all four discourses (i.e. master, university, hysteric and analytic discourses) each involve four positions, namely, those of 'agent', 'other', 'product' and 'truth'. In the discourse of the analyst, these positions are occupied as follows: *a* as agent, $ as other, S_1 as product and S_2 as truth. That is to say, in analytic discourse, the analyst is an agent whose specific agency is to function as an embodiment of the analysand's object(s)-cause-of-desire (i.e. *a* as *objet petit a*) through transference phenomena. This analyst-agent, whose position is underpinned by the 'truth' of analytic knowledge (S_2) as a savoir faire apropos letting the unconscious speak, addresses his/her interventions and interpretations to the analysand-other's intrasubjective conflicts and inconsistencies, namely, to this other's status as a split subject ($). Through the labour of the analytic process unfolding thusly between analyst and analysand, the master signifiers

(S_1s) grounding and organizing the structure of the analysand's subjectivity are 'produced', that is, brought to light as bits of contingent, factical senselessness nonetheless pivotal in the vicissitudes of the subject's life history.

Much of this is foreshadowed in, for instance, *Seminar XI* (*The Four Fundamental Concepts of Psychoanalysis* (1964)). The June 17 session therein contains some statements about analytic interpretation and 'nonsense'. Lacan asserts that 'the effect of interpretation is to isolate in the subject a kernel (*un cœur*), a *Kern*, to use Freud's own term, of *non-sense*'.[45] Such interpretation 'has the effect of bringing out an irreducible signifier (*faire surgir un signifiant irréductible*)'[46] (i.e. of producing a master signifier qua S_1). Although such signifiers are meaningless, they are not, for all that, without relation to highly organized and intricate unconscious formations – 'What is there is rich and complex, when it is a question of the unconscious of the subject, and intended to bring out irreducible, *non-sensical* – composed of non-meanings (*faits de non-sens*) – signifying elements'[47] (with Lacanian analyst Serge Leclaire's disguised self-analytic dream interpretation of the nonsensical signifier '*Poordjeli*' as a key example here for Lacan[48]). The primary-process mentation of an unconscious that thinks differently than consciousness, but truly thinks all the same, could be said to indulge in the rigorously structured nonsense of chains of signifiers in their pure meaningless acoustic and/or graphic materiality (i.e. the both infantile- and Joycean-style babble Lacan subsequently baptizes '*lalangue*'[49]). This is what Lacan is referring to when, at the same moment in the eleventh seminar, he maintains, speaking of the analysand, that, 'What is essential is that he should see . . . to what signifier – to what irreducible, traumatic, non-meaning (*non-sens, irréductible, traumatique*) – he is, as a subject, subjected (*assujetti*)'.[50]

Lacan then, at the very start of his 1976 'Preface to the English-Language Edition' of *Seminar XI*, sees fit to underscore how alighting upon such core signifiers in their irreducible meaninglessness/nonsensicality (or, perhaps, irreducible stupidity [*bêtise/connerie*]) signals with certainty that analysis really has managed to touch the very heart of the unconscious. He begins these prefatory remarks by proposing that, 'When the space of a lapsus no longer carries any meaning (*sens*) (or interpretation), then only is one sure (*alors seulement on est sûr*) that one is in the unconscious. *One knows* (*On le sait, soi*)'.[51] The reduction to a senselessness underpinning all sense and significance, the time and place of the circulating buck of meaning and its interpretation finally stopping, would appear to be the necessary and sufficient condition for the proper termination of a Lacanian analysis, the sine qua non of a thorough analytic experience.

To return to the issue of Lacan's characterization of S_1s as stupid: With the matheme of the discourse of the analyst now in view, the preceding quotation from the twentieth seminar readily can be understood as involving Lacan identifying the master signifier, S_1 as the product of this discourse, with stupidity (*bêtise*). Similarly, in *Seminar XVI*, Lacan proclaims, 'the master is an idiot (*con*)'.[52] And, in *Seminar XXIII* (*The Sinthome* (1975–1976)), he once again proposes that analysis produces stupidity (*connerie*):

> That's what analysis is. It's the response to a riddle. Moreover, it's a response . . . that is quite especially daft (*spécialement conne*). This is precisely why one must keep a firm hold on the rope (*il faut garder la corde*). I mean that, if one has no idea where the rope ends, namely, in the knot of sexual non-relation (*nœud du non-rapport sexuel*), one runs the risk of floundering (*bafouiller*).[53]

The answers produced by psychoanalysis are 'especially daft'. Moreover, analysis orients its movement in the direction of this *bêtise/connerie*, rather than fleeing from anything smacking of stupidity (as is the case, according to *Seminar XX*, with discourses other than that of the analyst). The desire of the analyst definitely should not include a yearning to be seen as clever, erudite, infallible, ingenious, witty and the like – lest the analyst counterproductively play into analysands' transferential investments in the figure/function of 'the subject supposed to know' (*le sujet supposé savoir*). But what exactly is Lacan's master signifier (S_1), the product of analytic discourse, in this 1970s context? And what renders it, for Lacan, peculiarly and intensely stupid (*bête/con*)?

As seen, in both the twentieth and twenty-third seminars, Lacan invokes his '*il n'y a pas de rapport sexuel*', his 'sexual non-relation' (*non-rapport sexuel*), as regards *bêtise/connerie*. And, as I already argued, this is because human sexuation is, for Lacan, ultimately 'stupid' qua a matter of meaningless factical contingency. It is central but inexplicable. No signifiers of the socio-symbolic big Other ever adequately answer questions along the lines of: Why is there sexual difference? What is it to be sexed? What is it to be masculine or feminine? As the earlier Lacan of the third seminar (*The Psychoses* (1955–1956)) likewise already observes about finitude and thrownness (*als Geworfenheit*), 'The question of death and the question of birth are as it happens the two ultimate questions that have precisely no solution in the signifier. This is what gives neurotics their existential value'.[54]

The later Lacan comes to depict neurotics as afflicted by a 'retardation', a 'mental debility' (*une débilité mentale*), in which their conscious thinking labours in vain to repress the irrepressible (and also the *bête/conne*) truth of '*il n'y a pas de rapport sexuel*'[55] (yet, at the same time, he avows that his own teaching is no less '*débile*' than such *débilité mentale*[56]). In *Seminar XXII* (*R.S.I.* (1974–1975)), Lacan even defines 'mental debility' in his sense as any worldview overtly or covertly assuming the existence of the harmonious, balanced sexual relation Lacanian psychoanalysis denies exists.[57] Examples of such worldviews would include ontologies of being as All, One, Whole and so on and cosmologies of yin-yang-style complementarities and equilibriums.

Is this to say that subjects are forced to choose between stupidity and retardation? Is this a choice between, on the one hand, the *bêtise/connerie* of the sexual non-relation as the ultimate *vérité* of the analytic unconscious and, on the other hand, the *débilité mentale* of neurotic defenses against this truth? At the close of the 11 January 1977 session of *Seminar XXIV* (*L'insu que sait de l'une-bévue, s'aile à mourre* (1976–1977)), Lacan asserts that, 'We have only the choice between madness and retardation' (*Entre folie et débilité mentale, nous n'avons que le choix*).[58] But, what does this assertion entail?

Reasonably inferring that by 'madness' (*folie*) Lacan means psychosis, one can hypothesize that there is an initial, primordial 'choice', an (unconscious) *Ur*-decision, for the subject(-to-be) between psychosis and neurosis (with the latter as *débilité mentale*). Assuming a subjectifying decision in favour of neurosis rather than psychosis, there subsequently can be another choice, that between retardation as mental debility (i.e. perseverating in an established neurotic modus operandi) and stupidity (i.e. opting for an exhaustive analytic experience leading to a confrontation with the senseless, idiotic truth(s) at the core of the unconscious). Lacan's indications along these lines suggest that humans are forced to choose between being mad, retarded or stupid, with foolishness and knavery as two ways of being retarded.

At least some of the S_1s serving as quilting points (*points de capiton*) for the unconscious subjectivity of the speaking being (*parlêtre*) are tantamount to this subject's always inadequate and unsatisfactory answers to impossible-to-answer questions about sexuality, mortality and related matters, as questions with 'no solution in the signifier'. Beneath these 'master signifiers', these pseudo-solutions to the insoluble enigmas of sexuation and much bound up with it, is nothing more than the faceless emptiness of pure subjectivity ($) as negativity. This helps account for why, in Lacan's matheme for the discourse of the master, $ is positioned as the (primally repressed) truth beneath the (false) agency of S_1. These S_1s subjectify the void of $, filling in this anonymous blank with semblances of identity, essence and substance, with the appearance of grounded being (i.e. this is the true meaning of being alive, sexed, etc.). Each subject could be said to be an idiot, including in the etymologically original ancient Greek sense of ἰδιώτης, in his/her self-subjectifying choice of idiosyncratic master signifiers as foundations of his/her fictitious selfhood and singularity.

However, as regards the topic of stupidity, more still remains to be said about Lacan's S_1 and, in connection with this, his general theory of the signifier. Tellingly, Lacan highlights, also in *Seminar XX*, two dimensions of the signifier converging in, and epitomized by, the master signifier qua S_1: on the one hand, the senselessness of the signifier in its acoustic or graphic materiality divorced from any signifieds as meaning-making referents of recognized linguistic signs; on the other hand, the idiocy of *jouissance*, of the compulsively repetitive looping circuit of the drives lying at the base of the libidinal economy. These two dimensions coinciding and condensed in the speaking subject's S_1s, the quilting points of his/her sexuated subjectivity and its accompanying symptoms, constitute the supremely stupid nucleus of the *parlêtre*, the nonsense grounding the subject's very sense of being. Hence, in *Seminar XXI*, Lacan claims that 'stupidity (*la connerie*) is our essence'.[59] To paraphrase the above-quoted, Heideggerian-style observation by Lacan (in *Seminar XVI*) according to which 'the truth of stupidity (*la connerie*) is not without posing the question of the stupidity of truth', the essence of stupidity is the stupidity of essence. But, how so, precisely?

During the 19 December 1972 session of the twentieth seminar, Lacan says a few things about stupidity and the signifier. To begin with, he bluntly maintains that, 'The signifier is stupid' (*le signifiant est bête*).[60] He soon adds, 'analytic discourse introduces an adjective made into a noun, "stupidity" (*la bêtise*), insofar as it is a dimension of the signifier at work (*une dimension en exercise du signifiant*)'.[61]

This stupidity of the signifier (at work) is operative on both sides of the analytic couple. On the analyst's side, and as per the discourse of the analyst as I gloss it above, he/she listens to the analysand's associations with an ear to arriving eventually at the master signifiers quilting, organizing and anchoring the field of these associations. Such an arrival is the production of S_1s as a result of analytic discourse, of analysis as a peculiar 'social link' (*lien social*). These S_1s are like the refrains of the mood music accompanying the analysand's day-to-day life.

What is more, as Lacan never tired of stressing starting with his 1950s-era fusing of Freud's psychoanalysis with Ferdinand de Saussure's structural linguistics, the analyst should register the analysand's speech not (only) as a series of signs (i.e. as meanings aimed at referents intended by the speaker on the couch), but (also) as a chain of pure signifiers (i.e. as meaningless sounds and images establishing associational connections unconstrained by conscious concerns with the sensible, the communicable, the logical or the grammatical). Only thereby is the analyst able to hear the machinations of an unconscious that speaks in and through homophonies, puns, double entendres, punchlines and the like (especially when these are consciously unintended). This would be Lacan's Saussurian rendition of a Freudian 'evenly-suspended attention'[62] attuned to 'primary processes'[63] and the 'false verbal bridges'[64] established by these processes characteristic of unconscious thinking (as distinct from conscious thinking, with its secondary processes).[65] For secondary-process-level conscious cognition, the primary-process-level unconscious, as voicing itself through the (apparent) nonsense of dreams, jokes, slips of the tongue, parapraxes and free associations, cannot but seem to be profoundly stupid in its failure to conform to familiar criteria for meaningfulness and rationality.

Apropos the stupid signifier being at work on the analysand's side, the analytic golden rule for the analysand is none other than the injunction to associate freely, to say whatever comes to mind as it arises without concern for appropriateness, clarity, importance, manners, relevance or whatever else might lead to intentional or unintentional self-censoring. Again in the 19 December 1972 session of *Seminar XX*, Lacan brings up free association by the analysand, noting the impossibility of fully living up to what it enjoins – 'The subject is precisely the one we encourage, not to say it all (*tout dire*), as we tell him in order to charm him – one cannot say it all – but rather to utter stupidities (*bêtises*). That is the key (*tout est là*).'[66] He then adds:

> For it is with those stupidities (*bêtises*) that we do analysis, and that we enter into the new subject – that of the unconscious. It is precisely to the extent that the guy (*le bonhomme*) is willing not to think anymore that we will perhaps learn a little bit more about it, that we will draw certain consequences from his words (*dits*) – words that cannot be taken back (*se dédire*), for that is the rule of the game.[67]

Soon after, Lacan notes of the analytic method of interpreting free associations, 'in analysing anyone, no matter how stupid (*bête*), a certain real (*réel*) may be reached (*atteint*)'.[68] At this point, one could say that, in Lacan's view, both the means and the ends of analysis for analyst and analysand alike involve stupidities (*bêtises*). In terms of ends, and as observed, the 'certain real' that 'may be reached' through the meanderings of the analysand's speech would be the idiotic master signifiers (S_1s) produced by analytic discourse. The attainment of this Real is, as Lacan indicates, in no way dependent upon the intelligence of the analysand ('no matter how stupid').

In terms of means, the parallel labours of analyst and analysand during the work of the analytic undertaking are also bound up with stupidities. The analyst must not presume him/her-self to know (too) much and attune his/her ears to the senseless materiality of signifiers, rather than the sensible meaning of signs. The analysand, for his/her part, must allow him/her-self to speak 'stupidly', namely, to babble, confuse, curse, digress, joke, mumble, mutter, offend, pun, ramble, slip and so on. Moreover, none of these 'stupid' words can 'be taken back (*se dédire*)'. That is to say, no analyst is willing to comply with analysands when they implore him/her to disregard and set aside anything they have said ('Never mind, that was dumb'). On the contrary, such pleas to ignore encourage further analytic attention instead of neglect (although one could imagine a knavish manipulation of this by a sufficiently savvy analysand).

Before addressing the stupidity of master signifiers (S_1s) as involving idiotic *jouissance* in addition to meaningless materiality, it should be noted that Lacan identifies certain of the signifiers of his own teaching with *connerie*. In *Seminar XIX* (*. . . or Worse* (1971–1972)), he brings up the topic of his doctrine of the 'matheme'. This neologism, echoing structural anthropologist Claude Lévi-Strauss's own neologism 'mytheme' (itself echoing in turn the term 'phoneme' as it features in structural linguistics, especially as per Roman Jakobson),[69] harks back to the ancient Greek '*ta mathēmata*'[70] (i.e. the etymological origin of 'mathematics' and related words). The Greek *ta mathēmata* is that which can be transmitted without ambiguity, distortion, vagueness and so on. When pedagogy succeeds in this sense, there is a perfect identity between what is taught and what is learnt. When the learner has truly learnt in this way, his/her knowledge, as both what is known and how it is known, is exactly the same as that of the teacher.

Hence, in the nineteenth seminar, Lacan remarks, 'I posited that this *matheme* is the pivotal point of all teaching. The rest is banter (*plaisanterie*)'.[71] He is anxious to avoid the distorting and even falsifying receptions Freud's ideas and texts suffered at the hands of most audiences and readers, whose commentary as 'banter' (mis)attributes various meanings to Freud. Lacan for a while invests hope and effort in attempting to distill his own core concepts and theories into integrally transmissible formalizations, namely, into mathemes as signifiers purified of ambiguous or vague meanings.

In the same session of *Seminar XIX* (15 December 1971), right after invoking the original ancient connection between the mathematical and the teachable, Lacan associates the matheme with stupidity. He avers that, 'my own *matheme* invariably verges of doltishness (*mon mathème . . . confine toujours à la connerie*)'.[72] So, not only are both parties of analytic practice, the analyst and the analysand, caught up in stupidities – analytic theory too, as a metapsychology crystallized into mathematical-style symbolizations, likewise veers into *connerie*. In Lacan's framework, instances of *bêtise* and *connerie* proliferate. Stupidity multiplies.

Later, in the twenty-second seminar, Lacan depicts long-held cultural traditions as stupid (*conne*).[73] As with the matheme *qua ta mathēmata*, so also with tradition: transmission is what is essential. That which is traditional as well as that which is *ta mathēmata* is transmitted through teaching. And, Lacan's various remarks here indicate that the price to be paid for thorough or complete transmissibility, for high-fidelity transmission, is a reduction to stupidity (*connerie*). Why?

From the default non-psychoanalytic standpoint of secondary-process-style conscious thinking, that which is not stupid is inseparable from that which is meaningful on the combined syntactical and semantic bases of common sense, natural language and/or classical bivalent logic. Yet, for Lacan, such non-stupid meanings, as bound up with signs in Saussure's sense (with their pictured signifieds), are inseparable from the experiences of idiosyncratic consciousnesses internal to the register of the Imaginary. As such, these meanings are non-transferrable; they cannot be transmitted (at least not 'integrally' transmitted as per the standards of *ta mathēmata*).

Only elements of the Symbolic shorn of residues of the Imaginary's *sens*, and the Real dimension inseparable from these Symbolic elements, can be passed on without the loss of anything crucial from subject to subject through teaching, tradition and so on. Lacan's mathemes are intended by him to function, on behalf of his theoretical pedagogy, as precisely such Symbolic elements (although, starting in 1976 and at the very end of his intellectual itinerary, the final Lacan abandons the paradigm of the matheme, deeming this project to be ultimately futile and doomed[74]). Yet, insofar as conscious cognition considers (Imaginary) meaning as necessary for non-stupidity, these mathemes must look to be just as (if not more) stupid as the nonsense at play in both the psychopathology of everyday life and the drivel rolling off analysands' tongues session after session.

As an aside, the later Lacan also ties the register of the Imaginary, with the solipsism of its not-integrally-transmissible phenomenal and affective experiences, to retardation, to mental debility (*débilité mentale*). The Imaginary contains, among other things, the images of mind and thinking informing conscious cognition's conception of itself. Lacan dubs the mental as per the Imaginary's envisioning the 'senti-mental', namely, mindedness imagined on the basis of lived experience's 'sentiments', its feelings, emotions and the like.[75] In the very same context, Lacan similarly coins the neologism '*senti-ment*' so as to allege that affects (*senti*) lie (*ment*), that conscious sentiments can be deceptive.[76] This neologism thus also insinuates that the senti-mental of the Imaginary is a misleading rendition of the mind qua psychical subjectivity, a lying (*ment*) about the mental.

In the face of this, Lacan's mathemes are designed to provide an unsentimental (or un-senti-mental) model of the minded *parlêtre*. These stupid (*bête/con*), albeit not retarded (*débile*), mathematical-style formalisms are deployed so as to slice through the deceptive façades and erroneous superficialities of the Imaginary's sentimentality (or senti-mentality), what Lacan, in *Seminar XXII*, calls the '*imbécilité*' of sense/meaning (*sens*).[77] Even philosophy starting with Plato and Aristotle, insofar as its ideas (about the soul, the cosmos and God, for instance) are conditioned by Imaginary *sens*, is said by this Lacan to be afflicted with *débilité mentale*.[78]

GODS, ANGELS AND OTHER IDIOTS: STUPIDLY ENJOYING

So much for the sort of stupidity associated with material meaninglessness involved in the master signifiers (S_1s) produced by the discourse of the analyst. Now, what about the above-mentioned other sort of stupidity, that associated with idiotic enjoyment, also simultaneously involved in these very same signifiers? What of the *bêtise* or *connerie* of a *jouissance* embodied in the meaningless material signifiers of the speaking subject's symptoms (or, rather, *sinthomes* in Lacan's technical sense as symptoms the 'curative' removal of which would result in the destruction of the very subjectivity suffering from them)?

Already in *Seminar VIII* (*Transference* (1960–1961)), Lacan speaks of a kind of divine idiocy. Of course, much of this particular seminar is occupied with a close reading of Plato's *Symposium* dialogue in connection with a psychoanalytic account of love. As part of this focus on Plato, Lacan brings up the subject of the gods of antiquity. By contrast with Christianity's narrowing of the gap between humanity and divinity, the pre-Christian Greek pantheon consists of supernatural beings different-in-kind from human beings. Considering this, Lacan claims that the strict divide separating immortals from mortals means that the former are incapable of comprehending the this-worldly concerns of the latter. The gods, in their incomprehension of human preoccupations with love and the like, are stupid in a certain sense.[79] Lacan comments that, 'The expression "divine stupidity" (*une bêtise divine*) should, in my book, be more widespread'.[80]

In the twentieth seminar, this ancient Greek divine stupidity returns in the guise of Christianity's heavenly beings. On this occasion, Lacan speaks of angels:

> A stupid smile (*Une sourire bête*), as everyone knows – it suffices to visit cathedrals – is an angel's smile. Indeed, that is the only justification for Pascal's warning (*semonce*). If an angel has such a stupid smile, that is because it is up to its ears in the supreme signifier (*il nage dans le signifiant suprême*). To find itself on dry land (*un peu au sec*) would do it some good (*ça lui ferait du bien*) – perhaps it wouldn't smile anymore.[81]

There is quite a lot to unpack in these few sentences. To get underway with Lacan's references here, Bruce Fink, in a footnote to his superb 1998 English translation of *Seminar XX*, proposes apropos Lacan's mention of cathedrals that 'Lacan is evidently referring here to the statue *L'Ange au Sourire* (the Smiling Angel), the guardian angel of Saint Nicaise, at the Cathédrale de

Reims, dating back to the thirteenth century'.[82] Lacan undoubtedly is thinking of this. But, one additionally should bear in mind that Gian Lorenzo Bernini's seventeenth-century sculpture *The Ecstasy of Saint Teresa*, located in the Cornaro Chapel of the Santa Maria della Vittoria church in Rome, is both mentioned in the twentieth seminar and graces the cover of the Jacques-Alain-Miller-edited French version of this seminar published in 1975 as a book in Lacan's Champ freudien series by Éditions du Seuil.

The angel in Bernini's magnificent sculpture indeed is smiling. This winged being does so while simultaneously holding a spear about to pierce the body of Saint Teresa of Ávila. Saint Teresa's sculpted face cries out to be interpreted both as manifesting pain and as evidence of an unbearably intense orgasmic experience. Enjoyment and suffering appear both as the difference between the angel's smile (enjoyment) and Teresa's closed eyes and moaning mouth (suffering) as well as the simultaneous pleasure-in-pain expressed by Teresa's face on its own. Clearly, for Lacan, the spear-wielding angel and the sixteenth-century Christian mystic saint depicted by Bernini artistically incarnate Lacan's concept of *jouissance* as a paradoxical unenjoyable enjoyment, the overwhelming 'too muchness' of a painful pleasure beyond the pleasure principle.[83] Teresa's own recorded testimony of one of her mystical experiences emphasizes the combination of agony and ecstasy.[84]

As regards *jouissance*, Lacan's associations of it with the Greek gods (*Seminar VIII*) as well as with Christian angels and mystics (*Seminar XX*) clearly suggest that it is something inhuman, otherworldly and fundamentally foreign to subjectivity. This enjoyment is reserved for immortals, cherubs and saints, but not for frail mere mortals. Yet, why does Lacan qualify such excessive enjoyment as stupid?

Before answering this question through further parsing the above quotation from the twentieth seminar, Lacan's somewhat obscure reference to Blaise Pascal in this same quotation calls for elucidation. In a translator's footnote to the sentence referring to Pascal, Fink draws attention to the word he renders as 'warning' (*semonce*). Fink recommends that readers interested in its significance consult 'Lacan's favorite dictionary', namely Oscar Bloch and Walther von Wartburg's *Dictionnaire étymologique de la langue française*[85] (indeed, Lacan once declared that Bloch and Wartburg's dictionary is the book he would take with him to a deserted island if he had to go to such a place with only one book to read, preferring it even to the Bible in such a circumstance[86]). The entry for '*semonce*' in this particular dictionary traces it back to the fourteenth century as a word for the summoning of vassals and men-at-arms. It goes on to become, in the seventeenth century, 'a juridical term designating a sort of summons (*convocation*)'.[87]

So, given this etymology, what is Pascal's 'warning' (*semonce*) qua call to arms, summons and/or convocation? My best guess is that Lacan is thinking of a handful of passages in the *Pensées* about angels, beasts and humans. Speaking of the human creature, Pascal at one point observes, 'He is neither angel nor beast (*bête*), but man'.[88]

Two other passages in the *Pensées*, cautionary in tone and content, appeal to this in-between status of humanity. One of these draws attention to a certain danger:

> It is dangerous to explain too clearly to man how like he is to the animals (*bêtes*) without pointing out his greatness (*sa grandeur*). It is also dangerous to make too much of his greatness without his vileness (*sa bassesse*). It is still more dangerous to leave him in ignorance of both, but it is most valuable to represent both to him.[89]

Pascal immediately adds in the same fragment, 'Man must not be allowed to believe that he is equal either to animals or to angels, nor to be unaware of either, but he must know both'.[90] Another of Pascal's aphorisms is more precise about at least one version of this danger – 'Man is neither angel nor beast, and it is unfortunately the case that anyone trying to act the angel acts the beast' (*L'homme n'est ni ange ni bête, et le malheur veut que qui veut faire l'ange fait la bête*).[91] I am confident that these 'thoughts' constitute the Pascalian 'warning' (*semonce*) Lacan gestures at during the twentieth seminar in connection with the angelic smile.

Since the etymology of '*semonce*' involves a juridical dimension (a dimension noted by Fink[92]), Pascal could be said here to touch upon what Lacan, as evinced throughout so much of his work, takes to be a sort of law one ignores at one's own peril. The general form of this law is none other than G. W. F. Hegel's dynamic of dialectical self-subversion first fully exhibited in 1807s *Phenomenology of Spirit*. Pascal's warning, according to which 'anyone trying to act the angel acts the beast', is an instance of the dialectics of an intention bringing about the opposite of what it intended to accomplish, a law of antithetical-to-intention consequences (rather than simply unintended consequences).

Lacan's variations, brought into association with Pascal in *Seminar XX*, on the fearsome necessity of Hegelian-style dialectical self-subversion have to do specifically with libidinal economics. Even more precisely, they have to do, in the later period of his teaching, with *jouissance*. Perhaps the angel's smile could be said to be a lure seducing mortal subjects into pursuing the supposed enjoyment expressed by this 'stupid' (*bête*) grin, namely, divine qua Absolute, unbarred fulfilment. But, desiring and divided subjectivity ($), in aiming at the fantasized heavenly ecstasy of angelic '*jouissance* expected', ends up getting instead the actualized hellish agony of beastly '*jouissance* obtained' (to employ Lacan's distinction from the twentieth seminar between these two categories of *jouissance*).[93]

This would be the Lacanian version of the Pascalian 'anyone trying to act the angel acts the beast': Anyone trying to enjoy like an angel suffers like a beast. Reinforcing this interpretation, Bloch and von Wartburg's entry for '*bête*' explains that this French word for 'stupid' originates in the classical Latin '*bestia*'.[94] Lacan, perhaps thanks specifically to Bloch and von Wartburg, likely is well aware of this etymological relationship between the stupid and the bestial/beastly. Indeed, his reference to 'Pascal's warning (*semonce*)', with this warning's use of the word '*bête*', hints at this very awareness.

Incidentally, and before leaving Pascal behind, another of the *Pensées* has him acknowledging the difficulty of discerning the difference between mysticism and nonsense (*sottise*).[95] The significant pronouncements of the Christian mystic, due to their mysterious, oracular quality, risk seeming indistinguishable from senseless babble to the untrained ear. But, Pascal maintains, such a Christian indeed is able to articulate truly 'angelic things' (*choses angéliques*) endowed with 'mystic meaning' (*être mystérieux, mystère*).[96]

Lacan could be said to recast the figure of the analyst, with his/her 'babbling practice', as one who gets others to voice 'angelic things' precisely in and through 'talking nonsense' (*disent de sots contes*).[97] Indeed, the opening session of *Seminar XXV* (*Time to Conclude* (1977–1978)) christens psychoanalysis '*une pratique de bavardage*'.[98] Via the 'foolish tales' (*sots contes*) of the free associating peculiar to the strange babbling practice that is analysis, the analysand, assisted by the analyst, comes to say angelic things specifically as nothing other than key bits and pieces of contingent, factical meaninglessness (i.e. the master signifiers (S_1s) in their pure structuring materiality produced by the analytic discourse).

By contrast with Pascal's Christian mysticism, Lacanian analysis zeroes in on a zone of indistinction in which the seeming opposites of profundity and superficiality, of significance and senselessness, overlap and intermingle. Especially in the concluding moments of the analytic process, worthless stupidities and invaluable truths can, should and do become indistinguishable. The master signifiers hitherto governing the vicissitudes of the *parlêtre*'s life history (*à la* Freud's '*Wo Es war, soll Ich werden*'[99]) – these are made explicit thanks to the work of analysis – may very well strike the parties to analysis like the disappointing and/or funny punchlines to bad jokes.

Pathos thereby turns into *bathos*, neurotic into ordinary suffering.[100] Correspondingly, the figure of the Lacanian analyst, in the eyes of an analysand experiencing the terminal dissolution of the transference, shifts from seeming to be the sublime, indispensable subject supposed to know to being the ridiculous, superfluous bystander, just another miserable schmuck, quietly witnessing the analytic endgame from the sidelines. The analyst is thereby rendered as the waste product (*déchet*), the garbage, to be disposed of by the analysand at the end of the labour of analysis, as the final clean-up concluding a job done well enough.[101]

Returning again to the exact words of the above quotation from *Seminar XX* (in which Lacan refers to Pascal), Lacan's stupidly smiling angel is described by him as being 'up to its ears in the supreme signifier' (*il nage dans le signifiant suprême*). A more literal translation would be 'swimming in the supreme signifier'. Retranslating it thus brings out the cross-resonance with Lacan's talk of 'dry land (*un peu au sec*)' in the immediately following sentence. There is a clear contrast here between the (presumed) fluidity of otherworldly *jouissance* and the aridity of earthly desire. Although the dryness and thirst of the all-too-human condition of *désir* are enough to wipe the smile off anyone's face, angels included, it still is better and more livable than actually turning fantasized enjoyment from the expected to the obtained ('To find itself on dry land (*un peu au sec*) would do it some good (*ça lui ferait du bien*) – perhaps it wouldn't smile anymore').

The 'supreme signifier' in which Lacan's angel swims (or, at least, appears to swim) is an S_1 – more precisely, the signifier of the unbarred, uncastrated Other, S(A). This S_1, as S(A), stands for (the fantasy of) a complete, undiluted enjoyment (i.e. an expected, but never obtained, absolute *jouissance*). Such (supposed) *jouissance* is condensed into the form of the signifier, into a supreme, master signifier. These S_1s are, to use a phrase from Žižek, 'metastases of enjoyment'.

Like René Descartes's pineal gland interfacing mind and body, the supreme master signifier, S_1 as S(A), is a knot functioning as a *sinthome* binding together the dual dimensions of energy and structure, fluidity and solidity, and pleasure and pain. Hence, in the same session (19 December 1972) of the twentieth seminar in which Lacan invokes the angel's smile, he also adds a third dimension to Cartesian ontological dualism. In addition to *res cogitans* (thinking substance) and *res extensa* (extended substance), there is, for Lacanian psychoanalysis, enjoying substance (*la substance jouissante*) too – with the signifier as the substance, the substantialization qua condensing crystallization, of this enjoying.[102]

The libidinal side of the stupidity of S_1s is quite clearly explained by Lacan at the start of the this same 19 December 1972 session of *Seminar XX*. Lacan's opening sentence of this session, right before he begins rendering homage to Jakobson, confesses, 'It seems to me that it is difficult not to speak stupidly (*bêtement*) about language (*langage*)'.[103] He then soon goes on to observe:

> to nourish oneself is part and parcel of stupidity (*la bêtise*). Need I say more to the people present in this room where one is, ultimately, at a restaurant and where one imagines that one is being nourished because one is not at the

university cafeteria? One is nourished by the imaginative dimension (*La dimension imaginative*).[104]

Lacan continues:

> I trust you remember what analytic discourse (*le discours analytique*) teaches us about the old bond with the wet nurse (*la vieille liaison avec la nourrice*), a mother as well, as if by chance, and behind that the infernal business (*l'histoire infernale*) of her desire (*désir*) and everything that follows from it. That is what is at stake in nourishment – some sort of stupidity (*bêtise*), but one that analytic discourse puts in its rightful place (*assoit dans son droit*).[105]

Whether the infant at the breast or the listener in Lacan's seminar room (a place ostensibly distinct from the academic lecture hall ('the university cafeteria')), both weave fantasies around what they consume in unsublimated oral or sublimated aural manners: mother's milk in the one case, psychoanalytic teaching in the other. Moreover, in each case, one is dealing with two intersecting types of stupidity (*bêtise*): natural and more-than-natural stupidity.

On the one hand, there is the natural stupidity of nourishment itself. The original, biologically dictated condition of the prematurational helplessness (*Hilflosigkeit*) in which one needs to be nourished without being able to nourish oneself is at root a matter of brutish (even bestial) *bêtise à la* meaningless organic facticity. This is the *bêtise* of a mere, sheer givenness involving all the accidents of birth as well as the much larger background constellations of natural history, with its countless contingencies leading to the evolution of human beings and their distinctive peculiarities. One enters the world senselessly condemned to such natural, beastly stupidity.

On the other hand, 'the imaginative dimension' invariably mediating the living being's rapport with both nourishment and nourishment's provider also is overflowing with more-than-natural stupidities. These would be the ideational representations (whether as Freud's *Vorstellungen* or Lacan's signifiers) having nothing to do with the natural purposes of biological survival and adaptation. Neither the nursling's fixations on aspects of breastfeeding other than the nourishing quality of what it is ingesting (aspects such as the motor movement of repetitive sucking, the sensory-perceptual features of the breast, the gaze and voice of the breastfeeder, etc.) nor the seminar auditor's preoccupation with envisioning contrasts between analytic and university discourses evidently are essential to the purposive activities these cathexes inevitably accompany. They are stupid qua superfluous.

Additionally, there is the more-than-natural stupidity introduced into all of this by the figure who is not just the nourisher (*la nourrice*) of the infant but also its mother – with no apparent necessity for the one also to be the other ('the wet nurse (*la nourrice*), a mother as well, as if by chance'). As also a mother, a subject-position shaped by socio-historical Imaginary-Symbolic reality, the nourisher brings with her the more-than-natural stupidities associated with her own libidinal economy, subjectivity, unconscious and so on ('the infernal business (*l'histoire infernale*) of her desire (*désir*)'). Then there is 'everything that follows from' this primordial influence of the libidinally-charged maternal Other. This 'everything' includes the traces left behind in the psychical subjectivity of the speaking being, dating back to this being's prolonged childhood helplessness, of the maternal Other's conscious and unconscious desires (and, relatedly, her dreams, drives, enjoyments, fantasies and the like).[106] The most potent of these traces are *les signifiants maîtres sinthomatiques* holding together the very structure of the subject as this subject's load-bearing (yet stupid) S_1s. Through the *discours* that is analytic practice, the analysand can come to situate these fateful traces in their 'rightful place'.

In the language of *Seminar XVII*, these S_1-type truths (*vérités*) produced in and through the discourse of the analyst amount to all the 'bullshit' (*déconnage*) from the analysand's past burdening him/her (with '*déconnage*' being closely related to "*connerie*"). Indeed, the seventeenth seminar, echoing Lacan's equations elsewhere of truth with stupidity, contains the claim by Lacan that, 'bullshitting (*déconnage*), as I have always said, is truth (*la vérité*). They are identical'.[107] Psychoanalysis, as a knowledge qua familiarity (*connaissance*) with this bullshit (*déconnage*), is thus a '*déconnaissance*' (a neologism Lacan coins in *Seminar XV* that combines *connaissance* and *déconnage*).[108]

Despite Lacan enjoying a reputation as exceeding cerebral, perhaps even too clever for his own good and his audiences' comprehension, stupidity plays a surprisingly central role in his thinking. As seen throughout all of the preceding, Lacan's teaching invokes numerous kinds of stupidity: foolishness, knavery, ignorance, doltishness, meaninglessness, imbecility, dupery, retardation, bullshit, nonsense and the like. With Lacan, psychoanalysis is an especially radical *reductio ad absurdum* of subjects' realities. Seen from the standpoint of Lacanian analysis, the world is veritably overflowing with, and ultimately grounded upon, stupidities of myriad sorts. It is all so very stupid on so many levels. Yet, for psychoanalysis, this constitutes the most essential stuff of the human condition, its spade-turning base. Analysis requires an appreciation of the tragicomic ridiculousness of life.

NOTES

1. *SE* 1: 297, 324–27
SE 5: 602
2. Adrian Johnston, *Adventures in Transcendental Materialism: Dialogues with Contemporary Thinkers*, Edinburgh: Edinburgh University Press, 2014, pg. 191–92, 197, 288
3. Jacques Lacan, "Discours à l'École freudienne de Paris," *Autres écrits* [ed. Jacques-Alain Miller], Paris: Éditions du Seuil, 2001, pg. 277
4. Lacan, "Discours à l'École freudienne de Paris," pg. 277
5. Jacques Lacan, *Le Séminaire de Jacques Lacan, Livre XXIV: L'insu que sait de l'une-bévue, s'aile à mourre, 1976–1977* [unpublished typescript], sessions of 14 December 1976, 11 January 1977, 19 April 1977
Jacques Lacan, *Le Séminaire de Jacques Lacan, Livre XXV: Le moment de conclure, 1977–1978* [unpublished typescript], session of 11 April 1978
Jacques Lacan, ". . . *ou pire: Compte rendu du Séminaire 1971–1972*," Autres *écrits*, pg. 551
Jacques Lacan, "Television" [trans. Denis Hollier, Rosalind Krauss, and Annette Michelson], *Television/A Challenge to the Psychoanalytic Establishment* [ed. Joan Copjec], New York: W.W. Norton and Company, 1990, pg. 10
Adrian Johnston, "Misfelt Feelings: Unconscious Affect Between Psychoanalysis, Neuroscience, and Philosophy," in *Self and Emotional Life: Philosophy, Psychoanalysis, and Neuroscience* [eds. Adrian Johnston and Catherine Malabou], New York: Columbia University Press, 2013, pg. 143–46
6. Jacques Lacan, *Le Séminaire de Jacques Lacan, Livre XVII: L'envers de la psychanalyse, 1969–1970* [ed. Jacques-Alain Miller], Paris: Éditions du Seuil, 1991, pg. 104
Jacques Lacan, *The Seminar of Jacques Lacan, Book XVII: The Other Side of Psychoanalysis, 1969–1970* [ed. Jacques-Alain Miller; trans. Russell Grigg], New York: W.W. Norton and Company, 2007, pg. 91
7. Lacan, *The Seminar of Jacques Lacan, Book XVII*, pg. 20, 29, 31, 43, 54, 152
Adrian Johnston, *Žižek's Ontology: A Transcendental Materialist Theory of Subjectivity*, Evanston: Northwestern University Press, 2008, pg. 251–53. 257–60
8. Lacan, *The Seminar of Jacques Lacan, Book XVII*, pg. 87, 102
9. Lacan, *Le Séminaire de Jacques Lacan, Livre XIV*, session of 26 April 1967
10. Jacques Lacan, *The Seminar of Jacques Lacan, Book XX: Encore, 1972–1973* [ed. Jacques-Alain Miller; trans. Bruce Fink], New York: W.W. Norton and Company, 1998, pg. 22
11. Jacques Lacan, *Le Séminaire de Jacques Lacan, Livre XX: Encore, 1972–1973* [ed. Jacques-Alain Miller], Paris: Éditions du Seuil, 1975, pg. 25
Lacan, *The Seminar of Jacques Lacan, Book XX*, pg. 22
12. Jacques Lacan, *Le Séminaire de Jacques Lacan, Livre XVI: D'un Autre à l'autre, 1968–1969* [ed. Jacques-Alain Miller], Paris: Éditions du Seuil, 2006, pg. 41
13. Lacan, *The Seminar of Jacques Lacan, Book XX*, pg. 12
14. Lacan, *Le Séminaire de Jacques Lacan, Livre XX*, pg. 17

Lacan, *The Seminar of Jacques Lacan, Book XX*, pg. 12

15. *GW* 16: 99

SE 23: 252

16. *GW* 16: 99

SE 23: 252

17. Jacques Lacan, "D'une question préliminaire à tout traitement possible de la psychose," *Écrits*, Paris: Éditions du Seuil, 1966, pg. 549

Jacques Lacan, "On a Question Prior to Any Possible Treatment of Psychosis," *Écrits: The First Complete Edition in English* [trans. Bruce Fink], New York: W.W. Norton and Company, 2006, pg. 459

18. Jacques Lacan, *The Seminar of Jacques Lacan, Book VII: The Ethics of Psychoanalysis, 1959–1960* [ed. Jacques-Alain Miller; trans. Dennis Porter], New York: W.W. Norton and Company, 1992, pg. 182

Jacques Lacan, "Remarks on Daniel Lagache's Presentation: 'Psychoanalysis and Personality Structure,'" *Écrits: The First Complete Edition in English* [trans. Bruce Fink], New York: W.W. Norton and Company, 2006, pg. 554

19. Lacan, *The Seminar of Jacques Lacan, Book VII*, pg. 182–183

20. Jacques Lacan, *Le Séminaire de Jacques Lacan, Livre VII: L'éthique de la psychanalyse, 1959–1960* [ed. Jacques-Alain Miller], Paris: Éditions du Seuil, 1986, pg. 215

Lacan, *The Seminar of Jacques Lacan, Book VII*, pg. 183

21. Lacan, *Le Séminaire de Jacques Lacan, Livre VII*, pg. 215

Lacan, *The Seminar of Jacques Lacan, Book VII*, pg. 183

22. Slavoj Žižek, *The Plague of Fantasies*, London: Verso, 1997, pg. 45

23. Alain Badiou, *Trump*, Paris: Presses Universitaires de France, 2020, pg. 48–51

24. *SE* 19: 235–36

25. Jacques Lacan, *Le Séminaire de Jacques Lacan, Livre XXI: Les non-dupes errent, 1973–1974* [unpublished typescript], session of 19 March 1974

26. Lacan, *The Seminar of Jacques Lacan, Book XVII*, pg. 61

27. Lacan, *Le Séminaire de Jacques Lacan, Livre XVII*, pg. 68

Lacan, *The Seminar of Jacques Lacan, Book XVII*, pg. 61

28. Lacan, *Le Séminaire de Jacques Lacan, Livre XVII*, pg. 68

Lacan, *The Seminar of Jacques Lacan, Book XVII*, pg. 61

29. Lacan, *Le Séminaire de Jacques Lacan, Livre XVII*, pg. 68

Lacan, *The Seminar of Jacques Lacan, Book XVII*, pg. 61

30. Johnston, *Adventures in Transcendental Materialism*, pg. 70–72

31. Lacan, *Le Séminaire de Jacques Lacan, Livre XX*, pg. 92

Lacan, *The Seminar of Jacques Lacan, Book XX*, pg. 101

32. *SE* 8: 115

33. *SE* 8: 115

34. *SE* 8: 115

35. *GW* 2/3: 163–64

SE 4: 157–58

36. *SE* 19: 235

37. Lacan, *Le Séminaire de Jacques Lacan, Livre XVI*, pg. 134

38. Jacques Lacan, *Le Séminaire de Jacques Lacan, Livre XIX: . . . ou pire, 1971–1972* [ed. Jacques-Alain Miller], Paris: Éditions du Seuil, 2011, pg. 14

Jacques Lacan, *The Seminar of Jacques Lacan, Book XIX: . . . or Worse, 1971–1972* [ed. Jacques-Alain Miller; trans. A.R. Price], Cambridge: Polity, 2018, pg. 6

39. Lacan, *Le Séminaire de Jacques Lacan, Livre XIX*, pg. 198

Lacan, *The Seminar of Jacques Lacan, Book XIX*, pg. 174

40. Jacques Lacan, *Le Séminaire de Jacques Lacan, Livre XV: L'acte psychanalytique, 1967–1968* [unpublished typescript], session of 19 June 1968

41. Lacan, *Le Séminaire de Jacques Lacan, Livre XIX*, pg. 198

Lacan, *The Seminar of Jacques Lacan, Book XIX*, pg. 174

Lacan, *Le Séminaire de Jacques Lacan, Livre XX*, pg. 17

Lacan, *The Seminar of Jacques Lacan, Book XX*, pg. 12

42. Lacan, *The Seminar of Jacques Lacan, Book XX*, pg. 13

43. Lacan, *Le Séminaire de Jacques Lacan, Livre XX*, pg. 17

Lacan, *The Seminar of Jacques Lacan, Book XX*, pg. 13

44. Lacan, *Le Séminaire de Jacques Lacan, Livre XX*, pg. 18

Lacan, *The Seminar of Jacques Lacan, Book XX*, pg. 13

45. Jacques Lacan, *Le Séminaire de Jacques Lacan, Livre XI: Les quatre concepts fondamentaux de la psychanalyse, 1964* [ed. Jacques-Alain Miller], Paris: Éditions du Seuil, 1973, pg. 226

Jacques Lacan, *The Seminar of Jacques Lacan, Book XI: The Four Fundamental Concepts of Psychoanalysis, 1964* [ed. Jacques-Alain Miller; trans. Alan Sheridan], New York: W.W. Norton and Company, 1977, pg. 250

46. Lacan, *Le Séminaire de Jacques Lacan, Livre XI*, pg. 226

Lacan, *The Seminar of Jacques Lacan, Book XI*, pg. 250

47. Lacan, *Le Séminaire de Jacques Lacan, Livre XI*, pg. 226

Lacan, *The Seminar of Jacques Lacan, Book XI*, pg. 250

48. Serge Leclaire, *Psychoanalyzing: On the Order of the Unconscious and the Practice of the Letter* [trans. Peggy Kamuf], Stanford: Stanford University Press, 1998, pg. 70–87

Lacan, *The Seminar of Jacques Lacan, Book XI*, pg. 212, 250

Jacques Lacan, *Le Séminaire de Jacques Lacan, Livre XII: Problèmes cruciaux pour la psychanalyse, 1964–1965* [unpublished typescript], sessions of 27 January 1965, 24 March 1965, 7 April 1965, 28 April 1965

49. Jacques Lacan, *Le Séminaire de Jacques Lacan, Livre XIX: Le savoir du psychanalyste, 1971–1972* [unpublished typescript], sessions of 4 November 1971, 2 December 1971

Lacan, *The Seminar of Jacques Lacan, Book XX*, pg. 138–139

Lacan, *Le Séminaire de Jacques Lacan, Livre XXI*, session of 11 June 1974

Jacques Lacan, *The Seminar of Jacques Lacan, Book XXIII: The Sinthome, 1975–1976* [ed. Jacques-Alain Miller; trans. A.R. Price], Cambridge: Polity, 2016, pg. 98

Lacan, *Le Séminaire de Jacques Lacan, Livre XXIV*, session of 19 April 1977

Lacan, *Le Séminaire de Jacques Lacan, Livre XXV*, sessions of 15 November 1977, 11 April 1978

Jacques Lacan, "Alla Scuola Freudiana: Conférence à Milan," *Lacan in Italia, 1953–1978*, Milan: La Salamandra, 1978, pg. 112–15

Jacques Lacan, "Joyce le symptôme II," *Joyce avec Lacan* [ed. Jacques Aubert], Paris: Navarin, 1987, pg. 36

Jacques Lacan, "Conférence à Genève sur le symptôme" [ed. Jacques-Alain Miller], *La cause du désir*, no. 95, 2017, https://www.cairn.info/revue-la-cause-du-desir-2017-1-page-7.htm

Jacques Lacan, "*Conférences et entretiens dans des universités nord-américaines: Columbia University Auditorium School of International Affairs*," *Scilicet*, 6/7, 1975, pg. 47

Johnston, "Misfelt Feelings," pg. 141–46, 195–200

50. Lacan, *Le Séminaire de Jacques Lacan, Livre XI*, pg. 226

Lacan, *The Seminar of Jacques Lacan, Book XI*, pg. 250–51

51. Jacques Lacan, "Préface à l'édition anglaise du Séminaire XI," *Autres écrits* [ed. Jacques-Alain Miller], Paris: Éditions du Seuil, 2001, pg. 571

Lacan, *The Seminar of Jacques Lacan, Book XI*, pg. vii

52. Lacan, *Le Séminaire de Jacques Lacan, Livre XVI*, pg. 385

53. Jacques Lacan, *Le Séminaire de Jacques Lacan, Livre XXIII: Le sinthome, 1975–1976* [ed. Jacques-Alain Miller], Paris: Éditions du Seuil, 2005, pg. 72

Lacan, *The Seminar of Jacques Lacan, Book XXIII*, pg. 57

54. Jacques Lacan, *The Seminar of Jacques Lacan, Book III: The Psychoses, 1955–1956* [ed. Jacques-Alain Miller; trans. Russell Grigg], New York: W.W. Norton and Company, 1993, pg. 190

55. Lacan, *Le Séminaire de Jacques Lacan, Livre XVI*, pg. 173–75

Lacan, *Le Séminaire de Jacques Lacan, Livre XXV*, session of 11 April 1978

56. Jacques Lacan, *Le Séminaire de Jacques Lacan, Livre XXII: R.S.I., 1974–1975* [unpublished typescript], session of 10 December 1974

57. Lacan, *Le Séminaire de Jacques Lacan, Livre XXII*, session of 17 December 1974

58. Lacan, *Le Séminaire de Jacques Lacan, Livre XXIV*, session of 11 January 1977

59. Lacan, *Le Séminaire de Jacques Lacan, Livre XXI*, session of 11 December 1973

60. Lacan, *Le Séminaire de Jacques Lacan, Livre XX*, pg. 24

Lacan, *The Seminar of Jacques Lacan, Book XX*, pg. 20

61. Lacan, *Le Séminaire de Jacques Lacan, Livre XX*, pg. 24

Lacan, *The Seminar of Jacques Lacan, Book XX*, pg. 21

62. *SE* 12: 111–12

63. *SE* 1: 297, 324–27

SE 5: 602

64. *SE* 1: 355

SE 2: 67–70

SE 3: 51–53, 218

SE 5: 530

SE 14: 229

65. Jean Laplanche and Jean-Bertrand Pontalis, *The Language of Psycho-Analysis* [trans. Donald Nicholson-Smith], New York: W.W. Norton and Company, 1973, pg. 339–41

66. Lacan, *Le Séminaire de Jacques Lacan, Livre XX*, pg. 25
Lacan, *The Seminar of Jacques Lacan, Book XX*, pg. 22

67. Lacan, *Le Séminaire de Jacques Lacan, Livre XX*, pg. 25
Lacan, *The Seminar of Jacques Lacan, Book XX*, pg. 22

68. Lacan, *Le Séminaire de Jacques Lacan, Livre XX*, pg. 25
Lacan, *The Seminar of Jacques Lacan, Book XX*, pg. 22

69. Roman Jakobson, *Six Lectures on Sound and Meaning* [trans. John Mepham], Cambridge: MIT Press, 1978, pg. 24, 27–28, 32, 57, 61–62, 64–67, 76, 82, 99, 102–3
Claude Lévi-Strauss, "The Structural Study of Myth," *Structural Anthropology* [trans. Claire Jacobson and Brooke Grundfest Schoepf], New York: Basic Books, 1963, pg. 210–11
Lacan, *Le Séminaire de Jacques Lacan, Livre XIX: Le savoir du psychanalyste*, session of 3 February 1972
Jacques Lacan, "Intervention après un exposé de Claude Lévi-Strauss à la Société française de philosophie, 'Sur les rapports entre la mythologie et le rituel', avec une réponse de celui-ci," *Le mythe individuel du névrosé ou Poésie et vérité dans la névrose* [ed. Jacques-Alain Miller], Paris: Éditions du Seuil, 2007, pg. 103
Jacques Lacan, "La troisième," *Lettres de l'École freudienne*, 16, 1975, pg. 180–81
Dylan Evans, *An Introductory Dictionary of Lacanian Psychoanalysis*, New York: Routledge, 1996, pg. 108
Élisabeth Roudinesco and Michel Plon, *Dictionnaire de la psychanalyse*, Paris: Fayard, 2011 [fourth edition], pg. 977–78

70. Lacan, *The Seminar of Jacques Lacan, Book XIX*, pg. 17, 126
Lacan, *Le Séminaire de Jacques Lacan, Livre XIX: Le savoir du psychanalyste*, session of 4 May 1972
Lacan, "Television," pg. 38
Jacques Lacan, "*Du discours psychanalytique*," *Lacan in Italia*, pg. 54

71. Lacan, *Le Séminaire de Jacques Lacan, Livre XIX*, pg. 27
Lacan, *The Seminar of Jacques Lacan, Book XIX*, pg. 17

72. Lacan, *Le Séminaire de Jacques Lacan, Livre XIX*, pg. 27
Lacan, *The Seminar of Jacques Lacan, Book XIX*, pg. 17

73. Lacan, *Le Séminaire de Jacques Lacan, Livre XXII*, session of 11 March 1975

74. Johnston, "Lacan's Endgame," pg. 156–87

75. Lacan, *Le Séminaire de Jacques Lacan, Livre XXIII*, pg. 37
Lacan, *The Seminar of Jacques Lacan, Book XXIII*, pg. 26
Lacan, *Le Séminaire de Jacques Lacan, Livre XXIV*, session of 19 April 1977

76. Lacan, *Le Séminaire de Jacques Lacan, Livre XXIII*, pg. 66
Lacan, *The Seminar of Jacques Lacan, Book XXIII*, pg. 51
Johnston, "Misfelt Feelings," pg. 141, 146

77. Lacan, *Le Séminaire de Jacques Lacan, Livre XXII*, session of 10 December 1974

78. Lacan, *Le Séminaire de Jacques Lacan, Livre XXII*, session of 11 March 1975
79. Jacques Lacan, *The Seminar of Jacques Lacan, Book VIII: Transference, 1960–1961* [ed. Jacques-Alain Miller; trans. Bruce Fink], Cambridge: Polity, 2015, pg. 74–75
80. Jacques Lacan, *Le Séminaire de Jacques Lacan, Livre VIII: Le transfert, 1960–1961* [ed. Jacques-Alain Miller], Paris: Éditions du Seuil, 2001 [seconde édition corrigée], pg. 95

Lacan, *The Seminar of Jacques Lacan, Book VIII*, pg. 74

81. Lacan, *Le Séminaire de Jacques Lacan, Livre XX*, pg. 24

Lacan, *The Seminar of Jacques Lacan, Book XX*, pg. 20

82. Bruce Fink, "Translator's Footnotes," *The Seminar of Jacques Lacan, Book XX: Encore, 1972–1973* [ed. Jacques-Alain Miller; trans. Bruce Fink], New York: W.W. Norton and Company, 1998, pg. 20
83. Lacan, *The Seminar of Jacques Lacan, Book XX*, pg. 76
84. Teresa of Ávila, *The Life of Teresa of Jesus: An Autobiography of Teresa of Ávila* [trans. E. Allison Peers], New York: Doubleday, 1991, pg. 244–45
85. Fink, "Translator's Footnotes," pg. 20
86. Lacan, *Le Séminaire de Jacques Lacan, Livre XVI*, pg. 179
87. Oscar Bloch and Walther von Wartburg, *Dictionnaire étymologique de la langue française*, Paris: Presses Universitaires de France, 2016 [4e tirage], pg. 584
88. Blaise Pascal, *Pensées* [ed. Léon Brunschvicg], Paris: Flammarion, 1976, 140-522 [pg. 91]

Blaise Pascal, *Pensées* [trans. A.J. Krailsheimer], New York: Penguin, 1966, 140-522 [pg. 214]

89. Pascal, *Pensées*, 418-121 [pg. 161]

Pascal, *Pensées*, 418-121 [pg. 60]

90. Pascal, *Pensées*, 418-121 [pg. 60]
91. Pascal, *Pensées*, 358-678 [pg. 151]

Pascal, *Pensées*, 358-678 [pg. 242]

92. Fink, "Translator's Footnotes," pg. 20
93. Lacan, *The Seminar of Jacques Lacan, Book XX*, pg. 111

Adrian Johnston, *Time Driven: Metapsychology and the Splitting of the Drive*, Evanston: Northwestern University Press, 2005, pg. xxxiv–xxxv, 239, 282–83, 298, 324–25

94. Bloch and von Wartburg, *Dictionnaire étymologique de la langue française*, pg. 69
95. Pascal, *Pensées*, 691-276 [pg. 250]

Pascal, *Pensées*, 691-276 [pg. 115]

96. Pascal, *Pensées*, 691-276 [pg. 250]

Pascal, *Pensées*, 691-276 [pg. 115]

97. Pascal, *Pensées*, 691-276 [pg. 250]

Pascal, *Pensées*, 691-276 [pg. 115]

98. Lacan, *Le Séminaire de Jacques Lacan, Livre XXV*, session of 15 November 1977

Jacques Lacan, "Intervention de Jacques Lacan à Bruxelles," *Quarto*, 2, 1981, pg. 7

99. *GW* 15: 86

SE 22: 80

100. *SE* 2: 305

Adrian Johnston, *Irrepressible Truth: On Lacan's "The Freudian Thing"*, Basingstoke: Palgrave Macmillan, 2017, pg. 209–211

101. Lacan, *Le Séminaire de Jacques Lacan, Livre XV*, session of 6 December 1967

102. Lacan, *Le Séminaire de Jacques Lacan, Livre XX*, pg. 26

Lacan, *The Seminar of Jacques Lacan, Book XX*, pg. 23

103. Lacan, *Le Séminaire de Jacques Lacan, Livre XX*, pg. 19

Lacan, *The Seminar of Jacques Lacan, Book XX*, pg. 14

104. Lacan, *Le Séminaire de Jacques Lacan, Livre XX*, pg. 19

Lacan, *The Seminar of Jacques Lacan, Book XX*, pg. 14

105. Lacan, *Le Séminaire de Jacques Lacan, Livre XX*, pg. 19

Lacan, *The Seminar of Jacques Lacan, Book XX*, pg. 14

106. Lacan, "Joyce le symptôme I," pg. 22–23

107. Lacan, *Le Séminaire de Jacques Lacan, Livre XVII*, pg. 127

Lacan, *The Seminar of Jacques Lacan, Book XVII*, pg. 111

108. Lacan, *Le Séminaire de Jacques Lacan, Livre XV*, session of 22 November 1967

Chapter 9

Can One Be Less Stupid?

Luis Izcovich

I begin with intellectual disability. Lacan made it into a clinical category that does not take the general conception into account, which approaches intellectual disability in terms of intellectual capacity. What justifies us in taking up Lacan's conception of disability? Our interest in focusing on the disabled subject is linked to the fact that he/it gives the interlocutor the impression that one is dealing with stupidity incarnate.

Hence, it is important to posit the specificity of the clinical category and to distinguish it from what we could call the speaking being's stupidity. So, let's begin with the fundamental point, which involves figuring out the reasons why it is the case that one clinical category most especially incarnates stupidity, that is, most particularly brings it to light.

Lacan puts forth an idea that lets us better grasp the specificity of intellectual disability in terms of how it involves the subject's relation to discourse: 'the fact of being a speaking being who is not solidly installed in a discourse; that is the price paid by the debile subject'.[1] This proposition already shows us how Lacan's position goes against the general idea that understands intellectual disability in terms of a deficit in intelligence.

According to Lacan's conception, what is essential is to determine for each speaking being not only its relation to language but – and this is even more complicated – whether the subject is installed in a discourse or not.

Moreover, the subject's relation to discourse is what leads Lacan to rearrange the analytic clinic. With some exceptions, the speaking being is in language. In this respect, the term 'speaking being' is clear enough. But it is something else to be in a discourse.

To be in a discourse it is not enough to speak, and it does not suffice to enter into a discourse; it is necessary, further, that one anchor oneself in one. What is essential is that a neurotic be someone who is installed in a discourse, while Lacan defines psychosis as being outside discourse. Here, discourse is to be understood as one of the four discourses put forward by Lacan: that of the hysteric, the master, the analyst and the university. In other words, his proposal is that, according to what is said by the subject, and how, we can locate the discourse in which the subject is inscribed. Except that there are subjects who do not inscribe themselves in any. This leaves the subject outside discourse. In these cases, one notices a gap between language and discourse. While language is a condition for entering into discourse, one can be in language without for that reason being in a discourse.

Being installed in a discourse assumes that the subject is caught up in one of these discourses. Certainly, one discourse can be left behind in order for another to be entered into. This is what we see in an analysis. It is a fact that analysis allows for a change of discourse. For example, a passage from the discourse of the hysteric into analytic discourse, which is necessary for the entry into analysis. But the analytic arrangement allows for another change of discourse, connected to the advent of a real that is proper to analysis, which entails a departure from the discourse in which the subject is caught up with the analyst. A question imposes itself here: outside of analysis, is it possible to change discourse? This might be observed sometimes, but often what is seen is a transitory change that then reverts back to the prior discourse.

The difficulty in passing from one discourse to another shows us that the subject installs itself quite durably in one discourse. This does not prevent a subject from being able to go from one discourse to another. But essentially, the subject remains anchored in one. It is in light of this view that we can grasp Lacan's suggestion about the subject in intellectual disability: 'there is no other definition that can be given it except that of being a bit off track, that is, floating between two discourses. To be solidly installed as a subject, it is necessary to stick to one, or else to be well aware of what one is doing'.[2]

But three years earlier, in the seminar *D'un Autre à l'autre*, he broached the topic of a floating subject who was not excluded from being able to be analysed.

> I was awestruck by the bouquets of flowers, flowers of truth, that I received when, by accident, I took into a psychoanalysis a type that Freud – wrongly! – seemed to avoid, namely, someone with an intellectual disability.[3]

What changes between 1969 and 1972 is essentially Lacan's introduction of the concept of discourse. In it we find a demonstration of what it means to say that a discourse has not taken hold of a subject. To float between two discourses is to have the freedom to pass freely from one to the other. If there is floating, it is precisely because something about the subject's mark is missing, a mark that comes to it from the Other.[4]

The relationship between freedom and intellectual disability should be made clear, since psychosis also, equally, assumes freedom. How is the freedom in psychosis distinguished from that found in an intellectual disability? Moreover, is it not the hallmark of a certain stupidity to hold on to an idea of absolute freedom? In psychosis, the fact of being outside of discourse entails, for the subject, the absence of any consent to the Other's commandments. Either the subject is excluded from them, as in the case of schizophrenia, or the subject proclaims itself their master, as in the case of the paranoiac.

Sometimes this can bring psychosis and stupidity together. Consider the case of a paranoiac. If one is not addressed by, that is, if one is not under the command of a paranoiac, the extravagance of his megalomaniacal statements may provoke laughter.

And sometimes the excessive, senseless statements of certain politicians would make us laugh if we did not also have to think about their dramatic consequences. But this is not the laughter of comedy, connected to the phallus. It's the laughter of the absurd, a laughter connected to statements disconnected from the phallus.

Consider certain contemporary statements, especially about the management of the crises connected to coronavirus. How can we explain the fact that on one day a health care policy can be advanced that goes against everyone's opinion, especially the scientific community's, and then just a few days later the position is completely changed?

It is not a matter here of trying to diagnose politicians. It's a matter of showing that we are dealing here with a stupidity that does not make us laugh, because it affects us. Is this the stupidity of someone who believes himself to be above the laws of nature, or is it that of a subject who floats between discourses? Because, in fact, there is also the stupidity engaged in by the statements of the subject of an intellectual disability. In the floating of an intellectual disability, we do not find the contradictions that are common among speaking beings. For, we can observe that contradiction seems to be part of the essence of speaking beings. It is remarkable that Lacan clearly articulated the relation between contradiction and the end of analysis when he raised a question about the emergence of religious belief in an analysis: 'Is psychoanalysis capable', Lacan asks, of making 'a viable atheist, that is, someone who would not contradict himself at every turn'?[5]

What can we deduce from this?

That, on the basis of analysis, it is possible to find a way to leave contradiction behind. The exit involves another relation to belief. It is not ceasing to believe, but ceasing to believe in an illusion that can function as a cork stopper when it comes to the desire to know.

So, let's address the contradictions that we find in certain political discourses. They seem to be oriented entirely around personal benefit. What gives us the impression of stupidity is the way in which the advice of the scientific community can be systematically neglected, along with the belief that one's own word is above everything.

Lacan dealt with the position of believing oneself to be above everything, and exerting a fascination on everyone else, in his discussion of Freud's *Mass Psychology and the Analysis of the Ego*. Regarding identifications with leaders, Lacan demonstrates 'how an object, reduced to its stupidest reality . . . can bring about an identification of the ideal ego with [its???] very moronic power'.[6] Then Lacan deals with the Führer. In retrospect, one can wonder: 'How could an entire people be so stupid'? Psychoanalysis gives us the key, with its view of the subject's relationship to the Ideal. The Ideal is placed outside: Freud clarified this in the text just mentioned, *Mass Psychology and the Analysis of the Ego*, about a collective function in which a group of individuals, the mass, acts so as to place outside of them, around one person, a common element that serves them as a model. The example is Hitler's moustache. This is the model for identification with the leader of the crowd. Capital I, the signifier of the Ideal, is posited onto the One who incarnates it for a community, such that all its members have at the same time the same ideal. Here, we are dealing with a special form of human stupidity. Without using other examples that have appeared in our history with often devastating consequences, we can linger a bit on the subject's relation to stupidity.

Stupidity can be loved. Socrates gives us an example of this, and Lacan highlights it in his Seminar on Identification: 'Why didn't Socrates love Agathon, if precisely in his case, as in that of Monsieur Teste, stupidity is what he is missing'?[7] In fact, Lacan highlights Socrates's statement that 'stupidity is not my strong suit'.

But again, what Lacan highlights is how power can go astray. Thus, he emphasizes Socrates's statements to Alcibiades: 'My good friend, keep talking, because it's that one, you too, whom you love. This whole long discourse is for Agathon. Only the difference is that you do not know what it is at stake. Your force, your mastery, your wealth deceives you.'

The neurotic, illustrated here by Alcibiades, is the one who repeats without knowing it. How can we not see this as a form of stupidity, someone tirelessly running into the same thing without knowing why? This is why Lacan in the same seminar refers to the neurotic as someone who is an innocent.

But what does the neurotic's confusion consist of? Wanting to catch the object of desire with the image, placing it on the side of an object of love or on the side of what incarnates, for the subject, the One who is worthy of identification. Notice that this is the very principle of hypnosis, and sometimes an entire community can fall under the charm of an object, producing a collective hypnosis. This is what renders idiotic, indiscriminately, blindly, but with one great benefit: one avoids having to take a position. So, the image functions as a lure for the subject.

This is what founds our interest in external trappings and forms the basis of our stupidity.

It is also why a woman's stupidity can exert a certain charm. The other's stupidity is noticed, which lets us avoid a confrontation with our own. This is also the foundation for the prevalence of love among speaking beings. We believe that we can leave lack behind by reducing the other in a couple, such that One is made with the subject. This is the foundation for beatitude in love. But what escapes is the real of desire. Between the subject and the real of its desire, the shadow of fantasy intervenes. This is what creates the goals of the Lacanian orientation in psychoanalysis. The shadow-effects would be dissipated by the wanderings of signifiers. By allowing for the wandering of signifiers, one can accede to true desire. But there is also another sort of stupidity, that of the strong Ego, which is all the more stupid since it is the foundation for misrecognition. Consider Socrates's elegy at the end of *The Symposium*, addressing 'the idiot of idiots, the most idiotic of all, and even the only complete idiot'.[8] Alcibiades is the one being called an idiot here, and if Socrates, in the place of the analyst, is less of an idiot, it is because he knows that his discourse on love is addressed to another object, in this case Agathon. But there is also the stupidity of the wealthy person, the one who cannot give what he does not have: love.

This is seen in the analytic clinic. A wealthy person thinks he is giving everything to a woman, but what she asks him to do is to give love, namely, what he does not have. The lack of understanding regarding women renders him stupid. At bottom, stupidity could be summed up in Lacan's statement about the idiot's connection to unity. What makes the stupid person stupid is an adherence to form, to the illusion of completeness.

This is why Lacan says that matter is a swindle: 'Matter presents itself to us as "*corps-sistance*" [body-consistency], I mean what is under the "sub-sistance" of the body, that is under what is con-sistant.'[9]

There is a play on words here between consistence and con-sistance.[10] The stupid thing to do is to believe in consistence, in the unity of the body, whereas the essence of the body is that it is filled with holes. Stupidity is not noticing that unity is conferred by the image that the subject fabricates of himself. In this respect, Lacan observes that everything that attracts us about unity is idiotic. Basically, the idea is that everything that is not included in the dimension of the real leads us to idiocy.

There is equally the stupidity of meaning. It is a cork stopper; it closes off instead of opening up. It is the stupidity of understanding, which stops us on the way to the real of desire. There is again another form of stupidity which is that of optimism. This is in the service of the subject's carelessness. More fundamentally, there is the stupidity that consists in letting oneself be guided by affects that are not a guide to the real. Lacan makes a play on words about this: he writes sentiment as '*senti-ment*' [feel-lying]. Letting oneself be guided by sentiments is to let oneself be guided by a sham. He also says it in another way: '*Senti* as *mental*, the sentimental, is stupid.'[11] The sentimental is stupid because in every way its existing coordinates are reducible to the imaginary. Thus, there is the stupidity of the imaginary, and then the stupidity connected to the belief in semblants.

A question arises: How does psychoanalysis allow one to escape from stupidity? We have seen that Lacan gave many examples of a generalized stupidity among human beings. First of all by giving figures of the idiot, such as the butcher in relation to his beautiful wife, who does not understand why she remains unsatisfied even though he satisfies her every demand. The stupidity is found in the fact that he does not notice the disjunction between demand and desire. In fact, satisfying demand crushes desire, if one does not leave the other, the sexual partner, unsatisfied every once in a while, when it comes to desire.

This is what makes Lacan say that this husband is 'a perfect idiot'.[12] This is not the only time Lacan uses this expression. He expresses himself in the same terms with respect to Sacher-Masoch: he 'was an idiot', although not for the same reasons.[13] The term designates something else in this case: it marks the invention of masochism, namely what Sacher-Masoch invented in order to fill in the hole in the real. This allows us to take up again the question of stupidity from another perspective: a stupidity that is a knowledge invented for covering up the real. Are there knowledges that are less idiotic? Certainly. Sacher-Masoch invented a knowledge based on moral suffering. When it comes to inventions, one can do better.

Let's consider different traditions. Lacan's idea is that traditions, like religions, are myths that cover over the real of the subject. This is why Lacan designates myth as the 'field of bullshitting'.[14] This bullshitting is the truth. In reality, bullshitting is believing that there is an ultimate truth. On this basis, we can understand why Lacan posits that 'idiocy is our essence'.[15] But it must be noted that analytic discourse is also considered by Lacan as a stupidity. For this reason: 'the signifier is stupid'.[16] Lacan puts it this way: 'an adjective made into a noun, "stupidity", . . . is a dimension of the signifier at work'.[17] So is it possible to leave stupidity behind, and how? The question becomes all the more pressing since Lacan says that we encourage the subject to utter stupidities. Let's say then, that if analysis is a practice that encourages the uttering of stupidities, it is because it is the way to secure a grip on the real that founds the subject. 'It is with . . . stupidities that we do analysis.'[18]

This demonstrates at once that analysis aims at the real but also that it is only by agreeing to go through stupidities that we find out that the signifier is not so stupid.[19] And Lacan even makes a relation to stupidity into the essence of analytic discourse: Doesn't this discourse (analytic) hold together by supporting itself on the dimension of stupidity?

So, there is stupidity and stupidity. True stupidity is believing that one is master of oneself. In this respect, we can refer to the following statement by Lacan: 'I am the master (*m'être*), I progress along the path of mastery (*m'êtrise*), I am the master of myself (*moi*) as I am of the universe. That is what I was talking about earlier, the vanquished idiot (*con-vaincu*).'[20]

Lacan makes this play on words between *con-vaincu* and convinced in many places. When he says, for example, that it is idiotic [*con*] to look to convince.

Lacan distinguishes between analytic discourse and other discourses regarding their positions with respect to stupidity, claiming that 'in other discourses stupidity is what one flees'.[21] The other discourses see stupidity reign supreme.

For psychoanalysis, by contrast, a choice is possible, and it is formulated in these terms: 'between madness and intellectual disability, we only have a choice'.[22] What is pointed out here is that the choice of intellectual disability is the choice of uniformity, conformity, homogeneity. It is the choice to conform oneself to the Other who prescribes, whereas taking a position, assuming one's singularity, entails a dimension of madness. It is madness that consists at least in part of going in the opposite direction of the norm.

We see in these reflections the difference that Lacan emphasizes between psychoanalysis and other speech practices. Psychoanalysis leads one to become the dupe of the unconscious.

But what is a dupe? Lacan takes this up in his seminar *Les non-dupes errent*:

'It seems that the dupe is the bird that one catches precisely because it is stupid.'[23] Here Lacan is referring to all those who are not dupes of the unconscious, that is, those who do not do all they can to stick to it.

But he is going to suggest a possible exit when he points out regarding idiocy that there is 'a chance to leave it behind. This is even why you are counting on me. Except that idiocy makes up part of this demand'.[24]

Lacan's position is that it is not enough to be a dupe not to err! He affirms that the non-duped err, but it is necessary not to be a dupe of just any old thing. Then to stake out his position, Lacan evokes Freud:

'Freud, and this is certainly something we need to consider very closely; he was a dupe of the Real.'[25] Just prior to this in the same seminar, Lacan evoked the thinking of imbeciles. This means that thinking is not what guarantees that we are leaving stupidity behind; rather, the exit is found in our relation to the real. This is why Lacan says that Freud was a dupe of the Real, even if he did not believe in it.

In other words, the Lacanian orientation in psychoanalysis does not aim at completeness, nor form, nor ideas. It goes against the common measure and common sense. It does not flee stupidity but tries to apprehend the real that certainly renders us less stupid. Because in fact there is a paradox of analysis: the signifier is stupid and we encourage the subject, through free association, to utter stupidities. Even in the case of the good dupe, the one who does not err, there must somewhere be a real of which he is the dupe.

What would be then the speech practice that gets us out of stupidity? Nothing allows us to be sure there is one, unless it is based on the following idea: that it is a practice of chit-chat, which means a practice of stupidities that aim at a real.

At the same time, we can deduce that there is a politics of psychoanalysis that cannot be based on naiveté. Naiveté is in the service of the illusion of believing in optimism. Enthusiasm as an affect of the end of an analysis is not the same thing as optimism; on the contrary, it assumes the collapse of false optimisms. Enthusiasm is an affect that is not a nostalgia for the claims of a better past, nor the belief in a future marked by the idea of progress. This point seems to me to be fundamental for understanding the implications of psychoanalysis, because psychoanalysis wishes to hang on to the marks of the past, without any nostalgia for better times. In other words, it is about hanging on to the real of experience without the myths that cover it over. This is what an analysis teaches us, and this is what it can thus teach politics. Because politics is a way of covering over the real.

I turn now to a current way of covering over the real. Lacan in fact created the expression 'current disk' (*disque-ourcourant*),[26] which is a play on words between discourse and a disk going around, highlighting the disk-like quality of what goes around in current discourse. This is about the repetition of formulas, as in a refrain, while avoiding the taking of a position. This is what happens when the subject uses a phrase while withdrawing itself from it as a subject. In French, often in order to avoid assuming the I, the subject says 'on' [TN: 'one', or the passive voice]. Well, in French there is also a proverb that goes: 'when one says "*on*" one is an idiot [*con*]'. What is idiotic, in fact, is not being able to assume one's own speech.

In other words, just as Lacan mocks the notion of 'common sense', he demonstrates that the disc-that-turns aspect of current discourse is a way to escape something structural, namely, the fact that there is no sexual relation.

Let's note that, according to Lacan, if there were no analytic discourse, the subject would continue to 'sing the disque-ourcourant'. Consequently, he makes a major opposition between participating in the current discourse on the one hand, and entering into analytic discourse on the other. If the latter gives the subject a chance of extracting itself from the stickiness of the current discourse – this is the disc-dimension – it is because of the production of a singularity in desire. To believe in structure means, in this sense, to let oneself be guided by a fact of experience, the effect of an encounter in transference, namely, a failure in the quest for meaning. It is on this condition that a passage is possible from the stupidity of the signifier to the real of the subject. This passage results in the emergence of what is most singular about a subject: its saying [*dire*].

This saying is what emerges from a subject, and it ex-sists in relation to the said, but it nevertheless has consequences on the totality of things said. We see again here why Lacan gave stupidity such an important position. Because encouraging a subject to utter stupidities is the royal road for the advent of a saying [*dire*]. Lacan formulates it in yet another way when he suggests, regarding the consequences of a saying on what is said: 'this is the proof that, in someone's analysis, as stupid as he is, a certain real can be attained'.[27] Uttering stupidities, which is the paradigm of the subject's consent to free association, ultimately implies a touch on the real. In fact, it is about drawing out the consequences of what could become an endless experience: psychoanalysis without the real.

Contrary to the experience of Achilles, who only catches up to the tortoise in infinity, putting the real at the heart of analysis is what extracts the analysand from the destiny that weighs Achilles down.

We come now to the following fact about analytic experience. A subject says: 'Ah, now I understand!'. Except the next day he continues to do the same stupid things as before! After that, we hear this recurring phrase: 'I understand but things are not changing.' Certainly, for psychoanalysis, a change assumes a reorganization of signifiers. At the same time, nothing changes just by understanding. The subject can say 'I know it, but . . .'. Stupidity is related to meaning, to believing that one would be different because one has understood. In this respect, the quest for meaning renders us stupid. This is the stupidity of *jouis-sens*.[28] But there is another relation between jouissance and stupidity that Lacan formulates about the practice of masturbation: he calls it 'the jouisance of the idiot'.[29]

Lacan thus takes up the theme of an auto-erotic jouissance. S1 is the index of the signifier of even the most idiotic jouissance, in the sense of the idiot's jouissance but also of the most singular jouissance: the most singular because S1 alone is the signifier without S2, which would be the bearer of meaning.

Notice that Lacan returns to the topic of intellectual disability at the end of his teaching, suggesting in the Seminar *Moment pour conclure* that there is an affinity between intellectual disability and thought, affirming that thought 'is something that verges on intellectual disability', as opposed to what he suggests is the result of the act: 'there must exist an act that is not an intellectual disability'.[30]

Such a logic confronts thinking as always stupid because it does not catch the real. There remains one thing that makes a speech practice consequential: an act that would detach the subject from its tendency towards stupidity.

To say that it would detach the subject from this tendency is not to say that psychoanalysis cures stupidity. Moreover, Lacan affirms: 'I've been advised that psychoanalysis is a remedy against ignorance: but it has no effect on idiocy.' Further on: 'It is up to us, as analysts, that it lets something be known, something that has its limits. And the limit that idiocy imposes, as I just said, is one we do not cross.'[31]

Translated by Ed Pluth

NOTES

1. Lacan, J. *Le Séminaire, Livre XIX, Ou Pire . . . .* Paris, Seuil, 2011, p. 131.
2. Ibid.
3. Lacan, J. *Le Séminaire, Livre XVI, D'un Autre à l'autre*, Paris, Seuil, 2006, p. 175.
4. There is an extensive discussion of the notion of a mark on the subject in my book *The Marks of a Psychoanalysis*, London, Routledge, 2018.
5. Lacan, J. "Conférences et entretiens aux Universités américaines," *Yale*, 24 Novembre 1975, Scilicet 6/7, Paris, Seuil, 1976.
6. Lacan, J. "Remarque sur le rapport de Daniel Lagache," in *Ecrits*, Paris, Seuil, 1966, p. 677.
7. Lacan, J. "Le Séminaire, Livre IX, L'Identification," Leçon du 21 Feb 1962, unpublished.
8. Lacan, J. *Le Séminaire, Livre VIII, Le transfert*, Paris, Seuil, p. 460.
9. Lacan, J. "Le Séminaire, Livre XXIV, L'insu que sait de l'une-bévue s'aile à mourre," unpublished.
10. TN: "*Con*" in French means *idiot.*
11. Lacan, J. *Le Séminaire*, *Livre XXIII*, *Le Sinthome*, Paris, Seuil, 2005, p. 37.
12. Lacan, J. *Le Séminaire*, *Livre XVII*, *L'Envers de la pyschanalyse*, Paris, Seuil, 1991, p. 84. [Eng. Trans. 74.]
13. Lacan, J. "Le Séminaire, Livre XXI, Les non-dupes errent," session of 19 Feb 1974, unpublished.
14. Lacan, J. *Le Séminaire*, *Livre XVII, Op. Cit.*, p. 127. [Eng. Trans. 111.]
15. Lacan, J. *Le Séminaire*, *Livre XXI*, *Les non-dupes errant*, session of 11 December 1973, unpublished.
16. Lacan, J. *Le Séminaire*, *Livre XX*, *Encore*, Paris, Seuil, 1999, pp. 17–18.
17. Ibid., p. 24. [Eng. Trans. P. 21.]
18. Ibid., p. 25. [Eng. Trans. P. 22.]

19. Ibid., p. 27. [Eng. Trans. P. 25.]
20. Ibid., p. 53. [Eng Trans. Page. 56. And some added . . .]
21. Ibid., p. 18. [Eng. Trans. Page 13.]
22. Lacan, J. "Journal d'Ornicar?" *Ornicar?* 17/18, 1979, p. 278.
23. Lacan, J. *Le Séminaire, Livre XXII, Les non-dupe errant. Op. Cit. Session of 11 December 1973.*
24. Ibid.
25. Ibid.
26. Lacan, J. *Le Séminaire, Livre XX, Encore, Op. Cit.*, p. 35.
27. Ibid., p. 25.
28. TN: *Jouissance* is enjoyment, roughly: *jouis-sens* suggests an enjoyment in or of meaning.
29. Ibid., p. 75. [Eng. Trans. 81.]
30. Lacan, J. *Le Séminaire, Livre XXV, Le moment pour conclure*, unpublished.
31. Lacan, J. 1975 dans La Letter de L'École Freudienne, n. 15, p. 235.

Chapter 10

A Paradigmatic Case of Brazilian National Stupidity

Christian Ingo Lenz Dunker

OLAVO DE CARVALHO

Stupidity has acquired pretensions to universality with the registration of Fake-News and Post-Truth. But in each case and culture, stupidity admits to specific, historical and unique forms. This chapter analyses the trajectory of Olavo de Carvalho, a Brazilian writer who became an intellectual mentor and master of ideas for Jair Bolsonaro's family and government,[1] acquiring a reputation as a thinker against all odds. Such influence is examined for its exemplification value, which is perfectly in accordance with the spirit of the new digital language, capable of making uncontrolled stupidity, lack of education and misinformation a mass phenomenon. These, alongside dangerous political valour, induce new forms of authoritarianism and fascism. The trajectory of this former communist militant and astrologer, who eventually became involved with Islamic radicalism, as well as having held positions in the newsrooms of numerous relevant print media in Brazil during the 1980s, will be the object of inquiry, especially for the way in which he reverses the obvious criticism against himself on a platform of denunciation. de Carvalho is a perfect example of successful stupidity, not only because of his millions of books sold and his influence in culture and politics, but also for his capacity of grouping, generalizing, socially expanding and being recognized for stupidity from beginning to end.

Although de Carvalho finished at high school levels, he was influenced by the traditionalism of Aleksandr Dugin and René Guenon. de Carvalho's most-read books, *O Mínimo que você precisa saber para não ser um Idiota*[2] (*The Minimum You Have to Know in Order Not To Be an Idiot*), *Apoteose da Vigarice*[3] (*Apotheosis of Swindle. Letters from an Earthling to Planet Brazil*), *A Fórmula Para Enlouquecer o Mundo*[4] (*The Formula to Drive the World*

Crazy), *O Dever de Insultar*[5] (*The Obligation to Insult*) and *O Imbecil Coletivo*[6] (*The Collective Imbecile – Current Events in Brazilian Uneducated*), are collections of truisms, commonplaces and quotations capable of shaming any average intellectual: Hobbes is mixed with the devil, Marx is peppered with swear words and the use of erudite authors lends itself to attack all who are in positions of respect and merit in the Brazilian academy and universities.

In a context of rising middle classes during the years 2002–2010 and with significant advances in the inclusion of children in schools as well as the expansion of universities, involving quota systems and greater access by the black and poor population, Olavo de Carvalho became a best-selling author of a phenomenon of online philosophy courses denouncing the falsity of intellectuals and their systems for recognition. It could be said that he repeats the formula of Roger Scruton and Theodore Dalrymple (Anthony Daniels) in England, Rush Limbaugh in the United States or Jordan Peterson in Canada. However, the problem of stupidity does not lie in their conservative, regressive or right-wing ideas, but rather in the way these acquire conspiratorial contours, aggressive rhetoric, poor articulation and the combination of erudite quotations with shady political interests, culminating in the incitement towards violence. They are not only sophists selling palatable ideas in a good format, but they are also thinkers of a preventive right-wing counter-revolution. That's why the key to their rhetoric consists of inverting key content, signifiers, narratives and discourse from the radical left. To understand this type of stupid anti-intellectual, we must take into account the unity he forms between his character, his concepts as inverted notions, his legal expression and his aesthetic efficiency.

The academy has always dealt with such phenomena with a certain amount of reserve, decorum and discretion, hoping that isolation and the lack of foundation would reduce the pyrotechnics of such ideas to their self-imposed bubble. However, this approach only seemed to constitute a strategic error because it unwittingly serves to confirm the conspiratorial ivory tower theory that universities are composed of arrogant subjects who are insensitive to criticism and indifferent to the actualities of people's lives.

Olavo de Carvalho was responsible for choosing the ministers of Foreign Affairs, Education and Citizenship; participated in President Jair Bolsonaro's entourage during his visit to meet with Donald Trump; and is the direct mentor of numerous decisions in Brazil, especially in the context of culture. His nominee for the Ministry of Culture, Roberto Alvim, was able to record a message to the population replicating the speech of Goebbels (Nazi German minister) in both its form and content.

With the transformation of politics into administration along with the reduction of public spaces to scenes of private interests, a gap emerges around the ideological underpinning of power, particularly power in a neoliberal form. We can say that this gap is occupied by stupidity, a stupidity which is elevated to the dignity of a figure of thought. In 2016, Donald J. Trump called Olavo de Carvalho 'one of the greatest conservative intellectuals in the world'[7].

Olavo de Carvalho died in 2022, two days after the diagnosis of COVID-19, 'an invention' and 'the vastest manipulation of public opinion that has ever taken place in human history',[8] in his ranch in Richmond, Virgínia. His legacy includes a film-maker company named *Brasil Paralelo*, which made his biographical movie *The Garden of Afflictions*.[9] They still produce fake-new films about science and politics. His ideas still strong influenced many people on the internet through his 1.2 million participants on his YouTube channel.[10]

A CONCEPTUAL FORM OF STUPIDITY

All regimes, worse or better, have their ideologues. In general, such a figure is not very respected in his area or is situated peripherally in relation to his peers. His function is twofold: first, to justify the arbitrariness to those he uses to create projection and second, to translate the leader's messages in order to create strategic advantages for his supporters in the exercise of small daily power. In general, the ideologist does not form himself in the ranks of the party or in the direct ideas of his master but takes advantage of the fluctuation of his points of view to fit an affinity of circumstances. This is possible because the role of the ideologist is above all suspend or destabilize the systems that guarantee the legitimacy and authority that we attribute to certain forms of knowledge.

For example, legal knowledge of the Weimar Republic was neutralized by an ideologist like Roland Freisler during the rise of Nazism; American university knowledge was controlled by an ideologist like Joseph McCarthy at the beginning of the Cold War; Soviet artistic and intellectual knowledge was destroyed by Andrei Jdanov during the rise of Stalinism. Although they were all mediocre thinkers, they knew how to use a swing of tone that allowed them to make impressive allusions alongside pimping words, generating an effect of authenticity. While they were scholars and experts in only one area, they tended to transfer their authority to problems in which they were not knowledgeable.

Olavo de Carvalho has a long record of unmasking and refutations marked by the continued exercise of philosophical improbity. The fact that he has no regular education, such as a degree in humanities, neither a master's nor doctorate, should not be an obstacle; after all there were many good thinkers who came from outside the university system or remained in its periphery.

That is why the fact that his first works focused on astrology and claims that he was a communist militant and adept of the sectarian Tariqa Islamic (who today lives as a refugee in the United States) do not disgrace him but rather, serve to create ideal traits to represent the role of someone who purports to be anti-system, independent and outside of the academy. He has what seems to be enough for others to believe in him and passages through the great world of newspapers and magazines, where like-minded people respond positively. This offers a great advantage to the perceived integrity of his character because he can undo complex erudite and always relatively controversial knowledge, such as science and professional philosophy, and represent the wisdom of the 'common man'. This stance confirms his prejudices while transferring conviction and authority to supporters.

Ideologists feed on oppositions, controversies and offenses because this creates enemies necessary to keep belief alive; moreover, it installs a solidarity composed of hatred and takes advantage of the feeling of intellectual inferiority that inhabits many people. Any attack on his work only confirms his position as a pariah and intellectual injustices only increase the aura of persecution, which he uses to tune into the masses. The trick of the pique works like this: to influence followers, the ideologist uses difficult words, quotes and extravagant titles, or makes use of his participation in semi-scientific events such as the Brazil Parallel Congress.[11] Notice that the key word, *influence*, even if it comes from the association with the suspicious notability of those listed. The idea here is that you can become wise by contagion, as if culture and thought work similarly to gossip magazines: when the inconsistency of the ideologist's ideas is scrutinized, the ideologist simply looks towards their followers or critics for responses, or where inconsistency is irrefutable, the ideologist resorts to deliberate obfuscation. If neither of these works, then the ideologist appeals to profanity: *ass*, *pussy* and *shit* are recurrent expressions in our case in point as ways to express his concepts and qualify his opponents, as far as it happens in many of Donald Trump's speeches.

Knowing all of this, problems arise for those of us wanting to expose that Olavo de Carvalho is a fake thinker. Any criticism of this kind will be neutralized by one simple assertion: I am a full professor at the University of São Paulo (USP) and part of the uncultured leftists propagated by the Working Party system. Anything I say can only be out of personal interest to preserve my privilege, and perpetuate a cultural hegemony, as proposed by Marx and Gramsci. In other words, both anything and nothing would have any real impact outside of the ideologist's discursive parameters. It is a deliberate no-win situation: on the one hand, I criticize relativism and postmodernity; on the other hand, I allow myself to speak anything because the truth has become trivial and subject to cynicism. His ideological operation begins by capturing the signifier 'ideology' as synonymous with 'left wing' thought.

Here, truth, or the very idea of it, becomes a matter of majority opinion and number of supporters. The human sciences comprise a variety of traditions and understandings, which gives room for the most heterodox positions.

Let us examine the problem a bit closer from a very crude and elementary but nevertheless objective point of view. From the community of scientists, there is an impartial system that aggregates and compares a variety of positions to the field of science, which serves to validate the value and legitimacy of the knowledge that is already produced. It seems that peer review is determined by no less than Twitter, Facebook, Instagram and Google Scholar, especially when it pertains to indexing, recognition and relevance of one's scholarship. Therefore, it is hardly worth saying that the university system, or indeed Brazilian philosophy, does not recognize or pursue so-called innovative and often misunderstood ideas of Olavo de Carvalho.

Of course, the 'system' has several deserving criticisms, but at the same time, it serves as a kind of generic sieve to talk about 'who is who' when it comes to science, knowledge and truth. The advantage is that anyone can enter this system and check the quantity and quality of the quotations of an author. For example, a left-wing professor like Vladimir Safatle has an i-10 of 40, in Google Scholar's[12] index of books and articles that have been cited by other authors. Vladimir,[13] one of the ascending figures of the left in Brazil, has 282 citations, resulting from his main work until 2016. A renowned right-wing author such as José Guilherme Merquior has 331 quotations from his best-known work. In 2016, Olavo de Carvalho had thirty citations from his magnum opus *O Mínimo que você precisa saber para não ser um Idiota*[14] (*The Minimous You Must Know in Order Not To Be an Idiot*) twenty-eight of these being references to research on the emergence of conservative thought in Brazil, speeches against corruption and research on political journalism. Carvalho's most 'technical' work, *Theory of Discourses in Aristotle*,[15] has only three citations in the field of philosophy, all of which disgrace the work of the ingenious polymath and philosopher, Aristotle.

Such low citations do not at all mean that all of Carvalho's ideas are rejected, but rather that his thinking is considered irrelevant to the field in which he is situated. This shows up his technical errors, his inconsequential lessons and other weaknesses of someone 'who can't think straight' and is akin to putting an amateur in lieu of a professional. A selection of Olavo de Carvalho's erratic statements includes the following: the UN supports terrorism; Pepsi is made with aborted foetuses;[16] there exists a global communist conspiracy of which the gay movement is a part; the Law of Inertia is false; and Isaac Newton was dumb.[17] Another outrageous claim is his claim of the existence of books written to teach children to perform oral sex on elephants.[18] And so he goes on: Brazil today is a communist dictatorship; the media supports gays to promote population control;[19] Marxism was born of

Satanism; Darwin is the father of Nazism;[20] the internet was created to fight atheism; human beings do not need brains to live; Nazism and the Forum of São Paulo are left-wing;[21] Bill Clinton was an agent from Beijing; the United States entered Vietnam to lose; there are 40 million communists in Brazil;[22] cigarettes do not cause cancer (he is an inveterate smoker);[23] there is no genetic difference between humans and chimpanzees during pregnancy; the business world was never politically organized; the dictatorship in Brazil was mild and still had democratic elections; and General Geisel (general and dictator president) was communist.[24]

His books include such titles as *The Duty to Insult*, a manifesto and invitation to insult your opponents; even I have had a taste.[25] In *The Collective Imbecile II*, another 'masterpiece', best seller with more than five hundred pages.[26] His *Theory of the Twelve Layers of Personality* is a ridiculous and pretentious summary of some of the most common psychological conceptions in psychology.[27] These are texts that serve to shame others and denounce the defenceless provincialism of the average Brazilian in non-school subjects. Even when his own daughter published a book denouncing his atrocities[28] and bad behaviours as a father, it did not diminish Olavo's popularity.

It certainly appears that ideologues serve mainly in disqualifying symbolically or strategically important knowledges and authorities. Therefore, it's no use to simply dismissing them as not serious because doing this only confirms, in the language of alienation, that they are outsiders and 'anti system'. Fernando Haddad (left-wing candidate in the 2018 presidential elections) has been criticized as an incompetent mayor and as a member of a corrupt party or as someone who plays the guitar very badly,[29] but he is also one who can't dispute his high Google indexing against Olavo de Carvalho. His work plan for the development of education has been cited 127 times and always in a technical or scientific context. Haddad completed his law degree at the USP, then studied for a master's degree in economics followed by a doctorate in philosophy. Haddad studied at McGill, one of the best Canadian universities, whereas Olavo de Carvalho did not finish his master's, as he did not see the merit in studying abroad. For over ten years, Haddad did what was decisively lacking in Olavo de Carvalho's education: he gave classes to enrolled undergraduate students. But, again, what is the value of this task? After all, USP has never appointed a self-respecting philosopher (a textual statement by de Carvalho). Haddad gave classes which were assessed, attended by restless or indolent students or what we might call, real classes. These were public classes, open and free and not paid courses over the internet. In 2022, Haddad became the economy minister of Lula, who defeated Bolsonaro by less than 2 per cent votes in the election. Olavo died one year before from respiratory problems and arguably with serious legal issues against him. The full irony remains in the fact that before he died, he returned to Brazil from his resident ranch in the United States in order to be treated by the public Brazilian health system, one which he had criticized for most of his life.

It is in this context of capital inequality, which bears witness to the ignorance of many regarding the recognition of the difference between a true teacher and researcher, or to put a finer point on it, one who is committed to serious intellectual curiosity and an 'asshole' who stands behind the table talking and hunting ducks in the United States. It is in this literal and metaphorical sense that we can examine and refute Olavo de Carvalho's statements and presumptions about Haddad's book:

1. 'The Worker's Party (PT) breaks images, rubs the crucifix on the genitals, urinates [*sic*] in the Bible and now wants Catholic support.'[30] The statement is grotesquely false. We can simply ask for whom can this message be persuasive, to the point of being restudied by the son of MP Jair Bolsonaro? It seems to be targeted at someone who will never read this text, who does not understand what research is or rather who merely understands that we should give credit to famous or potentially famous people. The more spectacular the plea, the more it renders an effect. Really, it begs the question: What is the difference between this and lying to be elected?

2. As Caetano Veloso once said: 'I consider Olavo's text to be an incitement to violence. I call upon my fellow citizens to repudiate it. Here are we going to pretend that this candidate has already won the election, so he can have those who did not vote for him be killed?'.[31] The communist conspiracy, the cultural hegemony of the university left and everything else that the duck hunter denounces seem to be exactly what he is immediately willing to practice. An intellectual who defends violence as a method immediately loses the right to use such a qualification and thus becomes an 'idiot' fulfilling the motto that people become what they hate most.

3. However, the champion of inconsequence of the highest award, *Nonsense of the Year*, (which incidentally inspired this very chapter) goes to his statement that Haddad wanted to overcome the 'taboo of incest' by implanting socialism in Brazil. Haddad would do his 'incest apology', probably as an extension of the 'gay kit'[32] (which never existed) and the 'gender ideology'. After the immediate repercussion of such a mistake was easily verified by the press, Olavo de Carvalho withdrew the post and replaced it with another presumptuous claim that Haddad 'fully subscribed to the erotic society and is a lawyer at the Frankfurt School who advocates the erotization of the relationship between mothers and children'.[33]

To qualify, the taboo of incest is an expression used by Freud in his 1913 text *Totem and Taboo* to designate that in all known human cultures there is a restriction on marriage within the structure of family. From this tradition, Freud infers that there is an existence of a potential desire of the child for the mother, which gives rise to his Oedipus complex hypothesis. This desire is consciously repressed, giving rise to the process of socialization as recognition of a larger law and authority that prevents us from accomplishing everything we want. According to Freud, many cultures and some family patterns exaggerate repression, creating children who are too forbidden in their desires and erotic lives. That is why any social transformation should pay attention to less rigid standards of repression, authority and law enforcement. This simple and widespread thesis, both among right-wing and left-wing thinkers, has been misappropriated to justify the 'erotization of childhood' and the 'apology for incest'. This is how a 'fake' thinker, a false thinker and hunter of ducks, operates: he takes an idea and deforms it without rigor, only to use it to instil fear in others. This is not a question of interpretation or point of view; the human sciences may admit variations and varieties, but they have one criterion, which is that rigour be sustained and maintained. In this case, it is crystal clear that neither psychoanalysis nor the Frankfurt School, nor Haddad advocate 'incest apology' or 'childhood erotization'.

This misappropriation of concepts is far from being just an academic all-rounder; it is a specific practice of relating signifiers to imaginary popular fantasies. Olavo criticizes postmodernism, multiculturalism and political correctness because he is its greatest practitioner, in the most corrupt sense of the term. Thus, here we arrive at the precise thinking cultivated by Olavo de Carvalho: such thinking not only consists of a lack of rigor or rhetorical pyrotechnics but also of political corruption and intellectual irresponsibility.

Teachers are not necessarily those who seem informal, or who transmit at the limit of their possibilities and their training, but rather are those who deliberately tell lies. Disinforming people in a country so lacking in teachers and teaching, doing it purposefully and for political purposes (remember the direct adhesions of Bolsonaro and his children to Olavo de Carvalho), harsh words and practicing lack of academic decorum only deserve a judgement worthy of one response, as Captain Nascimento would say: a willingness to leave!

THE LEGAL FORM OF STUPIDITY

In 2026, Olavo de Carvalho issued a criminal complaint against me for slander, defamation and insult based on a column published in the Boitempo Blog (and reproduced in the first section of this article), in which I present him as 'Bolsonaro's ideologist'[34]. The complaint is based on the alleged claim that I said that Olavo does not have a university degree. He says:

> the challenged, in a macabre relay, in thesis, with other mercenaries, incautious or subservient to the rotten Bolivarian populist powers, add with emphasis that;

Master Olavo would not have recognized course, as if this prevented us from admiring Jô Soares,[35] Silvio Santos,[36] Pelé,[37] Ronaldo Phenomenon,[38] Santos Dumont[39] and so many other geniuses in their areas.

The petition can be thought of as an aesthetic-legal example of the Brazilian curse, which testifies to the so-called textual rigor we find in Olavo de Carvalho's arguments, since I explicitly state that:

> The fact that he has no regular education, such as a degree in human sciences, neither master's nor doctorate, should not be an obstacle, after all there are many good thinkers who came from outside the university system or remained in its periphery.[40]

In other words, Olavo's paranoia entails that he inadvertently repeats my argument as part of his own complaint, as if anticipating a criticism that I did not make, but which perhaps torments him. This is a precise example of what can be described as a lack of rigor. In philosophy, rigor is the criterion of method, whether in the precision, understanding, interpretation or criticism of texts. Instead, disqualifying terms such as 'mercenary' and 'Bolivarian' abound, as does the typical 'humility' that places oneself next to 'Ronaldo Phenomenon'. Drawing a comparison is simple: Olavo would be for philosophy as Santos Dumont is for aviation. Complement this with Eike Batista and the owners of JBS 'do not have basic academic backgrounds'.

However, what I declare here first-hand is that Olavo de Carvalho lost his case against me,[41] as he has lost all seven other cases that have been tried so far.[42] The terms outlined by the judge who decided the case in my favour were clear: thus, de Carvalho was ordered to pay for a lawyer as well as court costs and other incidentals:

> It is incompatible, with the pluralism of ideas (which legitimizes the divergence of opinions), the view of those who intend to deny the media (and their professionals) the right to seek and interpret information, as well as the prerogative to express pertinent criticism.[43]

But let us return to the primary cause. I have stated that the problem was not in the absence of a formal diploma, but rather the irrelevance of Olavo's scholarship production, according to quantitative criteria that are valid for any researcher and that any reader can verify by himself in computer databases that count how many times someone's work is mentioned by others, indicating its consequence or importance for that area. The book *The Least You Need to Know in Order Not to Be an Idiot* has been cited thirty-nine times by specialists; *The Collective Imbecile*, only twenty-eight times; and *The Garden of Afflictions*, thirty-six times – all are examples of the rise of the new Right

Brazilian irrationalism. To have a basis for comparison, Paulo Freire, who the government wants to dismiss as the patron of education, is currently the most cited Brazilian author with 342,711 mentions. Marilena Chaui, one of the authors preferably attacked by Olavo and who is comparable in age to his, has 24,095 quotations to date. That is, read carefully, now in full: twenty-four thousand and ninety-five works mention her as a reliable source of research.

The whole work is a prime example of the current Brazilian trajectory in legal marketing. The self-titled 'greatest thinker in Brazil' had at his disposal several arguments. He could have argued that citation count is a very technocratic index, but apparently, he could not understand the criticism and turned it into a 'word count' in a published book. Further, he also could have argued that the number of citations would simply reflect what he supposedly already knew: all university students, not only Brazilians, are involved in this great red conspiracy that has taken over the world. Moreover, he could have illustrated textually how the Frankfurt School defends the erotization of the relations between mother and child (contrary to what I objected in my initial criticism). But instead, the 'vacillation' he chooses is to defer to legal intimidation. In other words, he confesses that his arguments are not enough and thus cowards his ideas. He takes up the challenge set by Débora Diniz so that he accepts the invitation to debate in Brazil. This kind of warlike empathy is based on what the rhetorical arms are made of: cowardice.

THE AESTHETIC FORM OF STUPIDITY

Tosco is a Portuguese word with two semantic roots: that which presents itself in a natural and authentic way, but also an act which is undertaken without refinement, that is, something rustic or coarse. It is estimated that the concept is illusory to the inhabitants of Tuscany, a region of Italy where the Etruscans lived. As the oldest inhabitants of the Italian peninsula, they were considered barbaric, rude and yet somewhat relaxed people (*toscu*). Onde can say '*shearing a sheep*' as '*tosquear* a sheep'. So *Toscu* can be a verb, not just an adjective, which translates as the proximate gaze of seeing from afar, a sighting from afar or perceiving from a distance. Here one can see immediately how a quick idea, without approaching the object, or deepening the experience, can truly look. The act of doing something in a *tosco* way seems perfect for the art of transmitting great ideas without detail, of forming blunt judgements without examining their consequences or of declaring things that cannot be translated into real transformations when seen up close.

It is possible that ten or fifteen years from now art historians might well characterize this period, between 2016 and 2022, as the apogee of the Brazilian *Tosco*. Such an expression can be compared to English romanticism,

American postmodernism or German baroque as a small contribution to the universal concert of nations. The philosophical question that beckons *Tosco* is, *what is it (good) for?* Such a provocation is not new to the history of art and Brazilian sensibility. Rather, it starts with questioning the relevance of incomprehensible forms, those opaque functions or segregated languages which determine the position of a certain *elite*. However, what characterizes the new Brazilian *Tosco* is the appropriation of this questioning by another type of *elite*, which functions as parasites of the denunciation as a mode of production of a certain authority and, at the same time, mimics the ethics of work and production. This kind of *elite* is not necessarily altogether popular but arguably emergent and gaining power. It possesses a disdain for culture and education as means of social ascension and mobility, since such members descend from the ancient aristocracy, for whom being in a place with uneducated people is a symptom of decadence and identity uncertainty. For this reason, the new Brazilian *Tosco* is basically the return of the recalcitrant kernel of ingenuity against the imposter of the well-behaved liquidator. That is why the new Brazilian *Tosco* is an aesthetic and philosophical expression of our shock of incivilities.

It is part of *Brazilian Tosco* (Brazilian Crude) to practice a kind of absolutist relativism. As all opinions are equally valid and as all points of view are equalized according to a very simple or minimal difference, of the left or right type, the strength of my enunciation is absolute as such. Hence, the fundamental method of Tosco Brasileiro is *gambiarra*, a term that originally refers to the irregular extension of a lighting line or a 'fraudulent connection', which is in any way precarious, ugly and improvised or made according to circumstances, in the archetypal 'Brazilian way' style (maybe 'handlamp' in English). *Gambiarra* is perceived as the crude return of the recalculated corruption. For example, *gambiarra* theatre consists of a style where front lighting is used to reduce unwanted shadows so that the artist does not lose concentration. This artifice of the limelight covers the audience, turning it into a faceless mass so the *gambiarra* protects the actor from his own intentioned malpractices. In the field of computing, the concept of *gambiarra* refers to procedures that reach their end without any elegance or concision within their own operations.

The crude (*tosco*) is not a popular republican expression, in the sense of the São Paulo arts quarter, but nor is it necessarily naïve, although the collective voice of the middle classes is interested in denouncing (in an interpassive way) the imposture of the *elites*. It is thus understood that every *elite* must be recognized as being within quotation marks, because only the authentic and true *elite* is also the rough *elite*, without quotation marks.

The characteristic trait of the *Brazilian Tosco* is an a-plus gesture, which makes average and responsible work an intolerable exaggeration. Through an involuntary parody, the artist produces a denouncing effect while at the same time defending himself by affirming his irrelevance. Such a method also serves the ambiguous formula of fake-news: for believers it seduces and warns against condescending self-irony. This re-appropriation of materials according to circumstances is a technical reproducibility that even Benjamin never intuited.

The *Brazilian Tosco* is an involuntary national re-reading of the aesthetics of precariousness. The word precarious derives from the Latin *precarious*, 'obtained through prayer; granted by revocable grace; taken as loan; alien, stranger; passenger'. Here precarious means, among other things, 'little, insufficient, scarce' or 'that has little or no stability; uncertain, contingent, inconsistent'.[44] Baudelaire had already defined aesthetic modernity in terms of a precarious search for the transitory, the fugitive and the contingent.

For Nicolas Bourriaud,[45] precariousness is an ethical reflection on contemporary art closely linked to the definition of reality. Judith Butler[46] also themes precarious lives as those lives worthy of care, especially given their parentage and vulnerability. According to Hal Foster,[47] no concept includes all art from the past decade better than precariousness.

In 2004 at the Albinet Precarious Museum, Thomas Hirschhorn[48] moved original works from Duchamp, Malevich, Mondrian, Warhol, Beuys, Le Corbusier, Léger and Dali to the outskirts of Paris. Sheltered in wooden shacks and small open-air shops, combined with cheap copies and utensils in the periphery, the out-of-place effect of ambiguity and displacement constructed the refuge ethic. Francesc Torres' '25%' which was exhibited at the fifty-fifth Venice Biennale[49] we find eight 'precarious' citizens representing the vast army of unemployed, young and old, men and women, of different origins and professions whose lives are losing value. Ana Gallardo's 'A place to live when we come', exhibited at the Mamba, consisted of five headphones hanging from the ceiling which provide narratives of receptionists, telephonists, sales promoters and jewellery smugglers. The installation '*Construction materials for the pavilion of Spain*' by Lara Almarcegui[50] is held at the pavilion of a building built in 1922 and is occupied with crushed construction rubble, piles of bricks, cement, earth and glass.

No such aesthetic provocations are to be found in *Tosco Brasileiro*, which rather consists of the negation of the experience of precariousness and the refusal to recognize precariousness as an aesthetic without a place (foreigner, migrant, immigrant), of the animal (hybrid, inhuman, without law, without rule) and of the monster (invisible and indiscernible body). That is why historically the rise of *Tosco Brasileiro* is preceded by the ostensive repression of exhibitions such as the Queermuseum in Porto Alegre,[51] of the History of Sexualities at MASP[52] and the performance on nudity at La Béte at MAM in São Paulo.[53] The *Brazilian Tosco* is deliberately a non-dialectic inversion of the aesthetics of precariousness. Moreover, it serves as a parasite for the force of authenticity contained in the notion of helpless lives but does so in the name of a warlike recovery of power. *Tosco Brasileiro* operates according to a logic of resentful inversions: *machism* is a non-dialectic inversion of *feminism* and presumes that violence justifies violence.

Instead of the recognition of Freudian helplessness (*Hilflosichkeit*) as a common and universal condition, such a reversal creates a split between those considered 'good citizens' and who deserve the protection of the State, and 'enemies of the people' who threaten our children. In this measure, the *Brazilian Tosco* finds its roots in the rhetoric of socialist realism. Everything that is shown must possess the power of example: the logic follows that if a claim harbours no pedagogical propensity, it must be suppressed.

Education presumes the imitative assimilation of myths and heroes, holding little room or place for anti-model, criticism or indetermination. Privileging simplicity over complexities which are deemed unnecessary, we choose accessible demonstration patterns and iconic or geometric language. The idea of a central, paternalistic type of hero who communicates with the people directly in the manner of an omnipresence contrasts directly with the image of the model-worker, who must be represented one-dimensionally as a kind of entrepreneur of himself.

Here, art and its various functions must, above all, be useful to the system. The thesis will also be found in Nazi allegorism, with its return to mythological heroes and warriors, but also in fascism and its glorification of a military and imperial state. But in the case of the national crude, the system is represented discursively by an anti-system (such as the swastika is a direct inversion of systematic praxis for Buddhist enlightenment). Art as a field of freedom, with distinct and polyphonic tendencies, is thus redefined as dangerous. Here, the anti-intellectualist schemes of Hitler pursuing degenerate art, Stalin boycotting the constructivists and Fidel's position against American pop art are repeated. An example of 'international crap' is the independence museum, donated by North Korea to Namibia. Three majestic floors, in the centre of Windhook,[54] are filled with a heroic, militaristic narrative with illustrative puppets as an aspiration for modernity. The affinity between crude and realistic nationalism is confirmed by the exaltation of symbols such as the flag, sporting and Olympic idols. Such images are specifically symbolic, marked by green and yellow, with images of dawn inferring new beginnings. Here is an allusion to the new man who is going to emerge, in the restart of history, in which the corruption of the past will be abandoned.

As in the urinophilic aesthetic of the presidential post on the Golden Shower,[55] it is a question of returning to the true national values of the Brazilian carnival through the denunciation and the rustic authenticity of the criticism. The *Brazilian Tosco* is above all a failed virile aesthetic, in which the sharing of a chocolate becomes a homosexual allegory. Educating by arms and Christianizing by violence are strategies by which the *Tosco* explores ontological feelings of insecurity. The impermanence of this project resumes the ephemerality of the 1960s vanguards. The erratic discourse recovers the automatic writing of the surrealists.

Much is discussed in the authorship of this new era, inaugurated in 2018, regarding the use of university courses in Philosophy or Sociology, as well as the usefulness of museums and other cultural repositories: 'we have never won a Nobel Prize and we suffer from chronic hypertrophy of the human sciences'.[56] These assertions carry the typical trace of exaggeration and imprecision that we have already seen being the tonic of this style. In the name of taxpayers' money and the fight against corruption, it is not being said that philosophy and the arts are useless, only that they are luxury items that are not for the State to sponsor. Their logic is as follows: the rich and privileged may well continue their historic dedication to these contemplative pleasures. But the poor need food and schools; they demand material needs met and jobs restored. But who speaks for the poor? The affinities with the most vulnerable are dangerous and manipulative and it is here we contemplate the opportunistic affiliation between *Brazilian Tosco* and post-war socialist realism.

It would be a mistake to agree that the fundamental propositions of *Tosco* are anti-philosophical or counter-cultural. To affirm that Nazism is left-wing, to arm the population to diminish violence or to rewrite the history of torture in Brazil and the *Statute of the Child and Adolescent*[57] involves a kind of excess of philosophy: philosophy without method, history without rigor, sociology without criticism, psychology without ethics, anthropology without diversity. All of this is already available intuitively and free of charge to those who came from a good family, who developed the religious synthesis of universal thought and who were formed in the abundance of digital knowledge.

Career intellectuals were awakened from their dogmatic sleep of their irrelevance by the poisonous kiss, directly from 1964.[58] This *Sleeping Beauty* effect cannot be ignored; it reveals the ignorance or indifference towards the emergence of a new aesthetic-philosophical attitude in Brazil. Never in this country has the importance of names like Gramsci, Marx or Paulo Freire been so vehemently discussed. Moreover, never before has it been so important to define political guidelines with real and painful consequences for the dynamics of families, friendships and love.

Clumsy, though it might be to say that 'what presents itself as coming from nature', is authentic, uncut and transparent. But it is also presumptuous to offer that what 'is done without refinement or with refinement, with rudeness or in a crude way', harbours a certain ostentatious and an exhibitionist pride in unthinking. The logic is structured as a mockery: nothing can last longer than the natural effect of its inconsequence, underlined by the offensiveness of words and concepts. The *Tosco Brasileiro* claim it is necessary to ignore any seriousness concerning education, culture or universities as they make accusations against gender ideologies, cultural Marxism, protection of human rights or black or LGBT minorities to produce and reproduce new internal enemies. Moreover, they argue that it is necessary to denounce privileges of any protection for children, indigenous people or those suffering from mental health issues. Here the strength of *Tosco Brasileiro* lies in its attitude of denunciation and imitation. This prodigal formula in the history of the arts carries the enunciation of resistance against the tyranny of the sensitive personality and the invisible customs of the 'little intelligent people' of high Brazilian culture, perceived as a club for the exchange of favours and the cross-maintenance of privileges. In the background of this is traditional music with American translations, such as *Toghether e Shalow Now*[59] by Paula Fernandes and Luan Santana, conveying the strength of simplicity, which is just enough to entertain us.

The *Brazilian Tosco* style serves as a revolt against illusion. Not only is it against the specific illusions of a certain political programme that preceded and conditioned it, but also against the very status of illusion because it speaks from reality's point of view. Illusions make us believe in different futures of the past. Moreover, illusions betray us and make us hate the work of illusion itself. If incompleteness typifies illusive production, it follows that stereotype and caricature are its non-dialectic inverses. *Tosco Brasileiro* appear to hate art and science as realized in the figure of the teachers of the *elite*, who are considered impostors and inauthentic. That is why it is essential for *Tosco Brasileiro* to present themselves as 'without a party', 'without ideology', 'without obscure or ambiguous points', 'the same things in life as she is'. All local ambiguity is a certainty doubled in the second instance by the aesthetic community of taste. Hence, the *Brazilian Tosco* is a religious aesthetic, in the Kantian sense of a community of taste and in the Lacanian sense of a community of *jouissance*. The leap from the judgement of taste automatically and problematically presumes something sublime because the object itself is representative of outward and palatable beauty.

Just as the old *Tosco Brasileiro* does not recognize art or culture, education or philosophy, which are not equally rough, the new *Brazilian Tosco* is a creation and creature produced to sanction the self-recognition of a new *elite*, which has suddenly resized its parameters and importance. It may be a passing trend, like so many others, but it will certainly leave scars in the history of Brazilian civilization. Hopefully, it will be the last song, stronger than all the others, that the swan pronounces before it disappears.

NOTES

1. Jair Bolsonaro (born 21 March 1955, Glicério, Brazil) is a Brazilian politician who served as President of Brazil from 2019 to 2023. He was a right-wing nationalist, law-and-order advocate and former army captain who expressed admiration for the ruling military Brazilian government between 1964 and 1985. Bolsonaro came into office on a wave of populist antiestablishment indignation stirred up by the massive Petrobras scandal that had tainted much of the country's political class.

2. Carvalho, Olavo de (2013) *O Mínimo que você precisa saber para não ser um Idiota*. São Paulo: Record.

3. Carvalho, Olavo de (2016) *Apoteose da Vigarice: Cartas de um Terráqueo ao Planeta Brasil*. São Paulo: Record.

4. Carvalho, Olavo de (2015) *A Fórmula Para Enlouquecer o Mundo*. São Paulo: Record.

5. Carvalho, Olavo de (2015) *O Dever de Insultar*. São Paulo: Vide.

6. Carvalho, Olavo de (2021) *O Imbecil Coletivo – Atualidades Inculturais Brasileiras*. São Paulo: Vide.

7. Nicas, Jack (26 de janeiro de 2022). "Olavo de Carvalho, Bolsonaro's Far-Right Guru, Dies at 74". *The New York Times* (em inglês). ISSN 0362-4331. Consultado em 11 de fevereiro de 2022.

8. Reinaldo Azevedo (23 de março de 2020). "Olavo de Carvalho sobre coronavírus: 'A endemia simplesmente não existe'". Uol. Consultado em 9 de abril de 2020.

9. *The Garden of Afflictions* (2017) directed by Brazilian film-maker Josias Teófilo, with executive production by Matheus Bazzo and cinematography by Daniel Aragão. It was the biggest crowdfunding campaign for a film in Brazil's history.

10. https://www.youtube.com/channel/UC6RQhzm93SterWntL7GzqYQ

11. https://www.youtube.com/channel/UCKDjjeeBmdaiicey2nImISw The Congress was attended by more than sixty influential participants, among them Ronaldo Caiado, Onyx Lorenzoni and Gilmar Mendes, who provided seminars about the reality of Brazil from the liberal-conservative point of view.

12. https://scholar.google.com/

13. https://scholar.google.com/citations?hl=pt-BR&user=fw3hwBYAAAAJ

14. Carvalho, Olavo de (2013) *O Mínimo que você precisa saber para não ser um Idiota*. São Paulo: Record.

15. Carvalho, Olavo de. (2013) *Aristóteles em nova perspectiva: introdução à Teoria dos Quatro Discursos*. Campinas/SP: Vide Editorial.

16. Carvalho, O. *Pepsi Cola e o uso de fetos abortados*. [S.l.], 2018a. 1 vídeo [1min. 10 seg]. Publicado pelo canal Cheirando Moura. Disponível em: https://www.youtube.com/watch?v=ju0sSdseqXA&ab_channel=ANovaLoiradoChan. Acesso em: 24 jan. 2021.

17. rasil247.com/geral/terra-plana-pepsi-com-fetos-cigarro-faz-bem-e-pandemia-e-mentira-confira-8-frases-bizarras-de-olavo-de-carvalho

18. https://valor.globo.com/brasil/coluna/por-que-e-essencial-entender-o-olavismo.ghtml

19. Mário Jorge de Paiva (2020) Análise introdutória sobre a relação de Olavo de Carvalho com as pautas LGBTI+. Revista Brasileira de Estudos da Homocultura 7(22), 1–23.

20. José Colucci Jr. (2004) O fantasma de Darwin. Observatório de Imprensa. *Edição* 297. https://www.observatoriodaimprensa.com.br/ciencia/o-fantasma-de-darwin-2/

21. https://olavodecarvalho.org/comunismo-versus-nazismo-o-charlatanismo-de-esquerda/

22. https://olavodecarvalho.org/tag/midia/

23. https://www.diariodocentrodomundo.com.br/cigarro-faz-bem-disse-olavo-de-carvalho-internado-em-estado-grave-em-sp-com-infeccao-generalizada/

24. https://olavodecarvalho.org/incomparaveis/

25. Carvalho, O. Donkey: analfabeto e mentiroso. [S.l.], 1 jul. 2019. 1 vídeo [49 min. 39 seg.]. Publicado pelo canal Olavo de Carvalho. Disponível em: https://www.youtube.com/watch?v=mHVcLO2WC74. Acesso em: 24 jan. 2021.

26. Carvalho, O. (1996) *O imbecil coletivo: atualidades inculturais brasileiras.* Rio de Janeiro: Faculdade da Cidade, 1996.

27. An example of what I would ask a third-year student to tell me in nineteen pages is a precise of all that has been noted thus far about the concept of personality. For example, get to know thirteen European capitals in four days and discover the truth of the millenary Western culture in a fast and cheap manner.

28. Carvalho, H.; Bugalho, H. (2020) *Meu pai, o guru do presidente: a face ainda oculta de Olavo de Carvalho*. Curitiba: Kotter Editorial; Editora 247.

29. https://www.youtube.com/watch?v=hZbFHDo3QvA

30. https://www1.folha.uol.com.br/opiniao/2018/10/olavo-faz-incitacao-a-violencia-convoco-meus-concidadaos-a-repudia-lo.shtml

31. https://www1.folha.uol.com.br/opiniao/2018/10/olavo-faz-incitacao-a-violencia-convoco-meus-concidadaos-a-repudia-lo.shtml

32. ‘Gay kit’ was the name given from right and adopted by Olavo de Carvalho to designate a manual made by PT to explain sexuality to students at school. The manual was never distributed, but it was associated with the ‘gender ideology’ which is going to kidnap ‘our’ kids with trans, gay and Other ‘dirty’ issues that come from left wing.

33. Dunker, Christian (2018) Olavo de Carvalho, o “ideólogo de Bolsonaro”, contra o professor Haddad https://blogdaboitempo.com.br/2018/10/15/olavo-de-carvalho-o-ideologo-de-bolsonaro-contra-o-professor-haddad/

34. Processo extinto sumariamente: Olavo de Carvalho sofre 4ª derrota consecutiva na Justiça (2019) https://www.diariodocentrodomundo.com.br/processo-extinto-sumariamente-olavo-de-carvalho-sofre-4a-derrota-consecutiva-na-justica-por-vinicius-segalla/

35. Brazilian TV showman.

36. Brazilian TV showman.

37. Brazilian soccer player.

38. Brazilian soccer player.

39. For Brazilians, the man who invented the aeroplane in the mid-1920s.

40. Quotation of the Juridic accusation peace. Case 1000175-60.2019.8.26.0050 according to the Initial Petition to the Court of the State of São Paulo: Special Criminal Court.

41. Werneck, Paulo (2019) Do lugar de fala ao lugar de escuta. *Revista* 451. https://quatrocincoum.com.br/noticias/psicanalise/do-lugar-de-fala-ao-lugar-de-escuta/

42. https://www1.folha.uol.com.br/ilustrissima/2018/12/esnobado-por-intelectuais-olavo-de-carvalho-dominou-video-e-redes-sociais.shtml

43. Quotation of the Juridic accusation peace. Case 1000175-60.2019.8.26.0050 according to the Initial Petition to the Court of the State of São Paulo: Special Criminal Court. The full text of accusation was as follows: 'Just from the above, any citizen with an intellect can clearly see that the activist, in theory, who signed and disseminated the aforementioned article, tries to distort the QUERELANT's words, inserting them in other contexts. In a cowardly and disguised way, in theory, he is trying to convey the image that Olavo is a fascist mentor to other supporters of authoritarian regimes such as A. Hitler, thereby the Honor of authorities constituted by the Noble Brazilian People, vide intelligence, because the Noble President of the Republic, Jair Messias Bolsonaro, and others are compared to (Joseph Goebbels).'

44. It is worth noting that during the 1640s the legality of a word was held up via the favor of another. This is from the precarious Latin phrase, 'depending on favor, pertaining to entreaty, obtained by asking or praying', from prex (genitive precis) 'entreaty, prayer' (from PIE root *prek- 'to ask, entreato'). The notion of 'dependent on the will of another' led to the extended sense 'risky, dangerous, hazardous, uncertain' (1680s), but this was objected to. Online Etymology Dictionary https://www.etymonline .com /word

45. https://www.google.com/search?q=Nicolas+Bourriaud+precarious&rlz=1C1RUCY_pt-BRBR695BR696&oq=Nicolas+Bourriaud+precarious&aqs=chrome.0.69i59.2249j0j8&sourceid=chrome&ie=UTF-8

46. Butler, Judith (2006) *Precarious Life: The Powers of Mourning and Violence*. London: Verso.

47. Foster, Hall (1996) The Return of the Real: The Avante-Garde at the End of the Century. Cambridge, MA: MIT.

48. http://www.leslaboratoires.org/en/projet/musee-precaire-albinet/musee-precaire-albinet

49. https://www.e-flux.com/announcements/32617/25-catalonia-a-venice-biennale-collateral-event/

50. https://theculturetrip.com/europe/spain/articles/transitional-places-lara-almarcegui-to-represent-spain-at-the-venice-biennale

51. https://g1.globo.com/rs/rio-grande-do-sul/noticia/mostra-queermuseu-e-desmontada-em-porto-alegre-e-deve-sofrer-uma-pausa-ate-ser-reaberta.ghtml

52. https://masp.org.br/exposicoes/historias-da-sexualidade

53. https://revistacult.uol.com.br/home/ensaio-polemica-la-bete-mam/

54. https://en.wikipedia.org/wiki/Independence_Memorial_Museum_(Namibia)

55. A 'Golden Shower' – refers to the act of being peed upon or peeing upon someone. It is a form of domination BDSM play that is mostly harmless, albeit a little

messy. It is a type of Urophilia, which is the sexual arousal and/or pleasure from the thought, sight, feel and/or smell of urine. Refer to Watersports for more information on this fetish.

56. https://www.gazetadopovo.com.br/rodrigo-constantino/artigos/olavo-de-carvalho-nem-precisa-sempre-ter-razao-para-estar-muito-frente-de-seu-tempo/

57. https://www.gov.br/mdh/pt-br/navegue-por-temas/crianca-e-adolescente/publicacoes/o-estatuto-da-crianca-e-do-adolescente

58. The Brazilian military dictatorship was the regime established in Brazil on 1 April 1964 and which lasted until 15 March 1985, under the command of successive military governments. Authoritarian and nationalist in character, the dictatorship began with the military coup that overthrew the government of João Goulart, the democratically elected president at the time. The regime adopted a nationalist, developmentalist and anti-communist policy. The dictatorship reached the peak of its popularity in the 1970s, with the 'economic miracle', at the same time as the regime censored all the country's media and tortured and exiled dissidents. In the 1980s, like other Latin American military regimes, the Brazilian dictatorship fell into decline when the government was no longer able to stimulate the economy, control chronic hyperinflation and deal with the growing levels of income concentration and poverty resulting from its economic project, which gave impetus to the pro-democracy movement. The government passed an Amnesty Law for political crimes committed by and against the regime; restrictions on civil liberties were relaxed and then indirect presidential elections were held in 1984, with both civilian and military candidates. The Brazilian military regime inspired the model of other dictatorships throughout Latin America by systematizing the 'National Security Doctrine', which justified military actions as a way of protecting the 'national security interest' in times of crisis.

Translated with DeepL.com (free version)

59. https://www.youtube.com/watch?v=MbdOTDCQiQE

Chapter 11

Seriously! That Is Fucking Stupid!

The Importance of Being Stupid, Earnestly

Cindy Zeiher

Does it produce insensibility?
By no means.
Not the least of its merits is,
that it is not an opiate.
It kills pain without killing feeling
You lie!
Some pains cannot be eased
but by producing insensibility,
and cannot be cured but by producing death.
(*The Confidence Man*)[1]

Why should we listen seriously to stupidity? Moreover, why should we listen to it again and again? When we decide to commit ourselves to psychoanalysis, we are at the same time admitting that we are, and certainly have been stupid, and probably always will be. This in itself is enough to trigger curiosity about stupidity, which presents initially as an overwhelming signifier. At times, we may feel or be a bit less stupid, but, in the end, we usually accept that we are basically stupid subjects interacting with other more or less stupid subjects, notwithstanding that we don't *want* to be stupid and certainly don't want to appear so. But although stupid, some of us are nevertheless longing to discover some hidden knowledge about our stupidity in order to be at least a little less stupid. The overwhelming effect of stupidity is that once we realize we have been repeatedly stupid, our longing not to be stupid hinges on what we think of as knowledge. Here, stupidity becomes more than an overwhelming signifier, as we realize this is precisely what is manhandling us so unbearably.

We should surely meet such subjective unbearability of stupidity with some degree of gracious understanding, not least because it presupposes a subject who is struggling with language. After all, stupidity is an unnamable thing at the limits of human experience yet is at the same time at the heart of that which organizes social life. As we live with others in the world, we are faced with a steady stream of meanings which are not necessarily linked and which – along with us – weave in and out of knowledge. We don't always fit neatly within the realm of discourse, especially at times when language can't be fully incorporated into our lived experience, for instance, when the failure of *savoir faire* results in stupidity. If only we had prior knowledge of our current stupidities so that we could at least properly enjoy the inevitable anguish they trigger! Although it seems stupid to be making a pact with stupidity in order not to be stupid, this is what we are doing when we commit to bringing the question of our desire to the clinic, when we bring to the couch a series of stupid questions, encouraged by our not wanting to appear stupid to our analyst, or anyone for that matter. What we are really doing here is elevating the signifier of stupidity into something more profound so that its stupidity falls away, disintegrates, vanishes. For Lacan, 'the signifier is stupid',[2] meaning that in the Symbolic stupidity presents any number of ways: by appearing dumb, arrogant, sanctimonious, hopelessly naïve, harbouring a loss of respect and so on. Yet in psychoanalysis, none of these much matter in the way they certainly do off the couch. Rather, the question in psychoanalysis is what the gaze of stupidity is demanding: the signifier is thus *necessarily* stupid. Of course, everyone is necessarily stupid, but perhaps there is a nuance here in the potential realization of one's singular stupidity. This might happen during escalating clashes between fantasy, the symbolic, ideology and so on, which engulf the subject.[3] Here it seems stupidity is what holds knowledge together. Nevertheless, stupidity remains frustratingly difficult to define; it can be anything at all, everything at once or nothing in particular. Yet it persists as part of being a subject in the world, as that which leads us to read Freud and Lacan, to lay our subjective anguish on the couch. It is stupidity's promise as intrinsic to transference which makes the subject willing to be a stupid one. Only within retrospective knowledge of having been stupid does one realize that it is now too late, that stupidity has already begun as part of one's subjective formation. But revelation of this dialectic is not the function either of stupidity or of the subject of stupidity but is rather a postscript which speaks directly to the signifier being revealed as stupid. Here Pushkin's description of stupid, dreamy desperation comes to mind,

> Whom, then, to love? Whom to believe?
> Who is the only one that won't betray us?
> (In Eugene Onegin[4])

In psychoanalysis, the other-side of stupidity is not the wisdom to avoid it, but rather the embracing of it as a particular knowledge one commits to live with rather than struggle against. This is why it is important to be 'knowingly' stupid. Perhaps what haunts us all is Adorno's take on stupidity: 'the almost insoluble task is not to let oneself be made stupid by the power of others, nor by one's own powerlessness'.[5] Even within such a devalued condition, it seems that stupidity retains sufficient capacity to be affectively divisive, rendering one an outlier to a particular group within which one can no longer occupy a position. In its strangely odd, vague and mercurial ambiguity, stupidity operates as an instrument to bring about consequences which affect one's experience of intimate, social and political arrangements. Regardless of whichever is the dominant in-crowd of the time, there is always a steady supply of stupidities to ensure that the laws of exclusivity can maintain their status quo.

There is much to be collectively gained politically, socially and culturally through deference to stupidity. Thus, smart people too can act in the name of stupidity, especially when surrounded by the 'right crew' who, in being willing to turn a blind eye, readily abandon awareness of their own folly. In this way, stupidity is embedded in the universality of discourse. Moreover, the logic of stupidity is necessarily tied to the social bond in that together they facilitate the chosen signifier whose lack is glossed over or reframed as 'fake-news'. As one journeys through life, it becomes abundantly clear that stupidity is not confined to those who do not necessarily know any better. Unlike good and bad ideas, stupidity doesn't divide but simply perpetuates unlinked meanings in its quest for discursive unity. This is paradoxical insofar as non-sense can normally be discerned only through its abstention from sense. Here, *non-sense* is recognizable from the very word which designates it, from the signifier which can be structured in a sentence. Absence of discernment is the trademark of (lack of) judgement concerning the wandering erring (stupid) person, as Descartes observes in his second meditation,

> I keep drifting towards that error because my mind likes to wander freely, refusing to respect the boundaries that truth lays down. Very well, then; I shall let it run free for a while, so that when the time comes to rein it in it won't be so resistant to being pulled back.[6]

This is an indication of stupidity's very function in its inability to recognize itself: that its signifier is wholly contained within a distribution of lack. Integral to stupidity is its truly libidinal quality, in which folly attaches to the body. For example, slapstick comedy presents an apparently stupid person who can nevertheless 'read the room' while tripping over, getting in the way of the non-stupid person, and generally playing the fool in order to generate laughter. Incarnations of stupidity can be found everywhere and provide no end of both entertainment and embarrassment (*jouissance* of the body). Contemporary cringe comedy is but a step away from Flaubert's or Melville's literary insight into arrogant fools delighting in vain *jouissance*. What makes a stupid person stupid is a question not of knowledge but of the means of its acquisition, namely language. After all, the Symbolic order – as Kant reminds us – is laden with rules, the most inescapable one being that the subject is required to make use of language as judgement. Discourse commands how one structures speech and language wherein stupidity can manifest enigmatically, when, for example, a stupid person's ill-conceived and ridiculous plans bestow light when all else has failed. What is notable about such a stupid endeavor is its spontaneous lack of calculation, its apparent naïve honesty and probable unawareness of folly. In being at the same time against conscious awareness yet outside thinking, the taken for granted certainty of stupidity puts the extravagance of thinking to the test by invoking those qualities most needed for it: doubt and curiosity.

What are we to make of the stupid bullshit artist (the knave among fools, the 'unmitigated scoundrel' *coquin fieffé* as Stendhal puts it), the one living only within the grandeur of their little world, cut off from exposure to the truth of their insignificance through despising knowledge beyond themselves? As Macbeth succumbing to pessimism, puts it,

> It is a tale
> told by an idiot,
> full of sound and fury,
> signifying nothing.[7]

Such a subject, in spite of speaking nonsense, as Macbeth reminds us, wants nevertheless to be seen as a speaker of majestic truths. Then again, there are those stupid people who think, with hyperbolic irreverence, that it would be foolish to, in fact, be reasonable. Here, folly manifests as a seductive *bourgeois* indulgence in rejection at all costs. Putting their arrogance aside, the question appropriate for such bullshit artists and *bourgeois* rejectionists as self-presumed superior subjects is not *who do you think you are?* as just ordinary, alienated subjects, which all they are, but *what do you think you are in terms of wish fulfilment*?[8]

There is a rumour that towards the end of his life Freud spent much time reading Balzac's hilariously forensic critique of the French *bourgeoise* in *La Comédie humaine* (1829–1848) which pierces the fantasies and upends the certainties traditionally associated with class and materiality. Balzac's insertion of doubt regarding the assumed worthiness of the rich, together with his depiction of the irrelevance and novel stupidity of *bourgeois* life, must have delighted Freud, not least because these are fantasies that we might all at various times occupy and wherein both the irrationality and excess of reason, which stupidity manifests, touch the very condition of humanity.

Such a claim of irrelevance risks being simply an existential throwaway remark, until we come to really appreciate the earnestness that stupidity demands from us. Being stupid is an important and serious undertaking for the subject because as a category of judgement, it is also holding the status of a master signifier. In order to appear less stupid, we redistribute stupidity via signifiers, either to make sense of or to hide its featurelessness. Stupidity knows no bounds and can be taken up in ascribing any number of qualities. As a parody of knowledge, stupidity is well attested: by ghostwriting, fabricating data and research findings, peer-reviewed manipulations and of course, the infamous New Sokal Hoax in 2018, where three academics collaboratively wrote twenty papers of completely fabricated research, including ridiculous methods and outrageous conclusions.[9] By the time these academics revealed their deliberate duping of the wider academic community, seven articles had already been published in high-index journals and seven more were under consideration. The response from the academic community was divided, ranging from outrage towards this cheap attempt at notoriety to quiet amusement in the knowledge that arrogant fraudsters are always to be found in the academy. What we might glean from this incident, apart from the immediate question of why, given even the minimal freedom to pursue an intellectual curiosity, one would choose to simply 'make stupid shit up', is that far from being divorced from reason, stupidity can sometimes bask in its excess. Stupidity demands that an act takes place even when this is the entirely reasonable highlighting of disturbing intellectual complacency.

Melville put the absurdity of stupidity to work in *The Confidence Man*, in which a stranger stowed away on a Mississippi steamboat emerges to test the trust and patience of some of the passengers using confidence trickery. In the name of the illusion of trust, how far are some passengers willing to be duped? Moreover, how far are others willing to go along with so-called objects of truth in the name of saving face?

> One who has confidence in nature, and confidence in man, with some little modest confidence in himself.
> That's your Confession of Faith, is it? Confidence in man, eh? Pray, which do you think are most, knaves or fools?
> Having met with few or none of either, I hardly think I am competent to answer.
> I will answer for you. Fools are most.
> Why do you think so?
> For the same reason that I think oats are numerically more than horses. Don't knaves munch up fools just as horses do oats?
> A droll, sir; you are a droll. I can appreciate drollery – ha, ha, ha!
> But I'm in earnest.[10]

One would prefer to identify with a knave than with an earnest fool, as Lacan reminds us in *Seminar VII, The Ethics of Psychoanalysis*.[11] After all, the knave at least embodies the egoic wish fulfilment. Might we then say that the fool is the exception to the law? The fool certainly destabilizes the symbolic and (un)knowingly violates the law for the sake of the law – that is, complies with the law but without embracing its spirit. The fool can also be incredibly bold as Mark Twain famously observes: 'They did not know it was impossible, so they did it.' Furthermore, the fool is not necessarily bereft of poetry or expansive vision (Camus asks, was Sisyphus actually stupid(ly bold?)[12]). It seems that stupidity is simply nondiscriminatory and has the potential to fully and unintentionally embrace the status of curiosity and doubt.

Further on in Melville's story, a confident young peddler offers free, counterfeit detectors to customers who buy enough sundry items, a hilarious scene that also disturbingly resonates with contemporary marketplace 'step-right-up' techniques – peddlers come in all shapes and sizes, guises and disguises perhaps some of us are duped more often than we care to admit. However, Lacan gives us all a bit of latitude when he says,

> What is at stake in being a dupe is not a matter of being the dupe of ideas, because these letters [of the analyst's discourse] are not ideas. They are not ideas at all. The proof is that it is very, very difficult to give them a meaning. Which does not mean that one cannot make something of them. This is what is inscribed from a certain elaboration of what I will call [. . .] the mathematics of Freud, what is locatable in the logic of his discourse, in his own wandering. Namely, the way he tried to render this analytic discourse adequate to the scientific discourse. That was his *erre*.[13]

In *Knowing Nothing and Staying Stupid: Elements for a Psychoanalytic Epistemology*,[14] Dany Nobus and Malcolm Quinn explain how the discourse of the university always serves as a master. They point out that with discourse, despite apparent reasonableness, there is no guarantee because in the marketplace the economy of ideas can always be leveraged to prevent these appearing stupid. In stating this, they point out the significant function of discourses: '[which] are not to be used as keys to the meaning of speech, but as a means of separating speech from meaning'.[15]

The New Sokal Hoax is an apt example of stupidity acting in the name of stupidity itself and thereby revealing the subversive effects of over-compliance with the law (arguably, the strangest *jouissance*). After all, only a stupid person would transgress the law or vehemently refuse it. Either way, the associated pleasure engendered by both options represents a pathway to the *jouissance* of the obedient. One thing the New Sokal Hoax revealed was that intellectual freedom and integrity all hinge on not appearing stupid and perhaps this was its unintentionally ironic point. Although in the end they made fools of themselves, these academics chose to write rubbish and in attempting to articulate the part of the duper, they exposed how frightfully easy it is to feign authentic thinking. Yet in this process, they were doing nothing exceptional in that they did what at times we all do: allow the *jouissance* of drive to dictate speech: 'Don't be the stupid barbaric one, be the smart one and fall on the side of cynicism! After all, being called cynical is more palatable than being thought of as stupid!' It seems, however, that the inverse of the Sokal motive is more revealing: those social and political structures in which we are interpellated do not always reveal stupidities but rather arouse suspicions; authenticity is not characterized by either a freedom from stupidity or a willingness to be duped. In the end, all the Sokal academics created were stupid fictions and a cynicism regarding knowledge and truth. Perhaps that is really not so much a crime as just a rather dull outcome. Nevertheless, they did at least reveal enjoyment in their collective fetishization of the university discourse. They took their own game seriously to the point that the shame and contempt that was anticipated (and received) was, in the end, worth it. They appeared perversely proud of the enjoyment their deliberate uptake of symbolic stupidity generated. Perhaps this scandal might be thought of as just another *bourgeois* stupidity; then again, it is a stupidity one can count on continuing to be enjoyed behind the name-of-the-father's back.[16]

The New Sokal Hoax – and perhaps figures such as Trump – reveals something further. Intrinsic to the master's discourse is not only identification with knowledge but also a different command, that 'you shall enjoy!' Obedience to the latter is actually quite stupid as it purports style over substance and form over content. It is an act that marks its intention by separation from discourse. The New Sokal Hoax emerged from the given ideal of intellectual freedom just as the figure of Trump emerged from the American ideal of unfettered capitalism. Admittedly, these are to some extent successful stupid mistakes in which discourse works against itself, and where *jouissance* lies in implicating other bad academics and even worse politicians in stupid discourse as a passage to the act. Stupidity may not be so perceptible to the observer but is highly perceptible and thus crucial to disavowal. One would think that one does not know what one is doing in the repetitive act of stupidity. After all, there was the inaugural Sokal Hoax of 1996, a stupid embarrassing moment in academia. Its presumed fantasy that anyone could be praised for writing something stupid is even today no mere fantasy: it happens all the time in many different fields and throughout history. Such purveyors of stupidity are active among us, repeating stupidities which then become doxa. Stupidity is in service to repetition where its interventions in the social bond can be at least imagined if not always called out. If stupidity flees from sense, then sense is not grasping something of the absence of interpretation of the symptom.

Nobus and Quinn claim that the consequence of the original Sokal Hoax[17] is logical and makes complete sense because it is an exchange of nonsense for nonsense. The hoax underlines how the stupidity of some signifiers of the university discourse renders those outside the academy stupid because such signifiers speak, if they do at all, only to those inside the academy. For Nobus and Quinn, this illustrates the Lacanian point that speech and meaning are separate, and it is from the gap between them that subjects are compelled to make something meaningful from it.

It seems as if the function of stupidity is to masquerade as something different, which exceeds the lack in discourse. After all, stupidity champions lack as something to be avoided. However, stupidity is more than simply the passage to the act of being stupid; it is also the subjective uptake of something which qualifies this act. Stupidity is the *a priori* condition of an inconvenient, embarrassing and misplaced superego. As we have seen, being stupid is not contained simply by intellectual inadequacy but is rather a condition that allows for the uncertainty of lack to be obfuscated. The question now beckons, is being stupid a choice? Lacan's clue to answering this lies in his *les non-dupes errent* ['the non-dupes go astray'].[18] We can read this as decisive: stupidity occurs as a circular course with no beginning or ending. It commands the unchanging drive in the body towards an object which may change. Moreover, stupidity functions as a lapse where language unreflexively goes along with the instinct of the drive. Indeed, stupidity colonizes language as it traces its way to the real of the body. Stupidity is thus a demand for which a gap must be provided before a response can be made to it: that is, a demand that, for stupidity to be structured as stupidity, something stupid must be allowed to present itself in speech and be thereby symbolically represented.

Psychoanalysis is keenly invested in stupidity, which plays out in what is at first an unconscious act in the analysand's repetition. In analysis, the analysand has plenty of time not to pretend to be something else or, indeed, anything in particular. The couch is what Lacan calls a 'habitat', which offers stability and is where the analysand has a duty to say everything, especially stupidities, thereby repeating whatever they think they know in a cycle of stupidities, all the while being driven by a (stupid) injunction towards complex fantasies emanating from conscious reasons. The analyst listens over and over again to various iterations of the same (lapse in) conscious reason until it becomes unbearable for the (hysterical) analysand. As Freud points out, transference is based on this very process of stupidity:

> Since we demand strict truthfulness from our patients, we jeopardize our whole authority if we let ourselves be caught out by them in a departure from the truth.

> Besides, the experiment of letting oneself go a little way in tender feelings for the patient is not altogether without danger. Our control over ourselves is not so complete that we may not suddenly one day go further than we had intended. In my opinion, therefore, we ought not to give up the neutrality towards the patient, which we have acquired through keeping the counter-transference in check.[19]

Lacan puts Freud's problem of counter-transference to rest by also insisting that the analysts' desire is to remain neutral while listening for the analysand's stupid signifiers, repeating them and putting them to work. The analysts' position must be to occupy the place of the void where the curiosity of stupidity is privileged, thereby enabling the once-stupid analyst to be a little less stupid. Such is the invitation of psychoanalysis: to accept being stupid oneself in order to be interested in taking up another knowledge position in which one hopes to be a bit less stupid.

What specifically do we become less stupid about? Nothing more than a rather modest realization that stupidity is neither the alternative to being sensible nor the other side of reason. Here the impossible choice of Kant's fantasy comes to mind: either sleep with the women of your dreams and go to the gallows, or refuse desire and live. On the face of it, this frames desire as a conscious choice between the rational judgement to live, or to give ground to stupid desire and die. But we can also think of Kant's impossible choice as not only proposing the act as an ethical event (judgement) in the life of a subject, but also as revealing libidinal desire to be as unfathomable as lived conscionability. Here Kant reveals an inner contradiction between serving the higher good (that is, enjoying one's morality and moderate forms of normative prescriptions) and confining desires to the closet of stupid fantasy. Perhaps for Kant, stupidity is the ultimate category of persecution. But as Freud reminds us, we cannot avoid being stupid through logical choice. Rather, stupidity emerges as the unconscious revelation of a force which needs to be reckoned with in the symbolic, on a par with those incoherent moments of *lalangue*, that part of language which doesn't quite fit but is needed in order to explicate the absurdity of language itself. *Lalangue* works as traces of the viscosity of the libido in which a possible change in enunciation is anticipated. For example, Dora, the mother of psychoanalysis, who coughed out her desire until she could articulate it as a question of feminine desire. Or Little Hans, who developed an unsayable phobia of horses in order to preserve the life of his father. It seems stupidity strongholds a logic of its own beyond being the consequence of lack, howsoever this manifests – immaturity, inability to 'read the room' or failure to anticipate outcomes. Something further is required for stupidity to attain a coherent subject position as something recognizable. Consider as an obvious example the stupidity of love, that unnamable ocean we all want to swim in. If only, says Bruce Fink,[20] we realized that our chosen lover was a reminder of our first love object – our mother or father! How embarrassingly and horrifyingly stupid we would feel! In the liberation of the libido, even stupidity must play a part.

Whether or not we can be less stupid is a question taken up by Luis Izcovich when he explores to what extent the analytic experience encourages the analysand to utter stupidities.[21] During analysis, the stupid analysand recollects, reminisces, remembers and so on. These are incarnations of the temporal subject-supposed-to-know about their own stupidities. Izcovich suggests that the dilemma regarding stupidity and its counterpoint knowledge, which confronts the analysand through their utterance, is this: Is the signifier they employ stupid (thereby implying that they too are stupid), or is the signifier just pretending to be stupid and thereby simply duping them? During analysis, the analyst is a co-conspirator, a de facto accomplice in this witnessing of one stupid utterance after another. That is the agreement between analysand and analyst: the analysand is duty-bound to speak stupidity and the analyst must listen out for stupid signifiers. There is knowledge to be gleaned from being stupid, which in turn pivots on the discourse being taken up. For example, within the discourse of the master or the university, really smart yet (nevertheless sometimes stupid) people can convey knowledge of sorts which not only fits but is also validated and rewarded. After all, such discourse is not going to employ signifiers that do not make sense, and if by chance it does, then it would probably be called mad or psychotic. In the polite symbolic, we take care not to talk past one another, we try to read one another and so on. Whatever our work, we attempt to engage a certain logic of transmission in which what we say to others is taken up. There is always on both sides certainty that this is a shared discourse and because such discourse is understood, no one is intentionally being stupid. However, when discourse demands something else from the speaking subject, for example, during analysis, then there is a shift not only in the transmission between two speaking subjects but also (especially for the analysand) a seeking of something extra, the nature of which is insistent yet obscure. In yearning for a different knowledge, the analysand must risk not only being stupid in speech, but must also understand that as soon as analysis proceeds, so the uptake of stupidity begins. Questions inevitably beckon: What is this procedure of stupidity all about? What does it mean when a speaking-subject-supposed-to-know (the analyst) takes very seriously the analysand's stupid utterances? Does the analysand repeatedly return to the couch simply to be heard, or is it rather to confront stupidity in terms of desire for a different discursive arrangement, perhaps a less stupid one?

The field of language runs a tight agenda, but for *jouissance*, anything goes. This is the contradiction we are all stuck with. As Lacan offers, folly speaks as a stupidity which firstly, privileges irrationality against reason and purpose; secondly, firmly insists upon the letter as an unconscious logic; and finally, purports that reason is anyway fundamentally unconscious.[22] The upshot of this is that although we are subordinated to *jouissance*, we are not wholly in deference to it and in the context of analysis, our lack of dependence on and deference to reason shapes the *jouissance* we experience.

No sense (meaningful nonsense) is the product of a lapse in judgement. For Lacan, there is not only the truth of stupidity but also the stupidity of truth. Furthermore, the law renders itself to stupidity as much as it does to truth; indeed, the greatest truth cannot contend with the *jouissance* of stupidity. We see this all the time: the most simple and stupid truths lie in the order of the everyday. Happiness, trauma and the sexual act (one does not have to be particularly intelligent to perform it, even well) all exhibit the truth of stupidity, which fixates the libido and makes apparent the symbolically derived organized credentials to which we must yield. Yet at the same time the truth of stupidity is ambivalent in that in recognizing stupidity, symbolic structures coordinate and limit enjoyment. For Lacan, even magical thinking is still valid thinking, although it explains nothing.[23] All cultures have practices that, for example, propagate placebo effects that are not locked into the rational. We can understand – as Freud reminds us – that jokes and witticisms[24] are an attempt to promote the statement to the level of the discourse of the Other. Here, witticisms and absurd statements elevate the symptom as a way to foreclose the subject. Ignorance leads to statements that are not always quite wrong. These do not lie outside discourse but exist to supplement our understanding of the perplexing, enigmatic nature of truth and thus, stupidity.

Stupidity is not only a parapraxis of the tongue, but also the *jouissance* of stupidity is what characterizes our resistance to the symbolic, spilling over into anxiety, except when we feel duped. In order not to be duped, we take up the strongest available subject position, that of the Name-of-the-Father, wherein we are no longer surprised to hear, or even to utter, stupid words ourselves. In explicating this, consider the colloquialism 'stupid is as stupid does'. Stupidity consists of being within an act, often one that is understood as (largely) going against the social bond. Here, a certain *näivety*, lack of knowledge or assumed cleverness becomes insistent to the subject. That one is stupid on account of a stupid deed or utterance is how stupidity is usually understood and, on this basis, even the smartest person in the world can sometimes be stupid. Furthermore, stupidity reveals itself through symbolic authority.

Referencing Lacan, Izcovich says of the stupid subject,

> So, there is stupidity and stupidity. True stupidity is believing that one is master of oneself. In this respect, we can refer to the following statement by Lacan: 'I

> am the master (*m'être*), I progress along the path of mastery (*m'êtrise*), I am the master of myself (*moi*) as I am of the universe. That is [. . .] the vanquished idiot (*con-vaincu*).'[25]

What then are the implications of being stupid? Here we can look to Lacan's *Les Non Dupe Errent* where he talks about what it means to be duped and asks if we have a choice in the matter. Arguably, as Lacan signals, we have at least an unconscious choice. For example, Lacan claims that the masochist 'invents' himself through a particular interpellation of the knotting of the symbolic order, which enables the masochist as a speaking subject to speak meaningfully. We can say that the duper too operates within the same symbolic structure in a procedure which provides the dupee with – if nothing else – Phallic enjoyment. Here the dupee must be willing to be duped: the duper is deliberately staging an error which, although not in itself a mistake for the duper, certainly is for the dupee. In making this mistake, the dupee literally misses the duper's insight that their willingness to be duped is fuelled by their desire not to be overlooked. The dupee's mistake becomes a retrospective error only after realizing they have in fact been duped, precisely because the fantasy of choice was never available to them until after the duping. This procedure is the Name-of-the-Father in action, whose job is to institute and ensure the regulation of the law via *jouissance* of the drives. In doing this, it establishes which *jouissance* is available and which is not, thereby making its function both credible and enforceable. If there is no law, there is no prohibition and therefore as an unintended consequence, the function of the name-of-the-Father entails that any transgression of the law is meaningful. Stupidity, however, is a law unto itself: it disavows the threat of castration by ridiculing meaning in the name of transgression. Stupidity is the logical end point of castration, for it had not only never purported wholeness, but wholeness is the last thing stupidity would stand in the name of. Stupidity calls out the Name-of-the-Father as one who dupes us into the fiction of meaning.

However, Lacan offers a bit of mercy and a possible way out for the dupee:

> Precisely, your demand, the one that herds you in here, is how to have a chance to get out of this stupidity. This is even what you are counting on me [psychoanalysis] for. Except for the fact that this demand forms part of the stupidity.[26]

Lacan is not saying that non-dupes do not make mistakes: we can say that the mistake is the destiny for the non-dupe. Rather, he is engaging how any subject harbours the extimate space provided by the nexus of the three registers of imaginary, symbolic and real as a location in which even the non-dupe cannot avoid mistakes. We are prone to be duped and only then can we understand that we have been, asserts Lacan. Therefore, what differentiates the dupe from the non-dupe is not some additional awareness or insight, but rather a willingness to distinguish between the three registers of the symbolic order as a way of comprehending different aspects of what might constitute the possibility of knowledge.

Lacan understands the symbolic order as an intra-psychic structure made up of the three aforementioned registers. (See figure 11.1.) The imaginary is described by Jacques-Alain Miller as the relation 'between the ego and its images'. In this relation, the subject's post-mirror stage conscious sense of self is exposed as deliberate misrecognition; its apparent internalized egoic self-image of being made whole through identification with the Other, being a fiction. The symbolic, on the other hand, relies upon the formation of a web of signifiers which in language 'determine[s] the order of the subject'. Lacan claims that 'man speaks therefore, but it is because the symbol has made him man'.[27] Furthermore, Lacan states that 'symbols in fact envelop the life of man in a network so total that they join together, before he comes into the world, those who are going to engender him'.[28] The function of the symbolic is through discourse (including the unconscious discourse of the Other) which is what organizes the speaking subject in the world in relation to other speaking subjects. By contrast, the real refers to that which, in resisting all representation in the symbolic, cannot be totally symbolized. What keeps these registers knotted together and in relation to each other is the central point, a hole at the centre which is called *objet a* or the object cause of desire, as in figure 11.1.

We can best think of the *objet a* as a partial object, insofar as it is the image of an object generated by alienation and reconfigured through fantasy. It is this fantasy of an object which, in standing in for desire, is also its cause. For Lacanian psychoanalysis, desire is problematic in that its object is ambivalent

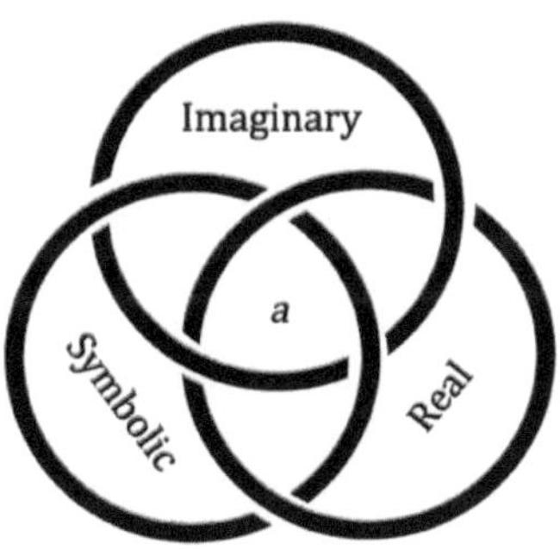

Figure 11.1 Borromean Knot. *Source*: Adapted from Jacques Lacan, *Seminar XXIII*, 1975–6; ed. J-A Miller, *Ornicar?* 6–11, 1976–7. Translated from the *texte établi* by Luke Thurston.

and opaque: we are not quite sure what desire is, but it nevertheless apprehends us. We know that there is something to be desired, but this something cannot be wholly encapsulated in any specific object. We go on searching for an elusive object which maybe doesn't even exist, knowing full well that whatever object we might locate as a placeholder for the *objet a* will never fully satisfy. Yet in this quest to know desire, we remain willing to take the risk of being duped by the partial object. It is this willingness to be duped by the strange, albeit false freedom proffered via the *objet a*, that, for example, Trump exploited when encouraging his followers to abandon wearing face masks during the pandemic – he is not going to be duped by a face mask, which after all would only muzzle him!

In the scenario of being duped, we feel permitted to wander, as Lacan observes even 'the unduped wander/are mistaken'.[29] What exactly are we wandering around? The most probable answer is around phallic enjoyment, the insistence of the Other that we enjoy the Other's *jouissance*. Lacan is clear that not only is the Phallic signifier one of *jouissance* but also that it represents an exception in the signifying chain because without it, other signifiers would be impotent to signify anything. We might say that in circulating (wandering around) the *objet a*, this false freedom set up by command of the master, we are circulating in 'his' *jouissance*. When we think of the master, it is of a specific discourse which claims to represent all other discourses. The master purports that 'he' alone is the master signifier and therefore the subject for all signifiers. However, reference to figure 11.1 reveals that it is the *objet a* which holds the symbolic order together. Moreover, it is the *objet a* which, in standing in for desire, produces an abundance of meaning, maybe too much, in fact what we might call a surplus of stupid *jouissance*.

This background enables us to consider how the Name-of-the-Father is not merely a supplement to imagining stupidity but an absolute necessity if we are to understand stupidity. Drawing on Lorenzo Chiesa's work, Gioele Cima puts this succinctly:

> Language no longer carries out a humanizing function but, on the contrary, a profoundly de-stabilizing one. This change of direction turns the philosophical anthropology of the early Lacan into a negative, or even monstrous, anthropocentrism [. . .] in which the cut of the signifier no longer compensates for the impasse of the biological but produces an irreducible perpetual disorientation that the very last seminars would rename 'mental debility'.[30]

What Cima is saying here is crucial to stupidity having the ability to destabilize language. Such disorientation is so confusing that it causes mental debility, in which the Symbolic is over-privileged by its ceasing to register in the imaginary to leave nothing more than an affective response. This is precisely the enigmatic character of stupidity.

What then follows is Cima's second point,

> [T]he unconscious is redefined as a knowledge [savoir] that has to be invented starting from the assumption of the hole of the Real: to invent this knowledge, and avoid becoming prey to the bottomless freedom of the psychotic, it becomes necessary to let oneself be 'duped' by the viscosity of structure, abiding by it as best as one can.[31]

Paralysed with or by stupidity, the subject, whether being stupid or simply witnessing stupidity, is left with no choice but to accept stupidity as a willingness to be duped by language. Here we might observe the homophony between Lacan's *Les non-dupes errent* and *Les noms du père* (the two Names-of-the-Father). The function of the Name-of-the-Father is straightforward: by insisting on the incest taboo, its signification confers identity to another subject. Lacan explicitly says in *Écrits*:

> It is in the name of the father that we must recognize the support of the symbolic function which, from the dawn of history, has identified his person with the figure of the law – as distinct from the narcissistic relations, or even from the real relations, which the subject sustains with the image and action of the person who embodies it.[32]

Here, Lacan plays on the homophony *non* and *nom*: the Name-of-the-Father (*le nom du père*) is also the Father's command, 'no' (*le 'non' du père*) to the child's incestuous desire for its Mother. Here, the two Names-of-the-Father (symbolic and imaginary) keep in check obedience, misrecognition and alienation as well as not being caught up in falsities. In this context, stupidity might be seen as the impossible object propelling the two Names-of-the-Father. That language is the natural by-product of being human is vehemently denied by Lacan. We are, he argues, constantly confronted by the failure of the word, constantly reminded how limited it is, how stupid we are *vis-à-vis* language because we simply can't grasp it well enough – as he explains,

> It is when the Word is incarnated that things really start going badly. [The speaking subject] is no longer at all happy, he no longer resembles at all a little dog who wags his tail or a nice monkey who masturbates. He no longer resembles anything. He is ravaged by the Word.[33]

Being ravaged by the Word, especially in the context of stupidity, is obviously a place of castration for the subject. Perplexingly, stupidity does not stop the subject from continuing to speak ever more stupidities. Given this compulsion, where does it leave the hypothesis that stupidity can be a placeholder for the *objet a*? Do we desire to be stupid, even if only a little? What springs to mind here is the ultimate hysterical question, *Che Vuoi?* What do you want from me? What do I need to be for you? Arguably, this is the most stupid question, not least because it is unanswerable. It is stupid on two fronts: first, the subject asking this stupid question knows full well it is a stupid one; second, it is a question directed to another stupid subject, who feels the need to answer it notwithstanding the impossibility of this. Thus, within this transmission, a double-duping is occurring: the subject acts as if they are the big Other, all the while knowing they are not. The subject asking the stupid question knows that the subject to whom this question is directed is similarly a subject grappling with lack. This is a question that goes nowhere, never gets answered adequately, consistently or with any satisfaction. It is the ultimate stupid question. Yet that does not prevent it from being asked again and again because it is the question that directs and orients the subject's will towards desiring and being desired. Because achieving some sort of literacy of desire is such hard work, in its place we supplement our ambivalence and unknowingness with the placeholder of stupidity from which to hinge our subjectivity. We do it all the time without perhaps unknowingly but more often by knowingly subscribing to the promise of stupidity's *jouissance*. We willingly dupe ourselves when we act one way while knowing very well that, both for ourselves and others, any signification of certainty, stupid or otherwise, is anything but certain.

In *Knowing Nothing and Staying Stupid*, Nobus and Quinn put this question to work. They claim that *Che Vuoi?* is a question directed towards the analyst by the analysand in full awareness of the analyst's 'passion of ignorance' not as an absence of knowledge but rather as a recognition of its limits. The stupidity of the pact of transference between analyst and analysand lies in its being always just out of reach.

Even the mythical proto-Father in the Freudian myth, *Totem and Taboo*, is arguably stupid in its simplistic function of disrupting the transmission of the mother-child relation by insisting that he too matters, a stupidity which Lacan sees as fundamental to discourse. Rather, the (contradictory) function of the name-of-the-Father is to set up forbidden desire alongside what the subject is desiring, while all the time insisting that although this desire may be stupid and perverse (no, you won't be able to fuck your mother or your father) nevertheless feel free to give it a go (dream it or act it out by falling in love with someone like them). It's a stupid idea but a necessary one regarding the unanswerable question, *Che Vuoi?*

Returning now to knowledge afforded by the analytic procedure and in particular to how this is in a pact with stupidity. In *Encore*, Lacan inverts the classical conception of stupidity, stating that it is in fact the signifier which is stupid.[34] Similarly, Izcovich claims that in order to fully appreciate the stupidity we are willing ourselves into, we must stay with the question of discourse:

> Being installed in a discourse assumes that the subject is caught up in one of these discourses. Certainly, one discourse can be left behind in order for another to be entered into. This is what we see in an analysis. It is a fact that analysis allows for a change of discourse. For example, a passage from the discourse of the hysteric into analytic discourse, which is necessary for the entry into analysis. But the analytic arrangement allows for another change of discourse, connected to the advent of a real that is proper to analysis, which entails a departure from the discourse in which the subject is caught up with the analyst. A question imposes itself here: outside of analysis, is it possible to change discourse? This might be observed sometimes, but often what is seen is a transitory change that then reverts back to the prior discourse.

To be in analysis means to be anchored in the analyst's discourse, one where the unconscious is privileged. Lacan emphasizes that the subject in analysis can float between discourses whenever there is a different contention with stupidity. Consider misogyny, for example. Many misogynistic acts and utterances, we can say, appear stupid since they manifest within the shady areas of discourse and thus (dis)connected to the Other. Here, such stupidity is obviously concerning because it contradicts the social bond. Furthermore, by manifesting as a desire to be free from the demands (and commands) of contending with contradiction and by placing itself as an all-knowing authority, this stupidity of misogyny mimics the dual function of the name-of-the-Father by resisting the Other in order to insist – misogyny is a stupidity designed to hurt. Yet hopefully, as Lacan says, 'If Freud's discovery has any meaning, it is that truth grabs error by the scruff of the neck in the mistake'.[35] If we consider Freud's proto-Father as the one establishing the law, this could easily imply a standard masculine symbolic fantasy of misogyny. Such an incarnation of the misogynist's fantasy reveals that the misogynist has access to unending *jouissance*, which they can get away with because it is their right and beyond punishment. Stupidity arises when otherwise supportive bystanders are blinded or seduced by misogynistic acts and rhetoric, thereby becoming collaborators. Although seduced onto the side of the misogynist's fantasy, such collaborators become stupidly inadequate politicians of their own *jouissiance*. Their stupidity is truly disturbing: that the law is discarded in favour of the real of the other's body reduced to a plaything.

In writing 'how an object, reduced to its stupidest reality . . . can bring about an identification of the ideal ego with its very moronic power',[36] Lacan is saying that one relation with an ideal is premised in part on stupidity and the strange enjoyment resulting from it. For example, in the case of Trump, many of us vacillate between rolling our eyes in mock disgust and feeling genuinely outraged – after all, how can an adult with so much power also be so childishly stupid?! The function of stupidity is to hystericize, to thrust the subject into confusion and disarray, which in turn challenges the subject not to be stupid. In other words, when faced with stupidity, the subject must take a position that cannot be sidestepped. For the analysand, this position is one in which lack cannot be left behind or ignored. The analysand must confront not only fantasy but also the effects of repetition, which enable the fantasy to be sustained. For example, the seemingly innocent, well-intentioned yet perhaps somewhat stupid declaration, 'I believe in honesty and therefore this makes me a good person' can only ever be a phantasmatic position. The most obvious form of stupid misrecognition is an overly strong ego. As Izcovich says, 'What makes the stupid person stupid is an adherence to form, to the illusion of completeness'.[37] Here stupidity is not on the side of desire because its investment is in satisfaction, not in possibilities. We walk into the clinic with a desire for different knowledge, every time leaving with perhaps more insight into our own stupidity, yet in the end realizing that not only are we still stupid but so also are the signifiers we have been hinging our subjective desires on. Why then even bother entering into analysis?! First, it is not only the ego that is put to work but the whole schema of our subjectivity which constitutes the truth of our desires. Second, whether we like it or not, knowledge is simply not enough in the face of our yearning for a certain truth to be revealed, one which puts our stupidity to work. During analysis, we are allowed to be stupid – with our words, our desires, our half-baked ideas, our nonsensical moments which can ironically be so revealing. We are allowed to produce *semblant* after *semblant* which we articulate as truth, only to have the rug pulled from beneath us by an analyst who takes our words seriously and never holds them against us. That would indeed be stupid! We can be what Lacan calls, 'the perfect idiot'; our idiocy is singular and its function is clear, being based, as Izcovich claims, on 'stupidity that is a knowledge invented for covering up the real'. Thus stupidity really needs to be put to work over time, again and again. As it is unveiled, the signifier is stripped of its stupid props to reveal for the subject that it no longer needs these in order for it to be convincing. A prime example of this is love. It would seem that all we have to do is to remain dupes and stick with stupidity as the secretary of the unconscious, rather than aim at subjective completeness or wholeness. We should listen to stupidity because it allows us to take – with a pinch of salt – the comically malleable nature of the law despite its apparent gravitas and tethered knowledge. Stupidity confronts us with our alienation within language, also with how we treat the effects of this. Here, the word is synthetic, having the ability to break apart, fracture, and in doing so reveal itself as precarious and dependent on our gaze and articulations. If we give ourselves fully to language, then stupidity gives language back to us in a new form. Stupidity operates as more than just a word processor spitting out revealing language, because it not only demands that we make sense of language and our precarious relation to it, but also shows how it is a chaser of *jouissance*. In this way, stupidity is two-fold: a protective container reminding us in an ironic way of the importance of language, yet at the same time allowing us to enjoy acting out. Stupidity is not merely the bread-and-butter command of psychoanalysis but ultimately its paradox: either to make a pact with the anguish of stupidity in order to be a little less stupid, or to be earnestly, seriously, anything but.

NOTES

1. Herman Melville (1857). *The Confidence-Man*. Dix, Edwards & Co.
2. Jacques Lacan (1999). *Le Séminaire, Livre XX, Encore*. Paris, Seuil, pp. 17–18.
3. Note wonderful French playwright, Honoré de Balzac, who says in *Father Goriot* (1835, part II): *Le secret des grandes fortunes sans cause apparente est un crime oublié, parce qu'il a été proprement fait.* Translated as 'The secret of great fortunes without apparent cause is a crime forgotten, for it was properly done'. There is something a trifle comforting in knowing that cunning people are not so deserving, and yet, those of us who don't envelop ourselves in great fortune are perhaps a bit stupid when it comes to being a half-decent criminal.
4. The Project Gutenberg (1881 [2007]). *Eugene Onéguine [Onegin]: A Romance of Russian Life in Verse*, ed. Aleksandr Sergeevich Pushkin and trans. Henry Spalding. London, Macmillan and Co.
5. Theodor Adorno (1974). *Minima Moralia: Reflections on a Damaged Life*, trans. E. F. N. Jephcott. London, Verso, p. 34.
6. René Descartes (1639). *Meditations on First Philosophy in Which Are Demonstrated the Existence of God and the Distinction between the Human Soul and the Body*, trans. Johnathon Bennet. Cambridge, Cambridge University Press.
7. Act 5, scene 5, lines 16–27.
8. These questions refer back to Lacan's claim that 'the subject of the unconscious is the subject of the signifier' (Jacques Lacan (2000). *Écrits*, trans. Bruce Fink. New York, W. W. Norton & Co., p. 430). The constitution of the subject as one who only thinks is problematic because one does not arrive into existence, thinking. Rather, fundamental signifiers (work, family, etc.) render the subject one of identification, which entails alienation as fundamental to thinking.
9. https://www.theatlantic.com/ideas/archive/2018/10/new-sokal-hoax/572212/
10. Herman Melville (1857 [2002]). *The Confidence Man: His Masquerade*. London, Penguin, pp. 130–131.
11. *The Ethics of Psychoanalysis* (1959–1960), edited by Jacques-Alain Miller. London, Routledge, p. 172.

12. Albert Camus (1942). *The Myth of Sisyphus*. Paris, Éditions Gallimard.

13. Jacques Lacan (1974). *Book XXI,* Seminar 15, *Les Non Dupe Errent,* trans. C. Gallagher (Unpublished Manuscript), pp. 37–38.

14. Dany Nobus and Malcolm Quinn (2005). *Knowing Nothing and Staying Stupid: Elements for a Psychoanalytic Epistemology*. London, Routledge, pp. 37–38.

15. Ibid., p. 128.

16. It is worth quoting Lacan here in full to fully appreciate the close encounter between the figures of the knave and the fool: 'The fool is an innocent, a simpleton, but truths issue from his mouth that are not merely simply tolerated but adopted, by virtue of the fact that this fool is sometimes clothed in the insignia of the jester. And in my view, it is in this happy shadow, this fundamental foolery, that one finds the true value of the left-wing intellectual.' Lacan goes on to clarify the knave's apparent self-awareness when he says that, '[e]veryone knows that a certain way of presenting himself, which constitutes part of the ideology of the right-wing intellectual, is precisely to play the role of what he is in fact, namely, a knave. In other words, he doesn't retreat from the consequences of what is called realism; that is, when required, he admits he is a knave'. *The Ethics of Psychoanalysis* (1959–1960), edited by Jacques-Alain Miller. London, Routledge, p. 10.

17. Where Alan Sokal published an article, *Transgressing the Boundaries: Towards a Transformative Hermeneutics of Quantum Gravity* in 1996 as entirely fabricated.

18. Jacques Lacan (1974). *Book XXI,* Seminar 15, *Les Non Dupe Errent,* trans. C. Gallagher (Unpublished Manuscript).

19. Sigmund Freud (1911–1913). "Observations on Transference- Love", in *The Case of Schreber. Papers in Technique and Other Works*, trans. James Strachey. London, Hogarth Press, p. 164.

20. From *The Lacanian Subject: Between Language and Jouissance* (1995). Princeton, Princeton University Press.

21. Please see Luis Izcovich's contribution to this collection, *Can One Be Less Stupid*?

22. Jacques Lacan (1974). *Book XXI,* Seminar 15, *Les Non Dupe Errent,* trans. C. Gallagher (Unpublished Manuscript).

23. Lacan says, 'Magic tempts you only insofar as you project its characteristics onto the subject with which you are dealing in order to psychologise it, that is, misrecognise it. So-called "magical thinking", which is always attributed to someone else, is not a stigma with which you can label the other. To be more explicit, recourse to magical thinking explains nothing – what must be explained is its efficiency'. Jacques Lacan (2002). *Écrits*, trans. Bruce Fink. New York, W. W. Norton & Co., p. 744.

24. Sigmund Frued (1905). *Der Witz und seine Beziehung zum Unbewußten*, F. Deuticke. Leipzig und Wien Franz Deuticke Verlag.

25. Please see Luis Izcovich's contribution to this collection, *Is the Signifier Stupid*?

26. J. Lacan (1973 [1998]). *Four Fundamental Concepts of Psychoanalysis*, trans. A. Sheridan. New York, Norton and Norton, p. 60.

27. Ibid., p. 279

28. J. Lacan (1956). "Symbol and Language", in *The Language of the Self.* Baltimore, John Hopkins University Press, p. 42.

29. Jacques Lacan (1974). *Book XXI,* Seminar 15, *Les Non Dupe Errent,* trans. C. Gallagher (Unpublished Manuscript), p. 21.

30. Please refer to Cima's contribution to this collection, *Natural Born Dupes: A Lacanian Theory of Stupidity.*

31. Ibid.

32. Jacques Lacan (2002). *Écrits*, trans. Bruce Fink. New York: W. W. Norton & Co., p. 67.

33. Jacques Lacan (2015). *The Triumph of Religion.* Cambridge, Polity Press, p. 74.

34. Jacques Lacan (1999). *Le Séminaire, Livre XX, Encore.* Paris, Seuil, pp. 17–18.

35. Jacques Lacan (1975). *The Seminars of Jacques Lacan: Freud's Papers on Technique,* trans. J. Forrester. New York, Norton, p. 265.

36. Jacques Lacan (1966). "Remarque sur le rapport de Daniel Lagache," in *Ecrits.* Paris, Seuil, p. 677.

37. Please see Luis Izcovich's contribution to this collection, *Is the Signifier Stupid*?

Index

NOTE: Page numbers in *italics* refer to figures.

About the Contributors

Gioele P. Cima is an independent researcher. He has published several books in Italian on the thought of Jacques Lacan, Georges Bataille and Elvio Fachinelli. He is also the author of the critical introduction to the life and work of Elvio Fachinelli in E. Fachinelli, *On Freud*.

Christian Ingo Lenz Dunker, born in 1966, is a psychoanalyst, full professor at USP's Institute of Psychology, coordinator of the Laboratory of Social Theory, Philosophy and Psychoanalysis (LATESFIP-USP) and member analyst of the Lacanian Field Forum. Doctor and lecturer at USP, post-doctorate at Manchester Metropolitan University, youtuber (Falando Nisso) and a UOL-TILT columnist. He is the author of more than hundred scientific articles and has been a guest lecturer at over fifteen foreign universities. He has made a name for himself by renewing Jacques Lacan's thinking on the basis of ideas from critical social philosophy, post-structuralist anthropology and the language sciences. His critique of traditional psychoanalytic psychopathology and the hegemony of the statistical diagnostic systems prevalent in psychiatry (such as the DSM-5) involves the introduction of concepts such as suffering of determination, pathologies of the social and calculation of jouissance. He has made contributions to psychopathology, involving the revision of the notions of neurosis, psychosis and perversion. He values diagnostic criteria such as 'freedom and truth', as well as researching the political impact of psychoanalytic practice and the social experiences of suffering in Brazil. He is the author of *Structure and Constitution of the Psychoanalytic Clinic*, *Mal-Estar, Sofrimento e Sintoma* and *Reinvenção da Intimidade*, *O Palhaço e o Psicanalista*, *Autobiografia da Depressão*, *Lacan e a Democracia* and *Lutos Finitos e Infinitos*.

David Ferraro is a psychoanalyst practising in Melbourne, Australia. He is a member of the Lacan Circle of Australia and has published numerous articles on psychoanalysis, biopolitics and contemporary mental health in magazines and academic journals.

Luis Izcovich is a psychiatrist, psychoanalyst and founding member of the School of Lacanian Field Forums. He taught at the Department of Psychoanalysis of Paris VIII and currently at the College of Psychoanalytic Clinic in Paris. He is the author of numerous books in French, Spanish, Italian, Portuguese, Romanian and Turkish. He regularly gives seminars on psychoanalysis in Europe, South America and Australia. He is the *directeur of Editions Stilus* in France. He currently practices as a psychoanalyst in Paris.

Adrian Johnston is a distinguished professor in the Department of Philosophy at the University of New Mexico at Albuquerque and a faculty member at the Emory Psychoanalytic Institute in Atlanta. He is the author of *Time Driven: Metapsychology and the Splitting of the Drive*; Žižek's *Ontology: A Transcendental Materialist Theory of Subjectivity*; *Badiou, Žižek, and Political Transformations: The Cadence of Change*; *Prolegomena to Any Future Materialism, Volume One: The Outcome of Contemporary French Philosophy*; and *Prolegomena to Any Future Materialism, Volume Two: A Weak Nature Alone*, all published by Northwestern University Press. He is also the author of *Adventures in Transcendental Materialism: Dialogues with Contemporary Thinkers*, *Irrepressible Truth: On Lacan's "The Freudian Thing"* and *A New German Idealism: Hegel, Žižek, and Dialectical Materialism*. He is the co-author, with Catherine Malabou, of *Self and Emotional Life: Philosophy, Psychoanalysis, and Neuroscience* (2013). He recently co-edited, with Boštjan Nedoh and Alenka Zupančič, *Objective Fictions: Philosophy, Psychoanalysis, Marxism*. His latest books are *Infinite Greed: The Inhuman Selfishness of Capital* and, with co-author Lorenzo Chiesa, *God Is Undead: Psychoanalysis for Unbelievers*.

James Martell is an associate professor of French at Lyon College. His books, editions and co-editions include *Beckett and Derrida*; *Modernism, Self-Creation, and the Maternal*; *Tattooed Bodies*; *Samuel Beckett and the Encounter of Philosophy and Literature*; a special issue of *Samuel Beckett Today/Aujourd'hui*; and the forthcoming *Understanding Sade*, *Understanding Modernism*. He is currently co-editing the volume *Beckett and Nature* and writing a book on surfaces of thought in French philosophy.

Dany Nobus is professor of psychoanalytic psychology at Brunel University London, founding scholar of the British Psychoanalytic Council and former chair and fellow of the Freud Museum London. He has published widely on the history, theory and practice of psychoanalysis; the intersections between psychoanalysis, philosophy and the arts; and the history of ideas, with special reference to the Renaissance and Early Modern periods. Recent books include *Critique of Psychoanalytic Reason: Studies in Lacanian Theory and Practice* (2022); *Thresholds and Pathways between Jung and Lacan: On the Blazing Sublime*, edited with Ann Casement and Phil Goss; and *The Law of Desire: On Lacan's 'Kant with Sade'*. In 2017, he was the recipient of the Sarton Medal of the University of Ghent for his outstanding contributions to psychoanalytic historiography. He is currently working on a new, in-depth biography of Jacques Lacan.

Jean-Michel Rabaté, professor of English and comparative literature at the University of Pennsylvania, co-editor of the *Journal of Modern Literature*, co-founder of *Slought – Public Trust Foundation*, is a fellow of the American Academy of Arts and Sciences. He is the author or editor of fifty books on modernism, psychoanalysis, philosophy and literary theory. Titles from the past decade include *Crimes of the Future*; *The Cambridge Introduction to Literature and Psychoanalysis*; *The Pathos of Distance*; *Think, Pig!: Beckett at the Limit of the Human*; *Les Guerres de Jacques Derrida*; *Rust*; *Kafka L.O.L.*; *Rire au Soleil: Lacan*; *les affects et la literature*; *Beckett and Sade*; *Rires Prodigues: Rire et jouissance chez Marx, Freud et Kafka* (Paris, Stilus, 2021); *James Joyce, Hérétique et Prodigue*; *Lacan l'irritant*; *Jacques Lacan against Psychoanalytic Obsolescence*, and the edited collections *After Derrida*, *New Beckett*, *Understanding Derrida/Understanding Modernism*, *Knots: Post-Lacanian Readings of Literature and film*, and the co-edited volumes with Angeliki Spiropoulou, *Historical Modernisms: Time, History and Modernist Aesthetics*, *Encounters with Soun-Gui Kim: Writings, 1975–2021*, *S-Journal special issue: Hélène Cixous and Psychoanalysis.*

Samo Tomšič is a professor of philosophy/aesthetics at the University of Fine Arts Dresden. His research areas comprise modern and contemporary European philosophy, psychoanalysis and critical theory. Selected publications include *The Capitalist Unconscious: Marx and Lacan* and *The Labour of Enjoyment: Toward a Critique of Libidinal Economy.*

Antonio Viselli is head of French studies as well as translation and interpreting at the University of Canterbury (Aotearoa/New Zealand). His research is in Comparative Literature, mainly on intermediality and translingualism in a Romance-language context, with a strong focus on French Symbolism and European Modernism. Authors that figure prominently in his work include, among others, Tristan Corbière, Paul Verlaine, James Joyce, Ezra Pound,

André Gide and Cesare Pavese. He has published on musico-literary writing, on the polysemy, polyphony and interdisciplinarity of fugue in the works of authors from the nineteenth to the twenty-first century, in English, French and Italian. His research in Francophone Studies includes publications on French-Canadian writers outside Quebec, such as Alexandre Amprimoz and Jean Chicoine; on theorizing North-African carceral narratives in relation to the writings of Behrouz Boochani and his translator, Omid Tofighian; and on Kanak voices in New Caledonia as well as gender and ecopoetics in Oceania. His work has appeared in several journals and collected volumes, including the *University of Toronto Quarterly*, *French Studies*, *the Australian Journal of French Studies*, *Dix-neuf*, *Romantisme*, *Voix plurielles*, *Continental Thought & Theory: A Journal of Intellectual Freedom and Pacific Dynamics*. In 2019, he co-edited *Iconoclasm: The Breaking and Making of Images*. He currently leads a research project funded by the French Ministry of Foreign Affairs entitled '*Humanitarian and Ecological Crises: (De)Constructing Minorities and Freedoms*'.

Cindy Zeiher is a Lacanian psychoanalyst in training and senior lecturer at Te Whare Wānanga o Waitaha/University of Canterbury, Aotearoa/New Zealand, where she teaches modernism and postmodernism in the human services program. Her work explores psychoanalytic interventions and interpretations relating to subjectivity, ontology, politics and creativity, especially music. With Ed Pluth, she co-authored *On Silence: Holding the Voice Hostage* (2019) and co-edited a collection of essays with Todd McGowan, *Can Philosophy Love?* (2016) Her journal articles have appeared in *S-Journal, Diacritics, Filozofski vestnik, Pacific Dynamics* and *Penumbr(a)*. She has contributed essays to *The Politics of Desire: Foucault, Deleuze, and Psychoanalysis; Reading Lacan's Seminar VIII*; and *Understanding Sade, Understanding Modernism* among other collections. She is finalising a book manuscript which interrogates musicologist and philosopher Vladimir Jankélévitch's radical refusal of German culture from the perspective of Lacan's theory of the speech act.

www.ingramcontent.com/pod-product-compliance
Ingram Content Group UK Ltd.
Pitfield, Milton Keynes, MK11 3LW, UK
UKHW040858081026
15587UKWH00016B/755

9 781786 616203